DE CARLE'S
WATCH AND CLOCK
ENCYCLOPEDIA

WATCH & CLOCK ENCYCLOPEDIA

by
Donald de Carle, F.B.H.I.
Author of *Practical Watch Repairing*, etc.

Illustrations by
E. A. AYRES, F.B.H.I.

BONANZA BOOKS • NEW YORK

Author's Additional Works:

PRACTICAL WATCH REPAIRING.
PRACTICAL CLOCK REPAIRING.
WITH THE WATCHMAKER AT THE BENCH.
BRITISH TIME.
THE WATCHMAKERS' LATHE.
COMPLICATED WATCHES AND THEIR REPAIR.
PRACTICAL WATCH ADJUSTING AND SPRINGING.
CLOCKS AND THEIR VALUE.

CONTENTS

The contents are arranged in alphabetical order, except for the last section, "Workshop Hints and Helps." For ease of reference, the chief sections are given in index form below.

A

ABACUS. *See* Antique Clock and Clock Case Terms.

ABRASIVE. A substance used for polishing and grinding; such as carborundum, diamantine, Montgomery stone, oilstone dust, red stuff, rouge, rubytine, Water-of-Ayr stone (*q.v.*).

AC. Abbreviation of Alternating Current (*q.v.*).

ACANTHUS LEAVES. *See* Antique Clock and Clock Case Terms.

ACCELERATE. To increase the rate of time keeping; or to speed; to make faster. The term " to accelerate on its rate " means that a timepiece gains on its usual time-keeping. *See* Rate.

ACCELERATION. The rate of increase in velocity of a moving body.

ACCUMULATOR. A secondary type of voltaic cell which yields electrical energy by a reversible electro-chemical action after being charged from an external supply. Produced in single units of approx. 2 volts and in combinations of 2, 3, 4, etc., cells giving 4, 6, 8, etc., volts, generally referred to as a battery (*q.v.*).

ACETIC ACID. Formula $C_2H_4O_2$. More conventional is the formula $CH_3.6OOH$, which indicates the *type* of acid (" aliphatic " acid). In dilute form, the principal content of vinegar. Used in removing broken-in screw stubs or other steel parts from watch plates, cocks etc. Immersion for 24 hours is usually sufficient to rot the steel and does not affect the gilding. In concentrated form, a syrupy colourless liquid known as glacial acetic acid. Used as an adhesive for Perspex and similar plastics.

ACIER. (French) Steel.

ACIER FONDU. (French) Cast Steel.

ACORN. *See* Antique Clock and Clock Case Terms.

ACORN WATCH. A watch in the shape of an acorn; first produced in the early part of the seventeenth century in Germany.

ACOUSTICS. The science of sound. (An acoustic timing machine amplifies the beats of a timepiece so that the functioning may be plainly heard.)

ACOUSTIC TIMING. A method of measuring the beats of a timepiece by automatic comparison with those of a master instrument. *See* Timing Machine.

ACTION. A term used to denote the extent of the arc of vibration of the balance, or pendulum, *e.g.* " poor action "—the arc of vibration small; " good action " the arc of vibration brisk and ample. *See* Arc.

ACT OF PARLIAMENT CLOCK. Between 1797 and 1798 a tax was imposed on all clocks or time-keepers. During this period a distinct form of clock became popular, known as the " Act of Parliament Clock." This style of clock, however, received considerable attention and development from the middle of the eighteenth century, when improving coaching facilities required inns to have reliable time-pieces. While the tax was imposed innkeepers particularly, among others, invested in this form of " attraction."

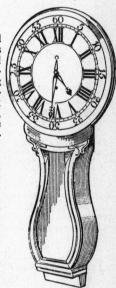

ACT OF PARLIAMENT CLOCK.

ACTIVATED or ACTIVÉE. Refers to oil or grease containing animal oil, *e.g.* stearic acid, olive oil, neat's-foot oil, etc.

ADAM STYLE. *See* English Period Styles, page 44.

ADDENDUM. The portion of a gear wheel tooth or pinion leaf external to the pitch circle.

9

ADDENDUM COEFFICIENT. The amount by which the addendum is corrected or modified, divided by the Module (*q.v.*) or multiplied by the Diametral Pitch (*q.v.*).

ADDENDUM CORRECTION, or modification. A departure from standard dimensions for the addendum, as employed in involute gearing.

ADHESION. The power of sticking. The frictional grip of two closely contacting surfaces.

ADJUSTED. (Watches, etc.) A term referring to the temperature correction and positional timing of a movement. An "Adjusted watch" usually refers to a high-grade movement which has been adjusted in five positions, *e.g.* dial up, dial down, pendant up, pendant right, pendant left for pocket watches, and, dial up, dial down, pendant down, pendant right, pendant up for wrist watches. Also in two temperatures usually 42° F. and 92° F. *See* Chronometer. (Clocks.) Refers to temperature correction; especially of pendulum types.

ADJUSTING. The art or act of regulating and adjusting watches or other timekeepers. *See* Adjusted and Chronometer.

ADJUSTING ROD. A tool consisting of a long rod carrying a movable weight used to determine the most uniform power development of the mainspring of a fusee watch, chronometer or clock, when "Setting up" (*q.v.*).

ADJUSTING ROD.

ADMITTANCE. The reciprocal of Impedance (*q.v.*).

AFFIX. The term usually applies to the supplementary bimetallic attachment to the "plain" Balance (*q.v.*). Its purpose is to compensate for the error of the balance itself in changes in temperature when an Elinvar or other self compensating balance spring is used. Invented by Paul Ditisheim.

AFFIX.

AIGUILLE (French). Watch or clock hand.

AIRCLOCK. A clock produced about the middle of the seventeenth century. Air was pumped by bellows similar to an organ and its gradual escape from a compartment regulated the fall of a weight which actuated a train of wheels as in other timepieces. *See* Hydrogen Clock.

AIR HARDENING. A method of hardening small steel pieces, *e.g.* fine drills, by heating to a cherry red and chilling suddenly by waving sharply in the air. Or, by blowing on to the steel and extinguishing the heating flame at the same time at one blast.

AIRY'S BAR. A bar with weights at each end which acted upon the limbs of a compensation balance to correct the Middle Temperature Error (*q.v.*). Invented by Sir George Airy, 1871.

AIRY'S BAR.

ALABASTINE. A proprietary product for use in filling cracks in stone, plaster, wood, etc., setting hard and stone-like.

ALARM OR ALARUM. A clock or watch which rings or "Alarms" at a pre-determined time. *See* Cricket Watch.

ALASKA STANDARD TIME. Ten hours slow of Greenwich Mean Time (*q.v.*).

ALBERT. A watch chain, used as a means

ALBERT.

of attaching a pocket watch to a garment; an article of jewellery, named after Albert, Prince Consort.

ALCOHOL. Pure spirit of wine—Common Alcohol C_2H_6O; also a general name for Ethyl Alcohol C_2H_5OH. Used as the final cleaning agent for watch etc., parts to remove the last vestige of resinous substances from the surfaces. Present-day benzines, etc., are usually contaminated with resinous impurities which dry out of solution in spots or a film and, in contact with fresh oil in sinks, etc., have a most deleterious effect. Alcohol is a powerful detergent of these residues. *See* also Carbon Tetrachloride.

ALL OR NOTHING PIECE. That part of a repeating watch mechanism which, by holding up the $\frac{1}{4}$ rack until the slide or push piece is fully home, ensures that All the hours and quarters, etc., are struck or Nothing. Probably invented by Julien Le Roy, or Sully about 1728. A form of all-or-nothing piece (found in a clock); is attributed to Tompion, who died in 1714.

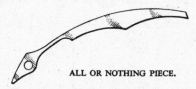

ALL OR NOTHING PIECE.

ALMANACK CLOCKS AND WATCHES. Another name for Calendar clocks and watches (*q.v.*).

ALOXITE. *See* India Oil Stone.

ALPHA CLOCK. A clock made for the Exhibition of 1851, in the shape of the letter " A."

ALTERNATING CURRENT. An electric current flow the direction of which periodically reverses. More exactly, an electric current flow the direction of which periodically and regularly reverses, each cycle occupying an identical period of time. The number of cycles per second identifies the " frequency " of the supply irrespective of the voltage. Abb.: A.C. *See* Oscillating Currents.

ALTERNATOR. A constant speed generator producing an alternating current of a particular frequency at that speed. Small types driven by a Direct Current

(D.C.) supply are sometimes known as " Converters." Compare with Dynamo.

ALTITUDE, TABLE OF. *See* next page.

ALUM. The name commonly given to one of the double salts of Aluminium (*q.v.*). A saturated solution in water can be used to rot broken-in, or wedged steel parts in watch and clock plates, etc., requiring about 12 hours immersion. The process can be hastened by heating. The process has the disadvantage of staining gilding etc.

AMERICAN SCREWS. Each of the American factories has its own screw threads, and screw plates etc. cannot be purchased in the usual manner. Details of threads can be found in " Machinery's Screw Thread Book."

AMMETER. Instrument for measuring the current flowing in an electrical circuit.

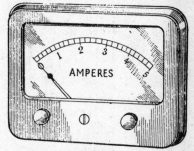

AMMETER.

AMPERE. Unit of electric current. The international ampere is defined as that unvarying current which deposits 1·118 milligrams of silver per second when passing through a solution of silver nitrate. The ampere is named after the French physicist Andre Marie Ampere 1775–1856. Abbreviated to amp., or A. Fractions of an ampere are usually expressed in milliamps or thousandths of an ampere. Thus,

500 milliamps $= \frac{1}{2}$ amp.
5 milliamps $= \cdot005$ amp.

AMPERE HOUR. An expression of quantity denoting the flow of 1 ampere of current for 1 hour; or an equivalent such as $\frac{1}{2}$ amp. for 2 hours, etc.

AMPERE HOUR CAPACITY. The discharge capacity of an accumulator or battery, reckoned at the rate of 1 amp. for a stated number of hours. Alternatively,

TABLE OF ALTITUDE

This table of altitude was plotted by Professor Sir G. B. Airy, K.C.B., late Astronomer Royal of England, at 50° F. mean temperature, and adopted by the National Physical Laboratory as the standard for meteorological and surveying aneroids in Great Britain.

NOTE.—For aeronautical height measuring instruments the I.C.A.N. or Isothermal scales are also used.

Aneroid or Corrected Barometer	Height in Feet	Aneroid or Corrected Barometer	Height in Feet	Aneroid or Corrected Barometer	Height in Feet	Aneroid or Corrected Barometer	Height in Feet	Aneroid or Corrected Barometer	Height in Feet
Hg. in.	ft.	in.	ft.	in.	ft.	in.	ft.	in.	ft.
31·00	0	28·28	2,500	25·80	5,000	23·54	7,500	21·47	10,000
30·94	50	28·23	2,550	25·75	5,050	23·50	7,550	21·44	10,050
30·88	100	28·18	2,600	25·71	5,100	23·45	7,600	21·40	10,100
30·83	150	28·12	2,650	25·66	5,150	23·41	7,650	21·36	10,150
30·77	200	28·07	2,700	25·61	5,200	23·37	7,700	21·32	10,200
30·71	250	28·02	2,750	25·56	5,250	23·32	7,750	21·28	10,250
30·66	300	27·97	2,800	25·52	5,300	23·28	7,800	21·24	10,300
30·60	350	27·92	2,850	25·47	5,350	23·24	7,850	21·20	10,350
30·54	400	27·87	2,900	25·42	5,400	23·20	7,900	21·16	10,400
30·49	450	27·82	2,950	25·38	5,450	23·15	7,950	21·12	10,450
30·43	500	27·76	3,000	25·33	5,500	23·11	8,000	21·08	10,500
30·38	550	27·71	3,050	25·28	5,550	23·07	8,050	21·05	10,550
30·32	600	27·66	3,100	25·24	5,600	23·03	8,100	21·01	10,600
30·26	650	27·61	3,150	25·19	5,650	22·98	8,150	20·97	10,650
30·21	700	27·56	3,200	25·15	5,700	22·94	8,200	20·93	10,700
30·15	750	27·51	3,250	25·10	5,750	22·90	8,250	20·89	10,750
30·10	800	27·46	3,300	25·05	5,800	22·86	8,300	20·85	10,800
30·04	850	27·41	3,350	25·01	5,850	22·82	8,350	20·82	10,850
29·99	900	27·36	3,400	24·96	5,900	22·77	8,400	20·78	10,900
29·93	950	27·31	3,450	24·92	5,950	22·73	8,450	20·74	10,950
29·88	1,000	27·26	3,500	24·87	6,000	22·69	8,500	20·70	11,000
29·82	1,050	27·21	3,550	24·82	6 050	22·65	8,550	20·66	11,050
29·77	1,100	27·16	3,600	24·78	100	22·61	8,600	20·63	11,100
29·71	1,150	27·11	3,650	24·73	6 150	22·57	8,650	20·59	11,150
29·66	1,200	27·06	3,700	24·69	6 200	22·52	8,700	20·55	11,200
29·61	1,250	27·01	3,750	24·64	6 250	22·48	8,750	20·51	11,250
29·55	1,300	26·96	3,800	24·60	6,300	22·44	8,800	20·47	11,300
29·50	1,350	26·91	3,850	24·55	6,350	22·40	8,850	20·44	11,350
29·44	1,400	26·86	3,900	24·51	6,400	22·36	8,900	20·40	11,400
29·39	1,450	26·81	3,950	24·46	6,450	22·32	8,950	20·36	11,450
29·34	1,500	26·76	4,000	24·42	6,500	22·28	9,000	20·32	11,500
29·28	1,550	26·72	4,050	24·37	6,550	22·24	9,050	20·29	11,550
29·23	1,600	26·67	4,100	24·33	6,600	22·20	9,100	20·25	11,600
29·17	1,650	26·62	4,150	24·28	6,650	22·16	9,150	20·21	11,650
29·12	1,700	26·57	4,200	24·24	6,700	22·11	9,200	20·18	11,700
29·07	1,750	26·52	4,250	24·20	6,750	22·07	9,250	20·14	11,750
29·01	1,800	26·47	4,300	24·15	6,800	22·03	9,300	20·10	11,800
28·96	1,850	26·42	4,350	24·11	6,850	21·99	9,350	20·07	11,850
28·91	1,900	26·37	4,400	24·06	6,900	21·95	9,400	20·03	11,900
28·86	1,950	26·33	4,450	24·02	6,950	21·91	9,450	19·99	11,950
28·80	2,000	26·28	4,500	23·97	7,000	21·87	9,500	19·95	12,000
28·75	2,050	26·23	4,550	23·93	7,050	21·83	9,550	19·241	13,000
28·70	2,100	26·18	4,600	23·89	7,100	21·79	9,600	18·548	14,000
28·64	2,150	26·13	4,650	23·84	7,150	21·75	9,650	17·880	15,000
28·59	2,200	26·09	4,700	23·80	7,200	21·71	9,700	17·235	16,000
28·54	2,250	26·04	4,750	23·76	7,250	21·67	9,750	16·615	17,000
28·49	2,300	25·99	4,800	23·71	7,300	21·63	9,800	16·016	18,000
28·43	2,350	25·94	4,850	23·67	7,350	21·59	9,850	15·439	19,000
28·38	2,400	25·89	4,900	23·62	7,400	21·55	9,900	14·883	20,000
28·33	2,450	25·85	4,950	23·58	7,450	21·51	9,950		

Courtesy: Messrs. Short and Mason.

This table is intended more particularly for the graduation of Aneroids with a circle of measures in feet concentric with the ordinary circle of barometric height measured in inches. The circle of feet is to be read off, at the upper and lower stations, by the index ; and the rule for measuring the height will be: Subtract the reading at the lower station from the reading at the upper station; the difference is the height in feet.

EXAMPLE: Barometer at Upper Station, 23·50 .. 7,550 feet.
Barometer at Lower Station, 24·20 .. 6,750 ,,

Actual height .. .. 800 ,,

a greater current may be drawn for a correspondingly shorter period.

AMPERE TURNS. A term applied to the calculation of Magnetomotive Force (*q.v.*), especially in construction of Electro-magnets (*q.v.*), Transformers (*q.v.*), etc. The M.M.F. is directly proportional to the current flowing in each turn of a winding and the number of turns.

AMPLITUDE. The extent or swing of a pendulum or balance. Strictly, the extent of swing from the rest point, or the semi-arc. Also an electrical term. Also, the angular distance measured from due east or due west at which a heavenly body rises or sets.

ANCHORAGE. The means whereby a part is fastened or held.

ANCHOR ESCAPEMENT. Another name for the Recoil Escapement (*q.v.*), usually attributed to Dr. Robert Hooke (about 1656–7). While he was still at Oxford he stated he had invented " a device for continuing the motion of pendulums." Also attributed to Wm. Clement. The action of the escapement is as follows:—The escape wheel is rotating

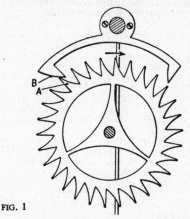

FIG. 1

in a clockwise direction. The pallets are fixed to the pallet arbor (*q.v.*) and the crutch (*q.v.*) is fixed to the pallet arbor. The crutch controls and gives impulse to the pendulum. As the pendulum swings to the left it allows the tooth A of the escape wheel to slide along the impulse face B of the pallet pad and at the same time imparts impulse to the pendulum. Eventually the tooth A drops off the pallet pad and the tooth C drops on to the pallet pad D and

as the pendulum continues to swing to the left this locking becomes deeper and by reason of the curve of the pad the escape wheel is made to recoil. When the pendulum has reached the end of its journey and starts to return the escape tooth C will then give impulse to the pallet and so to the pendulum. This cycle is repeated on the pallet pad B. Fig. 1.—Pendulum about to swing to the left. Fig. 2.—Tooth about to escape from left hand pallet and drop on to right hand pallet. Fig. 3.—Impulse imparted to right hand pallet.

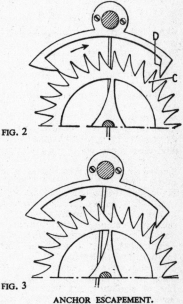

FIG. 2

FIG. 3

ANCHOR ESCAPEMENT.

ANCHOR PIN OR STUD. A pin, pip, or boss, by means of which two parts of an assembly are located and/or secured in their respective positions.

ANCHOR POINT. The position (ideally, the optimum) having regard to the design, in which the base of movable pieces, clicks, fingers, etc., or the fulcrum of a lever, crank, pawl, etc., must be planted to obtain the required action.

ANCHOR RELEASE. A term for the forms of recoil escapement as used in alarms to drive the hammer.

ANEROID. A thin metal box hermetic-ally sealed and exhausted of air so that the ends recede or approach each other with changes in the pressure of the atmosphere. Used as a barometer or altimeter.

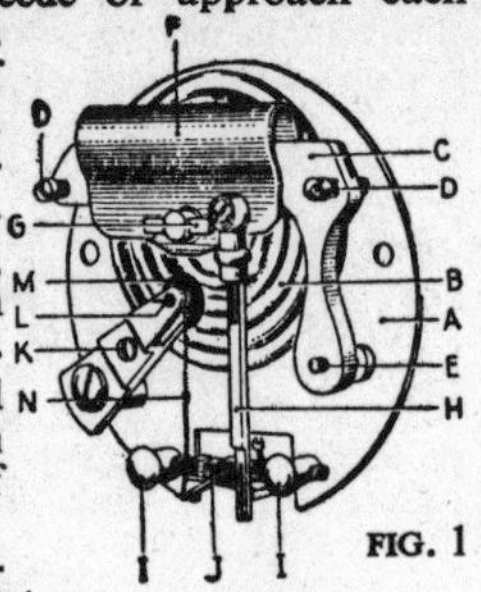

FIG. 1

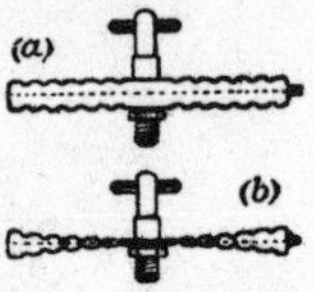

FIG 2.
(a) open; (b) closed.
ANEROID.

A. Base plate, on which parts are set.

B. Corrugated vacuum chamber of nickel-silver (metal thickness 0·004 inches), from which all air is exhausted.

C. Bridge which spans vacuum chamber "B."

D.D. Adjusting screws, which are used to raise or lower the bridge, thereby altering the tension on chamber "B."

E. Adjusting screw which raises bridge "C" up or down.

F. Steel spring, which slides in back of bridge "C."

G. Knife-edge (triangular or square steel rod). This passes through the stud of the vacuum chamber and tends to open it by pulling strongly upwards.

H. Bar or arm, compensated for temperature, which at its ends magnifies movement of the spring "F."

I.I. Two supports or pillars, fitted to plate "A."

J. Bar or regulator, set between and working on steel points, or pivots, passing through supports "I.I."

K. Arm or cock.

L. Pin or arbor, passing through end of cock "K."

M. Hairspring, fitted to pin "L."

N. Chain of steel, one end of which is fitted to arm passing upward from regulator "L," the other end being secured to pin "L" to which the indicating hand is fitted.

The vacuum chamber "B" (known as a capsule) is similar to a small circular metal box (closely resembling two lids of a tin can soldered together at their edges) and will collapse when exhausted of air (Fig. 2). If we pull from the bottom and the top we pull it open (Fig. 2a), but directly we let go it collapses again (Fig. 2b). As the under side is secured to the base plate "A" and the upper side to the strong spring "F," the action is the same as in the case of the two tin can lids mentioned above. The strong spring "F" "opens" the vacuum chamber and holds it open. If we increase the pressure, or weight, on the vacuum chamber, it pulls this spring down with it; if we decrease the pressure the spring opens it up more than ever. It is easy to see, therefore, that the spring moves up or down as the air pressure decreases or increases. If we secure an arm "H" to the spring it will magnify the movement of the spring at the end of the arm. A small rod is shown in the illustration, passing from the end of the bar or arm "H" to the edge of the bar or regulator "J." If the arm "H" moves downward it will tend to move the bar, or regulator "J" outward, and if the arm "H" is elevated, the bar, or regulator "J" will turn inward toward the vacuum chamber "B." An arm is set in an upward direction from regulator "J," which at its upper end greatly magnifies the movement. Aneroid barometers should not be expected to indicate present weather conditions, but may be depended upon generally to foretell weather changes 6 to 18 hours in advance. Do not hang the barometer outside. It will work better inside, but to get the best results it should be kept in as even a temperature as possible, unless it is a "compensated" instrument, in which case temperature changes will not affect its operation. Do not put faith in the weather words "rain," "change," and "fair" when they appear on the dial, as they are approximate only, and if the hand points to "rain" it does not follow that that condition must exist. The figures "31," "30," "29," "28," etc., represent inches of pressure. Between these inch points on the dial there are lesser divisions, sometimes $\frac{1}{10}$th of an inch, sometimes $\frac{1}{20}$th of an inch, or even $\frac{1}{50}$th or $\frac{1}{100}$th of an inch. It is usual to use longer graduation lines at the $\frac{1}{10}$th points and to figure the dial at those points. The barometer dial should be studied carefully before an attempt is made to read it. The description of the aneroid is by courtesy of Messrs. Short and Mason.

ANGLE. The inclination of one line to another in the same plane, measured in degrees (°). A term referring to the lever escapement. The angle at which the pallets are set in relation to the lever. The lever escapement is said to be "in angle" when the locking and unlocking of each pallet occupies an equal arc of movement of the lever about its line of centres with the balance. " Angle " also refers to the total angle of movement of the lever; hence, High Angle—where the lever describes a large arc as is experienced with the single roller escapement; and, Low Angle—where a lesser arc is required as in the double roller escapement.

ANNEALING. A process of controlled heating and cooling, especially of metal and glass. Widely employed to soften metals to enable them to be worked cold. Also to relieve internal stresses after working.

ANNE, QUEEN STYLE. See ENGLISH PERIOD STYLES, page 44.

ANNULAR BALANCE. The circular balance as fitted to watches, etc.

ANODE. The positive pole of a cell or battery. An Electrode (q.v.) which is connected to the positive terminal or pole of a supply towards which Electrons (q.v.) will migrate from a Cathode (q.v.). See Valve. An electrode connected to A.C. will be alternately an Anode and a Cathode as the current alternates.

ANODE LOAD. The inductance etc., or plain resistance across which the anode current of a valve develops the required voltage for the operation of apparatus, a succeeding stage, or other circuits.

ANTE MERIDIEM. Denotes the hours before noon before the sun reaches the Meridian. Abbreviated a.m. See Post Meridiem).

ANTI-MAGNETIC. Resistant to magnetism. Device to screen from or prevent magnetisation (as Mu-metal, q.v.). A descriptive term applied to watch, etc., construction to denote the use of non-magnetic materials in those parts subject to the disturbing effect of magnetism (e.g. Balance, Balance Spring, Lever).

ANTIPHASE. Phase relationship of two alternating motions or quantities so that one is exactly 180° retarded or advanced with respect to the other.

ANTIQUE CLOCKS
Antique Clock and Clock Case Terms

Many of the terms used to describe antique clock cases are not standard, some being borrowed from the furnishing trade.

One authority will use one term and another something quite different to describe the same article. Similarly there seems to be no standardisation regarding the sizes of clock dials; a 10 inch dial may mean the actual size of the dial, the size of dial visible—or sight line—or the size of the glass covering the dial, a difference of an inch or more. The size of a dial should refer to the sight line since a dial measuring say, 12 inches, could have an aperture exposing 10 inches of the dial only, and to refer to such a dial as 12 inches would be misleading. Also the height of a clock should exclude all ornaments, e.g., handle of a bracket clock and finials of a long-case clock.

It is hoped that the terms included in this glossary will help, in some measure, to standardise this nomenclature.

ABACUS. The uppermost member of the capital of a column.

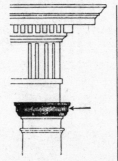

ABACUS.

ACANTHUS. Celebrated among the Greeks and Romans for the elegance of its leaves. Represented conventionally in decoration.

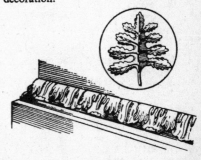

ACANTHUS.

ANTIQUE CLOCKS—Cont.

ACORN. The turned brass decoration in the shape of an acorn, used on clock cases.

ACORN.

APPLIQUE. The decorative brass work applied to the top, and other parts of bracket clock cases. Originally the top of the cases were cut open to allow the sound of the bells to emit and the aperture was covered with brass work, lined with silk, to prevent dust penetrating.

APPLIQUE.

APRON. The decorative drop piece attached to the pallet cock of some of the old bracket clocks. Also, the decorative drop piece between the feet or legs of a clock case, sometimes referred to as Apron Plinth.

APRON.

ARABESQUE. Late style of marquetry, fantastic decoration with intertwining of leaves, scroll-work, etc. *See* Strap-work for an illustration of arabesque.

ARCH. As its name indicates, part of a circle. There are " arch " topped clock cases and also " arch " dials.

ARCH.

ARCHITECTURAL STYLE. In horology,

ARCHITECTURAL STYLE.

ANTIQUE CLOCKS—Cont.

it refers to the style of clock case, where the design is based on Classical architecture. The superstructure, supported on columns, is a feature.

ATROPOS. A figure used in decoration. The eldest of the Three Fates. Clothe spun the thread of life ; Lachesis distributed men's lots and Atropos cut the thread.

BALL FOOT. Flattened ball used for the feet of clocks.

BALLOON CLOCK. The name is derived from its balloon-like shape and was introduced about 1760.

BALLOON CLOCK.

BANDING. A strip or band of veneer in a panel or round the edge of a door, the grain of the wood can be either across or with the banding.

BANDY LEG. Another name for Cabriole (*q.v.*).

BANJO BAROMETER. Another name for Wheel Barometer (*q.v.*).

BANJO CLOCK. A clock of American origin, being first made, it is reputed, by Simon Willard, about 1802. The name is derived from its banjo-like appearance. It is suggested that the English Act of Parliament Clock (*q.v.*) gave Willard the idea.

BARLEY TWIST. Refers to the form of twist decoration where a rectangular section is twisted, similar to sticks of barley sugar. *See* Twist.

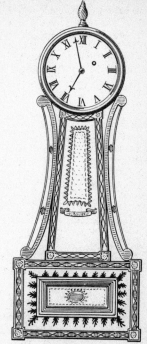

BANJO CLOCK.

BARLEY TWIST.

BAROQUE. Italian ornate style of the first part of the 18th century, ornamentation without restraint.

ANTIQUE CLOCKS—Cont.

BASE. The lower member at the base of a column, in clock cases it is frequently of brass. The word base is also used to define the Plinth (*q.v.*).

BASE.

BASKET TOP. The open-work metal top to a clock case, when there are two tiers it is termed a " double basket top." Sometimes referred to as Bell Top (*q.v.*).

BASKET TOP.

BAS-RELIEF. Relieved from the base: where in carving, metal casting, etc., the figures stand out or project from the base a little and have a flat appearance.

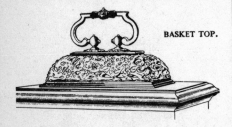

DOUBLE BASKET TOP.

BEAD. A small half round moulding. One of the nine classical mouldings. *See* MOULDINGS.

BELL TOP.

BELL TOP. The bell-like top to a clock case; the hand or turret clock bell cut in half has a convex and a concave curve, and the ordinary bell, *i.e.*, the bell of a clock, has just one curve. For examples of the latter type *see* Bracket Clock. When the top of a clock has a dome-like shape, it is termed Basket Top (*q.v.*).

BLEACHED. Whitened; a term used in woodwork to define a style of finish where the colour is bleached out, leaving the wood as white as possible.

BLIND FRET. A style of decorative carving effect, which is achieved by fret cut wood applied on to the base. A carved effect of equal depth with the incisions made with straight sides.

BLIND FRET.

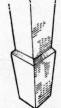

BLOCK FOOT. When the form of a foot is an oblong or cube, *see* Spade Foot.

BLOCK FOOT.

BLOCK-FRONT. Where the front of a solid door projects, or is a panel.

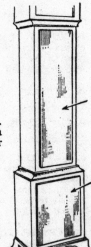

BLOCK-FRONT.

ANTIQUE CLOCKS—Cont.

BOB PENDULUM. Where the pendulum of a clock is a fixture to the pallet arbor. Generally associated with antique clocks.

BOB PENDULUM.

BOLECTION. Refers to all the projecting parts of mouldings, collectively.

BOLT AND SHUTTER. A form of maintaining power, where a shutter covers the winding square; when the shutter is levered over to expose the square the maintaining device is brought into action.

BOMBÉ. A design that bulges as is sometimes found in Louis XIV and Dutch clock cases.

BOSS. A rounded projecting ornament sometimes found in the sides of clock cases.

BOW FRONT. A slow curved front, as distinct from bombé (*q.v.*).

BUHL OR BOULLE WORK. A style of decoration usually comprising a tortoiseshell base with brass inlay. Ivory, silver, etc., are also used. Andre Charles Boulle (1642–1732). A cabinet maker of great repute. At the age of 30 he was granted lodgings in the Louvre Galleries in Paris, 1672, by Louis XIV, the patent reading, "Chaser, gilder and maker of marquetry." Boulle was not the inventor of the style bearing his name, but the past master, improving on the renaissance artists of inlay brass into shell and wood.

BUHL, COUNTER. Counter Buhl is the reverse inlay to Buhl. Usually tortoiseshell inlaid with brass is Buhl work and brass inlaid with tortoiseshell is counter Buhl. When cutting the inlay both materials are cut together and to avoid waste the tortoiseshell cut out is laid into the brass left over.

BRACKET CLOCK. Originally, a clock

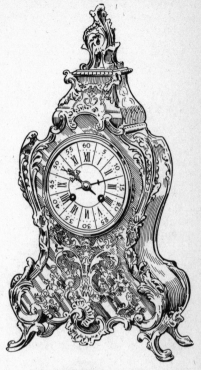

BUHL OR BOULLE WORK.

BRACKET CLOCK.

ANTIQUE CLOCKS—Cont.

made to stand upon a table and known in the seventeenth and eighteenth centuries as a table or portable clock. The bracket upon which the clock could stand was popular in the latter part of the eighteenth and early nineteenth centuries. The term Bracket still persists and is a broad term to define any of the larger wood clocks.

BRACKET FEET. Feet which have the appearance of a small bracket on the side of the main support or foot.

BRACKET FEET.

BRACTS. A decoration in the form of a small leaf or scale, *i.e.*, below the Calyx (*q.v.*) of the flower stem of plants.

BRACTS.

BREAK ARCH. An arch which termin-

BREAK ARCH DIAL.

ates at each side with a right-angle piece, the arch is then not complete, it is broken. There are " break arch " clock cases and also " break arch " dials.

BREAK ARCH CASE.

BREAK FRONT. Where the front is not an unbroken line, *i.e.* where the front line is broken by a projection or a recess.

BREAK FRONT.

BROKEN PEDIMENT. The triangular

BROKEN PEDIMENT.

ANTIQUE CLOCKS—Cont.

decorative facing over the cornice of barometer cases, etc., where the lines are broken at the top. *See* Pediment.

BUN FEET. The flattened, spherical or bun-shaped feet; one of the features of the seventeenth and early eighteenth century long-case clocks.

BUN FEET.

BURR. Also known as **BURL.** A growth or excrescence on the trunk of a tree, sometimes caused by an insect, disease or damage. Veneers cut from such parts usually have unusual figure, often of great beauty, as for instance, burr walnut.

CABOCHON. Part of a form of decoration in the form of a rounded protrusion.

CABRIOLE. The curved leg formed as a slender " S." Queen Anne and Chippendale periods.

CABRIOLE.

CALENDAR APERTURE.

CALENDAR APERTURE. The aperture in the dial of a clock through which the date of the month can be seen.

CALYX. A decoration in the form of a whorl of leaves, such as forms the outer case of a bud; serves as a protection of the unexpanded flower bud.

CALYX.

CAPITAL. The carved or moulded termination of a column.

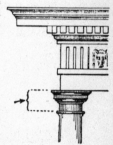

CAPITAL.

CARCASE. The frame or box of a clock case before the mouldings, etc., have been applied.

CARTOUCHE. A tablet or scroll unrolled, a form of decoration.

CARTOUCHE.

CARYATID. Sculptured female figures used instead of columns in architecture.

CARYATID.

ANTIQUE CLOCKS—Cont.

CAVETTO. A hollow moulding; one of the nine classical mouldings. *See* MOULDINGS.

CELLULOSE POLISH. A method of polishing wood by spraying with cellulose.

CERTOSINA. Inlay in the form of geometrical design employing small pieces of inlay.

CHAMBER CLOCK. Name usually given to the iron Lantern Clocks (*q.v.*) prior to the introduction of the pendulum.

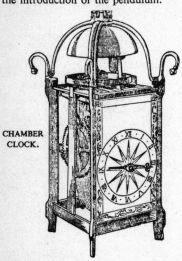

CHAMBER CLOCK.

CHANNELLING. Where grooves are cut into woodwork to form a pattern.

CHAPTER RING. *See* Hour Circle (General Dictionary Section).

CHECKER. Chess or checker board design; where inlay of light and dark woods is employed.

CHEEKS. That part of a long-case clock upon which the Seat Board (*q.v.*) rests.

CHEESE FEET. A foot in the form of a flattened sphere.

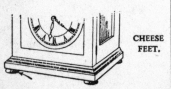

CHEESE FEET.

CHINOISERIE. Chinese ornaments.

CHIP CARVING. An early simple style of carving where a light cut is made.

CLAW AND BALL. A bird's claw clasped round a ball to form the termination of a leg of the Queen Anne and Georgian periods.

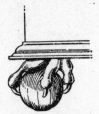

CLAW AND BALL.

CLUB FOOT. The bulb-like termination of the Cabriole Leg (*q.v.*). Queen Anne and Chippendale periods.

CONSOLE. An ornamental bracket in the form of a scroll. Another name for Corbel (*q.v.*) where the length or height is greater than its projection.

CONSOLE.

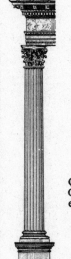

CORINTHIAN COLUMN. Grecian column with a most elaborate capital.

CORINTHIAN COLUMN.

CORONA OR LORMIER. A vertically faced upper member of a cornice, usually having considerable projection.

ANTIQUE CLOCKS—Cont.

CORBEL BRACKET. A bracket that juts out from the wall and is or has the appearance of being built into the wall.

CORBEL BRACKET.

CORNER PIECES. *See* Spandrels.

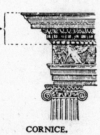

CORNICE. The topmost member of a structure; in a clock case it is the topmost moulding.

CORNICE.

COUNTER BUHL. *See* Buhl.

CRESTING. The carved addition above the uppermost moulding of early long-case clocks.

CRESTING.

CROMWELLIAN CLOCK. *See* Lantern Clock.

CURL. The natural figure in the grain of wood, found at the intersection of a large branch with the trunk of the tree.

CUSPS. The point formed by the intersection of two arcs, as in Gothic tracery. *See* Foil.

CYMA RECTA. An Ogee moulding in one of the classics. *See* Mouldings.

DENTILS OR DENTICKS. The ornamentation consisting of small rectangular blocks with spaces between them used on a cornice, etc.

DENTILS OR DENTICKS.

DIAL ARCH. The arch formed in the framework of a clock case to accommodate an arched dial movement.

DIAL FRAME. Where a wood door covers the dial of a clock, it is the frame into which the dial itself fits.

DIAL FRAME.

DIAPER. A rectangular arrangement of a repeating pattern in marquetry and inlay work. Strictly speaking composed of squares and diamonds.

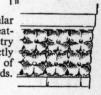

DIAPER.

DOG-TOOTH. A pyramidal like repeating ornamentation, used chiefly as part of a moulding.

DOG-TOOTH.

DOLPHIN FRET. A metal fret cut to resemble a dolphin and usually associated with the decoration of the Lantern Clock (*q.v.*).

ANTIQUE CLOCKS—Cont.

DOUBLE BASKET TOP. *See* Basket Top.

DOWEL. A wooden peg used in place of a nail.

DUTCH FOOT. Where the foot terminates in a bulge.

DROP HANDLE. A ring hanging from an ornamented boss.

EBONISE. To stain and polish wood black to resemble ebony.

EGG-SHELL FINISH. A term used to define a dull, flat, or egg-shell-like finish to paint work and French Polish.

ENCARPUS. A festoon of fruit and flowers on a frieze.

ENCAUSTIC. The art of burning in with heated wax, etc.

ENDIVE SCROLL. A form of carving derived from a species of leaf.

ENDIVE SCROLL.

ENRICHMENT. An ornamental term indicating that a moulding, column, etc., is enriched with ormolu, inlay or carving, etc.

ENTABLATURE. A term indicating the termination of a column, the frieze, moulding and cornice.

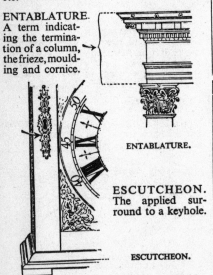

ENTABLATURE.

ESCUTCHEON. The applied surround to a keyhole.

ESCUTCHEON.

EXTRADOS. The outside curve of an arch. *See* Intrados.

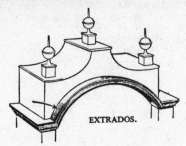

EXTRADOS.

FAUN. Half goat and half man, used as a decorative motif.

FAVAS. A form of decoration resembling the cells of a honeycomb.

FEATHER BANDING. Another name for Herring Bone (*q.v.*).

FAUN.

FESTOON. A decoration in a curved or draped form, another name for Swag (*q v.*).

FIDDLE BACK. The figure of veneer resembling the grain found on the backs of violins. *See* page 295.

FIELDED. A panel which is broken up into smaller panels.

FIELDED.

FILIGREE. Ornamental work made from wire.

FINIAL. A finishing point, such as the brass acorns, pineapples, balls, etc., used

ANTIQUE CLOCKS—Cont.

as decoration on clock cases; also the terminal of a column or spire.

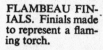

FINIAL.

FLAMBEAU FINIALS. Finials made to represent a flaming torch.

FLAMBEAU FINIALS.

FLASH. When wood has patches of brightly shaded figure.

FLEMISH FOOT. Where the foot is in the form of a scroll turning out and then in.

FLEMISH FOOT.

FLEUR-DE-LIS.

A   B

FLEUR-DE-LIS. French royal symbol, a decoration formed of three iris shaped parts tied at the base with a narrow band. A. Antique form of fleur-de-lis; B. The more modern form.

FLUTING.

FLUTING. Decoration by furrows or channels either lengthwise or across.

FOIL. The space between the cusps or points in Gothic tracery. Three cusps Trefoil, four Quartfoil, etc. (*q.v.*).

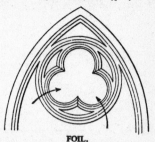

FOIL.

FOLIATED. When Foils (*q.v.*) are used, also to indicate enriched with leaves.

FRENCH POLISH. A method of polishing the surface of wood with a mixture of shellac and spirit. During the reign of Louis XIV (1643–1715) a method of polishing was introduced in which the surface to be polished was coated with lacquer and then polished with bees wax. About the last quarter of the 17th century this method was introduced into England and it was referred to as the *French Style* of polishing. At the beginning of the 19th century the method now employed was used.

FRET. Pierced wood or metal, used in clock cases to allow the sound to be emitted.

ANTIQUE CLOCKS—Cont.

FRIEZE. The middle member between the cornice and the supporting column, that part immediately below the upper moulding or cornice.

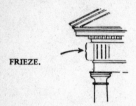

FRIEZE.

GADROON. A decoration resembling reeds or inverted flutes.

GADROON.

GALLERY. A decorative wood or metal edge.

GALLERY.

GLORY. Circle of light round figure or head; a halo.

GOTHIC. The pointed arch style, period twelfth to sixteenth centuries. The illustration is of a clock designed in the Gothic style.

GOTHIC.

GRAND-DAUGHTER CLOCK. A short, long-case clock; a miniature grandfather clock, usually about 3 feet 6 inches high. A style of clock case of recent introduction.

GRANDFATHER CLOCK. Originally known as a long-case clock; refers to the domestic clock of about 6 feet or more in height.

GRANDMOTHER CLOCK. A small edition of the grandfather clock. Standing about 5 feet high.

GRIFFIN. A decorative motif composed of a lion's body with an eagle's head and wings.

GRIFFIN.

GUILLOCHÉ. Ornamentation of curved and interlacing lines, usually of a circular form. The word guilloché means engine turned.

GUILLOCHÉ.

ANTIQUE CLOCKS—Cont.

GUILLOCHIS. Engine turning.

GUT PALLETS. Where the actual pad or active part of the pallets consists of a short length of cat-gut drawn taut. Used in the Anchor (*q.v.*, General Dictionary Section) and the crown wheel escapements. The crown wheel escapement illustrated here serves to show the treatment. Introduced by Justin Vulliamy about the middle of the eighteenth century. Its purpose is to make the escapement silent.

HERRINGBONE. A veneer cut obliquely into strips and placed together, resembling herringbone.

HERRINGBONE.

HOOD. The removable casing of the mechanism of the long-case clock; the hood rests upon the trunk or body of the case. It is either drawn forward or lifted up to remove. The earlier clocks were fitted with lift up of rising hoods or lifting hoods as they are known.

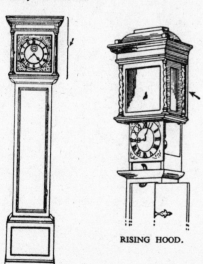

RISING HOOD.

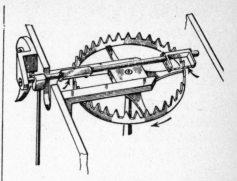

GUT PALLETS.

HUSKS. A form of decoration of the Sheraton period; consists of a series of open seed pods with a seed or small ball intervening. There are various styles, but the one illustrated is common.

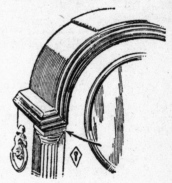

HUSKS.

IMPOST. That part of a pillar upon which arches rest.

IMPOST.

INCISED ORNAMENT. Cut in, engraved.

INLAYING. Where lines, bands, flowers, etc., are laid into a groundwork. *See* Marquetry and Intarsia.

INTARSIA. Insert or inlay where the design is cut out and fitted into corresponding cavities. Derived from the Latin *interserere* to insert. Intarsia is the earliest form of inlay work.

IN THE WHITE. Any wood, irrespective of colour, before it is polished or otherwise treated.

ANTIQUE CLOCKS—Cont.

INTRADOS. The underside of an arch. *See* Extrados.

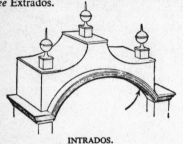

INTRADOS.

INVERTED BELL TOP. Refers to the Bell Top (*q.v.*) where the curve is inverted, *i.e.*, instead of the curve being convex and concave, it is concave and convex.

INVERTED BELL TOP.

IVES' CLOCK. *See* Wagon Spring Clock.

JARDINIÈRE. Ornamental pot or stand for display of growing flowers in room, on window-sill, etc.

KERF. The cut made by a saw, sometimes used as a form of decoration. Similar to some forms of inlay work but without the inlay.

KETTLE FRONT. Where the form takes the shape of the old fashioned kettle.

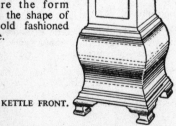

KETTLE FRONT.

LACQUER. A form of decoration resembling japanning. A kind of resinous varnish first used by the Japanese.

LAMINATE. Another name for " three-ply," " five-ply," etc. wood. Also used to indicate the intersection of another material such as laminated plastic, *i.e.*, plastic with section or sections of another material such as a fabric.

LANCET. Pointed arch of the thirteenth century or English Gothic.

LANCET.

HANGING LANTERN CLOCK.

28

ANTIQUE CLOCKS—Cont.

LANTERN CLOCK.

A metal-cased clock of the fourteenth to seventeenth centuries. Originally made to hang on the wall and to be weight driven. Also known as Cromwellian, bed post and bird cage clock. The first domestic clock. The cases of the earliest examples were made of iron; later, of brass. On the facing page is an example of the hanging type of lantern clock. *See* Sheep's Head Clock.

LANTERN CLOCK.

LATCH OR LATCHED PLATES.

A system employed in seventeenth century clocks of securing the front plate to the pillars by a latch or clip piece. This method is also used to secure the dial pillars to the front plate.

LATCH OR LATCHED PLATES.

LATTICE.

Interlacing work resembling network, in wood or metal, etc.

LIMED OAK.

Oak treated with lime which gives it a whitish-grey effect.

LION'S MASK AND RING HANDLES.

A decorative handle formed of a lion's head with ring passing through its mouth.

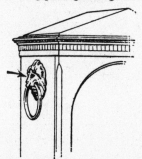

LION'S MASK AND RING HANDLES.

LOTUS LEAF.

A decorative motif resembling the water flower of that name.

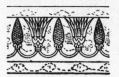

LOTUS LEAF.

LOW RELIEF.

Carving which is not cut deep.

LOZENGE.

Diamond shaped pattern.

LYRE CLOCK.

Refers to a clock where the case is in the form of a lyre, the musical instrument. Of French origin, dating from about the middle of the eighteenth century. Some are to be seen where the pendulum takes the form of a ring surrounding the dial of the clock, often set with pastes.

MARQUETRY.

A form of inlay work where the design or pattern is profuse. It employs a system where several sheets of different coloured woods (veneer) are placed together and cut to the same design; subsequently the sheets are arranged to fit one into the other and then glued. The word " marquetry " is from the French " marqueter " to spot or to mark. *See* Intarsia.

MASK.

An impression of the face in any material, used as a form of decoration.

MASK.

MATTING.

Refers to the finely punched centre of seventeenth and eighteenth century brass clock dials.

MATTING.

ANTIQUE CLOCKS—Cont.

MEDALLION. A decorative motif in the form of a plaque or medal, usually with figures or heads in low relief.

MEDALLION.

MOCK PENDULUM. *See* Pendulum Aperture.

MODILLIONS. Projecting decorative brackets forming part of the cornice of a column of the Corinthian order.

MODILLION.

MOSAIC. Decorative work formed by joining together minute pieces of stone, gems, etc., of different colour.

MOTTLED. A speckled or variegated grain in wood.

MUNTINS. The central vertical member of a door; that part of a door which divides the panels.

NECKING. The small band or moulding near the top of a column.

OBELISK. A tapering shaft or column of stone square or rectangular in section with pyramidal apex.

OGEE. A moulding; convex above and concave below, a continuous curve. *See* MOULDINGS.

OIL FINISH. Where the surface of wood is finished by polishing with several applications of boiled linseed oil.

ORMOLU. The word is of French derivation and should be spelt ormoulu. It means gold ground to a powder for amalgamation with mercury. The preparation was applied with a brush to the

OBELISK.

metal which was then heat treated to vaporise the mercury. The object was then burnished. Ormolu is now understood to refer to brass castings which have been gilt and are used as decoration on clock cases, furniture, and also complete articles such as clock cases, lamp stands, etc.

OYSTERED or **OYSTER.** A circular grain formation from cross sections of small branches of wood, *e.g.* oyster walnut; oyster olive wood, etc.

PAD FEET. A form of foot usually associated with the Cabriole Leg (*q.v.*).

PAD FOOT.

PARCEL GILT. Gilt in part. A form of decoration where, for purposes of design, certain parts only are gilt as distinct from a completely gilded surface.

PARLIAMENT CLOCK. *See* Act of Parliament Clock.

PARQUETRY. Refers to marquetry or inlay work where the design is formed by placing together pieces with straight sides, squares, rectangle, diamond shapes, etc. A draught board effect is an example. Taken from the word "Parquet" the wooden flooring.

PATERA. A small circular, elliptical, or other shape motif, carved or inlaid, used as a form of decoration.

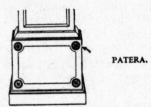

PATERA.

PATINA. The high polish acquired by old wood from long and constant polishing. Not to be confused with French polish (*q.v.*). Strictly, patina refers to the green incrustation on bronze coins and works of art.

PEDIMENT. Triangular, ornamental facing. In furniture and clock cases it has a rather loose term and refers to any decorative frontal structure above the cornice. Also referred to as Portico Top. The term also refers to the "Stick Barometer," where the readings are taken

ANTIQUE CLOCKS—Cont.

direct from the mercury in the tube. *See* also Broken Pediment.

PEDIMENT.

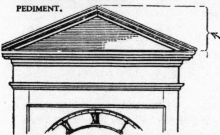

PEDIMENT BAROMETER. Refers to the type of barometer where the readings are observed direct from the level of the mercury in the tube; a scale is provided as a guide to enable the measurement of the mercury to be noted. The case is usually parallel with a bulbous part at the lower end to accommodate the "bag" of mercury and a "hood" shaped head for the scale, etc. Sometimes referred to as a stick barometer because of its stick-like appearance.

PENDULUM APERTURE. The aperture in the dial of a clock through which a small piece fixed to the pallets of the movement, can be seen to move to and fro when the pendulum is swinging. Usual in bracket clocks. Also known as mock pendulum.

PENDULUM APERTURE IN DIAL.

PENDULUM APERTURE, GLAZED. The glazed aperture in the door of a long-case clock, through which the bob of the pendulum can be seen. It is not usual for long-case clocks to have pendulum apertures in the dials.

PENDULUM APERTURE, GLAZED.

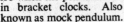

PERPENDICULAR STYLE. A design peculiar to England during the Gothic period at the end of the fourteenth century, its principal characteristic being its upright appearance and emphasis on the vertical line.

PIE CRUST EDGING. A decorative form of carving resembling the decoration given to the edge of a pie.

PIETRA DURA. Inlaying in marble.

PILASTER. A rectangular column.

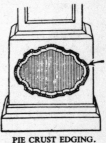

PIE CRUST EDGING.

PLANTED. Where mouldings are mitred and fixed separately, not stuck on to the ground work.

PLAQUE. Ornamental tablet of metal or porcelain, etc., either plain or decorated, usually circular or elliptical.

PLINTH. The lower part of a clock case upon which the case is built, also termed the base. Sometimes the skirting only is referred to as the plinth. Correctly the whole as indicated is the plinth. The base or stand upon which a cup or trophy stands.

POLLARD. A tree that has had its boughs and trunk lopped, causing a peculiar growth at the top which yields finely figured wood, usually cut as veneers.

PORTICO TOP. *See* Pediment.

POSTMAN'S ALARM CLOCK. A 30-hour, hanging clock; weight driven, long pendulum, circular dial. Case made of wood, fitted with alarm mechanism, usually of Dutch origin.

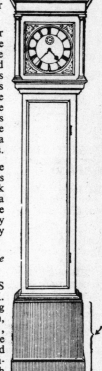

PLINTH.

ANTIQUE CLOCKS—Cont.

PULL QUARTER. Where the hours and the quarters are sounded by pulling the cord of a clock. In such clocks the quarters are not struck as the clock goes as in a chiming clock.

PUTTO. A cherub. When associated with clock case decoration it refers to a model of a cherub. The plural is putti.

PUTTO.

QUATREFOILS. A Gothic style consisting of four Foils (*q.v.*) within a circle.

QUIRK. The narrow groove or hollow at the side of a bead.

QUATREFOILS.

RAILWAY TIME. *See* Greenwich Mean Time. (General Dictionary Section.)

REEDING. Semicircular projections on columns or round the edges of a clock case, resembling reeds.

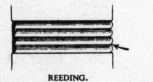

REEDING.

RENAISSANCE. A rebirth. The great 15th century European revival of interest in classic architecture.

RIBBON DECORATION. A form of decoration resembling ribbon.

RIBBON DECORATION.

RIBBON STICK. A form of decoration resembling ribbon wound upon a stick.

RISING HOOD. *See* Hood.

ROCOCO. A definite architectural period style, relating in the first place, to a style of landscape gardening. Also applies to a French ornamentation resembling shells and rock work. A term sometimes used to define a superabundance of ornament, after Baroque (*q.v.*).

ROE. A term referring to the figure sometimes found in wood; a spotty appearance not unlike Shagreen (*q.v.*).

ROUNDEL. The bull's-eye glass or bottle glass used in the doors of long-case clocks.

RUN OUT. Where a moulding runs out to a point; before mitres were used.

SATIN FINISH. A term used to denote a dull finish to French polish and a fine straight grain finish to metal work.

SCALLOP OR SCOLLOP. Carving resembling an escallop shell.

SCALLOP OR SCOLLOP.

SCROLL FOOT. *See* Flemish Foot.

SCROLL ORNAMENT. A form of ornamentation resembling a roll of parchment or other material.

SCROLL ORNAMENT.

ANTIQUE CLOCKS—Cont.

SCOTIA. *See* MOULDINGS.

SEAT BOARD. The piece of wood upon which the mechanism of a clock rests; usually the mechanism is secured to the seat board, which then stands in the case, as with a bracket clock, or upon the Cheeks (*q.v.*) of the long case.

SEAWEED MARQUETRY. Marquetry work which is composed of a large number of fine lines forming a profuse " all over " design.

SERPENTINE. When the front lines in plan, are of a curved in and out, or serpentine shape.

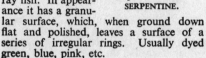

SHAGREEN. The skin of the horse, ass, camel, shark or ray fish. In appearance it has a granu-

SERPENTINE.

lar surface, which, when ground down flat and polished, leaves a surface of a series of irregular rings. Usually dyed green, blue, pink, etc.

SHEEP'S HEAD. A Lantern Clock (*q.v.*) with a very large dial.

SHEEP'S HEAD.

SKELETON DIAL. Refers to a dial where the hour ring has been cut away leaving the numerals standing in relief. A feature of some of the seventeenth and eighteenth century clocks.

SLIDE-UP HOOD. Refers to the way the Hood (*q.v.*) of the seventeenth century long-case clock was removed by sliding upwards, either to get at the mechanism or to wind it.

SPADE FOOT. The four-sided tapering foot. Also referred to as Block Foot (*q.v.*).

SPADE FOOT.

SPANDREL OR SPANDRIL. The triangular mount placed at the four corners of the dial of seventeenth century clocks, sometimes termed " corner-pieces." Usually the dial consists of a base plate, hour circle and then the four spandrels. Also known as corner pieces.

SPANDREL OR SPANDRIL.

SPOON FITTING. A fitting resembling a spoon, used in seventeenth century long-cases to lock the hood.

SPRUNG MOULDING. Referring to a curved moulding; where the moulding is sprung to take the form of a curve.

SPOON FITTING.

STICK BAROMETER. Another name for Pediment Barometer (*q.v.*).

ANTIQUE CLOCKS—Cont.

STRAP HINGES.
Used on the long
door of long-case
clocks and showing
straps inside the
door.

STRAP HINGES.

STRAP WORK. A style of decoration
forming bands, sometimes interlaced,
resembling straps. To be found in carving,
marquetry and fretwork. The style of
marquetry illustrated is referred to as
Arabesque (*q.v.*).

STRAP WORK.

STRINGING. Thin inlay of contrasting
colour with the main part of the panel.

SUNK PANEL.
Where a panel is
sunk below the sur-
rounding mould-
ings.

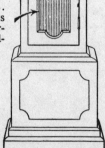

SUNK
PANEL.

SWAG. A swinging form of decoration,
such as drapery or festoons of flowers.

SWAG.

TERMINAL. The finish to a standard
or post.

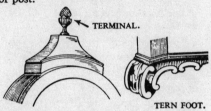

TERMINAL.

TERN FOOT.

TERN FEET. Referring to feet consisting
of a three scroll pattern.

THERM. A sort of trunk,
pillar or pedestal, often in the
form of an inverted obelisk, a
pedestal small at the base and
increasing upwards.

TORCHILUS. A moulding.
Also referred to as scotia.
See MOULDINGS.

TORTOISESHELL. The
tortoiseshell of commerce is
the shell of the Hawksbill
turtle. Used to make clock
cases and also as the ground
work for Buhl work (*q.v.*),
when a gilt, vermilion, or
yellow colour is given to the
work before the application
of the shell.

TORUS. A large bead, one
of the classical mouldings.
See MOULDINGS.

TRACERY. Fretwork in
wood or metal.

THERM

TREFOIL.

TREFOIL. A Gothic
design consisting of three
Foils (*q.v.*).

ANTIQUE CLOCKS—Cont.

TREILLAGE. Trellis work.

TRUNK. Refers to the body or main part of the case of a long-case clock. The case is formed of three parts, the trunk the Hood (*q.v.*) and the Plinth (*q.v.*).

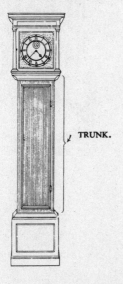

TRUNK.

TWIST PILLARS. The wood pillars of a twisted design found in the hood of seventeenth century long-case clocks.

TWIST PILLARS.

TYMPANUM. The triangular space forming the field of the Pediment (*q.v.*)

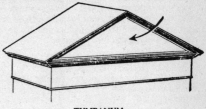

TYMPANUM.

URN FINIALS. Finials (*q.v.*) in the shape of an urn.

URN FINIALS.

VENEER. Thin sheets of wood used as a covering of other wood. Usually veneer is cut from a finer wood or wood with a beautiful grain or figure.

VIGNETTE. A Gothic ornamentation of vine leaves and tendrils.

VIGNETTE.

VINE ORNAMENT. Block under the corner of a Doric cornice.

WAGON-SPRING CLOCK. A leaf spring, similar to that used in wagons (and other vehicles) is employed as the motive power in place of a mainspring or weight. Clocks fitted with this device were made to run for 30 hours to 30 days with one winding. Invented by Joseph Ives, an American, about 1816–1818. This system of motive power is to be found in American clocks only. (Illustration on next page).

ANTIQUE CLOCKS—Cont.

WAX POLISH. Wood polished with beeswax and turpentine. Wax polishing was the only form of polishing before the introduction of french polish in the early part of the eighteenth century.

WHEEL BAROMETER. Refers to the type of barometer where the reading is indicated on a dial by a hand. A mercurial tube is used, and a glass float rises and falls on the mercury with the changes in atmospheric pressure. A cord attached to the float passes over a pulley and the hand is fixed to an extending pivot attached to the pulley. Invented by Dr. Robert Hooke, about 1686. This type of barometer is also referred to as a Banjo barometer due to the similarity of its case to a banjo.

WAGON-SPRING CLOCK.

English Clock Cases

DATE OF INTRODUCTION OF VARIOUS WOODS, ETC.

TUDOR	Iron or Brass.
JACOBEAN CROMWELLIAN	Oak (Mainly in the form of brackets for lantern clocks).
CAROLEAN QUEEN ANNE	Ebony; Pearwood ebonised; Marquetry; Kingwood, Walnut; Olive Wood.
GEORGIAN	Mahogany; Satinwood.
VICTORIAN	Rosewood

The date of the introduction of certain woods used in making clock cases is approximate. As an example:—although as a general guide, rosewood was introduced in the Victorian era a clock case has been found made of this wood and dated *circa* 1700; it may well be that a piece of rosewood was brought into this country specially. But such isolated instances do not necessarily alter the general rule.

The wood used for the manufacture of clock cases followed the furniture makers.

ANTIQUE CLOCKS—Cont.

English Clock Case Styles

Illustrations of typical examples of English clock case styles, intended to form a guide when assessing the age of clocks.

Notes on particular features in connection with antique clocks.

Illustrations on pages 38 to 43.

Quarter hour divisions only on dials (Clocks with hour hand only)	From 1600.
Portico or architectural top to long case and bracket clocks. *See* Fig. 1 ...	From 1600.
Minute hand made its appearance (?) ...	From about 1600.
Flat top to long case and bracket clocks. *See* Fig. 2	From 1670.
Signature of maker on dial at bottom of long case and bracket clocks	From 1670.
Straight columns to hood of long case and bracket clocks. *See* Figs. 1 and 11 ...	To 1670.
Twist or Barley Sugar columns to hood or long case and bracket clocks. *See* Fig. 3 ...	From 1670–1700.
Domed top to long case and bracket clocks. *See* Figs. 4 and 13 ...	From 1675.
Long or seconds, or Royal, pendulum introduced ...	1675.
Minute hand made its appearance (?) ...	From about 1660.
Basket dome top to bracket clocks. *See* Fig. 12 ...	From about 1680.
Signature of maker on chapter ring of long case and bracket ...	From 1690.
Straight columns introduced to long cases. *See* Fig. 1 ...	1700.
Double basket top to bracket clocks. *See* Fig. 18 ...	From about 1700.
Convex moulding under hood of long case clocks. *See* Figs. 1 and 2	Up to 1700.
Cupid spandrels (simple) on long case and bracket clocks ...	Up to 1700.
Foliated or more complicated design of spandrels ...	From 1700.
Concave moulding under hood of long case clocks. *See* Figs. 3 and 4	From 1700.
Inverted bell top with square dial to bracket clocks. *See* Fig. 16 ...	From 1710.
Arched hood to long case clocks. *See* Figs. 6 and 19 ...	From 1715.
Inverted bell top with break arch dial to bracket clocks. *See* Fig. 17	From 1720.
Broken arch dial to bracket and long case clocks. *See* Fig. 5 ...	From 1720.
Hour hand fitted to round pipe of hour wheel ...	From 1720.
Broken arch hood to long case clocks. *See* Fig. 6 ...	From 1730.
Bell top to bracket clocks (black or ebonised) ...	From 1740.
Bell top to bracket clocks (mahogany) ...	From 1740.
Round dial to long case and bracket clocks. *See* Fig. 19 ...	From 1760.
Painted dial to long case and bracket clocks ...	From 1760.
Dial silvered all over (straight grain) to long case and bracket clocks	From 1760.

The dates given can only be approximate. There was overlapping of some styles and features of up to 10 years, and there are instances where a feature may have appeared years before, i.e. there is a Tompion long case clock with broken arch dial assessed at 1695, but this does not necessarily make the general date of 1720 incorrect.

ANTIQUE CLOCKS—Cont.

English Long-Case Clocks

(See English Clock Case Styles, page 37.)

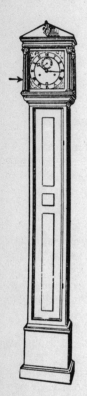

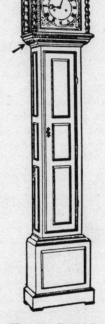

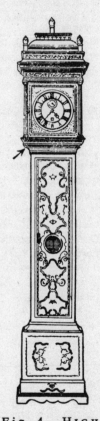

Fig. 1. PORTICO or ARCHITECTURAL (from 1660) Note: straight columns.

Fig. 2. FLAT TOP (from 1670).

Fig. 3. TWIST or BARLEY SUGAR COLUMNS (from 1670 to 1700). Note: convex moulding at top of trunk of case — under the hood. Also low dome.

Fig. 4. HIGH DOMED TOP (from 1705). Note: concave moulding at top of trunk of case— under the hood. Also built up dome.

ANTIQUE CLOCKS—Cont.

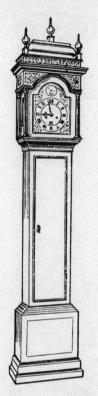

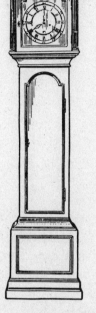

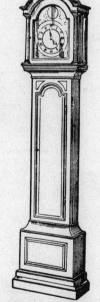

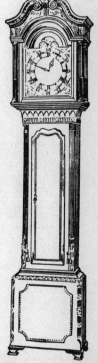

Fig. 5. BROKEN ARCH DIAL (from 1720).

Fig. 7. (From 1775.)

Fig. 6. BROKEN ARCH HOOD (from 1760).

Fig. 8. (From 1785.)

39

ANTIQUE CLOCKS—Cont.

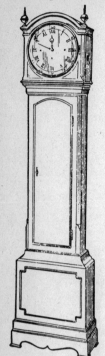

Fig. 9. (From 1810.)

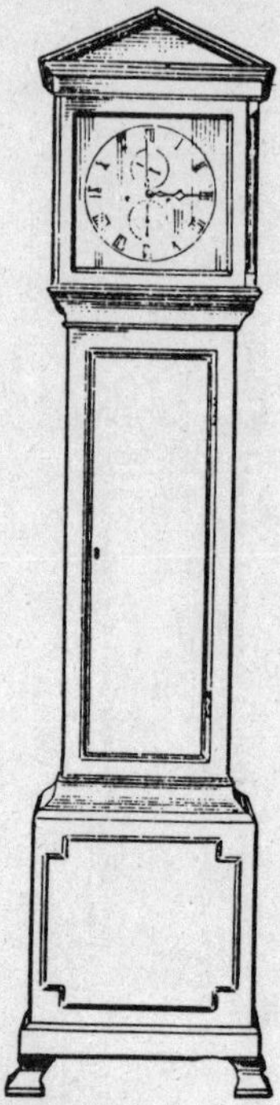

Fig. 10. (From 1825.)

English
Bracket Clocks

(See English Clock Case Styles, page 37.)

Fig. 11. ARCHITECTURAL
(*circa* 1665).

Fig. 12. BASKET TOP
(*circa* 1680).

ANTIQUE CLOCKS—Cont.

Fig. 13.   DOMED TOP
(*circa* 1685).

Fig. 14.   BELL BASKET TOP
(*circa* 1695).

Fig. 15.   INVERTED BELL TOP BROKEN
ARCH DIAL
(*circa* 1720).

Fig. 16.   DOUBLE INVERTED BELL TOP
(*circa* 1720).

ANTIQUE CLOCKS—Cont.

Fig. 17. BELL TOP (*circa* 1720).

Fig. 18. DOUBLE BASKET TOP
(*circa* 1770).

Fig. 19. BROKEN ARCH TOP (*circa* 1780).

Fig. 20. BALLOON (*circa* 1790).

ANTIQUE CLOCKS—Cont.

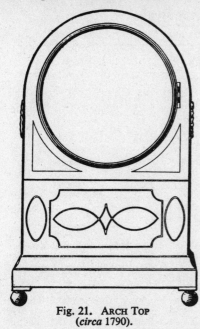

Fig. 21. ARCH TOP
(circa 1790).

Fig. 22. LANCET TOP
(circa 1800).

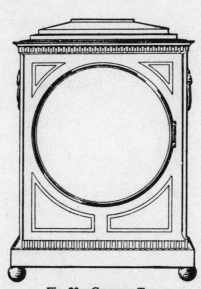

Fig. 23. CHAMFER TOP
(circa 1810).

ANTIQUE CLOCKS—Cont.
English Period Styles
For French Styles see page 134.

STYLE	PERIOD	DATE	REMARKS
TUDOR ..	Henry VIII	1509–1547	—
	Edward VI	1547–1553	—
	Mary	1553–1558	—
ELIZABETHAN ..	Elizabeth	1558–1603	—
JACOBEAN	James I	1603–1623	—
	Charles I	1625–1649	—
CROMWELLIAN ..	Cromwell	1649–1660	—
CAROLEAN	Charles II.. ..	1660–1685	—
	James II	1685–1688	—
QUEEN ANNE	William and Mary	1689–1702	—
	Queen Anne ..	1702–1714	—
	George I	1714–1724	—
GEORGIAN	George II	1724–1760	These reigns embrace Chippendale, Hepplewhite, Sheraton, English Empire and Regency.
	George III ..	1760–1820	
VICTORIAN ..	Queen Victoria ..	1837–1901	—
CHIPPENDALE I CHIPPENDALE II	—	1720–1779	The first Chippendale, Thomas, came to London in 1720. Furniture about 1750. Factory with about 30 workmen.
CHIPPENDALE III	—	1779–1805	Continued the business and became bankrupt 1805. Very small production.
ADAM	Adam brothers (Robert Adam was the principal).	1728–1792	Designers only, furniture made by Chippendale, Hepplewhite and others.
HEPPLEWHITE ..	George Hepplewhite.	1760–1800	Died 1786, the firm carried on under the title of A. Hepplewhite and Co.
SHERATON ..	Thomas Sheraton	1751–1806	Designer, made few pieces, but his designs used by many makers.
ENGLISH EMPIRE	—	1802–1840	This style was in vogue until the Victorian and is a poor copy of the French Empire style.
EMPIRE ..	—	—	French style of decoration based upon ancient Grecian and Egyptian forms.
REGENCY ..	—	1810–1820	The period during which, George, Prince of Wales (subsequently George IV) was Regent for his father, George III, during his incapacity. The style is a delicate form of the Victorian style.

ANTIQUE CLOCKS—Cont.

Periods of French Clock Styles

REIGN OF LOUIS
XIII
1610–1643

Clocks of Louis XIII style scarcely appeared at all before 1620; the style did not die out completely until the middle of the 17th century (i.e. 1650) or even later.

REIGN OF LOUIS
XIV, The Great
King
1643–1661 =
(Regency of his
mother)
1661–1715 =
(Louis XIV alone)

Clocks of Louis XIV period began to appear about 1650, their numbers increased greatly because Louis XIV encouraged craftsmen to produce more and more. This increased production continued for some time after the death of Louis XIV; up to about 1725.

ANTIQUE CLOCKS—Cont.

REIGN OF LOUIS XV
1715–1725 = (Regency)
1725–1774 = (Louis XV alone)

From 1725, the contorted style of Louis XV made itself evident, and was emphasised more and more up to the end of the 18th century. But already by about 1750 the first lines of the Louis XVI style made their appearance.

REIGN OF LOUIS XVI
1774–1791

Prodigious period of remarkable productions, thanks to the artists of the Court of Versailles and especially to their encouragement by the Queen, Marie Antoinette. The very pleasing Louis XVI style continued as late as the first quarter of the 19th century.

REVOLUTIONARY PERIOD
1789–1799

" Decimal " clocks showing decimal or " Republican " time. A decree was made during the French Revolution that clocks and watches should indicate decimal time. Dials of watches and clocks were made showing the dial divided into either five parts in the instance of the 12 hour dial or 10 parts in the instance of the 24 hour dial. The fashion was of short duration and there are no records that the decree was enforced. Clocks and watches are still extant with decimal dials.

ANTIQUE CLOCKS—Cont.

EMPIRE PERIOD
1799–1815   Particular period of gilt clocks, inspired by Greek and Egyptian styles.

RESTORATION
Louis XVIII

Charles X
1824–1830

Louis Philippe
1830–1848

Republique
1848–1852

Re-hash of the earlier styles arranged and grouped giving the style known as Rococo.

2ND EMPIRE
Napoleon II
1852–1870   Reproductions of old models—but of very economical manufacture and very cheap; this is what caused the loss of the art of the universally appreciated fine French clock.

Kings of France

Francois I	...	...	...	1515–1547
Henri II	...	...	...	1547–1559
Francois II	...	...	...	1559–1560
Charles IX	...	...	...	1560–1574
Henri III	...	...	...	1574–1589
Henri IV	...	...	...	1589–1610
Louis XIII	...	...	...	1610–1643
Louis XIV	...	...	...	1643–1715
Louis XV	...	...	...	1715–1774
Louis XVI	...	...	...	1774–1792
Louis XVII (Minor)	...			
Louis XVIII	...	...	...	1814–1824
Charles X	...	...	...	1824–1830
Louis Phillipe I	...	...	...	1830–1848
Napoleon I	...	...	...	1804–1814
Napoleon II Duke of Reich-stadt	...	...	...	1811–1837
Napoleon III	...	...	...	1850–1870

2ND EMPIRE

ANVIL. A steel stake, used when working metal, *i.e.*, hammering to make flat, etc.; also the stationary jaw of the micrometer.

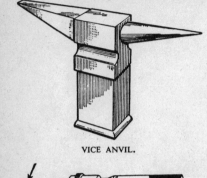

VICE ANVIL.

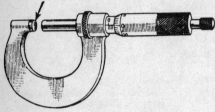

MICROMETER ANVIL.

APPARENT POWER. Superficial Wattage or Volt-Amperes. Volt-Amperes in a circuit especially if other than unity Power Factor (*q.v.*).

APPLIQUÉ. *See* ANTIQUE CLOCK AND CLOCK CASE TERMS.

APPROACH CONTACT. The phase in the action of a pair of mating gear teeth during which the point of contact is approaching the line of centres; also called Engaging Contact.

APRON. *See* ANTIQUE CLOCK AND CLOCK CASE TERMS.

AQUAFORTIS. Concentrated nitric acid used for testing platinum, gold, and silver. Chemical symbol $H N O_3$. Platinum and fine gold (24 ct.) are unaffected by it. As more alloy is used with gold, *i.e.* 22 ct., 18 ct., 14 ct., 9 ct., so the effect of the acid varies. By this means the quality of the alloy can be estimated. Silver turns black when touched with the acid. Brass turns green.

AQUA-REGIA. A mixture of nitric and hydrochloric acids. So named because of its ability to dissolve gold.

ARABIC. A style of numeral. The figures 1, 2, 3, etc., in contradistinction to the Roman numerals I, II, III, etc. The figure "0" is used with the Arabic numerals but is actually an ancient Hindu invention.

ARABESQUE. *See* ANTIQUE CLOCK AND CLOCK CASE TERMS.

ARBOR. The shaft or axle on which the wheel and pinion, etc., of watch and clockwork are carried. Pinions and arbors may be formed in one piece but the distinction remains. In the case of Pallets and Balance, the arbor is termed a "Staff."

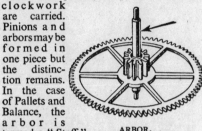

ARBOR.

Also, a tapering shaft fitted with a driving pulley, on which work is mounted for turning between centres. Similar devices for gripping work between brass, rubber, or cork flanges threaded on the shaft and other special holders of the same principle are termed arbors. *See* Turning Arbor; Pallet Arbor.

ARC (Electrical). The passage of current between separated conductors.

ARC. A segment of a circle. Also used to describe the extent of movement, *i.e.* arc of vibration of a balance or pendulum, etc., "Long and short arcs" usually refer to the arc of vibration of a balance when in the horizontal and vertical positions. Long arc in the horizontal position; short arc in the vertical position; *i.e.* the extent of the arc of vibration is greater in the horizontal position than the vertical position. More correctly, the "long and short arcs" represent respectively the vibrations over and under $1\frac{1}{4}$ turns although watch balances do not always attain that amplitude of vibration. In Marine Chronometers where the $1\frac{1}{4}$ turns are attained but varying positions are not taken, the long and short arcs are considered only in relation to the horizontal position. The variation if any, is due to fusee and mainspring discrepancies fully wound or down; also to thickening oil, faulty transmission of power, etc.

ARCH. *See* ANTIQUE CLOCK AND CLOCK CASE TERMS.

ARCHED DIAL. *See* ANTIQUE CLOCK AND CLOCK CASE TERMS.

ARCHIMEDEAN DRILL. An apparatus which causes the drill to rotate backward and forward. Jewellery mounters use the type where a cord is made to twine round the central rod and can be used with one hand. Horologists use a type consisting of a form of elongated quick-thread necessitating the use of both hands, one to operate the drill and the other to steady the instrument. Named after Archimedes, 287–212 B.C.

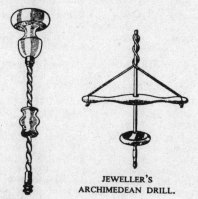

JEWELLER'S
ARCHIMEDEAN DRILL.

ARCHIMEDEAN
DRILL.

ARCHITECTURAL STYLE. *See* ANTIQUE CLOCK AND CLOCK CASE TERMS.

ARCHITECTURAL TERMS. Term applicable to clock cases. *See* ANTIQUE CLOCK AND CLOCK CASE TERMS.

ARGENTAN. *See* METALS USED IN HOROLOGY.

ARITHMETICAL CLOCK. An arrangement conceived in the early part of the nineteenth century where three clocks are so arranged and fitted that arithmetical calculation are possible. (Surely the forerunner of our modern automatic calculator.)

ARKANSAS STONE. A fine-grained, hard, whitish stone (Silicon) used for whetting tools to a fine edge. Quarried in the State of Arkansas, U.S.A.

ARMATURE (General). Part of an electro-magnetic circuit producing mechan-ical movement in the presence of a current. More particularly, a soft iron cap, plate, rod or other shaped piece which, under the influence of an associated electro magnet, produces useful mechanical movement, *e.g.* relay switches, lock actions, indicators, etc. Used in horology to impulse a specially constructed balance or, in pendulum clocks, to time, deliver, or control the impulsing of the pendulum and to " drive " the impulse dials.

ARMILLARY SPHERE. A skeleton celestial globe, made of metal rings representing the great circles of the heavens, including the equator, meridian, ecliptic and the tropics. The circles are divided into degrees for angular measurement. In the seventeenth and eighteenth centuries such models, were either suspended, rested on a stand or fixed to a handle. They were used to show the difference between the Ptolemaic theory of a central earth and the Copernican theory of a central sun. In a simple form they were used B.C. and at a later date the sun dial was incorporated. The armillary is used in the symbol of the British Horological Institute.

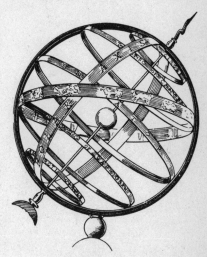

ARMILLARY SPHERE.

ASSAYING. The method of testing metals by refining. The metals composing an alloy are separated into their constituent elements.

ASSORTIMENT (French). The name given to the parts of an escapement, *e.g.* escape wheel, pallets, lever, etc.

ASTATIC. The arrangement of individual magnetic fields whereby the resultant of their mutual interaction is zero.

ASTRAGAL MOULDING. *See* MOULDINGS.

ASTRAL. A term applied to the dial of a clock or watch referring to a depiction of the heavens showing the constellations, etc., visible on a particular day.

ASTROLABE. An instrument used by the Greeks and Arabs and in medieval Europe to take altitudes and to mark the positions and movements of heavenly bodies, so to deduce time and latitude. It consists of a disc with a rotatable rule or scale carrying sights. The astronomical astrolabe is now superseded by the equatorial instrument. The example illustrated is of German origin and known as " Lynden's Heilbronn Astrolabe," it is 6¾ ins. diameter and ⅛ in. thick. It is illustrated by courtesy of the Oxford University Press from " The Astrolabes of the World," by Robert T. Gunther, M.A.

ASTRONOMER ROYAL. An official position; the head of the Royal Greenwich Observatory (*q.v.*).

ASTRONOMICAL CLOCK. A precision seconds pendulum clock driven by a weight; the dial is marked with separate hour, minute, and seconds circles and each circle has its own hand. Made to stand either on the floor or to hang upon a wall. These clocks are also referred to as Regulators. In practice astronomers today use the Quartz Crystal Clock (*q.v.*). *See* Regulator.

ASTRONOMY. The astronomers' contribution to horology (*q.v.*) is the determination of time. Historically the two have always been closely related.

ASYNCHRONOUS. Non-synchronous, *i.e.* not in exact step; out of phase. A term referring to electric clocks, etc.

ATLANTIC STANDARD TIME. Four hours slow of Greenwich Mean Time (*q.v.*).

ATMOS CLOCK. A clock which is wound by changes in the temperature. The 400 day type of pendulum is used. Originally the main spring was wound by the equilibrium of a drum being upset by a tube of mercury fixed to the drum and acted upon by the changes in temperature.

LYNDEN'S ASTROLABE.

About 90% of the power so obtained is due to changes in temperature and 10% to barometric change. The system employed to-day is in principle similar to the aneroid. The drum (1) is fixed to the movement support. An aneroid-like box (2) is contained in the outer drum. The drum (1) is filled with ethyl chloride C_2H_5Cl and hermetically sealed. The spring (3) tends to push the aneroid-like box out. With a rise in temperature the ethyl chloride expands, and causes the end of the box to press inwards, and with a fall in temperature, to press outwards. A spring (7) is fixed to the drum at the left-hand side and a chain (4) is attached to the free end. The chain operates on the mainspring winding mechanism (6) and it is the action of the spring (7) expanding (in low temperature) that winds the mainspring in the barrel (5). The contraction (in heat) of the spring (7) forms a back action ready for the forward winding movement. It is estimated that a variation of 2° F. in the temperature is equivalent to 48 hours running and, that when fully wound, the clock will run for 100 days. (8) is the pendulum supported by the spring (9). (10) Is the regulating piece.

The principle of the first Atmos clocks made is as follows: Mercury, a volatile liquid and its saturated vapour are contained in a Pyrex U-tube. One end of the tube is shielded by insulated material from ordinary temperature change, the other end is left exposed. The weather does the rest. Let the weather show a rise of temperature and the vapour in the exposed end expands. It pushes along the mercury to the insulated end of the tube at the same time compressing the gas in this arm. As the drum in which the tube is fixed is poised in the centre, the change of centre of gravity caused by the displacement of the mercury causes it to revolve slightly. If the temperature falls the action is reversed: the pressure of the gas in the insulated arm being greater, forces the mercury towards the exposed arm. It is this rocking motion of the drum which winds a light mainspring and so supplies the power to keep the pendulum in motion.
(1) U shaped glass tube.
(2) Mercury.
(3) Liquid gas.
(4) Saturated vapour.
(5) Insulating material.
(6) Outer Thermos-like chamber.
(7) Drum.
(8) Pivoted centre.
A variation of temperature of 1° gives 120 hours power.

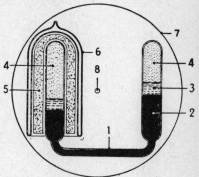

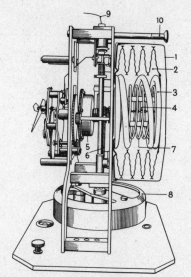

ATMOS CLOCK.
Made by the firm JAEGER-LE-COULTRE.

ATMOSPHERE. A unit of measurement of the average pressure exerted on the Earth's surface by the air, approx. 14.7 pounds per square inch. It is equivalent to the pressure of a column of water nearly 34 feet high and a column of mercury nearly 30 inches high. Used as a measure of water tightness of watch cases. The table below gives the relationship of different pressure scales. It is based on
1 atmosphere = 33·899 feet of water at 4° C.
= 14·696 pounds per square inch.
= 760 millimetres of mercury at 0° C.
1 inch = 25·3999 millimetres.

The table is made for water at a temperature of 4° C. and mercury at a temperature at 0° C. These are the usual temperatures used in making tables. However if the temperature were 20° C. then the maximum error in using this table would be less than 4/10ths of 1 per cent, so that for all practical purposes it may be taken to be correct.

CONVERSION TABLE—WATERPROOF WATCH CASES
ATMOSPHERES—FEET OF WATER—LB. SQ. IN.
INCHES Hg—MILLIMETRES Hg

Atmospheres	Depth of water in feet	Pounds per square inch	Inches of mercury	Millimetres of mercury
0·029	1	0·434	0·883	22·42
0·059	2	0·867	1·765	44·84
0·088	3	1·301	2·648	67·26
0·118	4	1·734	3·531	89·68
0·147	5	2·168	4·413	112·10
0·177	6	2·601	5·296	134·52
0·206	7	3·035	6·179	156·94
0·236	8	3·468	7·061	179·36
0·265	9	3·902	7·944	201·78
0·295	10	4·335	8·827	224·20
0·324	11	4·769	9·709	246·61
0·354	12	5·202	10·592	269·03
0·383	13	5·636	11·475	291·45
0·413	14	6·069	12·357	313·87
0·442	15	6·503	13·240	336·29
0·472	16	6·936	14·123	358·71
0·500	16·950	7·348	14·961	380·00
0·501	17	7·370	15·005	381·13
0·531	18	7·803	15·888	403·55
0·560	19	8·237	16·771	425·97
0·590	20	8·670	17·653	448·39
0·619	21	9·104	18·536	470·81
0·649	22	9·538	19·419	493·23
0·678	23	9·971	20·301	515·65
0·708	24	10·405	21·184	538·07
0·737	25	10·838	22·067	560·49
0·767	26	11·272	22·949	582·91
0·796	27	11·705	23·832	605·33
0·826	28	12·139	24·715	627·75
0·855	29	12·572	25·597	650·17
0·885	30	13·006	26·480	672·59
0·914	31	13·439	27·363	695·01
0·944	32	13·873	28·245	717·43
0·973	33	14·306	29·128	739·84
1·000	33·899	14·696	29·921	760·00
1·003	34	14·740	30·011	762·26
1·032	35	15·173	30·893	784·68
1·062	36	15·607	31·776	807·10
1·091	37	16·040	32·659	829·52
1·121	38	16·474	33·541	851·94
1·150	39	16·907	34·424	874·36
1·180	40	17·341	35·306	896·78

cont. on facing page.

Atmospheres	Depth of water in feet	Pounds per square inch	Inches of mercury	Millimetres of mercury
1·209	41	17·774	36·189	919·20
1·239	42	18·208	37·072	941·62
1·268	43	18·641	37·954	964·04
1·298	44	19·075	38·837	986·46
1·327	45	19·509	39·720	1008·88
1·357	46	19·942	40·602	1031·30
1·386	47	20·376	41·485	1053·72
1·416	48	20·809	42·368	1076·14
1·445	49	21·243	43·250	1098·56
1·475	50	21·676	44·133	1120·98
1·500	50·849	22·044	44·882	1140·00
1·504	51	22·110	45·016	1143·40
1·534	52	22·543	45·898	1165·82
1·563	53	22·977	46·781	1188·24
1·593	54	23·410	47·664	1210·66
1·622	55	23·844	48·546	1233·07
1·652	56	24·277	49·429	1255·49
1·681	57	24·711	50·312	1277·91
1·711	58	25·144	51·194	1300·33
1·740	59	25·578	52·077	1322·75
1·770	60	26·011	52·960	1345·17
1·799	61	26·445	53·842	1367·59
1·829	62	26·878	54·725	1390·01
1·858	63	27·312	55·608	1412·43
1·888	64	27·745	56·490	1434·85
1·917	65	28·179	57·373	1457·27
1·947	66	28·613	58·256	1479·69
1·976	67	29·046	59·138	1502·11
2·000	67·798	29·392	59·842	1520·00
2·006	68	29·480	60·021	1524·53
2·035	69	29·913	60·904	1546·95
2·065	70	30·347	61·786	1569·37
2·094	71	30·780	62·669	1591·79
2·124	72	31·214	63·552	1614·21
2·153	73	31·647	64·434	1636·63
2·183	74	32·081	65·317	1659·05
2·212	75	32·514	66·200	1681·47
2·242	76	32·948	67·082	1703·89
2·271	77	33·381	67·965	1726·30
2·301	78	33·815	68·848	1748·72
2·330	79	34·248	69·730	1771·14
2·360	80	34·682	70·613	1793·56

ATOMIC CLOCK. A time standard based on the natural frequency of the caesium atom. The first practical atomic clock was made by Dr. Louis Essen of the National Physical Laboratory, England, who was helped by pioneer work in the USA, and from June 1955, the quartz clocks at the National Physical Laboratory, England were checked by means of an atomic standard. This was the first time that quartz clocks had been calibrated with an atomic standard to an accuracy greater than that given by astronomical time. It was a complete break with the traditional system of time-keeping, which is, of course, based on the rotation of the earth. One complete rotation of the earth gives the day and this is divided into a more convenient and shorter unit by the steady swinging of a pendulum or, in recent years, the more rapid vibrations of a ring of quartz. In practice, because astronomical measurements are relatively inaccurate, the results are averaged over quite long intervals. The working standards of time are the quartz clocks, which are adjusted periodically to keep in step with the earth. This procedure is no longer good enough for some scientific work, because the earth's rotation itself is found to fluctuate during the year. To overcome these fluctuations the observations must be averaged over still longer intervals of several years. The quartz clocks cannot be relied upon to keep uniform time for such long periods. So, although it is possible to know the average value of the unit of time with great accuracy, the value at any particular instant can only be known with a much smaller degree of accuracy. There is the added disadvantage that the results can only be calculated some years in arrears, when sufficient astronomical data have been accumulated. A standard which is not only more accurate but gives results much more quickly seemed to be that offered by the natural vibrations of the atom. Not all atoms can be used but the caesium atom is particularly suitable because of its unusual magnetic properties. It behaves like a tiny compass needle, which can, however, set either along the direction of a magnetic field or in exactly the opposite direction. The state it is in can be recognised by the direction in which it is deflected by a magnet. It is possible to produce a change from one state to the other by applying a magnetic field which is reversing its direction very rapidly, but only when the frequency corresponds exactly to a particular value which is a fundamental constant of the caesium atom. The reason for this is that a small but very definite amount of work must be done to change the atom from one state to the other. The frequency required is very high. So far, the most accurate measurements made give it as 9,192,631,830 cycles per second. The first caesium standard was a copper tube 5 ft. in length supported on two heavy pedestals and a system of pipes and pumps maintains a very high vacuum inside it. Around the tube are a number of coils of wire which are used to apply the appropriate magnetic fields. A smaller copper tube leads away from the middle of the main chamber to a small transmitter, similar to that used in radar equipment, which supplies the rapidly alternating field.

The caesium atoms are evaporated from an oven at one end of the tube. They stream through the appropriate field and are focused on to a detector at the other end. When the frequency of the transmitter is just right, the tiny magnets spin round, as it were, and they are then deflected away from the detector so that there is a sudden drop in the number of atoms received. The transmitter can thus be set at the caesium frequency and then used in turn to calibrate the quartz clocks. The setting is so exact even with the first experimental model, the quartz clocks controlled by the caesium atoms kept time to 1 second to 30 years. The caesium standard also has many other scientific uses. One NPL version is employed as well to monitor the standard frequency broadcasts from the Post Office radio station MSF at Rugby on 2·5, 5, and 10 Mc/s. The accuracy of the latest atomic clock is in the region of one second in 3,000 years. It is not normally kept going continuously but is run when required for frequency comparison purposes.

ATROPOS. *See* ANTIQUE CLOCK CASE TERMS.

ATTRACTION. A force which is exhibited by any mass or tiny particle tending to draw others to itself. The force exhibited between unlike magnetic poles or electrical charges.

AUTOMATON. A clock with automatic figures working in conjunction with the mechanism of the clock. Distinct from the striking " Jacks " (*q.v.*) Clocks with automata are made as public and domestic clocks; the public clocks are usually of more simple design than the domestic ones. A popular type is, at each quarter and at the hours, a figure, *i.e.* St. George on horseback, gallops after the dragon. There are many schemes devised, and a representative example of a domestic automaton is as follows. A painted scene depicting a farmstead, with a clock in the tower, which indicates the time of day and chimes. In addition, at each quarter and at the hours, ducks swim by on a mill stream; a water-mill revolves; a man saws wood; birds fly overhead, a door opens, a man with a gun ready to fire appears at the open door, aims at a bird which immediately drops out of view; the man recedes through the door, which closes and completes the sequence. While this is enacted, twisted crystal columns fitted to the case, stars of crystal and faceted spheres, all revolve, stopping when the door closes as described.

AUTOMATIC LATHE. Generally referred in number as "automatics." "A bank of automatics" means a number of automatic lathes in a row together. A lathe in which the tools for cutting, threading and other purposes are advanced to the work automatically and the work is moved axially as required until it is finished, when a new piece of raw material comes into position and the cycle is repeated. Balance staffs, for instance, can be turned and cut to length one after the other from a steel rod automatically. Accuracy is possible normally to within ±0·0025 mm. and some automatics are accurate to within ±0·001 mm.

AUTOMATIC PUNCH. A spring-loaded, self-striking punch operated by hand pressure.

AUTOMATIC WATCH. *See* Automatic Winding.

AUTOMATIC WINDING. A device whereby the watch is wound automatically during wear. Its invention is claimed by the Swiss for the Swiss watchmaker. John Perrelet, 1729–1826. Since Perrelet's time, there have been many adaptions of the principle in "Automatic" and "Perpetual" watches. There is no record of a watch having been made by Perrelet; he did not patent his idea. John Harwood, an English watchmaker, was the first to apply automatic work to a wrist watch. The English claim the invention for a Swiss watchmaker resident in England, Louis Recordon. Letters Patent were granted him on July 15, 1780. "The History of the Self-Winding Watch" by Alfred Chapuis and Eugéne Jaquet is an exhaustive work on the subject. Breguet was, it is on record, the first man to put automatic winding into practice and this was adapted

to pocket watches. In recent years a pocket watch has been found fitted with automatic winding dating from about 1760 (no maker's name). It was not until the advent of the wrist watch that automatic winding was taken seriously. In recent years the self-winding watch has become commonplace. The Harwood system was patented in 1923. It consisted in principle of the "pedometer" action as introduced by Perrelet. Hatot of Paris introduced the Rolls watch shortly afterwards, the whole movement rocked or rolled backwards and forwards thus winding the mainspring. There followed systems in which the wrist movement worked upon the lug or strap supports of the case so that this slight movement wound the mainspring. Opening and closing of the case (hunter type) operating a rack engaging a wheel on the winding shaft is another system. There are other systems too numerous to mention. The systems most favoured are the pedometer and those in which there is complete rotation of the winding weight. There is much in favour of automatic winding for watches, the greatest advantage being a very constant mainspring torque thus obtained. Automatic winding is also applied to time switches, domestic clocks, and tower clocks. For time switches the arrangement is often to rewind the main-

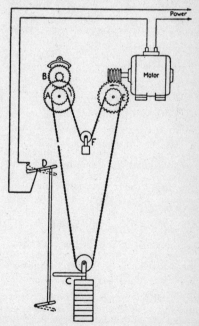

AUTOMATIC WINDING

spring by means of a synchronous electric motor. Domestic clocks are sometimes rewound at short intervals by a dry cell battery operating a solenoid and ratchet gear mechanism. Auto-wound turret clocks normally employ a Huygens endless chain with an electric motor, as shown in the diagram. The winding barrel and great wheel of the clock are dispensed with and the weight C drives the wheel A, and escape wheel B. As the weight falls it operates the bottom toggle of switch D which energises the electric motor, causing it to rotate wheel E and wind up weight C. When the weight reaches the top toggle of switch D, it switches off the motor. The object of the small pulley and weight F is to keep the chain taut.

AUXILIARY COMPENSATION. An attachment to a balance to reduce the " Middle Temperature Error." *See* Mercer's and Kullberg's Balance and Airy's Bar.

AUXILIARY REGULATOR. Also called an Auxiliary Index, this is a two part Index (*q.v.*). One part carries the index pins and the other the tail of the regulator. After the watch has been set to time by adjusting the part carrying the index pins, the part carrying the tail may be set to the centre of

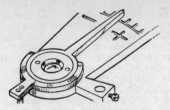

AUXILIARY REGULATOR.

its scale and further finer adjustment made by means of this.

AVANCE (French). Advance. " A " engraved on the balance cock of a Swiss or French watch or clock denotes " Avance," *i.e.* " Fast." " R " denotes " Retard," *i.e.* " Slow."

AXIAL PITCH. The pitch measured in the direction of the axis, of the teeth of helical, spiral or worm gears.

AXIAL THRUST. End pressure. Axial thrust bearings are fitted when no endshake is permissible (*e.g.*, lathe spindle).

AXIS. The stationary centre line of a rotating member.

AYR-STONE. Water-of-Ayr stone. A fine, slate like stone. Used to finish brass and similar soft metal surfaces. Obtained from Stair, Scotland. Montgomery stone (*q.v.*), is a finer cutting variety of Water-of-Ayr stone.

B

B.A. British Association screw thread. A standardisation of the sizes and pitches of screw threads as laid down by the British Association. Confined to small sizes; 6 mm. to 0·25 mm. in diameter and from 1 mm. to 0·072 mm. pitch. Numbered from 0 to 25.

B.H.I. *See* Horological Institute.

BACK COCK. The pallet cock of a pendulum clock. The term applies to both Anchor and Crown Wheel escapement clocks.

BACKLASH. The circumferential clearance between mating teeth. Backlash may be measured as a linear dimension at the

pitch circle as a fraction of the circular pitch or as an angle.

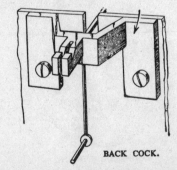

BACK COCK.

BACKSLOPE. That part of the balance staff which tapers from the balance on the underside; also refers to the cut at the back of a balance staff pivot.

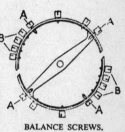

BACK SLOPE

BACK STOP. A form of Jumper Spring or lever (*q.v.*) the purpose of which is to prevent the part, usually a wheel, from turning backwards but at the same time not sufficiently strong to prevent backward movement if required, *e.g.* the piece engaging, the " escape wheel " of an Impulse Clock (*q.v.*).

BAGUETTE. *See* WATCH CASE STYLES.

BAIN'S CLOCK. The first electric clock, invented by Alexander Bain in 1840.

BALANCE. The controller or governor of a watch escapement such as the lever, chronometer, horizontal, duplex, etc. Sometimes referred to as " balance wheel," which is not good horological language. *See* Compensation Balance.

BALANCE ARC. The extent or amplitude of the vibration of the balance.

BALANCE CHUCK. Designed to hold the balance in the lathe.

BALANCE CHUCK.

BALANCE, PLAIN. A balance which is not cut, sometimes referred to as a Solid Balance, as distinct from the Compensation Balance (*q.v.*). A form of Plain Balance is used in Volet Balance compensating systems. *See* NOMENCLATURE OF WATCH PARTS, page 279.

BALANCE COCK. The bridge or bar

supporting the balance in position; it supports or holds the upper pivot in position. *See* NOMENCLATURE OF WATCH PARTS, page 276.

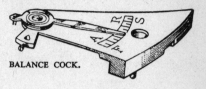

BALANCE COCK.

BALANCE COLLETS. *See* Timing Washers.

BALANCE SCREWS. The screws attached to the balance and used for the purpose of timing either for changes in temperature (B) or mean

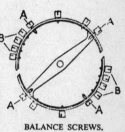

BALANCE SCREWS.

time (A). In the case of a plain uncut balance the screws then fitted serve to bring the balance to correct weight.

BALANCE SCREW FILING TOOL. A tool for the purpose of reducing the weight of balance screws without the necessity of removing the balance from the balance cock.

BALANCE SCREW REMOVING TOOL.

BALANCE SPRING. The spring controlling the balance; sometimes called the " Hairspring " owing to its similarity to a hair. The time of vibration of the balance is expressed by the formula:—

$$T = \pi \sqrt{\frac{Mk^2\ 12L}{Eht^3}}$$

where T=periodic time; L=length of

balance spring; h=height or breadth; t=thickness; 12=the constant applied to materials of rectangular section; k= radius of gyration of the balance, and M=its mass. E=the modulus of elasticity of the spring.

BALANCE SPRING (BREGUET). Where the outer coil is bent up and over the volute. Named after its inventor, A. L. Breguet. Also termed " Overcoil."

BALANCE SPRING (BREGUET).

BALANCE SPRING (CONICAL). Balance spring formed in the shape of a cone. Used by L. Berthoud.

BALANCE SPRING (CONICAL).

BALANCE SPRING (DOUBLE OVER-COIL). Similar to the Breguet spring but having two overcoils.

BALANCE SPRING (DOUBLE OVERCOIL).

BALANCE SPRING (DUO-IN-UNO). A helical balance spring with a flat spiral at one end: a combination of flat and helical forms.

BALANCE SPRING (DUO-IN-UNO).

BALANCE SPRING (HELICAL). Balance spring in the form of a helix: a spring wound round a parallel cylinder. Used in Marine Chronometers (q.v.) and occasionally to be found in pocket watches.

BALANCE SPRING (HELICAL).

BALANCE SPRING (SPHERICAL). Balance spring formed in the shape of a sphere; invented by F. HOURIET. Some times referred to as the " Bird Cage " spring.

BALANCE SPRING (SPHERICAL).

BALANCE SPRING (TRIA-IN-UNO). Similar to the " Duo-in-Uno " spring but having flat coils top and bottom. A com-bination of flat spring at upper and lower ends of a helically formed main body.

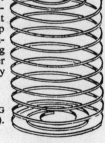

BALANCE SPRING (TRIA-IN-UNO).

BALANCE SPRING (VOLUTE). The flat balance spring.

BALANCE SPRING (VOLUTE).

BALANCE SPRING BUCKLE, GUARD OR FOOT. A small block or stud with projecting tongue, usually forming one of the two index pins, so that the tongue bridges the index pins and pre-vents two coils of the balance spring engag-ing between the pins. Sometimes two index pins are fitted and the guard is a separate piece. Also known as the " Boot."

BALANCE SPRING BUCKLE, GUARD OR FOOT.

BALANCE SPRING SIZES. The old method of sizing balance springs varied according to the makers but a more precise method was as follows. To suit the balance of a reasonably small watch, the maker would quote the diameter as size 0 and the weakest spring for this diameter, 00. The strengths then gradually

BALANCE SPRING ALLOYS

BALANCE SPRINGS FOR BI-METALLIC CUT BALANCES

Type of Balance Spring	Compensating Balance to be used	Quality	Colour	Temperature error over a range of approx. 32 deg. F. in 24 hours	Middle temperature error in 24 hours	Physical Properties
				Sec.	Sec.	
Tempered steel	Guillaume	Highest	Blue	0 to 0·36 approx.	0 to 1	Subject to magnetism and rust
Tempered steel	Steel and brass cut	1st grade	,,	0 to 1·8 ,,	0·5 to 3	,,
First tempering	,, ,, ,,	,, ,,	,,	0 to 1·8 ,,	0·5 to 3	,,
Hardened steel	,, ,, ,,	Fair	,,	0 to 1·8 ,,	0·5 to 3	,,
Soft steel	,, ,, ,,	Inexpensive	,,	0 to 1·8 ,,	1 to 4	,,
X-A-M	,, ,, ,,	1st grade	Yellowish	0 to 1·8 ,,	0 to 3	Non - magnetisable and rustless.
Melius	,, ,, ,,	Medium	,,	0 to 5·4 ,,	0·5 to 3	Only slightly magnetisable, rustless, good elasticity.

BALANCE SPRINGS FOR MONO-METALLIC BALANCES

Type of Balance Spring	Balance to be used	Quality	Colour	Temperature error over a range of approx. 32 deg. F. in 24 hours	Middle temperature error in 24 hours	Physical Properties
				Sec.	Sec.	
Elinvar 1	Glucydur	1st grade	White or blue	0 to 9·0 approx.	0 to 3	Only slightly magnetisable and rustless.
Elinvar 1	Glucidor with affixes (*see* p. 10)	,, ,,	,,	0 to 9·0 ,,	0 to 3	,,
Elinvar 2	Glucydur	Medium	,,	9·0 to 36 ,,	0 to 3	,,
Elinvar 3	Nickel	Fair	,,	36 to 72 ,,	0 to 4	,,
Parelinvar 1	,,	Inexpensive	,,	72 to 108 ,,	0 to 5	,,
Parelinvar 2	,,	,,	,,	90 to 108 ,,	0 to 5	,,
Melior	,,	,,	,,	90 to 108 ,,	0 to 5	,,
Metelinvar 1	Glucydur	1st grade	White or blue	0 to 9·0 ,,	0 to 3	Almost non-magnetic and rustless. Very good elasticity.
Metelinvar 2	Nickel	,, ,,	,,	9·0 to 36 ,,	0 to 3	,,
Metelinvar 2	,,	Fair	,,	36 to 72 ,,	0 to 4	,,
Nivarox 1 from 10½ ligne	Glucydur	Highest grade	Blue	0 to 9·0 ,,	0 to 4	Non-magnetic and rustless.
Nivarox 1 small movements	,,	1st grade	,,	0 to 18 ,,	0 to 8	,,
Nivarox 2	Nickel	,, ,,	Red brown	0 to 36 ,,	—	,,
Nivarox 3	,,	Fair	,, ,,	36 to 72 ,,	—	,,
Nivarox 4	,,	,,	White	72 to 108 ,,	—	,,
Nivarox 5	,,	Inexpensive	,,	108 and over ,,	—	,,

increased by $\frac{1}{4}$ sizes as shown in the following table.

Diameter	*Strength*
0	00
0	0
0	$\frac{1}{4}$
0	$\frac{1}{2}$
0	$\frac{3}{4}$
0	1
0	$1\frac{1}{4}$
0	$1\frac{1}{2}$
1	$1\frac{3}{4}$

As the size of the balance increased so a suitable range of strengths would be provided for each respective diameter and this would progress up to diameter 22, strength $12\frac{1}{2}$, which would be for a pocket watch of about 18‴. The modern method is based upon the diameter of the balance. A system of standardisation prevails in Switzerland and so uniform are the diameters with the weight of the balance, that balance spring makers are able to supply balance springs according to the diameter of the balance. Further, the diameter of the arbor of the balance staff, where the balance spring collet fits, is usually of a uniform diameter; as an example, a balance of 7·5 mm. diameter would have a collet fitting of 0·45 mm. The sizes of balance springs are also standardised, the packets containing the springs are numbered, the diameter of the balance is noted, and, if the spring is colletted the size of the hole in the collet is noted, *e.g.* a balance with a diameter of 7·5 mm. will need a spring from packet No. 17 and on the packet will be found 720 to 760, which means 7·20 to 7·60 mm. diameter balance. The sizes are arranged in steps of 0·4 mm. from packet to packet. No. 16 contains springs for a 6·8 to 7·2 mm. diameter balance and so on. The diameter of the balance is readily ascertained on the eighths gauge, a wheel gauge giving millimetres in $\frac{1}{8}$th mm. stages, *i.e.*, $7\frac{0}{8}$–$\frac{1}{8}$–$\frac{2}{8}$–$\frac{3}{8}$, etc., to $8\frac{0}{8}$ and so on. Convert the fraction into decimals and it is then possible to select the spring. If a ready colletted spring is required, the packet bearing the diameter of the hole in the collet will be selected, and if the movement is a modern one fitted with the original balance staff, the collet will fit. A useful table, issued by Fabriques Réunien, Switzerland, is appended here. The first column is the diameter of the balance and

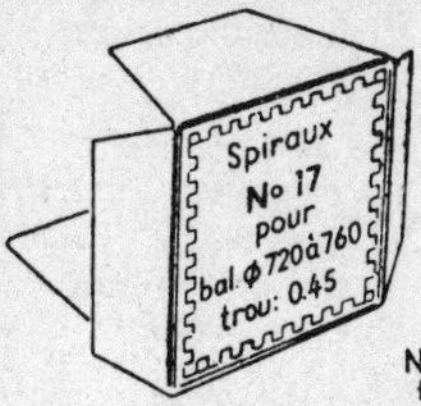

No 17
for
Bal. 7·20 to 7·60
Hole 0·45

BALANCE SPRING SIZES.

Balance	*Springs*	*Balance*	*Springs*
mm.	No.	mm.	No.
5·40	5 to 8	10·70	34 to 37
5·50	5 „ 8	10·80	35 „ 38
5·60	6 „ 9	10·90	35 „ 38
5·70	6 „ 9	11·00	36 „ 39
5·80	7 „ 10	11·10	36 „ 39
5·90	7 „ 10	11·20	37 „ 40
6·00	8 „ 11	11·30	37 „ 40
6·10	8 „ 11	11·40	38 „ 41
6·20	9 „ 12	11·50	38 „ 41
6·30	9 „ 12	11·60	39 „ 42
6·40	10 „ 13	11·70	39 „ 42
6·50	10 „ 13	11·80	40 „ 43
6·60	11 „ 14	11·90	40 „ 43
6·70	11 „ 14	12·00	41 „ 44
6·80	12 „ 15	12·10	41 „ 44
6·90	12 „ 15	12·20	42 „ 45
7·00	13 „ 16	12·30	42 „ 45
7·10	13 „ 16	12·40	43 „ 46
7·20	14 „ 17	12·50	43 „ 46
7·30	14 „ 17	12·60	44 „ 47
7·40	15 „ 18	12·70	44 „ 47
7·50	15 „ 18	12·80	44 „ 47
7·60	16 „ 19	12·90	45 „ 48
7·70	16 „ 19	13·00	45 „ 48
7·80	17 „ 20	13·10	45 „ 48
7·90	17 „ 20	13·20	46 „ 49
8·00	18 „ 21	13·30	46 „ 49
8·10	19 „ 22	13·40	46 „ 49
8·20	20 „ 23	13·50	47 „ 50
8·30	21 „ 24	13·60	47 „ 50
8·40	22 „ 25	13·70	47 „ 50
8·50	23 „ 26	13·80	48 „ 51
8·60	23 „ 26	13·90	48 „ 51
8·70	24 „ 27	14·00	48 „ 51
8·80	24 „ 27	14·10	49 „ 52
8·90	25 „ 28	14·20	49 „ 52
9·00	25 „ 28	14·30	50 „ 53
9·10	26 „ 29	14.40	50 „ 53
9·20	26 „ 29	14·50	51 „ 54
9·30	27 „ 30	14·60	51 „ 54
9·40	27 „ 30	14·70	52 „ 55
9·50	28 „ 31	14·80	52 „ 55
9·60	28 „ 31	14·90	53 „ 56
9·70	29 „ 32	15·00	53 „ 56
9·80	29 „ 32	15·10	54 „ 57
9·90	30 „ 33	15·20	54 „ 57
10·00	31 „ 34	15·30	55 „ 57
10·10	31 „ 34	15·40	55 „ 58
10·20	32 „ 35	15·50	56 „ 59
10·30	32 „ 35	15·60	56 „ 59
10·40	33 „ 36	15·70	57 „ 60
10·50	33 „ 36	15,80	57 „ 60
10·60	34 „ 37		

the second the number of the balance spring suitable, *e.g.* Balance φ 7 m/m, balance spring between numbers 13 and 16; if the balance is light, try No. 13 and if heavy, No. 16. Opposite the diameter of the balance (mm.) in the first column, will be found the reference numbers of the most suitable balance springs.

BALANCE STAFF. The axis, shaft, or spindle of the balance. *See* NOMENCLATURE OF WATCH PARTS, page 279.

BALANCE STAFF.

BALANCE STAKE. A stake used to rest the balance, complete with staff and rollers upon while fitting on the balance spring.

BALANCE STAKE

BALL CLOCKS. Several clocks employing a ball in the place of a pendulum or balance to unlock the escapement were invented by Grollier, a Frenchman, during the seventeenth century. A popular one is that in which a ball rolls in a groove along an inclined plane. The plate with the grooves is pivoted at its centre and is able to rock in a see-saw fashion. The plate is controlled by levers operated by clock mechanism which lock it when at the extremity of its angle of incline. As the ball (a large steel ball bearing) rolls down

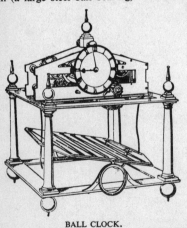

BALL CLOCK.

the plane, it contacts a lever which sets the clock mechanism into motion and the plate is unlocked and lifted to the opposite incline. The ball then starts to roll zig-zag fashion, along the grooves until it reaches the other end when it unlocks the plate and the cycle is repeated. It was developed by Congreve, the English scientist, after whom the clock is named.

BALL FOOT. *See* ANTIQUE CLOCK CASE TERMS.

BALLOON CLOCK. *See* ANTIQUE CLOCK CASE TERMS.

BAND. The central ring or body of a watch case to which the bezel, back and pendant are attached, and in which the movement is generally held. Also referred to as the " Middle."

BANDING. *See* ANTIQUE CLOCK CASE TERMS.

BANDY LEG. *See* ANTIQUE CLOCK CASE TERMS.

BANJO BAROMETER. Another name for " Wheel Barometer " (*q.v.*).

BANJO CLOCK. *See* ANTIQUE CLOCK CASE TERMS.

BANKING. When applied to the lever escapement it is that part on which the lever rests or " banks." In the cylinder escapement, the pin on the balance-cock or the sides of the cock upon which a pin affixed to the balance strikes or " banks " limiting the amplitude of the balance vibration.

BANKING, KNOCKING THE. A condition arising from an excessive arc of vibration of the balance; the Ruby Pin (*q.v.*) strikes the outside of the lever-notch causing a knocking sound. The timepiece will gain on its rate as a result of " knocking the banking."

BANKING, OVER. LEVER ESCAPEMENT: The circumstance in which the ruby pin passes to the wrong side of the lever notch. CYLINDER: The cylinder becomes locked on a tooth of the escape wheel due to the balance having exceeded its prescribed arc.

BANKING PIN. LEVER ESCAPEMENT: the pins upon which the lever banks or rests. CYLINDER ESCAPEMENT: the pins carried by the balance and balance cock to prevent overbanking. DUPLEX ESCAPEMENT: either a pin fitted to the balance spring or a kink or " knee " formed in the spring so that the protrusion touches or banks on a pin fitted to the balance arm. Also, a banking piece fitted to the staff so that it can rotate freely for $\frac{7}{8}$ths of a turn, banks against a pin projecting from the edge of plate. The pin in the plate and the banking piece fitted to the staff are indicated by arrows. CHRONOMETER ESCAPEMENT: a pin projecting up from the arm of the balance passes freely between two pins projecting down from the balance cock. A block attached to the balance spring has a pin projecting from it, and when the arc is excessive this pin bars the passage of the pin on the balance and so curtails the vibration of the balance. BANKING 'HORSESHOE.' This type of

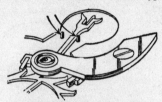

LEVER ESCAPEMENT BANKING.

CYLINDER ESCAPEMENT BANKING.

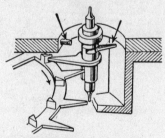

DUPLEX ESCAPEMENT BANKING.

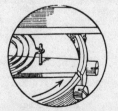

BALANCE SPRING BANKING.

banking is to be found in some of the high grade English $\frac{3}{4}$ plate chronometer pocket watches.

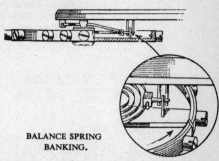

BALANCE SPRING BANKING.

BANKING SCREW. A form of banking in the chronometer escapement. The back of the head of a screw is used to regulate the amount of locking of the escape wheel teeth on the tube of the locking pallet, attached to the detent.

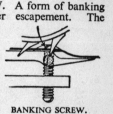

BANKING SCREW.

BANKING, SOLID. Where the banking of the lever in the Lever Escapement (q.v.) is solid; cut out of the plate, and not pins. See Banking Pin.

BANKING TO THE DROP. An American term. The banking pins, fitted eccentrically into screws, are adjusted so that the escape wheel teeth drop off the pallet stones: a system used during the testing of the lever escapement.

BARETTE. See Files.

BARLEY TWIST. See ANTIQUE CLOCK CASE TERMS.

BAR MOVEMENT. The type of construction employing bars or bridges to hold the train, etc., in position as distinct from the "Full," "Three-quarter," or "Half-plate" movement (q.v.).

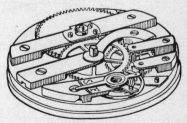

BAR MOVEMENT.

BAROGRAPH. An instrument which records changes in atmospheric pressure. Usually consists of a drum, carrying a sheet of specially ruled paper upon its exterior surface, which revolves once in seven days. A pen, operated by an Aneroid (*q.v.*), traces a line or graph on the paper thus recording the variations (or otherwise) of the atmospheric pressure.

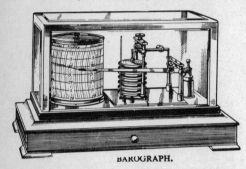

BAROGRAPH.

BAROMETER. An instrument to measure the atmospheric pressure. Either the Aneroid (*q.v.*) or the mercurial type, where the pressure of the air acts on a column of mercury. *See* Wheel Barometer, also Pediment Barometer.

BAROMETRIC ERROR. The error experienced in pendulum clocks due to variation in the density of the atmosphere. There are various devices to correct the barometric error, but generally speaking they are rarely used. Modern observatory clocks are fitted in strong airtight cases, so that the pendulum is operated in air of constant density and so the barometric error is eliminated. It is said that the Circular Error (*q.v.*) of the pendulum of Big Ben corrects its barometric error.

BAROQUE. *See* ANTIQUE CLOCK CASE TERMS.

BARREL. The box in which the main spring of a watch, clock, or spring driven instrument is coiled. Either without teeth (as illustration) when used with the Fusee (*q.v.*) or with teeth as Going Barrel (*q.v.*). *See* NOMENCLATURE OF WATCH PARTS, page 276.

BARREL.

BARREL ARBOR. The axis upon which the barrel rotates and around which the

mainspring is coiled being also attached thereto. *See* NOMENCLATURE OF WATCH PARTS, page 277.

WATCH BARREL ARBOR.   CLOCK BARREL ARBOR.

BARREL COVER. The cap or lid of the barrel.

BARREL COVER.

BARREL, GOING. A barrel having teeth cut in a strengthened periphery and thus driving directly, as distinct from the plain barrel driving a fusee through the medium of a line or chain.

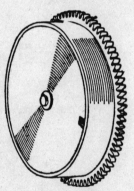

BARREL, GOING.

BARREL, GOING, MOVEMENT. A movement employing a going barrel and not a fusee.

BARREL HOOK. The hook fitted to the inside of the barrel to which the mainspring is attached.

BARREL HOOK.

BARREL RATCHET. The ratchet wheel attached to the barrel arbor or, in some instances (as in certain repeating watches) to the barrel itself. The purpose is to hold the mainspring when wound up, a pawl or click engaging with the wheel teeth and preventing a reversal of the winding motion.

CLOCK RATCHET WHEEL.

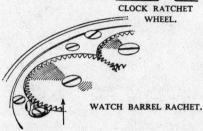

WATCH BARREL RACHET.

BARREL, SAFETY. *See* Safety Barrel.

BARREL STUD. The recessed shoulder or projecting piece formed in the wall of the barrel to provide an anchorage for the mainspring hooking in systems where the "hook and eye" method is not employed.

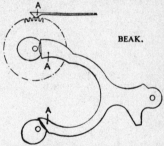

BARREL STUD.

BARRETTE FILE. *See* Files.

BASCULE ESCAPEMENT. Another name for the pivoted detent chronometer escapement. *See* Chronometer Escapement.

BASE. *See* ANTIQUE CLOCK CASE STYLES.

BASE CIRCLE. An imaginary circle upon which an involute (*q.v.*) curve is described, *e.g.*, by tracing the locus of a point in a piece of thin string as it is unwound from a drum of the same size as and coincident with the base circle.

BASIC RACK. The rack, or segment of gear wheel of infinite radius belonging to a system of gearing in which the tooth forms are such that any one wheel will mate with any other of the same pitch.

BASKET TOP. *See* ANTIQUE CLOCK CASE STYLES.

BAS-RELIEF. *See* ANTIQUE CLOCK CASE STYLES.

BASSINE CASE. The style of watch case in which the covers are quite plain without beads or ridges. *See* WATCH CASE STYLES.

BASTARD CUT FILE. A coarse cutting file.

BATON. The straight strokes or bars used on dials instead of figures.

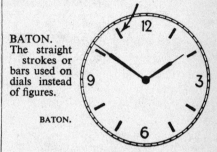

BATON.

BATTERY. Two or more primary cells or accumulators electrically connected. A large number of accumulators forming a common supply are referred to as a "bank."

BEAD. *See* ANTIQUE CLOCK AND CLOCK CASE TERMS, *Also* MOULDINGS.

BEAK. The shaped or pointed end of a finger, lever, click, or spring piece, etc., which effects or determines the action,

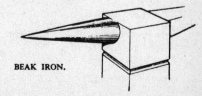

BEAK.

e.g. Chronograph, Calendar mechanism. The parts marked (A) are referred to as "Beak."

BEAK IRON. The pointed section of an anvil or a stake.

BEAK IRON.

BEARER. The piece of metal soldered to the inside of a watch case for reinforcement at the Joint (*q.v.*). *See* PARTS OF THE POCKET WATCH CASE, page 79.

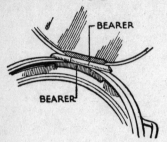

BEAT. The " tick " as an escape wheel tooth drops on to the locking face of the pallets. The escapes or beats take place when the balance or pendulum is moved through an equal arc on each side of the quiescent point. There are however, some exceptions, *i.e.*, the Chronometer and Duplex Escapements (*q.v.*) where impulse is given in one direction only. Beat also refers to amplitude of the arc, *e.g.*, a seconds pendulum takes one second to swing from the extreme right to the extreme left; it also takes one second to swing from the centre to the extreme right or left and back again to the centre. This movement is one-half Cycle (*q.v.*). A full cycle therefore is from the centre to the extreme right, through the centre and then to the extreme left, returning to the centre again, which equals two seconds. The same reasoning applies to the balance; the usual reckoning of the time of vibration of a balance is, in the case of an 18000 train, one fifth of a second for each swing in the same direction, *i.e.*, half-cycle.

BEAT, IN. The correct, equi-rhythmical action of the escapement. *See* Angle.

BEAT, OUT OF. The circumstance of the escapement discharging at unequal angles in the excursion of the balance or pendulum, relative to the line of centres, or dead centre. Frequently audible as an alternating light and heavy " tick " giving a halting, lame effect. *See* Angle. Often induced in pendulum clocks by mishandling of the pendulum and crutch, the case not being set vertically or the movement slipping in the case when being wound.

BED. Refers to the bar or base on to which fits the head and tail stock of a lathe.

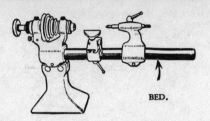

BED.

BELL CHUCK. *See* Box Chuck.

BELLOWS. A tool used to puff dust away during watch repairing, etc. That part of the mechanism of a cuckoo clock or bird box which produces the air blast to voice the call.

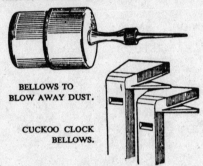

BELLOWS TO BLOW AWAY DUST.

CUCKOO CLOCK BELLOWS.

BELL PUNCH. A self-centring punch for marking a centre " pip " on the end of a round bar or rod.

BELL PUNCH.

BELL STANDARD. The standard or stem to which the bell of a clock is secured.

BELL STANDARD.

BELL TOP. *See* ANTIQUE CLOCK CASE TERMS.

BENT PALLET. *See* Exit Pallet.

BENZENE. A colourless, highly inflammable liquid. Obtained from coal tar, etc. or by chemical synthesis.

BENZINE. A distillate obtained from Petroleum. Very similar otherwise in characteristics to Benzene. Both are powerful solvents of grease, resins, etc., and are used in the cleaning of watch, clock, etc., parts.

BERGEON SCREWS. *See* Fine Metric Thread.

BERYLLIUM. *See* METALS USED IN HOROLOGY.

BEVEL WHEELS. Gearing, sometimes called "Skew gearing," in which the teeth are formed on the bevelled edge of the wheels. Used to transmit power to the motion work of

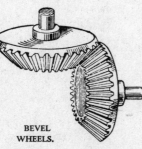

BEVEL WHEELS.

turret clocks; also in certain arrangements of keyless work in watches, etc.

BEZEL OR BEZIL. The ring or frame holding the glass of a watch or clock. Also the ring or frame without the groove for a glass. *See* PARTS OF THE POCKET WATCH CASE, page 79.

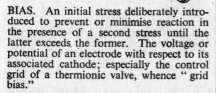

BEZEL OR BEZIL.

BIAS. An initial stress deliberately introduced to prevent or minimise reaction in the presence of a second stress until the latter exceeds the former. The voltage or potential of an electrode with respect to its associated cathode; especially the control grid of a thermionic valve, whence "grid bias."

BI-METALLIC. *See* METALS USED IN HOROLOGY.

BINDING. The condition obtaining when mechanical actions, parts, or surfaces, designed to work smoothly together, operate with excessive frictional losses due to maladjustment, lack of lubricant, poor fitting, etc. Term applied to the internal fouling of the mainspring in the barrel.

BIRCH KEY. A universal watch key named after its inventor. Sometimes referred to as Bench Key.

BIRCH KEY.

BIRD BOX. A form of musical box where, at will, a lid is made to open and a bird appears, turns from side to side, flaps its wings and opens and closes its beak while a tune is played on a flute or whistle arrangement or by a piston working in a tube resembling the singing of a bird.

BIRD'S BEAK MOULDING. *See* MOULDINGS.

BISEAU (French). A bevel. In horology it refers to the plates of a watch movement which have been bevelled to make the movement thin on the edge: a biseau movement.

BLACK POLISH. A peculiar polish, imparted to hardened or tempered steel by Diamantine (*q.v.*); a polish of great beauty and "depth" when contrasted to a polish which is merely a bright surface gloss.

BLANK. The oversize, unfinished, or roughly shaped piece from which a component is manufactured; especially a stamping. The operation is termed "Blanking."

BLEACHED. *See* ANTIQUE CLOCK CASE TERMS.

BLIND FRET. *See* ANTIQUE CLOCK CASE TERMS.

BLIND MAN'S WATCH. A watch so made that the time of day may be ascertained by the sense of touch alone. Usually fitted with protrusions on the dial in the place of figures and substantial, well fitting hands of a smooth character; also known as a Braille watch. Such watches have no glass to cover the hands and must of necessity be either hunter or half hunter. Another type, known as a "Tact," (*q.v.*), watch, has beads or small knobs soldered to the outer edge of the case to mark the hours; a hand fitted to the outside of the back of the case can be turned to a definite stop in one direction only, thus indicating the time. Repeating watches are also used.

BLIND MAN'S WATCH.

BLOCK FOOT. *See* ANTIQUE CLOCK CASE TERMS.

BLOCK FRONT. *See* ANTIQUE CLOCK CASE TERMS.

BLOCKING OSCILLATOR. A thermionic valve oscillator in which the anode, grid, and cathode circuits are tightly coupled. This arrangement gives the oscillator the peculiar ability to " divide " the frequency of a signal fed to its grid circuit. It is thus used to reduce a high and essentially stable frequency, such as given by a crystal controlled " master " oscillator, to a lower frequency of equal stability. Several such blocking oscillators may be used in cascade. Control of the " division " is simply and reliably obtained.

BLOWPIPE. A long tapered tube used for blowing a stream of air across or through a flame to direct it where required and increase the heat of the flame by improving combustion.

BLOWPIPE.

BLUEING. A colour finish given to steel by heating. The stages of colouring and tempering of hardened steel, polished white are:—

				F.
Pale straw	.	.	.	430°
Straw	.	.	.	460°
Yellow brown	.	.	.	490°
Red brown	.	.	.	510°
Purple	.	.	.	540°
Blue	.	.	.	560°
Dark blue	.	.	.	570°

BLUEING PAN. A container or holder especially made for the purpose of blueing steel by heating.

BLUEING PAN.

BOARD OF TRADE UNIT. The standard unit for the sale of electricity. It is one kilowatt hour. Abbreviated to B.T.U.

BOB. The weighted end which forms part of a pendulum; a heavy mass at the end of a pendulum rod. There are two forms of bobs in general use: (1) the cylindrical; (2) the lenticular.

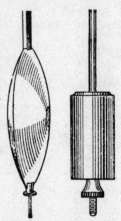

LENTICULAR   CYLINDRICAL
BOB.   BOB.

BOB PENDULUM. The type of pendulum where the rod is fixed to the pallet arbor and the bob screws direct on to the rod; usually found in antique Verge clocks and the Tic Tac French clocks (*q.v.*). *See* ANTIQUE CLOCK CASE TERMS.

BOBBIN. The spool or former upon which wire is wound, especially in construction of electrical components, *e.g.* electro-magnets, chokes, transformers. Also used as a term for the completed winding.

BOB
PENDULUM.

BOILING OUT PAN. A small saucepan-shaped pan, used for boiling out parts, *e.g.*, to remove shellac from a part after it has been mounted on to a chuck, the part is boiled in methylated spirit. (Illustrated on next page.)

BOILING OUT PAN.

BOLECTION MOULDING. *See* MOULD-INGS.

BOLT. *See* Pull-out-Piece.

BOLT AND JOINT. The hinge or joint and the snap fastener or bolt used in some watches, princip-ally the old Eng-lish type, to hold the move-ment in its case; sometimes referred to as a " Swing Move-ment." A, bolt; B, joint.

BOLT AND JOINT.

BOLT AND SHUTTER. *See* ANTIQUE CLOCK CASE TERMS.

BOLT TOOL. A tool used for holding small parts during Underhand Polishing (*q.v.*). Originally used to hold the bolt of the " Swing Movement " while polishing. It now has many applications.

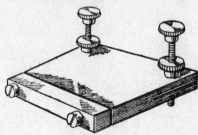

BOLT TOOL.

BOMBÉ. *See* page 19.

BOMBÉING. Producing a convex top on a watch jewel or instrument bearing by means of a special broach with a concave end used in a recessing machine.

BONE, BURNT. Used in place of chalk for cleaning the watch brush. It is more efficacious, especially on gilt plates, and is dustless. The best is a leg-of-mutton bone; it is placed in a red-hot fire and allowed to burn thoroughly. Carefully removed and allowed to cool, it will be found to be almost white. Used in the same manner as chalk, the brush being rubbed finally on tissue paper.

BONNIKSEN'S ESCAPEMENT. Another name for the Karrusel escapement (*q.v.*) invented by Bonniksen.

BOOT. *See* Balance Spring Buckle.

BORING. The process of cutting a hole or sink in the lathe, more accurate than drilling.

BORING CHUCK. Used in the lathe to hold the cutter while boring. *See* Chuck.

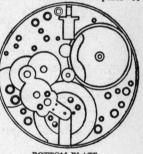

BORING CHUCK.

BOSS. A projection in the form of a cylinder usually for the purpose of addi-tional strength or bearing area. *See* page 19.

BOSS.

BOTTOM PLATE. The main plate of a watch; the founda-tion upon which the movement is built; the plate immediately behind the dial. *See* NOMENCLA-TURE OF WATCH PARTS, page 275. (Formerly called " Pillar plate.")

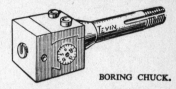

BOTTOM PLATE.

BOUCHON. *See* Bush.

BOULE. The pear-shaped mass of corundum formed in the manufacture of the synthetic jewel.

BOULE.

BOURGEAUX THREAD. *See* Martin Screw Plate.

BOW. That part of a watch case to which a chain, etc., is attached; sometimes a circular ring pivoted into the pendant; a shaped piece, square, rectangular, triangular, etc., pivoted to the pendant or to the case

WATCH CASE BOW.

and in some instances fixed solidly to the case. *See* NOMENCLATURE OF WATCH PARTS, page 289. *Also* PARTS OF THE POCKET WATCH CASE, page 79. Also, the strip of whale bone or cane to which gut or horse hair is attached and used to drive the work in the Turns (*q.v.*).

TURNS BOW.

BOW-FRONT. *See* ANTIQUE CLOCK CASE TERMS.

BOW OPENING AND CLOSING TOOL.

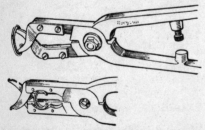

BOX CHRONOMETER. Marine Chronometer. *See* Chronometer.

BOX CHUCK. A chuck used in the lathe, where the work can be secured to enable it to be turned eccentrically and concentrically. Sometimes referred to as an " Eccentric Chuck " or " Bell Chuck."

BOX CHUCK.

BOX UP. A term referring to the final fitting of a watch movement into its case (also case up).

BOXING IN. A term used in the days of the old English watch manufacturing referring to the fitting of movements into their cases and, if keyless, to the necessary adjustments to fit the winding button and push piece, etc. " Boxing in " was a separate trade.

BOXING TIMER. *See* Timers.

BOXWOOD. A hard, almost grainless wood; used as a polishing medium, also as filing blocks, and for chucks, by watch-case makers.

BOXWOOD DUST. The sawdust of boxwood; used as a drying medium.

BRACE. An attachment for hooking the mainspring to the barrel; either a loose piece, riveted or pivoted. Also referred to as " T " piece.

BRACE.

BRACKET CLOCK. *See* ANTIQUE CLOCK CASE TERMS.

BRACKET FEET. *See* ANTIQUE CLOCK CASE TERMS.

BRACKET SUSPENSION. *See* Suspension Bracket.

BRACTS. *See* ANTIQUE CLOCK CASE TERMS.

BRAILLE WATCH. Braille was invented by Louis Braille (1809-52), a French professor who compiled the alphabet, numerals, and punctuation marks by the variation of arrangement of six raised dots. *See* Blind Man's Watch.

BREAD. Bread was used by the old English finishers as a means of cleaning the work during polishing. It is more efficacious than pith. The centre portion of a piece of bread without crust about the size of a golf ball was kneaded up with oil to the consistency of putty and used by dabbing on to the work.

BREAK ARCH OR BROKEN ARCH.
See ANTIQUE CLOCK CASE TERMS.

BREAK BEFORE MAKE SWITCH. A multiway switch so designed that any circuit through it is broken before another contact is made.

BREAK FRONT. *See* ANTIQUE CLOCK CASE TERMS.

BREGUET KEY. A watch key with a ratchet arangement, permitting winding in one direction only Invented by A. Breguet. Also known as a " Tipsy Key."

BREGUET KEY.

BREGUET SPRING. The overcoil form of balance spring, so named after its inventor A. L. Breguet. *See* Balance Spring Overcoil.

BRIDGE. A bar with two supports; with only one support, is termed a cock.

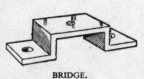
BRIDGE.

BRIDLE. A special attachment to a mainspring, which forms a friction clutch; or slipping device for a self-winding mechanism.

BRITISH HOROLOGICAL INSTITUTE. *See* Horological Institute.

BRITISH THERMAL UNIT. The quantity of heat or energy required to raise the temperature of 1 lb. of water by 1° F. (Abbreviated: B.Th.U.).

BROACH. To open out or enlarge a hole, particularly in exact fitting.

BROACH CUTTING. A long cutting tool, taper or parallel sided, the cutting edges being lengthwise. *See* Reamer.

BROACH ROUND. Similar to the cutting broach but of circular section without cutting edges. Used to " finish " holes by its burnishing action; especially in clock plates.

BROCOT ESCAPEMENT. The pin pallet escapement as used in clocks. Invented by Achille Brocot, Paris; b. 1817, d. 1878. The pins or pallets are usually made of agate secured to the pallet arms with shellac, sometimes they are of hardened steel. The action is similar to the Recoil Escapement (*q.v.*) but there is no recoil, it is a dead beat escapement since the point of contact of the pallets with the escape wheel teeth are on the radius of a circle and the faces of the teeth of the escape wheel are radial.

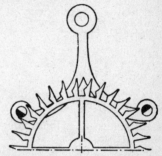
BROCOT ESCAPEMENT.

BROCOT SUSPENSION. A form of pendulum suspension whereby the length of the suspension spring may be altered by sliding chops, the adjustment being effected from the front of the dial.

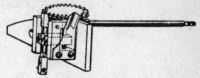
BROCOT SUSPENSION.

Invented by A. Brocot. *See* Brocot Escapement.

BROKEN PEDIMENT. *See* ANTIQUE CLOCK CASE TERMS.

BUCKLE. *See* Boot.

BUFF. An appliance for grinding or

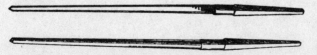
CUTTING BROACH.

ROUND BROACH.

polishing. The rotating form consists of a spindle on which is mounted a disc, built up of layers of linen, or a solid piece of felt, or a disc of wood surfaced with felt, leather, etc., and charged with an abrasive or polishing medium; emery paper mounted on wood is also used; the spindle is usually driven at high speed. For hand work, a parallel-sided stick of wood of circular, square, rectangular or triangular section is similarly dressed with a suitable material and charged in the same way; termed emery buff, rouge buff, etc.

BUHL OR BOULLE WORK. *See* ANTIQUE CLOCK CASE TERMS.

BULLE CLOCK. A battery driven clock where a permanent magnet passes through the pendulum bob, and the bob is an electro-magnet. Invented by Favre-Bulle.

BULLETIN DE MARCHE. Swiss rating certificate issued by the Swiss Bureau for testing watches.

BUN FEET. *See* ANTIQUE CLOCK CASE TERMS.

BUNSEN BURNER. A small, workshop or laboratory gas burner, giving a non-luminous flame of adjustable intensity. Particularly useful for moderate heating requirements such as hardening, tempering, melting lead, etc.

BUNSEN BURNER.

BURL. *See* ANTIQUE CLOCK CASE TERMS.

BURNISHER. A piece of hard steel of any suitable section (flat, round, oval, etc.) dressed with a cross grain. Used to " polish " metal, the smooth bright surface so obtained being also slightly hardened.

BURR. A rough or sharp edge thrown up up on metal after cutting, filing, etc. In

certain instances, particularly the cutting edges of tools, it can be referred to as " Feather Edge " (*q.v.*).

BURR WALNUT. *See* ANTIQUE CLOCK CASE TERMS.

BUSH OR BUSHON, OR BUSHING WIRE. Brass tubing or plugs used to refit worn holes in watch or clock plates, etc. Also referred to as " Bouchon."

BUTTING. The term used when a gearing is so arranged or constructed that the teeth catch on the incoming teeth or on the leaves of a pinion in the case of a wheel and pinion.

BUTTON. The knurled piece by which a watch, etc., is wound. Also termed " Crown." Generally termed " Winding Button " to differentiate from any similarly shaped knobs customarily called " buttons " but used for other purposes. *See* WINDING BUTTONS.

BUTTON.

BUTTON OR CROWN CHUCK. Designed to hold the button in the lathe during working.

BUTTON OR CROWN CHUCK.

BY-PASS CONDENSER. A capacitor, usually inserted in shunt or parallel with another impedance, to provide an earthing path for unwanted signal frequencies, *e.g.* Cathode by-pass, Screen by-pass, etc. (*See* De-coupling.)

C

CABRIOLE. *See* Antique Clock Case Terms.

CAESIUM CLOCK. *See* Atomic Clock.

CALENDAR. (Days of the week and months of the year of other countries. *See* pages 74-75.) During the 4th century b.c., the Greeks had a lunar calendar with years of 12 and 13 months. The Egyptians had a year of 12 months each with 30 days, making 360 days, but sometime before 330 b.c. another 5 days were added. In Roman times Julius Caesar reformed the calendar to make the year 365 days with an extra day added every 4 years. The months were alternately of 30 and 31 days except February which was of 28 and 29 in leap years. Pope Gregory XII reformed the Julian Calendar by making the last year of a century a leap year only if its number could be divided by 400. The reformed Gregorian Calendar was adopted by Catholic countries in 1582 and not until 1752 in England. There have been many movements to adopt a reformed calendar. The simplified version proposed by the

progression of the calendar. Simple calendars indicate the year, month, day of the week, date, and sometimes, the moon phases but have to be manually adjusted for leap years and the months of less than 31 days. The perpetual calendar effects these adjustments automatically.

CALIBRE OR CALIPER. The layout or design of a watch or clock movement. The size of a watch movement. (*See* also Ligne.)

CALIPERS. A comparative measuring instrument. A tool used to mount wheels, etc., while testing their truth and/or poise. A tool used in America not only for testing purposes but also to hold the wheel or balance during the operation of truing.

FOR TRUING.

JANUARY	FEBRUARY	MARCH
APRIL	MAY	JUNE
JULY	AUGUST	SEPTEMBER
OCTOBER	NOVEMBER	DECEMBER

S	M	T	W	T	F	S		S	M	T	W	T	F	S		S	M	T	W	T	F	S
1	2	3	4	5	6	7						1	2	3	4						1	2
8	9	10	11	12	13	14		5	6	7	8	9	10	11		3	4	5	6	7	8	9
15	16	17	18	19	20	21		12	13	14	15	16	17	18		10	11	12	13	14	15	16
22	23	24	25	26	27	28		19	20	21	22	23	24	25		17	18	19	20	21	22	23
29	30	31						26	27	28	29	30				24	25	26	27	28	29	30
																						W

W—World's Day (a world holiday), between Dec. 30 and Jan. 1 (365th day), *every* year. Leap Year Day (a second world holiday), between June 30 and July 1, occurs in leap years only.

World Calendar Association is shown. Each year and each quarter would always begin on a Sunday, and days of the week would always fall on the same dates every year; also each quarter would have the same number of days. As the year would comprise only 364 numbered days, the 365th day would have no number, only a name—"World's Day," which would be a world holiday. In leap years a similar Leap Year Day would occur between June 30 and July 1.

CALENDAR APERTURE. *See* Antique Clocks Case Terms.

CALENDAR WORK. The mechanism of a watch or clock which portrays the

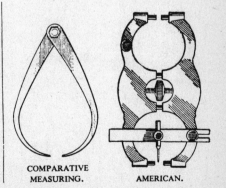

COMPARATIVE MEASURING.   AMERICAN.

DAYS OF THE WEEK IN VARIOUS LANGUAGES

	MONDAY	TUESDAY	WEDNESDAY	THURSDAY	FRIDAY	SATURDAY	SUNDAY
ENGLISH … …	MONDAY	TUESDAY	WEDNESDAY	THURSDAY	FRIDAY	SATURDAY	SUNDAY
CZECHOSLOVAK …	pondělí	úterý	středa	čvrtek	pátek	sobota	neděle
DANISH … …	MANDAG	TIRSDAG	ONSDAG	TORSDAG	FREDAG	LØRDAG	SØNDAG
DUTCH … …	MAANDAG	DINSDAG	WOENSDAG	DONDERDAG	VRIJDAG	ZATERDAG	ZONDAG
FRENCH … …	LUNDI	MARDI	MERCREDI	JEUDI	VENDREDI	SAMEDI	DIMANCHE
GERMAN … …	MONTAG	DIENSTAG	MITTWOCH	DONNERSTAG	FREITAG	SAMSTAG	SONNTAG
HUNGARIAN …	hétfő	kedd	szerda	csütörtök	péntek	szombat	vasárnap
IRISH … …	AN LUAN	AN MART	AN CHEADAOIN	AN DÉARDAOIN	AN AOINE	AN SATHARN	AN DOMHNACH
ITALIAN … …	LUNEDI	MARTEDI	MERCOLEDI	GIOVEDI	VENERDI	SABATO	DOMENICA
NORWEGIAN …	MANDAG	TIRSDAG	ONSDAG	TORSDAG	FREDAG	LØRDAG	SØNDAG
POLISH … …	PONIEDZIALEK	WTOREK	SRODA	CZWARTEK	PIATEK	SOBOTA	NIEDZIELA
PORTUGUESE …	segundafeira	terçafeira	quartafeira	quintafeira	sextafeira	sábado	domingo
*RUSSIAN … …	PONEDELNIK	FTORNIK	SREDA	TCHETVERG	PIATNITZA	SUBBOTA	VOSKRESENIE
SPANISH … …	LUNES	MARTES	MIERCOLES	JUEVES	VIERNES	SÁBADO	DOMINGO
SWEDISH … …	MÅNDAG	TISDAG	ONSDAG	TORSDAG	FREDAG	LÖRDAG	SÖNDAG
*RUSSIAN CHARACTERS	понедѐльник	вто́рник	среда́	четвѐрг	пя́тница	суббо́та	воскресѐнье

74

MONTHS OF THE YEAR IN VARIOUS LANGUAGES

	JANUARY	FEBRUARY	MARCH	APRIL	MAY	JUNE	JULY	AUGUST	SEPTEMBER	OCTOBER	NOVEMBER	DECEMBER	
ENGLISH	January	February	March	April	May	June	July	August	September	October	November	December	ENGLISH
CZECHO-SLOVAK	Lenden	Únor	Březen	Duben	Květen	Červen	Červenec	Srpen	Zárí	Říjen	Listopad	Prosinec	CZECHO-SLOVAK
DANISH	Janvar	Febuar	Marts	April	Maj	Juni	Juli	August	September	Oktober	November	December	DANISH
DUTCH	Janvari	Feburari	Maart	April	Mei	Juni	Juli	Augustus	September	October	November	December	DUTCH
FRENCH	Janvier	Février	Mars	Avril	Mai	Juin	Juillet	Août	Septembre	Octobre	Novembre	Décembre	FRENCH
GERMAN	Januar	Februar	März	April	Mai	Juni	Juli	August	September	Oktober	November	Dezember	GERMAN
HUNGARIAN	január	február	március	április	május	junius	julius	augusztus	szeptember	október	november	december	HUNGARIAN
IRISH	Eanair	Feabhra	Márta	Abrán	Bealtaine	Meithaine	Júl	Lughnasa	Meadhon Foghmhair	Deire Foghmhair	Samhain	Nodlaig	IRISH
ITALIAN	Gennaio	Febbraio	Marzo	Aprile	Maggio	Guigno	Luglio	Agosto	Settembre	Ottobre	Novembre	Dicembre	ITALIAN
NORWEGIAN	Janvar	Februar	Marts	April	Mai	Juni	Juli	August	September	Oktober	November	December	NORWEGIAN
POLISH	Styczeń	Luty	Marzec	Kwiecień	Maj	Czerwiec	Lipiec	Sierpień	Wrzesień	Październik	Listopad	Grudzień	POLISH
PORTUGUESE	Janeiro	Fevereiro	Março	Abril	Maio	Junho	Julho	Agôsto	Setembro	Outubro	Novembro	Dezambro	PORTUGUESE
*RUSSIAN	Janvar	Fevral	Mart	Aprel	Mai	Yune	Yule	Avgust	Sentyabr	Oktyabr	Noyabr	Dekabr	*RUSSIAN
SPANISH	Enero	Febrero	Marzo	Abril	Mayo	Junio	Julio	Agosto	Septiembre	Octubre	Noviembre	Diciembre	SPANISH
SWEDISH	Januari	Februari	Mars	Abrán	Maj	Juni	Juli	Augusti	September	October	November	December	SWEDISH
*RUSSIAN CHARACTERS	январь	февраль	март	апрель	май	июнь	июль	август	сентябрь	октябрь	ноябрь	декабрь	*RUSSIAN CHARACTERS

75

CALOTTE. A type of watch case which fits into a folding case; also known as " Portfolio." The outer case, usually made of leather, is the portfolio and the time-piece and its metal case, the Calotte.

CALOTTE CLOCK.

CALOTTE.

CALYX. See ANTIQUE CLOCK CASE TERMS.

CAM. A unit in a mechanism usually in the form of a disc, having all or part of its periphery set at varying distances from its pivotal centre so that upon revolving it transmits movement to, or exerts pressure upon, a contacting unit, e.g., the cams of a turret chiming clock are the discs operating the clappers.

CAM-PIPE. The pipe attached to the Heart Piece of a chronograph.

CAM-PIPE.

CANNON PINION. The pinion to which the minute hand is usually fitted, termed the " Snap on " cannon. Alternatively the cannon is fitted friction tight on to an arbor, the minute hand then being fitted direct on to the end of the arbor. See Hollow Centre Pinion. The cannon pinion drives the Motion Work (q.v.). See NOMENCLATURE OF WATCH PARTS, page 275.

CANNON PINION.

CANNON PINION TOOL. A tool for closing in the snap on cannon pinion.

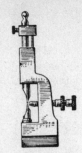

CANNON PINION TOOL.

CANNON PINION REMOVING TOOL.

CAP. In horology the term usually refers to a collet, such as a fusee cap, i.e., the collet which holds the fusee assembly together. Also, the cover to exclude the dust from a movement. End-stones are sometimes referred to as Jewel Caps or Capping Jewel Stones. See Capped Jewels.

CAP.

CAPACITANCE. The property of a body by virtue of which a charge or quantity of electricity has to be imparted to raise its potential above that of the surroundings. An American term for a Capacitor or Condenser. The former is now generally accepted. See Condenser.

CAPACITOR. An established American term for a Condenser (q.v.).

CAPACITY. The measure, or size of a condenser. Unit. micro-farad and micro-micro-farad. See Farad. The energy available from a cell or accumulator. See Ampere Hour.

CAPILLARITY. The property which causes liquids to be attracted. In horology it is associated with that property which causes oil to cling to pivots etc.

CAPITAL. See ANTIQUE CLOCK CASE TERMS.

CAPPED JEWEL. A jewel hole with an endstone. Properly this endstone or cap jewel takes the end thrust of the staff or arbor and forms part of the total bearing surface, and determines the Endshake (*q.v.*). There are instances of "false capping" in which the cap forms no part of the bearing, the endshake and thrust being borne by the pivot shoulders only.

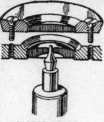

CAPPED JEWEL.

CARAT. The standard by which the quality or fineness of gold is defined, *i.e.* pure gold = 24 carats fine. The standard of weight for precious stones, *i.e.* 200 milligrams. *See* Hall Mark.

CARBON. A non-metallic element of great natural importance. Occurs in several forms, *e.g.* Diamond, Graphite, Lamp Black, Charcoal. Symbol C. (*See* Steel, page 183.) *See* Lamp Black and Charcoal.

CARBON TETRACHLORIDE, TETRACHLOROMETHANE. CCl_4. A colourless liquid highly volatile and having a sweetish smell. A powerful solvent of grease, fats and oils. Used in cleaning watch and clock parts. Sometimes especially useful in freshening gilt or silvered dials. Excellent also for cleaning electrical contacts, commutators, etc. Non-inflammable and electrically non-conducting.

CARBIDE. Cemented carbide tools for cutting steel, etc., are ultra hard; ideally suited for use as gravers, etc. Used extensively in America. Available from most machine tool dealers.

CARBORUNDUM. An abrasive; obtainable in various grades from coarse to fine. The latter being almost equal to diamantine. Made by Carborundum Co., Manchester. Quick cutting.

CARCASE. *See* Antique Clock Case Terms.

CARILLON. A set of bells tuned to octaves, which may be rung mechanically or by hand.

CARILLON MACHINE. A machine for ringing a carillon automatically.

CAROLEAN PERIOD STYLE. *See* Antique Clock Case Terms.

CARRIER. An accessory used to carry or rotate the work when turning in the lathe or turns. Also, a part of a watch case. *See* Parts of the Pocket Watch Case, page 79.

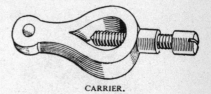

CARRIER.

CARRIER CHUCK. For use in the lathe to turn "between centres."

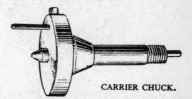

CARRIER CHUCK.

CARRIAGE. That part of a Toubillon or Karrusel Escapement (*q.v.*) which carries the escapement.

CARRIAGE CLOCK. A distinctive style of portable clock having a platform escapement (*q.v.*) The case usually consists of a brass base having four vertical corner pillars holding front and side panels of glass, or other material. The back is also of glass, carried in a brass frame hinged to the rear pillars to form a door to permit winding, etc. (The front may also be so arranged.) The top is

CARRIAGE CLOCK.

similarly constructed permitting a working view of the escapement and bearing a handle for portability. Solid brass, stone, enamel, or porcelain sides are also met with, there being numerous variations of the general construction.

CARTEL CLOCK. Usually refers to an ORMOLU clock, of French design, to hang upon a wall. *See* FRENCH PERIOD STYLES, page 45.

CARTEL CLOCK.

SWING RING

CARTOUCHE. *See* ANTIQUE CLOCK AND CLOCK CASE TERMS.

CARTRIDGE FUSE. A fuse having the fuse-link (*q.v.*) enclosed in a casing or tube resembling a cartridge. Usually fitted with metal end caps designed to be accommodated in spring clips or other means of holding and contacting to complete the electrical circuit yet allow easy removal and replacement.

CARYATID. *See* ANTIQUE CLOCK AND CLOCK CASE TERMS.

CASE. The container of a watch or clock movement.

Pocket Watch Cases

SCREW BACK AND BEZEL

BASSINE CASE

BISEAU

BASSINE HUNTER

78

PARTS OF THE POCKET WATCH CASE

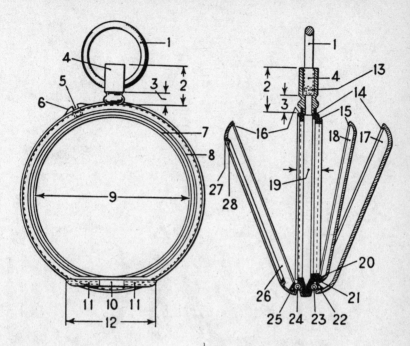

1. BOW.
2. PENDANT.
3. PENDANT NECK.
4. PENDANT PIPE.
5. PUSH-PIECE TUBE.
6. OLIVETTE.
7. DOME SNAP.
8. BACK SNAP.
9. MOVEMENT SEATING.
10. KNUCKLE.
11. CHARNIERE.
12. JOINT.
13. PENDANT HOLES.
14. BACK SNAP.
15. DOME SNAP.
16. FRONT OR BEZEL SNAP.
17. BACK COVER.
18. DOME.
19. MIDDLE. (This includes the whole centre part of the case.)

20. DOME JOINT CARRIER.
21. DOME JOINT.
22. BACK JOINT CARRIER.
23. BACK JOINT.
24. FRONT COVER OR BEZEL JOINT.
25. FRONT COVER OR BEZEL JOINT CARRIER.
26. FRONT COVER OR BEZEL.
27. GLASS GROOVE.
28. FLANGE.

Note.—With a hunter or half-hunter case the bezel carrying the glass covering the dial is termed the inside bezel. Where " Front Cover or Bezel " is noted, as in No. 26, it means that when the case is a hunter or half-hunter this part of the case is referred to as the hunter or half-hunter cover. When an open face, it is referred to as a bezel.

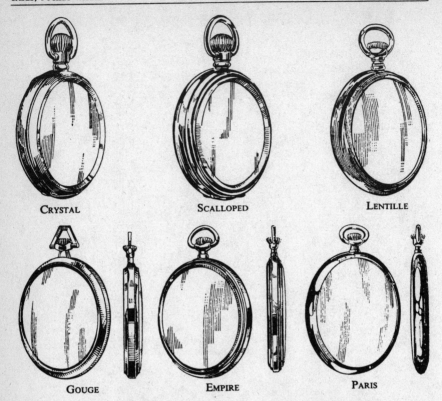

CRYSTAL   SCALLOPED   LENTILLE

GOUGE   EMPIRE   PARIS

WRIST WATCH CASE STYLES

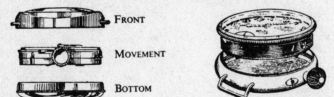

FRONT

MOVEMENT

BOTTOM

CACHECASE   BORGEL

MIRAGE. Refers to a round case where the front of the bezel only is shaped, to give the illusion of a shaped case.

OCTAGON MIRAGE   CUSHION MIRAGE

WRIST WATCH CASE STYLES

PARIS

CENTRIQUE

BISEAU

CUSHION OR CAMBRAI

SQUAT TONNEAU

OCTAGON

CURVY, SQUAT TONNEAU

RECTANGULAR WITH HORN LOOPS

TONNEAU

RECTANGULAR

RECTANGULAR OBTUSE CUT CORNER

RECTANGULAR CUT CORNER

RECTANGULAR CURVED CUT CORNER

OVAL

CURVY TONNEAU

COIN

CASE HARDENING. A chemical treatment whereby a thin skin of hard steel is given to iron or steel of low carbon content, chiefly by absorption under heat. The article to be treated is heated and dipped into the patent compound. A quantity of the powder will adhere. All is now heated to a cherry-red and chilled or quenched suddenly as when hardening steel. *See* WORKSHOP HINTS AND HELPS, page 304.

CASE SCREWS. The screws holding a watch movement in position in its case. The heads of such screws are sometimes reduced by about one half and are then known as " Dog Screws " (*q.v.*). *See* NOMENCLATURE OF WATCH PARTS, page 275.

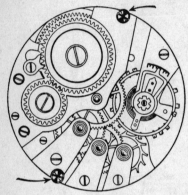

CASE SCREWS.

CASE SPRINGS. The springs of a watch case; such as the Fly-spring (B) that causes the cover to fly up and the Lockspring which locks the cover down (A). *See* PARTS OF THE POCKET WATCH CASE, page 79.

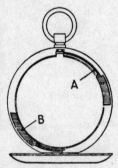

CASE SPRINGS.

CASE STAKE. A mushroom shaped boxwood or steel stake used in taking out dents or bruises in watch cases.

CASTLE RATCHET. *See* Column Wheel.

CASTLE WHEEL. The wheel operating on the winding shaft of a keyless mechanism. The ratchet teeth engage with similar teeth in the crown wheel (*q.v.*) to convey the power used to wind the mainspring, to the transmission and ratchet wheels. By means of a sliding action, the contrate teeth engage the hand setting mechanism.

CASTLE WHEEL.

CATCHING. The operation of finding the centre of, or re-aligning a mis-aligned hole, when marking or reboring it in a lathe.

CATGUT. Used as the line to carry the weights of weight driven clocks; also to convey the drive from the barrel to the fusee. *See* Gut. Wire is frequently used for the same purposes.

CATHODE. An electrode (*q.v.*) which is connected to the negative terminal or pole of a supply, from which Electrons (*q.v.*) migrate towards an Anode (*q.v.*) and to which positive Ions (*q.v.*) will migrate.

CATHODE-RAY TUBE. An electronic device consisting externally of an evacuated truncated glass cone, the base of which is coated upon its inner surface with a fluorescent material which, under bombardment by a thin electron beam, provides a visual indicator in the form of light. The device is based upon the transverse deflection by an external (signal) voltage of a narrow pencil beam of electrons, emitted from a hot cathode and propelled by an arrangement of electrodes termed an Electron Gun. The beam is directed through electrostatic or magnetic fields mutually at 90° wherein the deflecting signal voltages are impressed so that according to their relative strengths, sequence, or combination, the beam traverses the screen vertically, horizontally, or in any manner so determined, either in a single movement or in continuous repetition. The character or nature of this " trace " provides the means of examination of the signal. Screen materials possess varying powers of light emission the duration of which is termed the Afterglow. Thus, suitably chosen, a material will render visible a complete repetitive deflection even of a complicated nature, the electron beam retracing and re-activating its path before the preceding " trace " has faded. Used in horology in various makes of visual type watch timers (rate recorders). Signal voltages are generated electronically from any source under examination, *e.g.*, the amplified sounds of an escapement in action.

CAVETTO MOULDING. *See* MOULDINGS.

CELLULOID. A practically colourless thermoplastic material. Produced in sheets, etc. Used as the material for " unbreakable glasses." Highly inflammable and slowly discolours with exposure to light. *Compare* Perspex.

CELLULOSE FINISH OR POLISH. *See* ANTIQUE CLOCK CASE TERMS.

CEMENT. As used in horology is generally a form of gum or glue such as Le Page's or Seccotine or a cellulose acetate preparation such as Pear Drop Cement or St. Bride's Cement impervious to water. Shellac is also used to cement ruby pins, pallet stones, etc., in position, for which use it has special advantages. Glacial acetic acid is used as a cement for Perspex (*q.v.*), etc., and provides an invisible bond.

CEMENT CHUCK. *See* Wax Chuck.

CENTIGRADE TO FAHRENHEIT CONVERSION TABLE. *See* page 240.

CENTRAL EUROPEAN TIME. One hour fast of G.M.T. (*q.v.*)

CENTRAL STANDARD TIME. Six hours slow of Greenwich Mean Time (*q.v.*).

CENTRE ARBOR. The arbor, planted in the centre of a movement, which usually carries the cannon pinion and the minute hand and makes 1 revolution per hour. In some designs today however, with the centre, or sweep seconds hand, the arbor is hollow and concentric with the centrally planted seconds pinion. In other designs, both old and new, the centre wheel is planted to one side, out of centre, but the arbor of the wheel is still referred to as the " Centre Arbor."

CENTRE OF GRAVITY. The point through which the line of action of the weight of a body always passes irrespective of the position of the body.

CENTRE OF MASS. A point in a body coincident with the centre of gravity through which the resistive force acts when the inertia of the body reacts to acceleration.

CENTRE OF OSCILLATION. Determines the effective length of a pendulum, *i.e.*, if the centre of oscillation be at a constant distance from the centre of suspension, then the rate of vibration will be constant.

CENTRE OF PERCUSSION. Another term for the Centre of Oscillation.

CENTRE OF SUSPENSION. The theoretical point in the suspension system of a pendulum about which the pendulum oscillates. Known also as the " Centre of Motion."
Note.—The exact theoretical length of a pendulum to perform any given number of vibrations per second can be determined mathematically. Practical considerations of suspension, however, modify the calculation to a very close approximation.

CENTRE PINION. The pinion in a watch or clock train of the time-keeping part of the mechanism, driven by the great wheel, or barrel, if a " going barrel " movement (*q.v.*), or the fusee, in a fusee movement. Usually situated in the centre of the movement; the designation still remains if the wheel is to one side, *e.g.* the English centre seconds watch where the fourth wheel is planted in the centre of the movement and in some modern watches where the hour and minute hands are planted off centre.

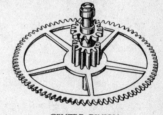

CENTRE PINION.

CENTRE PUNCH. A punch with a pointed end, used to mark the position for drilling, etc. *See* Bell Punch.

CENTRE SECONDS. Where the seconds

hand moves around the centre of the dial; termed "Sweep" seconds in America. *See* NOMENCLATURE OF WATCH PARTS, page 289.

CENTRE WHEEL. The wheel, usually in the centre of the movement to which the cannon pinion is attached. *See* Centre Pinion, also NOMENCLATURE OF WATCH PARTS, page 277.

CENTRELESS GRINDER. A machine for producing accurately ground cylindrical work, such as pallet pins for the Pin Pallet Escapement (*q.v.*). The pins are ground between two grinding wheels being rather closer together than the diameter required and the work is placed between them.

CENTRIFUGAL FORCE. The force with which a body resists being moved along a curved path. It acts from the centre of curvature. Centrifugal force is exemplified in horology in the cut balance, the limbs of which tend to move outwards in oscillation. Advantage is taken of this to obtain isochronism, particularly in the chronometer.

CENTRIPETAL FORCE. The force directed towards the centre of curvature, required to deviate a body along a curved path.

CERTOSINA. *See* ANTIQUE CLOCK CASE TERMS.

CHAIN, FUSEE. The steel chain connecting the mainspring barrel with the fusee. *See* Fusee Chain.

CHALK. Used by watch and clock repairers to clean brushes also for rubbing into the teeth of files to obtain smoother finishes.

CHAMBER CLOCK. *See* ANTIQUE CLOCK CASE TERMS.

CHAMFER. A sink or hollow, *i.e.* an oil sink. Also a bevel.

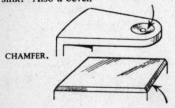

CHAMFER.

CHAMFER-HEAD SCREW. A screw with a back-sloping head.

CHAMFER-HEAD SCREW.

CHANNELLING. *See* ANTIQUE CLOCK CASE TERMS.

CHAPTER RING. The ring or circle bearing the figures and minute strokes, etc., and applied to the dial of a clock, sometimes referred to as a zone (*q.v.*). *See* Hour Circle, also ANTIQUE CLOCK CASE TERMS.

CHAPTERS. The hour figures on a watch or clock dial. More particularly refers to the applied enamelled plates bearing the hour numerals of some of the older French clocks.

CHARCOAL. Charred wood or coconut shell: used with oil as a surface finisher for brass, imparting a fine grain. Also used as a packing to exclude air in the hardening of fine steel parts likely to be burned in a direct flame or damaged by deep oxidation if heated in open air.

CHARGE. The electrical energy appearing as a potential or voltage across the terminals of a capacitor (condenser) during or immediately after the passage of a current. (Large capacitors may retain a heavy charge for several minutes after the circuit is switched off.) Also an abbreviated form of Charging Rate (*q.v.*).

CHARGE, FIRST. The initial rate of charge and procedure to be followed on bringing new accumulators into service. Is important in obtaining the maximum ultimate service.

CHARGING RATE. The normal rating of voltage and current at which accumulators in service are designed to be recharged. Dependent upon their type, capacity, construction, and mode of electrical connection.

CHARGING, TRICKLE. The system of providing a constant small recharging current, below the full charging rate, to enable accumulators to recuperate energy during alternating periods of rest and service. Thus giving an apparent increase in capacity and preventing internal damage due to the voltage falling below "discharged" value.

CHARIOT. The carriage or plate of a

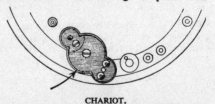

CHARIOT.

cylinder escapement on to which the balance, complete with its cock, is attached enabling the balance and cylinder to be moved bodily for purposes of adjustment.

CHASING. A form of decoration on metal, where an embossed or repoussé effect is obtained; no metal is removed in the process.

CHECKER. *See* ANTIQUE CLOCK CASE TERMS.

CHECK SPRING. The spring piece which holds the pull-out piece (*q.v.*) in a definite position either at hands set or to the winding position. *See* NOMENCLATURE OF WATCH PARTS, page 283.

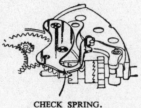

CHECK SPRING.

CHATELAINE. A ladies' fob watch.

CHATON (Fr.). A bushon, or a bezel or ring. In horology it refers to the ring or bushon into which is set a jewel hole, etc., or another metal bushon where the hole is relatively small. Some watches are fitted with brass chatons to the centre and other wheels, the object being that they can be renewed. They are usually fitted friction tight (no riveting).

CHEEKS. *See* ANTIQUE CLOCK CASE TERMS.

CHEESE FEET. *See* ANTIQUE CLOCK CASE TERMS.

CHEESE-HEAD SCREW. A screw with a cylindrical head.

CHELSEA CLOCK. Made by The Chelsea Clock Co. of America, a lever clock usually fitted into a metal case of nautical design. Makers of clocks striking Ships' Bell Time (*q.v.*).

CHEESE-HEAD SCREW.

CHENEER OR CHENIER. A metal tube similar to bushon wire; the term generally refers to watch cases where it is used to form the joints or hinges. English case makers termed it " Joint Wire."

CHENILLE. The plush-like material used as a dust seal at the base of glass clock covers.

CHEVÉE LENTILLE GLASS. A watch glass similar to a lentille but with a little more freedom at the shoulder. *See* Lentille. Also WATCH GLASS STYLES.

CHIMES. A peal, a succession of notes, distinct from a Strike, which is on one bell or gong, or a chord struck with one blow. Also distinct from an air such as played by a musical clock or watch, or on a carillon.

CHIMES

The information for this section of Chimes was compiled by permission from an article in the December, 1941, issue of the HOROLOGICAL JOURNAL.

TWO-BELL CHIMES

TING-TANG

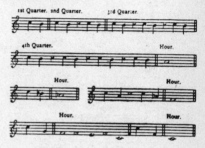

The most ancient form of chime used.

THREE-BELL CHIMES

HAMPSTEAD

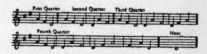

The chimes of Christchurch, Hampstead.

NAFFERTON

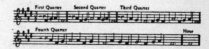

These chimes are not used in the village church at Nafferton. They appear in an old catalogue of Messrs. Potts, of Sheffield, as "Chimes for Nafferton Church" and may have been proposed and abandoned.

FOUR-BELL CHIMES
WESTMINSTER

The chimes of the great clock at Westminster. Big Ben was the name given to the hour bell, after Sir Benjamin Hall, the Chief Commissioner (afterwards Lord Llanover), and the clock itself has become to be known as Big Ben.

The chime was taken from the fifth bar of Handel's aria from the *Messiah:* " I know that my Redeemer liveth."

It was selected and expanded into the present chime by MR. CROTCH and DR. JOWETT and first used in St. Mary's Church, Cambridge (1793–94).

COPENHAGEN

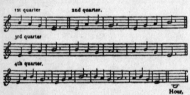

This chime is installed on the City Hall at Copenhagen. It is a modified form of the Westminster chimes.

Copenhagen plays this tune at twelve and at six.

PARSIFAL

The clock which uses this chime has not been identified. The phrase is played once at the first quarter, twice at the half hour and so on.

Referred to by KRUMM and BALTZER in their " Grossuhr-Schlagwerke," it is probably to be found in Germany.

Also to be heard at Riverside Drive Church, New York, or the Rockefeller memorial carillon.

SILCHESTER

These quarters are sounded by a group of figure jacks operated by a clock at Silchester House, the residence of T. M. HARTLEY, the maker of the clock.

LOSTWITHIEL

This chime is to be heard at Lostwithiel, Cornwall.

DORKING

The chimes of St. Michael's, Dorking, Surrey.

FIVE-BELL CHIMES
TENNYSON (OR CARFAX)

The chimes of Freshwater Church, Isle of Wight. Also to be heard at Uppingham and Maralin, Ireland.

CANTERBURY CATHEDRAL

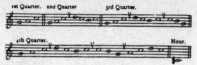

The chimes of Canterbury Cathedral were composed by the Rev. FREDERICK J. O. HELMORE.

LOURDES (AVE MARIA)

The chimes of Lourdes are founded on motifs taken from a composition of Liszt.

NORWICH

The chimes of Norwich Cathedral. Composed by the Rev. E. S. MEDLEY, 1876.

KEIGHLEY

The chimes of Keighley Parish Church.

R.C. CHURCH, CAMBRIDGE

R.C. Church, Cambridge—Cont.

The chimes of the Roman Catholic Church, Cambridge. Arranged by the Rev. Canon SCOTT, D.D., from an Alleluia song on Holy Sunday.

Also heard at the Redemptorist Church of St. Josephs, Dundalk.

PALMERS GREEN

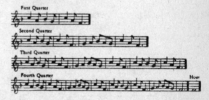

To be heard in the Bramley sports ground, near Palmers Green

FORT AUGUSTUS, N.B.

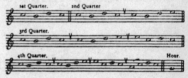

The chimes of Fort Augustus Abbey, New Brunswick.

STOKE ST. GREGORY

GONVILLE AND CAIUS

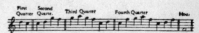

The chimes from the tower of Gonville and Caius College, Cambridge.

SIX-BELL CHIMES.

KROONSTAD

The chimes of the Dutch Reformed Church at Kroonstad, Orange Free State.

WINCHESTER

It is not known where these chimes are to be heard. They have come to be christened by clock manufacturers as Winchester, but they are not to be heard in that city.

CANTERBURY

This is not the chime of Canterbury Cathedral. It may be heard, it is stated, in the City of Canterbury but the name of the church is not disclosed.

TRINITY

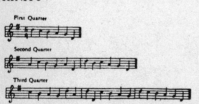

Trinity—Cont.

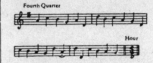

A traditional chime tune assumed to have been originally installed in a church of the Holy Trinity, London, now non-existent. The chime is used in clocks.

SEVEN-BELL CHIME

EATON SOCON

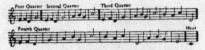

A unique chime of seven bells. Composed by S. G. WILKINSON in 1931 for the church at Eaton Socon.

EIGHT-BELL CHIMES

GUILDFORD

These chimes were composed by GEORGE WILKINS in 1843 for the Holy Trinity Church, Guildford, Surrey.

MAGDALEN COLLEGE

The chimes of Magdalen College, Oxford, originally set up in 1713. Also to be heard at Beverley Minster.

NEW COLLEGE

The chimes of New College, Oxford.

DENSTONE COLLEGE

The chimes of Denstone College, Staffordshire. Composed by R. J. DENTON in 1933.

ST. MICHAELS

This chime probably comes from St. Michael's Church, Hamburg.

CAIRO

The chimes of the King Fuad Hospital, Cairo. Composed by W. H. VIPOND BARRY.

NOTRE DAME

NOTRE DAME—Cont.

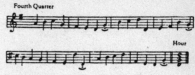

The chimes of Notre Dame, Paris.

TEN-BELL CHIMES
BEVERLEY

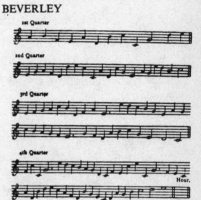

The chimes of Beverley Minster, Beverley, Yorks.

DERBY

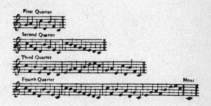

The chimes of All Saints' Church (now the Cathedral Church), Derby.

PRESTON

ELEVEN-BELL CHIMES
WHITTINGTON (BOW)

The chimes of Bow Church, composed by Sir CHARLES VILLIERS STANFORD in 1905 and based on the old six-bell tune.

WHITTINGTON
(AMERICAN VERSION)

This " American version " of the Whittington chime is typical of the undistinguished set of changes which pass for " A Whittington Chime."

TROWBRIDGE

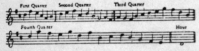

The Trowbridge chimes were composed by Sir W. G. ALCOCK in 1934.

CHIMING CLOCK. A clock which chimes on bells or gongs sounding the hours, half hours, and quarters in addition to striking the number of hours, at each hour. Distinct from the Striking Clock in which the number of the hour is sounded, sometimes the half hour with one blow. *See* also Ting-Tang.

CHINOISERIE. *See* ANTIQUE CLOCK ANL CLOCK CASE TERMS.

CHIP CARVING. *See* ANTIQUE CLOCK CASE TERMS.

CHIPPENDALE. *See* ANTIQUE CLOCK CASE TERMS.

CHOKE. An electrical device consisting of a single, or multi-layered winding, with or without a laminated iron core. An inductance used in alternating current circuits to discriminate between differing or superimposed frequencies present in a common circuit.

CHOPS. Term usually refers to the detachable linings of soft metal or wood used in the jaws of a vice. *See* Cycloidal Chops, also Clams.

WOOD CHOPS.

CHORD. A straight line between any two points lying upon a curve. The simultaneous sounding of several notes of a musical scale.

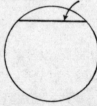

CHORD.

CHROMIUM PLATING. An electro-deposited skin or coating of chromium having a bluish appearance.

CHRONOGRAPH. A writer of time; Apparatus for registering the beats of a watch or clock so that they may be accurately compared with a standard time signal. Associated in horology with a mechanism that enables the seconds hand to be returned to zero at will. Invented by Adolphi Nicole in 1862. Such pieces are usually fitted with a centre seconds hand which can be started, stopped, and returned to zero. This is additional to the normal hour and minute hands indicating the time of day. This arrangement is distinct from a Timer (*q.v.*). Also refers to an instrument used in observatories, etc., for recording clock and watch beats, star transits, etc. For various calibrations of the chronograph dial *see* TIMERS, page 253. Also an apparatus for registering the beats of a watch or clock so that they may be

CHRONOGRAPH.

accurately compared with a standard time signal.

CHRONOGRAPHS. Drum and Tape. These chronographs are designed for many scientific and industrial purposes. Their main use is to facilitate the comparison of observation with a time base and at the same time provide a permanent record. The purpose is:—(a) to drive a drum or tape at a controlled speed by means of a mechanism driven by weight, spring or electric motor. Two speeds and a neutral are generally supplied; (b) to record by means of electrically driven pens or prickers on chart paper the impulses given out by the electrical contacts of the chrono-

meter in circuit with one pen or pricker to compare with another pen or pricker which is actuated with a tapping key (surveying) or by an instrument. Instruments of this kind are made by Thomas Mercer Ltd., St. Albans, England. The mechanisms are made as light as possible and supplied in a carrying case. Maximum number of pens or prickers on the tape model are five, and on the drum model, two.

CHRONOGRAPH DIALS. *See* TIMERS, page 253. *Also* NOMENCLATURE OF CHRONOGRAPH PARTS, next page.

CHRONOMETER. Time measurer. In England it is usually associated with the " detent " excapement as distinct from the lever escapement and was primarily made for the purpose of determining the longitude at sea. The chronometer escapement was invented by Le Roy and other French horologists and, in its present day form, by Arnold and Earnshaw simultaneously about 1780. The Earnshaw escapement is in use today. These marine instruments are known as " Box Chronometers " and consist of a fusee and chain movement fitted into a brass box which is slung in Gymbals (*q.v.*) fitted into an outer box of wood. In recent years the Admiralty have laid down a specification applying to a watch fitted with a lever escapement; it requires close rating and shall then be termed " Chronometer." In recent years the word " chronometer " has taken on a new meaning. The Swiss have decreed (and since the Swiss are the most important makers of watches in the world the ruling made by them affects all countries) that a watch having passed a certain prescribed test shall be known as a " chronometer." For some years and up to November 15, 1951, the Swiss Federation of Watch Manufacturers (Fédération Suisse des Associations de Fabricants d'Horlogerie), ruled that the term " chronometer " was descriptive of a precision watch regulated in different positions and various temperatures *capable* of obtaining an official timing certificate. On November 15, 1951, this same Federation modified its ruling which now reads as follows:—A precision watch regulated in different positions and various temperatures *having obtained* an official timing certificate. The entire Swiss watch industry is governed by regulations issued by the Swiss Federation of Watch Manufacturers and, although such regulations are not federal law they are considered as important by the watch industry. Therefore, anybody in Switzerland, using the word " chronometer " for a watch

Continued on page 97

CHRONOGRAPH.

NOMENCLATURE OF CHRONOGRAPH PARTS

THE NAMES OF THE PARTS AS NUMBERED ARE SHOWN IN THE CHART

(The numbers with the illustrations are the official Swiss spare parts numbers. *See* page 179.)

Where not already given, it is advisable to prefix the part name by the word Chronograph

SWISS OFFICIAL CATALOGUE NUMBER	No.	ENGLISH	FRENCH
8020	1	Minute Counter Wheel	Mobile Compteur des Minutes
8022	2	Minute Counter Heart Piece	Cœur Minutes
	3	Minute Counter Lever Screw	Vis de Bascule Compteur
	4	Return to Zero Lever Spring Screw	Vis de Ressort de Marteau
	5	Chronograph Push Lever Screw	Vis de Grande Bascule de Poussoir

92

Swiss Official Catalogue Number	No.	English	French
8140	6	Chronograph Push Lever	Grande Bascule
	7	Minute Counter Lever Shoulder Screw	Clef de Bascule de Compteur
8350	8	Return to Zero Lever Spring	Ressort du Marteau
8290	9	Friction Spring	Ressort de Friction
58290	10	Friction Spring Screw	Vis de Ressort de Friction
8220	11	Return to Zero Lever	Marteau
58070	12	Column Wheel Screw	Vis de Roue à Colonnes
8070	13	Column Wheel	Roue à Colonnes
8401	14	Eccentric Screw for Chronograph Wheel Depth	Excentrique Pivotement Bascule de Roue

Swiss Official Catalogue Number	No.	English	French
8200	15	Brake Lever	Bloqueur (Frein)
8335	16	Chronograph Push Lever Spring	Ressort de Poussoir
8345	17	Brake Lever Spring	Ressort du Bloqueur (Frein)
8355	18	Column Wheel Jumper	Sautoir de Roue à Colonnes
	19	Column Wheel Jumper Screw	Vis de Sautoir de Colonnes
	20	Brake Lever Screw	Vis de Frein
	21	Brake Lever Spring Screw	Vis de Ressort de Frein
	22	Chronograph Push Lever Spring Screw	Vis de Ressort de Crochet
	23	Intermediate Chronograph Wheel Shoulder Screw	Clef de Bascule de Roue
	24	Intermediate Chronograph Wheel Lever Screw	Vis de Bascule de Roue

Swiss Official Catalogue Number	No.	English	French
8080	25	Intermediate Chronograph Wheel Lever and Wheel	Bascule de Roue montée avec Roue
	26	Intermediate Chronograph Wheel Spring	Ressort de Bascule de Roue
	27	Intermediate Chronograph Wheel Spring Screw	Vis de Ressort de Bascule de Roue
8001	28	Chronograph Wheel	Roue Chronographe
8002	29	Centre Heart Piece (see No. 2)	Cœur Chronographe
	30	Intermediate Chronograph Wheel (see No. 25 above) Cock	Pont de Bascule de Roue
8083	31	Intermediate Chronograph Wheel	Roue Intermédiaire de Chronographe
	32	Intermediate Counter Wheel Lever and Wheel	Bascule de Compteur montée avec Roue

Swiss Official Catalogue Number	No.	English	French
8000	33	Centre Chronograph Wheel	Roue de Centre de Chronographe
	34	Intermediate Counter Wheel	Roue Intermédiaire de Compteur
	35	Minute Counter and Centre Chronograph Wheel Cock	Pont de Roue de Compteur et Roue de Centre de Chronographe
	36	Minute Counter Jumper Screw	Vis de Sautoir de Compteur
	37	Intermediate Counter Wheel Lever Spring Screw	Vis de Ressort de Bascule Compteur
	38	Intermediate Counter Wheel Lever Spring	Ressort de Bascule Compteur
8270	39	Minute Counter Jumper	Sautoir de Compteur
	40	Flirt Piece	Dard
	41	Heart Piece, Centre or Counter (see No. 2)	Cœur de Centre ou Compteur

96

unless it has been officially tested and granted a certificate, would be liable to prosecution. There are two official testing bodies, an Observatory and the Swiss Government Testing Station. Extracts from the regulations of the Swiss Government Testing Station (Bureaux Officiels) and the tolerances are given on page 247. The action of the chronometer escapement is as follows: The escape wheel is rotating in the direction as the arrow and the tooth A is arrested by the locking pallet B which is fixed to the spring detent C. The two rollers D and E are fixed to the balance staff and as they rotate to the left the discharge pallet F contacts the gold spring G, thus releasing the escape wheel and the tooth H drops on to the impulse pallet I and so gives impulse to the balance. The escape wheel continues to rotate and it is arrested by the escape wheel tooth J contacting the locking pallet B, which has by then sprung back into position to receive it. When the balance has completed its journey and returns, the discharge pallet F contacts the back of the gold spring G

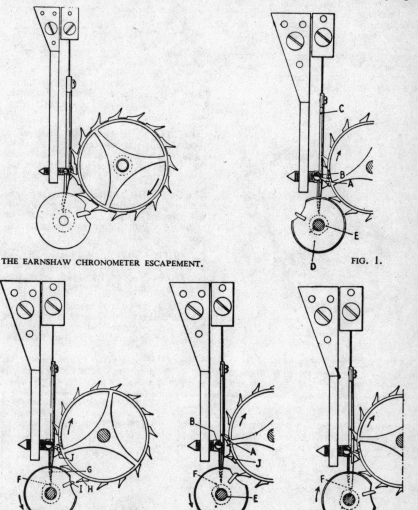

THE EARNSHAW CHRONOMETER ESCAPEMENT.

FIG. 1.

FIG. 2.

FIG. 3.

FIG. 4.

and lifts it free of the detent and the escape wheel is not unlocked, therefore the balance receives impulse in one direction only. *Fig.* 1—Escapement about to function. *Fig.* 2—Discharge pallet about to unlock escape wheel. *Fig.* 3—Escape wheel unlocked gives impulse to balance. *Fig.* 4—Discharge pallet flexing gold spring upon its return and " dead " journey. The Earnshaw escapement is more in use than the Arnold. The action of the Arnold escapement is similar to the Earnshaw, with the exception that the escape wheel rotates away from the foot of the detent and the shape of the escape wheel teeth are different. The active faces of the teeth are epicycloidal, so that when they contact the impulse face of the impulse roller, the action is in theory, rolling, and therefore frictionless. In practice the impulse is a sudden shock. The Earnshaw is a sharp impact and also frictionless.

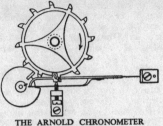

THE ARNOLD CHRONOMETER
ESCAPEMENT.

CHUCK. An accessory to the lathe for holding work to be turned. Sometimes termed a " Collet,"

THE BOX CHRONOMETER.

CHUCK.

" Wire Chuck " or " Split Chuck." *See* Box, Balance, Boring, Button or Crown, Lantern, Wood Screw, Universal, Wax, Self-Centring.

CIRCUIT. The whole, or part, of a conducting system connected to an electrical supply. Generally understood to be all the wiring, etc., immediately beyond the output terminals of a cell or generator.

CIRCUIT BREAKER. Any switch, especially an automatically operated or self-operated type, for interrupting or breaking off the supply to an electrical circuit.

CIRCUIT, OPEN. A break in the continuity of a circuit. To throw part of a circuit out of operation by disconnecting one side of the supply thereto.

CIRCUIT, SHORT. A fault in a circuit which enables the energy supplied to by-pass the intended circuit. To throw part of a circuit out of operation by bring-

CHRONOMETRE. The Swiss definition of the word " chronometre " (chronometer) is a watch that has passed the tests specified by one of the Bureaux Officiels at Bienne, La Chaux-de-Fonds, Le Locle, St. Imier or Geneva. The specification is as follows:—

	Without Mention	*With Mention*
1. Average daily rate in 5 positions.	0 + 15 sec.	0 + 15 sec.
2. Average daily variation in 5 positions	7 sec.	4 sec.
3. Greatest variation between two consecutive daily rates in the same position	12 sec.	8 sec.
4. Greatest difference between the average daily rate and one of the rates in 5 positions	± 26 sec.	± 16 sec.
5. Variation per degree centigrade (ranging from 1° to 32° C.)	± 1·4 sec.	± 0·8 sec.
6. Reverting rate	± 14 sec.	± 8 sec.

The sign + indicates fast and — slow. *See* pages 242-8 for other specifications.

ing both sides of its supply to a common potential; or, by-passing it with a conductor of relatively negligible resistance.

CIRCULAR ARC GEARING. A tooth form similar to the cycloidal, standardised by the British Standards Institute ; primarily evolved to reduce the number of cutters and hobbing tools required in the cutting of cycloidal gears.

CIRCULAR ARC GEARING.

" It has the advantage that a single hob of any given pitch can produce gears of any number of teeth of that pitch whereas the cycloidal form requires at least eight hobbs for each pitch."
Vide B.S. Specification 978—1941.

CIRCULAR ERROR. The error or difference of time caused when the pendulum describes a large arc: due to the pendulum tracing a circular instead of a cycloidal path. If the arc is 2° or less upon each side of the line of centre the circular error is practically negligible.

CIRCULAR FACES. The circular faces of the " Dead Beat " pallet, also called " Resting Faces." *See* Dead Beat Escapement. Sometimes referred to as " locking."

CIRCULAR GRAIN. Where the surface of metal is finished with a circular grain (circles of lines).

CIRCULAR LOCKING. Another name for Equidistant Locking (*q.v.*).

CIRCULAR PALLETS. The centres of impulse planes lie on the same circle. Pallets are " included " between two concentric circles. Known as Equidistant impulse. The locking faces are at an unequal distance from the centre motion

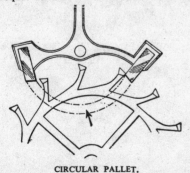

CIRCULAR PALLET.

thus causing an unequal and an increased resistance to unlocking which is not desirable, especially in small watches, where the balance is light. Watches fitted with circular pallets tend to " set " (*q.v.*). *See* Semitangental.

CIRCULAR PITCH. The distance from the centre of one tooth to the centre of the next tooth along the pitch circle.

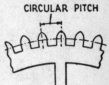

CIRCULAR PITCH

CIRCUMFERENTIAL PITCH. The pitch of a helical, spiral, or worm gear, measured along the pitch circle.

CLAMS. Refers to the metal linings (usually soft) used in the vice to protect work.

CLAMS.

CLAW AND BALL FOOT. *See* ANTIQUE CLOCK CASE TERMS.

CLEANING FLUID. A term given to a fluid used in watch and clock cleaning machines. A cleaning fluid is used first and then a rinse. *See* " Practical Watch Repairing."

CLEANING SOLUTIONS. *See* WORKSHOP HINTS AND HELPS, page 300.

CLEARANCE. Freedom. In gearing it refers to the distance between the tips of the teeth of one gear and the roots of the teeth of its mating gear, measured along the line of centres.

CLEPSYDRA. Water clock. There are various types of water clocks, from the plain vessel with an orifice at its base through which water percolates and, by the lowering of the surface of the water the passage of time is denoted, to the water clock with a mechanical device to cause a hand to rotate. The mechanical clepsydra shown overleaf is simple in operation. The cylindrical vessel is slowly filled with water and a float with a stem and rack engages the wheel to which the hour hand is attached. As the vessel fills so the float rises and the hour hand is made to rotate. When the vessel is full it is emtied and the process starts over again. While this type of clock is spectacular and one would like to think it

EGYPTIAN WATER CLOCK.

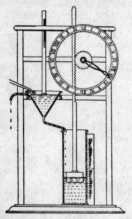

CLEPSYDRA (MECHANICAL).

is of ancient origin, it has to be recorded that no ancient example has been handed down to us. On the other hand, Egyptian water clocks, as illustrated, have been found and date from about 1400 B.C. Primitive water clocks of Saxon times have been found in the British Isles. They are of the " sinking bowl " type, where a bronze bowl with a hole in the bottom was placed upon the surface of the water, water percolated through the hole and eventually it sank which denoted a period of time. It is interesting to note that this system is still used in Algeria for timing periods of the supply of water for irrigation purposes.

CLICK. The piece of mechanism that allows the the ratchet wheel to travel in one direction only. *See* Back

Stop and Pawl. *See* WATCH PART NOMENCLATURE.

CLICK AND SPRING COMBINED.

CLICK, RECOIL. A form of click developed to prevent straining of the mainspring when fully wound thus eliminating " Knocking the banking " (*q.v.*). The locking surface or "Beak" (*q.v.*) engages only when the ratchet recoils (as the winding pressure is removed), thus preventing a dead tight winding.

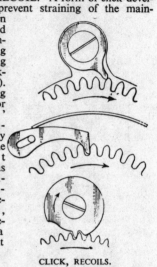

CLICK, RECOILS.

CLICK SPRING. A small spring acting

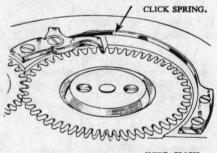

CLICK SPRING.

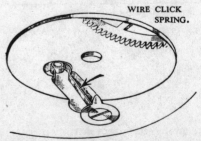

WIRE CLICK SPRING.

on a click. By suitable design and tempering a click may be made self-springing when it can be described as a "Spring Click." *See* NOMENCLATURE OF WATCH PARTS, page 275.

CLOCK. Derived from the Latin Clocca—a bell. Originally the passing of time was denoted by the striking of a bell, either by hand, or by mechanical means. A dial and hands were not used. To-day, generally, it refers to a time of day measuring instrument distinct from a Watch (*q.v.*) or Marine Chronometer (*q.v.*).

CLOCK WATCH. A watch that strikes the hours as it goes, as does a striking clock, and also repeats the hour, quarter, and minutes at will. Unlike a repeating watch, the strike train is wound, as is the going train. *See* Repeater.

CLOCKING - IN CLOCK. *See* Time Recorder.

CLUB FOOT. *See* ANTIQUE CLOCK CASE TERMS.

CLUB TOOTH. A "club-shaped" form of escape wheel tooth much used in lever escapements today. Compare with "Ratchet tooth " shape. *See* Lever Escapement.

CLUB TOOTH.

CLUTCH PINION. An American term for the Castle Wheel (*q.v.*).

CO-AXIAL. Lying about the same axis; concentric (*q.v.*).

COCK. A bracket with one support; as distinct from a "bridge" (*q.v.*) which has two supports.

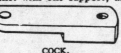

COCK.

COCKTAIL GLASS. The abnormally thick glass used in Cocktail Watches (*q.v.*).

COCKTAIL GLASS.

COCKTAIL WATCH. A term used to define an exotic type of wrist watch for ladies. Of gold and platinum, and steel, etc., often set with precious stones. A rather heavy bold style when compared with the conventional gem set watch for evening wear.

COCKTAIL WATCH.

COEFFICIENT OF ELASTICITY. The ratio of the stress set up within a body by a deforming force to the strain or deformation. Also termed Modulus of Elasticity. (*See* also Young's Modulus.)

COEFFICIENT OF EXPANSION. A numerical constant used as a multiplier to enable the expansion of a material to be calculated as a whole.

COEFFICIENT OF FRICTION. A constant factor between any two surfaces in contact. It is the ratio of Limiting friction to Normal Pressure.

COEFFICIENT THERMIQUE. *See* Temperature Coefficient.

COERCIVE FORCE. The inverse magnetising force required to reduce a residual magnetic condition to zero.

COHESION. The force of attraction between molecules, determining the mechanical strength or resistance to rupture of a material.

COIL. The general name for a winding of wire as used in an electrical component or circuit.

COIN WATCH. Where the case of the watch is made from a coin—a £5 or 100 Swiss Fr. piece, or 20 dollar piece.

COLLET. A circular ring, such as a balance spring collet; a split or solid collet by which the balance spring is held at the centre. *See* NOMENCLATURE OF WATCH PARTS, page 280. Hand collet, the collet fitted to assist in holding the hands in position. Sometimes the term Collet is applied to lathe chucks, wire chucks, or American chucks.

COLOUR TEMPERATURE TABLES. *See* Blueing.

COLUMN WHEEL. The castle-shaped wheel of the chronograph or timer mechanism, which causes the various levers to operate, so to set in motion, stop and return to zero the hands. Sometimes referred to as the Castle Ratchet. *See* WATCH PART NOMENCLATURE.

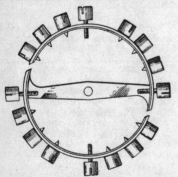

COLUMN WHEEL.

COMMA ESCAPEMENT. The Virgule escapement (*q.v.*).

COMMON NORMAL to two curved surfaces in contact, is a straight line passing through the point of contact, in a direction perpendicular to a tangent between the curved surfaces.

COMMON TANGENT to two curves in contact is a straight line passing through the point of contact, tangent to both curves.

COMPENSATING BALANCE SPRING. A balance spring made of Invar, Elinvar, Nivarox (*q.v.*) or such alloy, the modulus of elasticity of which remains unaffected (or only very slightly affected) by temperature changes. *See* Balance Spring Alloys.

COMPENSATION BALANCE. A balance made of steel or nickel steel having a brass layer fused on to its outer diameter and cut so as to form bi-metallic " limbs " which, under the influence of a rise or fall in temperature move correspondingly inwards or outwards relative to the centre. By this means compensation is effected for the varying elasticity of the balance spring due to the self-same temperature changes. *See* WATCH PART NOMENCLATURE.

COMPENSATION BALANCE.

COMPENSATION CURB. A device used in some early watches where one index pin is fitted to the index and the other is fitted to a bi-metallic strip, or the end of the strip acts as a pin. The action is

COMPENSATION CURB.

that in heat, for instance, the space between the pins is closed, thus making the watch gain when it would otherwise lose and so compensating for a loss in heat.

COMPENSATION PENDULUM. A pendulum employing some device to compensate its varying length in changes of temperature, or having a rod made of INVAR or other material, of similar properties. *See* Ellicott, Mercurial, Gridiron, Riefler.

COMPLICATED WORK. A term used to indicate other than a plain time piece; such as chronographs, repeaters, etc. " Triple Complication " refers to a watch fitted with chronograph, repeating, and calendar work.

COMTÉ OR COMTOIS CLOCK. A French clock made in the district known as Franche-Comté, usually in the towns of Morbier and Morez. *See* Morbier Clocks. They correspond to the English long case clock and are very heavily constructed with a special form of rack striking work and often with " Grande Sonnerie " (*q.v.*).

CONCENTRIC. Said of two or more circles having a common centre but different radii.

CONDENSER. An electrical component having two (or more) conducting surfaces separated by an insulating medium and capable of " holding " or " storing " a charge of electrical energy. An obsolescent term for a capacitance or Capacitor (American) (*q.v.*).

CONDUCTANCE. Facility offered to the flow of electric current. The reciprocal of Resistance (*q.v.*).

CONDUCTOR. That which carries or allows the flow of a current of electricity from one point to another.

CONGREVE CLOCK. *See* Ball Clocks.

CONICAL PENDULUM.

A pendulum the bob of which describes a circle. There is no escapement; the train wheels terminate with a wheel with an extended arbor to which is fixed a finger which touches an extension of the pendulum. In some clocks the finger terminates with a U-shaped end which embraces the extension. The pendulum is used in novelty clocks and also by astronomers to control equatorial telescopes. The virtue of the device is that the motion of the clock mechanism is continuous. There is no stopping and starting as with clocks having escapements. C. A. Crommelin in "The Clocks of Christiaan Huygens" says, when referring to

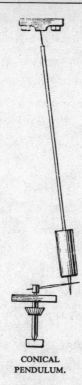

CONICAL PENDULUM.

inventions of Huygens, "the first clock after the invention of the pendulum clock was a timepiece with a conical pendulum invented probably in 1659 or 1660 and constructed about 1667 or 1668." The time of rotation of a conical pendulum is

$$T = 2\pi \sqrt{\frac{L \cos \alpha}{g}}$$

where L = length of pendulum.
α = angle of elevation.
g = acceleration due to gravity.

For small angles $T = 2\pi \sqrt{\frac{L}{g}}$ or the same as the time taken for a double swing by a plane pendulum of the same length.

CONICAL PIVOT.

A cone-shaped pivot, such as is used in a low grade watch or clock, working in a Vee-shaped hole or sink, more correctly a "Cone pivot." Also refers to the pivot which works in a through hole and fitted with an endpiece.

CONE PIVOT. CONICAL PIVOT.

CONJUGATE RACK.

The reciprocal, or inverse of the basic rack. The form used for generating tools such as hobs. *See* Basic Rack.

CONSOLE.

See ANTIQUE CLOCK CASE TERMS.

CONTACT RATIO.

The number of pitches over which load bearing contact is maintained.

CONTRATE TEETH.

An example of contrate teeth is to be found in the Castle Wheel (*q.v.*).

CONTRATE WHEEL.

A gear wheel the teeth of which stand at right angles to the plane of the wheel; such as the wheel driving the escape wheel pinion in a carriage clock where the Platform Escapement (*q.v.*)

CONTRATE WHEEL.

is fitted at the top and across the movement plates.

CONTROLLED FREQUENCY.

See Frequency Control.

CONVERSION TABLES.

See TEMPERATURE CONVERSION TABLE.

COPPER LOSS.

In electricity, the energy lost by dissipation as heat in windings, etc., due to resistance of conduction. Measured in Watts = (Current)^2 × Resistance.

COPPER OXIDE RECTIFIER.

An apparatus, based upon the uni-directional flow of current at the junction surfaces of a layer of cuprous oxide and copper, used to provide a source of Direct current from an alternating supply.

CORBEL.

See ANTIQUE CLOCK CASE TERMS.

CORE.

The soft iron or alloy centre or framework providing a path of low reluctance (*q.v.*) for the magnetic flux generated by a coil or winding. *See* Laminations.

CORE LOSS.

The energy lost due to Eddy-currents (*q.v.*) and Hysteresis (*q.v.*) in an iron core or magnetic circuit subjected to a varying Magnetic Flux (*q.v.*).

CORINTHIAN.

See ANTIQUE CLOCK CASE TERMS.

CORNER PIECES.

See Spandrels.

CORNICE. *See* ANTIQUE CLOCK CASE TERMS.

CORN TONGS. Tweezers used by jewellers and precious stone dealers for handling stones.

CORN TONGS.

CORONA. *See* ANTIQUE CLOCK CASE TERMS.

COTTER. A tapered pin used for locking or securing by virtue of its wedging action.

COULOMB. The practical unit of the quantity of electricity. One coulomb is that quantity of electricity which flows in one second through a conductor carrying current at the rate of one ampere per second.

COUNTER BUHL. *See* ANTIQUE CLOCK CASE TERMS.

COUNTERPOISE. A method of counter balancing. A weight attached to the hour or minute arbor of a turret clock to counter balance the weight of a heavy hand.

COUNTER POTENCE. In a verge watch, the stud which carries the Follower (*q.v.*) and supports the outer end of the escape pinion.

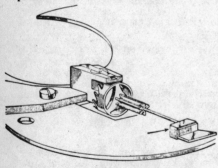

COUNTER POTENCE.

COUNTERSHAFT. A shaft fitted with pulleys to provide a range of speeds for a lathe driven by a motor or foot wheel, also termed Transmission.

COUNTERSINK. A recess or a blind hole with a smaller hole drilled through so that a screw head or other piece may be flush or sunk, *e.g.* the oil sink or reservoir of a clock or watch plate; the sinking of a screw into a click spring, etc.

COUNTERSINKING TOOL. A tool used to sink or chamfer a hole, *e.g.*, to take a screwhead or form an oil sink. The shape of the tool is determined by the form of sink required. *See* Rose Cutter.

COUNTING. The operation of counting the vibrations of the balance for purposes of checking, *e.g.* the " count " of a balance is 18,000 vibrations per hour. Also, to count the train, *i.e.*, the number of teeth in the wheels and leaves in the pinions to ascertain the required count of the balance or pendulum oscillations.

COUNT WHEEL. Another term for the Locking Plate (*q.v.*).

COUPLING. The transference of electrical energy from one circuit to another. Especially in valve circuits.

COVERED PALLETS. Where the pallet stone is set into the metal for its whole length. *See* Pallet Stone, English Pallets.

CRACKLE. A system of finishing given to metal where a covering enamel is applied and then baked until the surface is covered with small cracks or crackles.

CRAFTSMANSHIP TEST. *See* Kew.

CRAFTSMANSHIP WATCH TEST. *See* WATCH TESTING STANDARDS, pages 242–8.

CRAIG FREE PENDULUM. A free pendulum invented by E. E. Craig. It employs a system of two steel balls which, when released on to a platform attached to a bar fitted to the pendulum give impulse. *See* " Electrical Timekeeping," by F. Hope-Jones.

CRANK ESCAPEMENT. The double Virgule escapement invented by Lepaute. This escapement derives its name from the crank-like form of the balance axis. (*See* Virgule Escapement.)

CRANK ROLLER LEVER ESCAPEMENT. A form of lever escapement in which impulse is conveyed to the balance through a square notch in the lever to a pinion leaf form of projection in the roller. Invented by Massey of Liverpool.

CRANK ROLLER LEVER ESCAPEMENT.

CREAM OF TARTAR. *See* Potassium Acid Bitartrate.

CRESCENT. The hollow cut into the edge of the roller of the lever escapement to permit the passage of the guard pin.

CRESCENT.

CRESTING. *See* ANTIQUE CLOCK CASE TERMS.

CRICKET WATCH. The name given to an alarm wrist watch. Made by the Vulcain Watch Co., Switzerland.

CRICKET WATCH.

CROCUS. An oxide of iron. Used in polishing brass or steel. Rouge (*q.v.*) is a refined grade of crocus.

CROMWELLIAN CLOCK. *See* Lantern Clock, ANTIQUE CLOCK CASE TERMS.

CROMWELLIAN PERIOD STYLE. *See* ANTIQUE CLOCK CASE TERMS.

CROSS. A term denoting the extent of the arc of vibration of a balance, *e.g.*, a balance crosses 1½ turns, *i.e.*, a point on the balance passes through an arc of 273¾° on each side of a line of centre, or 547½° in all.

CROSSED AXIS HELICAL GEARS. Also known as Spiral Gears, they connect shafts which lie at an angle to one another but whose axes do not intersect. They are distinguished from Hypoid Gears (*q.v.*) in that their surfaces are cylinders and they are situated where the distance between the two shafts is a minimum.

CROSSING. The arms of a wheel, *e.g.*, the wheel shown has 5 crossings.

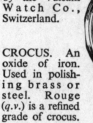

CROSSING FILE. *See* Files.

CROSSING.

CROSSING OUT. The act of shaping or cutting out the arms of a wheel from a blank (*q.v.*)

CROSSING OUT FILE. Specially shaped, flat oval files with thin edges and also thin edged flat files, used when crossing out the arms of a wheel.

CROWN. A winding button. *See* WATCH PART NOMENCLATURE.

CROWN WHEEL ESCAPEMENT. Refers to the escape wheel of the Verge Escapement (*q.v.*): when applied to a clock it is usually referred to as a Crown Wheel Escapement. This form of escapement is found in clocks dated about the middle of the 14th century and was still in use at the close of the 18th century and beginning of the 19th centuries. Although the anchor escapement (*q.v.*) was invented about 1671, it was used in domestic clocks of the long case or grandfather type only. The bracket type of clock was still fitted with the crown wheel escapement up to about 1800, the reason being that it was more robust and more or less portable; the clock could be moved from room to room without fear of damage to the escapement. The action is as follows:—
The escape wheel is rotating in the direction as arrow and the tooth A contacts the pallet or flag B and so gives impulse to the pendulum which is swinging to the right. When the tooth A drops off the pallet B, the pallet C is ready to receive the escape wheel tooth D and so impulse is imparted to the pendulum again as it swings to the left.

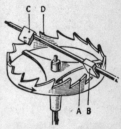

CROWN WHEEL ESCAPEMENT.

CROWN WHEEL ESCAPEMENT.

CROWN WHEEL. A wheel that operates with the Castle Wheel (*q.v.*) on the winding shaft (*q.v.*) in keyless mechanisms. *See* WATCH PART NOMENCLATURE.

CROWN WHEEL.

CRUTCH. That part of a clock mechanism which transmits the power from the escapement to the pendulum and maintains the pendulum vibrations. The crutch is also the medium through which the pendulum controls the instant at which the escape wheel is allowed to move forwards. This domination of the clock by the pendulum through the means of a crutch was the essence of the " invention of the pendulum ' 'by Christiaan Huygens, the Dutchman, for which a patent was granted in 1657.

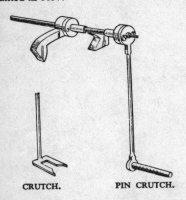

CRUTCH.   PIN CRUTCH.

CRYSTAL. A brilliant colourless quartz or rock; rarely used in horology owing primarily to the cost of working, there are instances of its use in the place of glass. Also a form of watch glass with a bevelled edge. Flat crystal, raised crystal, etc. *See* WATCH GLASS STYLES.

CRYSTAL CLOCK. *See* Quartz Crystal Clock.

CRYSTAL CONTROL. The application of a piezo-electric crystal (quartz) to frequency determination and/or stability involving more than one oscillatory circuit.

CRYSTAL OSCILLATOR. A thermionic valve oscillator notable for its constancy of frequency embodying a piezo-electric (quartz) crystal vibrating at its natural rate.

CUCKOO CLOCK
A clock first made by Anton Ketterer of Schönwald in the Black Forest, Germany, 1730. The feature of the clock is that at the hours and half hours a door at the top of the case opens and a cuckoo projects; the hours and half hours are sounded on a gong and by two bellows blowing pipes, which imitates the call of the cuckoo.

CUCKOO CLOCK.

CUCKOO-QUAIL CLOCK. A form of Cuckoo Clock (*q.v.*) in which the quarters are sounded by another bellows imitating the cry of the quail.

CUPPING MACHINE. *See* Recessing Machine.

CURB PINS. The pins, fitted to the index, which embrace the balance spring. Sometimes referred to as Index Pins.

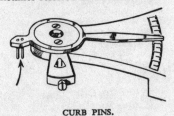

CURB PINS.

CURL. *See* ANTIQUE CLOCK CASE TERMS.

CURLED. A finish to brass. Usually employed on the edges of clock plates.

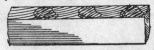

AN EXAMPLE OF CURLING.

CURRENT. The flow of electricity in a conductor, due to the passage of negatively charged electrons. Symbol I. Measured in amperes, milli-amperes, micro-amperes.

CUSPS. *See* ANTIQUE CLOCK CASE TERMS.

CUT BALANCE. *See* Compensation Balance.

CUT CARD WORK. Ornament in sheet metal, cut out and soldered on to a plain surface. Similar to "Blind Fret" (*q.v.*) in wood work.

CUT OFF OR CUT OFF POINT. A term referring to the cessation of anode current flow, especially in a thermionic valve. That value of negative voltage, or "bias" which, applied to the grid (or other electrode) determines the cessation of anode current.

CUT-OUT. An automatic self-operating switch; especially one designed to protect apparatus against an excessive current, failure or reversal of supply voltage.

CYCLE. A change from a position and back to the same position. With a balance or pendulum this equals two Beats (*q.v.*). In electrical horology it is a change of electricity from one direction to the opposite and back again. In Great Britain electric mains current alternates at 50 cycles per second. In the U.S.A. the frequency is 60 c.p.s. *See* Synchronous Motor.

CYCLOID. The curve traced by a point on the circumference of a circle (known as the generating circle) as it rolls along a straight line.

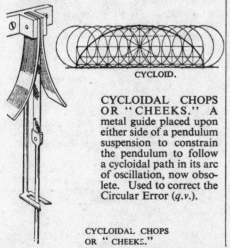

CYCLOID.

CYCLOIDAL CHOPS OR "CHEEKS." A metal guide placed upon either side of a pendulum suspension to constrain the pendulum to follow a cycloidal path in its arc of oscillation, now obsolete. Used to correct the Circular Error (*q.v.*).

CYCLOIDAL CHOPS OR "CHEEKS."

CYLINDER. The hollow staff carrying the balance in the cylinder escapement.

CYLINDER.

CYLINDER ESCAPEMENT. A frictional rest escapement invented by Tompion, Booth and Houghton in 1695, but, eventually improved by Geo. Graham. The cylinder is fixed to the balance which is controlled by the balance spring. A tooth of the escape wheel drops on to the outer side of the cylinder and as the balance rotates the cut away part allows the escape wheel to move forward to the left. The outer edge of the tooth presses against the lip of the cylinder and so gives impulse to the balance, which causes it to rotate to the left. Eventually the tooth leaves the entry lip and drops inside the shell of the cylinder and as the balance rotates back, to the right, the tooth is released, when impulse is imparted to the exit lip, and so the cycle continues. By reason of the cylinder there is no recoil of the escape wheel and the escapement is dead beat. No doubt it is this system which gave Graham the idea for his clock Dead Beat Escapement (*q.v.*). Fig. 1.—Tooth drops on inside of cylinder. Fig. 2.—Balance continues to rotate as arrow. Fig. 3.—About to give impulse. Fig. 4.—Imparting

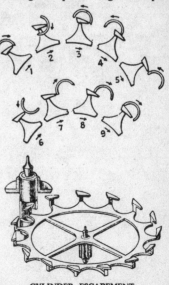

CYLINDER ESCAPEMENT.

impulse. Fig. 5.—Tooth drops on to outside of cylinder. Fig. 6.—Balance continues to rotate as arrow. Fig. 7.—About to give impulse. Fig. 8.—Imparting impulse. Fig. 9.—Completion of impulse and tooth drops on to inside of cylinder again. Also known as the Horizontal escapement.

CYLINDRICAL PENDULUM BOB. *See* Bob.

CYLINDER PLUG. The steel plug at each end of the cylinder on which the pivot is formed in the cylinder escapement.

CYMA RECTA MOULDING. *See* MOULDINGS.

CYMA REVERSA MOULDING. *See* MOULDINGS.

CYLINDER PLUG.

D

DAILY RATE. The amount that a clock or watch gains or loses on correct time. A gaining rate is shown as +, and a losing rate as −.

DAMASCENE. Ornamental work on metal. The flat keyless wheels of some watches are ornamented in a Damascene style. Watch plates and bars are also so treated. The word Damascene is derived from the word Damascus, once famous for its steel and the ornamental work thereon. The original Damascene work was to inlay metal and other material in steel, but in horology it refers to a complicated geometric design of fine etched lines on steel and cut lines on softer metal.

DART. Another name for the Guard or Safety pin in the lever escapement. Usually distinguishes the guard piece, which is made separately and fixed to the lever. *See* Guard Pin.

DART.

DATE OR CALENDAR LINE. The International Date Line is a line drawn on the 180° meridian in the Pacific to determine the change of the name of the day, or date. For instance, a traveller proceeding eastward to the Antipodes will anticipate the sun by 12 hours; another traveller journeying westward, will be 12 hours in arrear.

Thus there is a difference of 24 hours when they meet and, to avoid confusion, the 180° meridian is chosen as a convenient line of demarcation with the arrangement that the Aleutian Islands and Alaska come into the same dating as America, and sections of the South Sea Islands into the same dating as Australia and New Zealand. *See* TIME ZONES.

DATES. Important dates in horology. *See* pages 109-111.

DAWE WATCH RATE RECORDER. This instrument is quartz crystal controlled and the performance of the watch is permanently recorded on paper.

DAYLIGHT SAVING. Refers to the Act passed by Parliament in 1916, at the instigation of William Willett, by which the hour of the day is advanced by one hour during the summer months. Known as Summer Time to distinguish it from Greenwich Mean Time. An extra hour in addition, known as "Double Summer Time," is also brought into use, at times of emergency.

DEAD CENTRE. Where the centres of the lathe or Turns (*q.v.*) do not rotate, as distinct from the live centre, which rotates. Also the point on a crank where the application of power produces no rotational moment on the crank, *e.g.* top dead centre, bottom dead centre.

SOME IMPORTANT HOROLOGICAL DATES

B.C. 742 First authentic recorded mention of the sundial. There is however evidence of use of the sundial as early as 2000 B.C. Isaiah 38.8.
429 Clepsydrae used in Greece.
A.D. 330 Sand glasses known to be in use.
885 Alfred the Great used candles as " clocks."
1000 Haydn's " Book of Dates " records the first escapement, no mention of the type. May have been the verge.
1335 First escapement. Villard's rope escapement.
1360 The Henry de Vick clock. One of the first mechanical clocks.
1368 Clock making began in England.
1380 First domestic clocks, Italian.
1386 Earliest English clock. Salisbury Cathedral.
1500 Mainspring invented by Peter Hele, or Henlein, a locksmith of Nurnburg.
1500–1700 Lantern clock developed.
1510 Stackfreed made to equalise the pull of the mainspring.
1511 First small portable clocks; ascribed to Peter Henlein.
1525 Fusee, invented by Jacob the Czech of Prague.
1530 Brass plates were first used in clock movements.
1550 Screws, for metal work, made their appearance.
1565 About this time the fusee chain, first used in England, was substituted cat-gut. The exact date is obscure.
1581 Galileo, Italian Astronomer and Physicist, discovered the properties of the pendulum.
before 1600 Quarter hour divisions on clock dials.
1600 Watchmakers first active in London.
1600 The minute hand made its appearance.
circa 1600 Lantern clocks appeared in England, with balance or foliot.
circa 1600 Basse-taille enamel introduced.
1610 Enamel used to decorate watch cases.
1610 Glasses as protection for watch dials and hands introduced.
1630 Painted enamel watch cases introduced in Limoges, France.
1635 Enamel dials invented by Paul Viet, of Blois, France.
circa 1650 Puritan watches appeared.
1650 Form watches appear.
1650 Minute hand introduced but not general until 1670.
1656 Christiaan Huygens, Dutch physicist, designed the first practical pendulum controlled clock. It was made in 1657 by Salomon Coster.
1657 Endless rope or chain introduced for winding clocks.
1658 Pendulum clocks first made in England by Ahasuerus Fromanteel.
1660 Virgule escapement invented by Abbé Hauteville.
1660 Chains introduced in place of gut for fusee by Gruet.
1665 Long case clocks developed from hooded clock.
1666 Recoil or anchor escapement invented by Dr. R. Hooke. Also claimed for William Clement.
1670 Wheel cutting machine invented by Dr. Robert Hooke.
1671 First long pendulum clock made in England by Wm. Clement.
1671 Pendulum suspension spring introduced by William Clement.
1673 Seconds or Royal pendulum came into general use. Christopher Wren suggested it should be the standard of Measurement, i.e., 39.14 inches = 1 second.
1674 The coiled balance spring for watches introduced by Abbé Hauteville and Huygens.
1675 Royal Observatory at Greenwich founded. Edward Booth (later Rev. Edward Barlow) invented rack and snail striking mechanism for clocks.
1675 The pocket watch came into use with the introduction of the waistcoat.
1675 Rack and snail mechanism for striking clocks and repeating watches invented by Booth.
circa 1675 Repeating watch, invented by Edward Barlow.
1676 The concentric minute hand, with motion work similar to that in use to-day, was used by Daniel Quare, a famous London maker, and others.

A.D. 1680 Keyless mechanism for watches invented by R. Bowen.
1680 Watches made to go for 24 hours. (Previously they went for 15 hours).
1685 Bolt and shutter maintaining power for clocks.
1685 Gold watch cases Hallmarked.
1685 Night clocks appeared about this time.
1686 Dr. Robert Hooke invented the wheel barometer.
1690 Enamel watch dials made in England.
1694–1702 Jewelling introduced into watches by Nicholas Facio, F.R.S.
1695 Cylinder escapement invented by Tompion, Barlow, and Houghton.
1698 Act of Parliament passed obliging makers to put their names on watches lest discreditable ones might be sold abroad as English.
circa 1700 Egyptian style watch pillars appeared.
1715 George Graham invented the dead beat escapement.
1715 Seconds hand with tails; previously they had no tails.
1720 Hour hand fitted to round hour wheel pipe. Squared previously.
1720 Break arch dial and case first made their appearance.
1722 Rack lever escapement invented by Abbé Hauteville.
1724 Duplex escapement invented by Jean Baptiste Dutertre.
1725 John Harrison invented the grid-iron compensation pendulum.
1725 Dust cap used on watch movements.
1729 Automatic winding watch invented by Abraham Perrelet.
1730 The first cuckoo clock was constructed by Anton Ketterer, Black Forest, Germany.
1730 Grasshopper escapement invented by John Harrison. Attributed by some to James Harrison.
1730 Mahogany used for making English clock cases.
1734 Compensation for loss of elasticity of balance spring, by John Harrison.
1734 Maintaining power, invented by John Harrison.
1740 Silver watch cases Hallmarked.
1750 White enamel watch dials in general use.
1753 Pinwheel escapement invented by Lepaute.
1756 Compensation curb invented by John Harrison.
from 1760 Straight grain silvered dials for bracket and long case clocks.
1760–75 Painted dials on long case clocks appeared.
1761 John Harrison, originally a carpenter, awarded the £20,000 prize offered by the government for a marine timekeeper sufficiently accurate to determine longitude at sea.
1765 Centre seconds hand made its appearance.
1765 First compensation balance, invented by Le Roy. (Alcohol and mercury.)
1766 Pierre Le Roy invented a pivoted detent escapement for chronometers.
1770 Thomas Mudge invented the detached lever escapement by introducing the roller action. This English invention was the forerunner of all modern watches.
1770 Spring detent chronometer escapement invented by John Arnold.
1775 Helical balance spring invented by John Arnold.
1780 Abraham Louis Breguet came to the fore about this time, in Paris, and is acclaimed the greatest horologist of all times.
1780 Chronometer escapement perfected by Thomas Earnshaw.
1780 Automatic winding watch patented by Recordon, London.
1784 Josiah Emery and John Leroux applied " draw " to the lever escapement, making it more practical.
1790 Duplex escapement appeared in English watches.
1791 Rack lever escapement invented by Peter Litherhead.
1797 Act of Parliament clock.
1798 Pin pallet escapement invented by Louis Perron.
circa 1800 French carriage clocks made their appearance.
1801 Tourbillon escapement invented by L. A. Breguet.
1808 Congreve clock invented by William Congreve.
1840 Alexander Bain, an Edinburgh clockmaker, made the first electric clock.
1840 English skeleton clocks appeared.
1844 Adolphe Nicole invented the heart-shaped cam, as used in chronographs. He invented the modern chronograph.

A.D. 1852   Lord Grimthorpe invented the double three-legged gravity escapement. It was first used in the Great Clock at the Houses of Parliament, London, which was fixed and permanently set going in 1859.

1855   Gustavus Hugenin invented the rocking bar keyless mechanism for winding and setting the hands of a watch.

1865   Georges Frederick Roskopf invented the pin pallet escapement.

1872   First patent for water resisting cases.   First patent for shock resisting jewels.

1875   Postman's alarm clocks appeared.   Made in Black Forest, Germany.

1877   The first time signals instituted by Barraud & Lund, in London area only.

1880   Four hundred day clocks appeared.   Made in Germany.

1880   Greenwich Mean Time (G.M.T.) became the standard time for the U.K.

1884   The meridian of Greenwich was adopted by international agreement as the zero or prime meridian from which longitude is measured.

1891   Riefler, of Munich, invented an escapement for Observatory clocks.

1898   R. J. Rudd invented the first free pendulum.   Made practical by W. H. Shortt.

1900   Wrist watches appeared about this time.

1904   Dr. Charles Edouard Guillaume invented " Invar " for compensation pendulums and balance springs. Later he invented " Elinvar " for balance springs.

1906   Eureka electric clock appeared.

1916   Summer Time first introduced.

1918   The alternating current synchronous motor was first applied to clocks by H. C. Warren in the U.S.A.

1921   William Hamilton Shortt, an Englishman, invented the electric free pendulum.

1921   Study and development of the quartz crystal clock commenced by Dr. Warren A. Marrison, a Canadian who became an American citizen.

1924   The Six Pips wireless broadcasting of time signals started on February 5 by the British Broadcasting Corporation.

1924   John Harwood, a watchmaker born in Bolton, Lancs., in 1890, adapted the self-winding system to the wrist watch.

1936   " TIM," the Post Office Speaking Clock, was started at Holborn telephone exchange, London.

1937   Quartz crystal clocks introduced at the Royal Greenwich Observatory.

1946   Royal Greenwich Observatory moved from Greenwich to Herstmonceux Castle, Sussex.

1955   Caesium atomic clock invented by Dr. L. Essen, National Physical Laboratory, Teddington, England.

1957   First electric wrist watches marketed by the Hamilton Watch Co., U.S.A.

1960   Tuning fork watch invented by Max Hetzel.

1967   Quartz crystal watch (q.v.) developed in Switzerland and Japan.

DEAD BEAT ESCAPEMENT. Invented by George Graham, 1715. It is called Dead Beat because when a tooth of the escape wheel has dropped on to the pallet the escape wheel does not recoil but remains motionless, due to the faces of the pallets being arcs of a circle centred from the pallet arbor. This escapement is used in Regulators (q.v.). The action is as follows:—The tooth A of the escape wheel drops on to the face of the pallet B. The pendulum continues to swing to the right so that the depth of locking is a little deeper than the illustration. The pendulum then starts to swing to the left and when the tooth leaves the pallet face it slides along the impulse face and so imparts impulse to the pendulum; the pallets are fixed to the pallet arbor and the crutch—which is

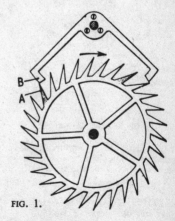

FIG. 1.

fixed to the pallet arbor embraces the pendulum. As the tooth drops off the impulse face the tooth C drops on to the pallet face D and the cycle starts again. Fig. 1.—Escape wheel locked. Fig. 2.—Escape wheel imparting impulse. Fig. 3.—Escape wheel arrested by right hand pallets. Fig. 4.—Pendulum at the end of it swinging to the left. The Continental clockmakers favour pallets where the pads are adjustable as in the Vulliamy (*q.v.*).

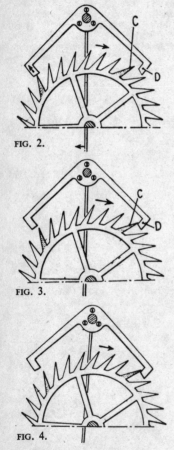

FIG. 2.

FIG. 3.

FIG. 4.

DEAD BEAT ESCAPEMENT.

DEAD SHORT. A commonly used term to denote an electrical short circuit of very low resistance and occurring unintentionally.

DEATH'S HEAD WATCH. A watch made in the shape of the human skull.

Introduced in the latter part of the sixteenth century.

DEATH'S HEAD WATCH.

DECIMAL COUNTER. *See* TIMERS.

DECIMAL WATCH. A watch with the dial divided into 10 instead of 12 hours; each hour into tenths and each tenth into hundredths of an hour. Watches and clocks of this kind were made in France after the French Revolution. *See* Decimal Clock, also TIMERS.

DECK WATCH. A precision watch used on board ship. Usually of large size (18 to 24 lignes) and contained in a wooden box, not dissimilar to the Box Chronometer but much smaller.

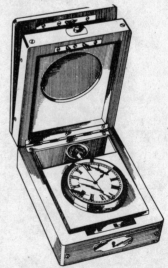

DECK WATCH.

DECLINATION. The angular distance north or south of the celestial equator, measured along the meridian. Used in setting transit instruments for time determinations in an observatory. *See* Time.

DECOUPLING. The avoidance or diminution of a common impedance between input and output circuits, especially thermionic valve circuits, *e.g.* Screen decoupling, Anode decoupling, Cathode decoupling, etc. May also be regarded as a form of filter to remove unwanted voltage components.

DEDENDUM. The portion of a wheel tooth or pinion leaf lying within the pitch circle.

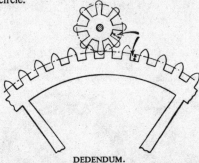

DEDENDUM.

DEFLECTION COILS. The windings or coils associated with the electro-magnetically controlled type of Cathode Ray Tube (*q.v.*). They are mounted externally and by reason of the signal voltages applied thereto, generate resultant magnetic fields, producing deflections of the (internal) electron beam. Also known as Scanning Coils. *See* Plates below.

DEFLECTION PLATES. The electrodes or plates in a Cathode Ray Tube of the electrostatic deflection type by means of which the electron beam is deflected according to voltages impressed upon them. The plates are arranged in two pairs mutually at 90°, the electron beam passing between them. The pair producing horizontal deflection are known as the horizontal or " X " plates but are actually mounted vertically. Similarly the vertical deflection, or " Y " plates, are mounted horizontally.

DEMAGNETISE. To remove magnetism. The system generally adopted by horologists when A.C. is available is to employ a demagnetising coil. Particulars of such a coil are given in " Practical Watch Repairing " also a system for use where D.C. only is available and a device requiring no power supply.

DEMAGNETISER. *See* Demagnetise.

DEMI-HUNTER. A watch with a half-hunter front cover. A full hunter refers to the front cover of a watch when it is fully covered, *i.e.*, solid or uncut. The half-hunter has a hole cut into the full-hunter cover so that the hands can be observed without opening the cover.

DEMI-HUNTER.

The half-hunter is attributed to Napoleon I who, it is said, cut a hole in the cover of his hunter with a knife to facilitate observation. The half-hunter is sometimes referred to as a " Napoleon." *See* WATCH CASE STYLES.

DENSITY. The degree of closeness in which the particles of a body are collected together; it is the mass of a unit volume of a substance, *e.g.* pounds per cubic inch of grammes per cubic centimetre.

DENTILS. *See* ANTIQUE CLOCK CASE TERMS.

DEPTH. The degree of intersection of a pair of gears. The depth is said to be correct when the pitch circles meet. The amount of locking of an escape wheel tooth on a pallet.

CORRECT DEPTH.

DEPTH TOOL. A tool for determining depths. The wheel and pinion or two wheels, etc., are mounted between two parallel pairs of runners, the distance of centres of which can be adjusted until the desired intersection is obtained. This position can then be transferred as a measurement to wherever the gearing is to function or to be planted.

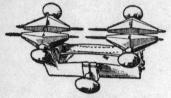

DEPTH TOOL.

DETACHED ESCAPEMENT. An escapement in which the balance or pendulum is free or almost free of its motive force, as opposed to a Frictional Rest Escapement (q.v.).
Examples of the Detached: Chronometer, Lever, and Gravity (in clocks).
Examples of the Frictional Rest: Horizontal, Duplex, Dead Beat, Pin-wheel.
(*See* the above under separate headings.)

DETACHED LEVER. Another name for the lever escapement (q.v.). In the early days of the lever escapement there were several variations, and it was not really "detached" until Josiah Emery introduced the "Draw." Thus the term "detached lever" really applies to the lever escapement as we now know it and not to its original form. *See* Draw.

DETENT. A form of click, or pawl, or stop. Also a name given to the Chronometer Escapement (q.v.) to avoid confusion with the lever escapement. *See* Chronometer. The term is closely associated with the maintaining power. It is the pawl which holds the maintaining power ratchet in position once wound up. As a rule no other term is applied to this pawl which is always spoken of as " the maintaining power detent." The term is also applied to certain parts of striking work.

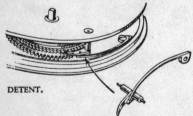

DETENT.

DEVELOPMENT. Refers to the number of turns made by the barrel arbor from fully wound until fully run down. If the arbor makes, say $6\frac{1}{2}$ turns, the mainspring is said to have $6\frac{1}{2}$ turns of development, or to " develop " $6\frac{1}{2}$ turns. Also applies to the force or " output " power of a mainspring as it unwinds or " develops."

DIAL. The " face " of a time piece from which the time or other functions performed by the mechanism can be observed. *See* NOMENCLATURE OF WATCH PARTS, Page 288. (*See* Date Dial, Moon Dial, Jumping Dial, Drop Dial, Double Sunk Dial, Snap-on Dial, Arched Dial, Silver Dial, Brass Dial, Braille Dial).

DIAL ARCH. *See* ANTIQUE CLOCK CASE TERMS.

DIAL CLOCK. A circular type of clock and case. Sometimes referred to as an Office or Kitchen dial. "English dial" usually refers to the familiar fusee movement fitted into a rectangular case bearing a large circular dial. *See* Drop Dial.

DIAL CLOCK.

DIAL FEET. The pins or pillars attached to the dial by which it is located and/or fixed in position.

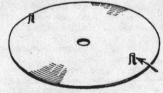

DIAL FOOT.

DIAL FRAME. *See* ANTIQUE CLOCK CASE TERMS.

DIALLING. The art or science of marking out and making sun dials. The term actually refers to the delineation of the hour markings.

DIAL, TO SILVER. *See* WORKSHOP HINTS AND HELPS, page 300.

DIAL SCREWS. Screws used to secure the dial to the movement. Commonly of a "waisted" pattern having a tall head rising from a wide flange, part of which is cut away to permit the passage of a dial foot through the plate. The screw, planted immediately at one side of the foot, is *unscrewed* to secure the dial, the flange biting into the foot as the screw turns and holding the dial firmly against the plate. *See* NOMENCLATURE OF WATCH PARTS, page 287. " Grub " screws are also employed with threaded radial holes drilled into the bottom plate to meet the dial feet holes.

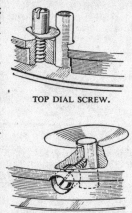

TOP DIAL SCREW.

SIDE DIAL SCREW.

DIAL SINKS. The sinks cut in the bottom plate to accommodate the slight thickening of the metal or enamel at the base of the dial feet.

DIAL TRAIN. Another name for Motion Work (q.v.).

DIAL WASHER. Very thin disc of metal fitted on to the hour wheel of a watch to control the up and down play of the hour wheel between the cannon pinion, upon which it rests, and the dial. The washers are curled to form a spring.

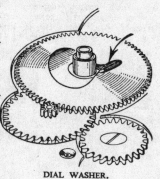

DIAL WASHER.

DIAMAGNETIC. Resists being magnetised. Refers to any substance having a Permeability (*q.v.*) less than that of a vacuum, *i.e.* less than 1.

DIAMANTINE. A white powder much used to polish steel. " The basic material used in the production of artificial stones. Is generally made from ammonia alum, a sulphate of aluminium and ammonia, and is specially manufactured to get the necessary purity. The alum is first calcined in a furnace at a temperature exceeding 1,000° C. This drives off the water of crystallisation together with the sulphuric acid and ammonia; pure alumina Al_2O_3 in the form of a white powder in an extremely fine state of subdivision remains. . . ." *See Horological Journal*, February, 1939.

DIAMETER. In gearing there are three diameters, the pitch circle diameter, abbreviated P.D., the outside diameter, abbreviated O.D. which is the diameter of a circle at the tips of the teeth, known as the addendum circle, and the root diameter, which is the diameter of a circle at the roots of the teeth known as the dedendum circle. Note, that for gauging purposes, tolerances are not applied to the P.D. which is a reference dimension from which tooth proportions are measured.

DIAMETRAL PITCH. The number of teeth divided by the pitch diameter in inches, *e.g.* a wheel of 48 teeth and 1" diameter has a D.P. of 48. *See* Module.

DIAMOND. Diamonds are little used in horology other than as decoration of watch cases. Rose diamonds are occasionally used as endstones; owing to the thickness of the stone it is as a rule, used only for the top balance pivot. Pulverised diamonds are used in the manufacture of jewels. *See* " Diamond Powder." Also, diamonds are used as " tool tips," for cutting steel. *See* STYLES OF GEMSTONE CUTTING, page 137.

DIAMOND POWDER. Finely crushed diamond used for working and polishing gems and watch jewels. Also used in American watch factories for producing a high finish to steel work.

DIAPER. *See* ANTIQUE CLOCK CASE TERMS.

DIAPHRAGM. Any relatively thin wall or boundary which can undergo flexure due to the stimulus of a force, *e.g.*:
(1) The magnetisable disc in a telephone receiver, influenced by the varying magnetic field generated by the pulsating speech currents.

(2) The sides or walls of an Aneroid Capsule (*q.v.*).

DIE. A thread cutting tool consisting of a steel block having a threaded hole of appropriate gauge, the walls of which are cut away to form cutting surfaces. The blocks are interchangeable in a two-handled holder, called a die-stock, which also serves a similar purpose for a set of taps. Dies of suitable gauge threads

DIE.

for horological purposes have been introduced. *See* Screw Plate.

DIELECTRIC. An insulating material or substance capable of supporting an electrical stress, *e.g.* mica, waxed paper, oiled silk, glass, perspex, air. Related particularly to capacitors (condensers).

DIELECTRIC CONSTANT. The ratio " K " of the capacity of a given capacitor with a dielectric other than air between its electrodes to the capacity of same with air.

DIELECTRIC STRENGTH. The stress, in voltage per millimetre, required to force a current through a dielectric. *See* Disruptive Potential.

DIFFERENTIAL BALANCE. *See* Volet Balance.

DIODE. *See* Valve.

DIRECT CURRENT. A uni-directional flow of electric current as distinct from an Alternating Current (*q.v.*). Abbreviated D.C.

DIRECTLY HEATED VALVE. A term referring to thermionic valves, etc., in which the heating current is applied directly to a filament which, treated with an emissive substance, also forms the cathode.

DISCHARGING PALLET. The exit pallet or stone of the lever escapement, *i.e.* the second or last pallet upon which the escape wheel teeth operate in their direction of rotation. Sometimes termed the Bent, or Left Hand or Exit Stone. Also the stone or part of

DISCHARGING PALLET.

the discharge roller of the chronometer escapement, which unlocks the escape wheel, as illustrated.

DISCHARGING SPRING. *See* Gold Spring.

DISENGAGING FRICTION. The type of friction set up when, for instance, a stick is drawn over a surface towards the holder (operator).

DISENGAGING FRICTION.

DISRUPTIVE POTENTIAL. The Voltage (*q.v.*) at which an Insulator (*q.v.*) breaks down permitting the passage of an electric current. *See* Dielectric Strength.

DISTANCE OF CENTRES. The distance on a straight line between the centres of bearings, or axes, of a wheel and pinion or of any two arbors.

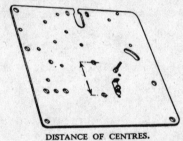

DISTANCE OF CENTRES.

DIVIDER OR DIVIDER CIRCUIT. An electronic device employing thermionic valves whereby a (high) frequency may be reduced or " divided " to any required frequency, as in the quartz clock.

DIVIDERS. A tool used for comparative measurement. Also a drawing instrument used for a similar purpose.

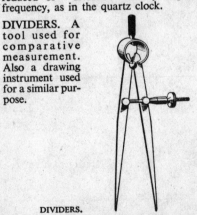

DIVIDERS.

DIVIDING PLATE. The plate of the wheel cutting machine by which the number of teeth to be cut is determined. Also an accessory to the lathe for dividing circles and spacing out.

DIXIÈME GAUGE. The dixième is a unit of measurement = 1 tenth millimetre. The dixième gauge is similar to the douzième gauge and has the same disadvantage: largely used by watch-case makers. The Dixième Gauge is similar in appearance to the Douzième Gauge (*q.v.*).

DOGS. The clamps or fixing pieces found on the face plate of the mandrel, uprighting tool, etc. *See* Mandrel.

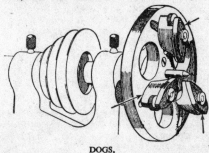

DOGS.

DOG SCREW. A watch movement fixing screw. Usually, a screw having part of its head cut away. *See* Case Screw. Also Watch Part Nomenclature.

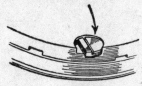

DOG SCREW.

DOG TOOTH. *See* Antique Clock Case Terms.

DOLPHINFRET. *See* Antique Clock Case Terms.

DOME. In horology, refers to the inside cover of a watch case, the cover or lid immediately next to the back cover. *See* Parts of the Pocket Watch Case, page 79.

DOME.

DOMINICAL LETTER. One of the seven letters A–G, applying to a given year. It relates the date to the day of the week.

DOUBLE ADDENDUM. The amount by which the outside diameter exceeds the pitch diameter circle (*q.v.*).

DOUBLE BASKET TOP. *See* Antique Clock Case Terms.

DOUBLE BOTTOM CASE. A watch case where the " dome " is solid with the case; the movement cannot be inspected from the back of the case, and the movement is usually secured by means of a Bolt and Joint (*q.v.*).

DOUBLE DEDENDUM. The amount by which the root diameter is less than the pitch circle diameter.

DOUBLE DIODE. *See* Valve.

DOUBLE-DIODE-TRIODE. *See* Valve.

DOUBLE LUNETTE. A thick, rounded type of watch glass. *See* Styles of Watch Glasses, page 139.

DOUBLE ROLLER ESCAPEMENT. The lever form of escapement in which separate rollers are employed for the impulse and safety actions; in contradistinction to the single roller form in which the impulse and safety actions operate on one roller. *See* Lever Escapement.

DOUBLE SPADE HAND. An hour hand having a double spade, one in series with the other: used in half hunter cases, the inner spade indicating the hours engraved on a circle around the centre glass. *See* Styles of Watch Hands, page 146.

DOUBLE SUMMER TIME. *See* Daylight Saving.

DOUBLE SUNK DIAL. A style of watch dial having the seconds dial and the centre of the main dial sunk below the main dial surface. Usually three separate portions are used in the construction, the two sunk dials—thinner than the main dial—being cemented into position.

DOUBLE SWELL HAND. A type of hand in which the stem is shaped with a double swell. Usually associated with Spade hands. *See* Styles of Watch Hands, page 146.

DOUBLE THREE-LEGGED ESCAPEMENT.

Invented by Lord Grimthorpe (1840) for the West-minster clock: (Big Ben) the first clock to be so fitted The arms A and B are pivoted at C. The escape wheel consists of two wheels of three teeth, or legs, each wlich are set at a distance apart so that the arms A and B can operate freely between them. Three pins—

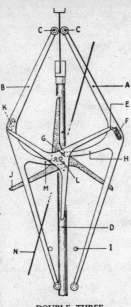

DOUBLE THREE LEGGED ESCAPEMENT.

equal to a three leaved pinion—are fitted between the wheels. As the pendulum D swings to the right it contacts the arm A and the leg E is unlocked from the block F. The pin G contacts the pallet H and lifts the arm A free of the pendulum rod. Eventually the arm A drops on to the pendulum and it is the weight of the falling arm gravity—which gives impulse to the pendulum and keeps it swinging. When the pendulum reaches the centre line the arm is arrested by the pin I. By this time the leg J (on the other side of the arms A and B) has reached and been arrested by the block K fitted to the arm B, on the other side. The pin L contacts the pallet M and the cycle is repeated as on the arm A. The fly or fan N is to relieve the shock of the legs dropping on to the blocks. The virtue of this escapement is that an excessive weight to create force can be applied, so as to ovecome obstruction such as snow, wind, etc., on to the exposed hands, without influencing the force necessary to drive the pendulum. An escapement of this description is used for turret clocks where the hands are exposed to the elements. Although the force arriving at the escape wheel may vary the falling weight of the arms remains constant, therefore, the arc of the vibration of the pendulum is constant and good time-keeping ensues, provided all things are equal, compensation, etc.

DOUBLE VIRGULE. *See* Virgule Double.

DOUZIÈME GAUGE.
The douzième is a unit of measurement—$\frac{1}{12}$ ligne; and ligne is $\frac{1}{12}$ French inch. ∴ douzième = 1/444 inch (French inch) = 0·0075 English inch = between 7 and 8 thousandths of an inch. The douzième gauge consists of two limbs pivoted near the jaws. One limb at its free end bears a quadrant engraved with the scale on which the other limb indicates the measurement. Any measuring instrument opening about a centre and having its divisions marked at equal intervals upon a circular arc scale has an inherent fault rendering it useless for absolute or proportional measurements. Some gauges, however, are so marked that the divisions are unequal round the circular arc so that the scale does correspond to equal distances between the measuring jaws. The douzième gauge is, however, a most useful conparative measuring instrument.

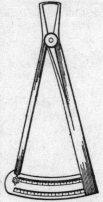

DOUZIÈME GAUGE.

DOWEL. *See* ANTIQUE CLOCK CASE TERMS.

DRAFT.
An American term for Draw (*q.v.*).

DRAW.
An important action in the operational sequence of the lever escapement whereby, after the instant of locking, the escape wheel tooth continues to advance drawing the pallets firmly to the banking and holding them against release by an external shock

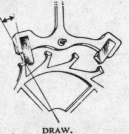

DRAW.

or other cause until unlocked by the balance and ruby pin action. The draw was introduced by Josiah Emery (about 1780). Draw imposes a slight drag or recoil on the train, but, it is essential to the correct functioning of the lever escapement and, in comparison to the advantage of freedom or detachment bestowed, it is negligible. (*See* Lever Escapement and "Practical Watch Repairing.") Draw is also present in the Chronometer Escapement (*q.v.*) where the escape wheel tooth draws the locking stone towards it.

DRAW FILING. A method of filing to finish a surface true in the flat, or to leave a fine grain. The file is drawn along the work at right angles to the length of the file. *See* "Practical Watch Reparing," (N.A.G. Press Ltd.).

DRAW PLATE. A tool for the purpose of reducing or drawing out wire. For round wire a series of graduated tapering holes are formed in dead hard steel plate. The wire is fed through successive holes until the required reduction of diameter is reached. Plates for various sections of wire are obtainable, *viz.* square, rectangular, star, etc., and also for drawing pinion wire.

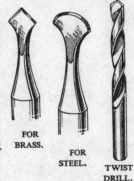

DRAW PLATE.

DRILL. A rotating cutting tool used for making holes. The operation of revolving the work, the tool being held, is generally referred to as boring. In engineering it is referred to as a process of machining a cylindrical hole, in a lathe

FOR BRASS.

FOR STEEL.

TWIST DRILL.

PIVOT.

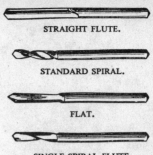

STRAIGHT FLUTE.

STANDARD SPIRAL.

FLAT.

SINGLE SPIRAL FLUTE.

or boring machine. Where great accuracy is required it is preferable to drilling. There are many terms used by engineers when describing drills, *e.g.*, diamond point, where the active part of the drill is diamond; spade drill, which horologists know as the ordinary drill, as illustrated for brass and steel.

DRILL STOCK. A device for rotating a drill by means of a Bow (*q.v.*)

DRILL STOCK.

DRILLING TAIL STOCK. A device used in the lathe for accurate drilling.

DRILLING TAIL STOCK.

DRIVEN. The wheel or pinion—usually the pinion in horology—that is being driven. Sometimes the wheel and the pinion with which it gears are termed the Driver and Driven. Also termed the Follower especially when applied to a *wheel* which is driven.

DRIVER. The driving wheel or pinion—in horology usually the wheel.

DROP. Usually refers to the action when an escape wheel tooth, released by one pallet, falls or "drops" on to the other pallet, or lips, when referring to the Cylinder Escapement (*q.v.*).

DROP DIAL.

A clock similar to the Dial Clock (*q.v.*) but having a short trunk to accommodate a longer pendulum. Sometimes referred to as a Trunk Dial.

DROP DIAL.

DROPHANDLE. *See* ANTIQUE CLOCK CASE TERMS.

DROP LOCK. An American term meaning Locking (*q.v.*).

DRUM. The name given to a clock when contained in a cylindrical case. Drum clocks usually fit into another outer case of wood or metal, etc. Also applies to the barrels of weight-driven turret or large house clocks.

DRUM.

DRUM ESCAPEMENT. *See* Tic-Tac Escapement.

DRY CELL. A primary type of voltaic cell for the generation of an electric current. Usually a LECLANCHÉ cell consisting of a central carbon anode, a zinc case forming the cathode and a paste form of electrolyte, and depolariser. Unlike cells of the secondary type (accumulators), these dry cells (commonly termed Dry Batteries) cannot be charged from an external supply. *See* WORKSHOP HINTS AND HELPS, page 300.

DUCTILE. Said of metals, etc., capable of being drawn out into long lengths when cold, *e.g.* when drawn out into wire.

DUCTILITY. The property which permits metals to be drawn out into fine threads.

DUMB REPEATER. A repeating watch in which the hammers strike, directly or indirectly, the side of the case instead of a bell or gong. The purpose is to indicate the time for the deaf, the striking being felt.

DUPLEX ESCAPEMENT. A frictional rest escapement where the escape wheel has a double set of teeth. Horizontal teeth for locking and perpendicular teeth to give impulse. Reputed to have been invented by Pierre Le Roy about 1750. Superseded by the Lever Escapement. The action is as follows:—As the escape wheel rotates in the direction of the arrow, a long tooth rests against the small cylindrical jewel roller A secured to the balance staff. This roller has a slit cut into it and, as the balance rotates the escape wheel is able to move forward when the slit arrives before the point of a tooth, at this precise moment

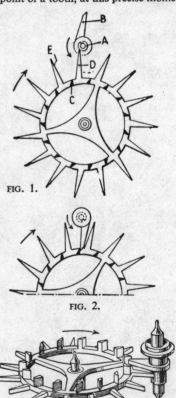

FIG. 1.

FIG. 2.

DUPLEX ESCAPEMENT.

the impulse pallet B, also fixed to the balance staff, is in such a position that an upright tooth of the escape wheel C imparts impulse to it and thus the balance is kept vibrating; when the tooth D drops off the impulse pallet the wheel is arrested by the succeeding long or locking tooth E dropping on to the locking roller. Most duplex escapements are fitted with a roller made of ruby, but there are exceptions where the roller is of steel. Like the chronometer, the balance receives impulse in one direction only, on its return journey the slit just passes by the point of the locking tooth. Fig. 1.—Balance rotating in direction of arrow to unlock escape wheel. Fig. 2.—Balance receives impulse.

DURINVAR. *See* METALS USED IN HOROLOGY.

DUST CAP. *See* Cap.

DUST CUP. The cup fitted on to the square of the fusee to prevent dust, from the key, being introduced into the fusee pivot bearing. *See* Fusee Cup.

DUTCH CLOCK. A style of wall clock popular in Holland over a period around 1700. Made principally in Zaandam and Friesland and known by these names. A style frequently met with in England has lead weights (going and striking) encased in brass, a brass pendulum bob (or similarly, brass faced) and a circular dial framed hexagonally in wood, sometimes with a glass cover and brass bezel.

DUTCH FOOT. *See* ANTIQUE CLOCK CASE TERMS.

DUTCH STRIKING. Where the clock strikes the hours at the preceding half hour on a high toned bell and at the hour in a low toned bell.

DUTCH STRIKING MECHANISM. Where the hammer strikes the bell by a twisting movement when compared with the conventional backward and forward movement. Many of these so called Dutch Clocks were made in the Black Forest, Germany.

DYNAMIC POISE. To be in poise while in motion. It is claimed that want of dynamic poise in the balance of a watch can have a detrimental effect on the rate when tested in the vertical positions. The claim is, however, problematical.

DYNAMICS. The study of force in action; of the motion of bodies.

DYNAMO. Any generator which converts mechanical energy into electrical energy by electro-magnetic induction. Particularly refers to a generator of Direct Current (*q.v.*). Compare with Alternator.

DUTCH CLOCK.

E

EARNSHAW'S ESCAPEMENT. Another name for the Chronometer Escapement (*q.v.*).

EARS OF PENDANT. The bushes used to plug the enlarged holes for the bow, in the pendant of a watch case. *See* PARTS OF THE POCKET WATCH CASE, page 79.

EARS OF PENDANT.

EARTH. The potential of the earth, referred to all other potentials, and usually regarded as zero. A direct connection into the soil itself, especially to complete a circuit. Nowadays also, a connection to any relatively large body which, in effect, is at or near earth potential. Thus an electric clock may be earthed to its frame if the latter is itself connected to a relatively much larger body. In radio, the term refers to any point in the circuit at which the potential does not vary at a radio frequency irrespective of the steady or low frequency potential of that point.

EASTERN EUROPEAN TIME. One hour slow of Greenwich Mean Time (*q.v.*).

EASTERN STANDARD TIME. Five hours slow of Greenwich Mean Time (*q.v.*).

ÉBAUCHE. An unfinished movement, *i.e.* the movement in the rough before the escapement is fitted, or the train has been pivoted, etc. In Switzerland to-day, there are Ébauche factories making movements which comprise plates, bridges, cocks, keyless work and the train. Other factories finish the movement and fit the main spring; pivot the train, and jewel it; make the escapement, the dial, the hands and the case.

EBONISE. *See* ANTIQUE CLOCK CASE TERMS.

ECCENTRIC. Non-concentric. Displaced in relation to the centre, *e.g.* the periphery of a cam and the motion of work mounted in a lathe or face plate off the line of centres.

ECCENTRIC ARBOR. A special arbor, used in turning fusee or barrel arbors, in the turns.

ECCENTRIC CHUCK. Another name for Box Chuck (*q.v.*).

ECCENTRIC RUNNER. A runner used in the lathe or turns to enable the work to be brought forward from the centre

ECCENTRIC RUNNER.

ECLIPTIC. The apparent path of the sun in the heavens.

EDDY CURRENT. A circulating current induced in the body of a conducting material by reason of the influence of a varying magnetic field.

EDGE ROLL MOULDING. *See* MOULDINGS.

EFFICIENCY OF A MACHINE. The ratio, over the same period of time, between the energy output of a machine and the energy put into it, consumed or absorbed.

EGG SHELL FINISH. *See* ANTIQUE CLOCK CASE TERMS.

EGG WATCH. Oval or egg shaped watches; the first pocket watches; made at Nuremberg, Germany, in the latter part of the fifteenth century.

EIGHTH'S GAUGE. *See* Wheel Gauge.

ELASTICITY. The power possessed by certain materials to resume their original form after subjection to a distorting force.

ELECTRIC CLOCKS. All clocks primarily driven or controlled by electricity. May be classified as follows: Battery operated; Impulse clocks; Self-winding; Synchronous. *See* " Electrical Timekeeping " by F. Hope Jones.

ELECTRICITY. The form of energy now generally considered as arising from the separation and/or movement of constituent parts of atoms, *i.e.* Electrons (*q.v.*).

ELECTRIC OSCILLATIONS. *See* Oscillating Currents.

ELECTROLYTE. A conductor, especially in solution in a liquid, in which the passage of an electric current is accompanied by movement of chemical elements or chemical decomposition, either complete, self-arresting, or reversible.

ELECTROLYTIC CONDENSER (CAP-
ACITOR). A condenser (usually of a
high capacity) in which the dielectric
between the plates is an electrolyte or, in
which the liquid electrolyte forms one
electrode and the container the other, the
dielectric being the exceedingly thin film of
oxide deposited upon the inner walls of the
container. Owing to the above construction,
such capacitors are " polarised," *i.e.* have
definite positive and negative terminals
and must be so connected in circuit, hence
they cannot be used in alternating current
circuits.

ELECTROLYTIC CORROSION. The
natural or intensified or forced corrosion
of one or both of dissimilar metals due to
the passage of a current between them
through an intervening or adjacent Electrolyte (*q.v.*). The current is frequently
self-generated due to the metals being in
close contact and forming, with the
electrolyte, a simple voltaic cell. Pure
water may become an electrolyte tempor-
arily by absorption of acid or alkaline
matter.

ELECTROMAGNET. A magnet, the
properties of which are exhibited under
and dependent upon, the energising influence of an electric current.

ELECTROMAGNETIC DEFLECTION.
The deflection of the electron beam of a
cathode ray tube by electromagnetic fields
acting across the path of the beam (and
through which it passes as generally
arranged). *See* Deflection Coils.

ELECTROMOTIVE FORCE. The force
which tends to cause a current of electricity
to flow in a circuit from one potential to
another. Usually expressed in Potential or
Voltage. Abbreviated: E.M.F.

ELECTRON. The smallest and most
numerous constituent of matter. An
electrically charged particle, possessing
inertia, and normally forming part of the
atom structure. It can exist separately,
however, as in Cathode Rays.

ELECTRON BEAM. Any narrow, controlled, or directed stream of electrons.
Especially that produced by the Electron
Gun (*q.v.*). Also the stream as directed
by special spacing of electrodes, etc., in
thermionic valves, *e.g.* Beam Tetrode.

ELECTRON GUN. The device which
produces a very narrow stream of electrons
as used in the Cathode Ray Tube (*q.v.*).
Consists of a cathode as the electron source
usually indirectly heated, an aperatured

anode to form, direct and accelerate the
stream, and one or more focusing electrodes which concentrate the beam. The
assembly in one unit is accommodated in
" neck " of the cathode ray tube.

ELECTRONICS. The study of the nature
and behaviour of Electrons. " That branch
of science and technology relating to the
conduction of electricity through gases or
in vacuo " (American Institute Electrical
Engineers). A general term somewhat
loosely employed but referring to the
application of electron phenomena and
properties to communications; measurement; control; lighting; power; and closely
associated with Thermionics.

ELECTROSTATICS. The study of electric
charges and potentials.

ELECTROSTATIC DEFLECTION. The
deflection of the electron beam of a cathode
ray tube by electrostatic fields set up
between pairs of plates and through which
the beam passes. *See* Deflection Plates.

ELIZABETHAN. *See* ANTIQUE CLOCK
CASE TERMS.

ELLICOTT
PENDULUM.
A compensated
pendulum de-
vised by John
Ellicott. In a
communication
to the Royal
Society, this is
mentioned as
" devised in
1732," exe-
cuted in 1738,
published in
1752." It was
shown to the
Royal Society
in 1738, but
publication
was deferred
until practical
trials could be
made. The
ultimate publi-
cation did not
take place in

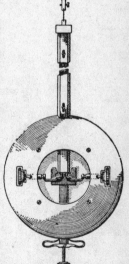

ELLICOTT PENDULUM.

1752. It is thought that Ellicott got the
idea from Harrison, whom he visited
frequently between 1736–1738. The downward expansion of the brass rod, attached
to the steel pendulum, presses on the
levers in the pendulum bob and so raises
the bob, thus keeping the centre of oscillation constant.

EMERY BUFF OR STICK. A wooden stick to which emery paper is glued. Obtainable in grades of coarseness as follows: 3/0 (*i.e.*, 000), 2/0, 1/0, 1, 2, 3. 3/0 is very fine and No. 3 is coarse.

EMERY STONE. A stone made of emery powder obtainable in grades of coarseness and made in various sizes.

EMISSION. The ejection of electrons from a conductor by the agency of heat, light, etc. The total electronic current emitted from a heated cathode.

EMPIRE STYLE. *See* FRENCH CLOCK STYLES, page 45.

EMPIRE GLASS. *See* STYLES OF WATCH GLASSES, page 139.

ENAMEL. A vitreous material fired in an oven or kiln after application. Much used for watch and clock dials and metal ornamentation.

ENCARPUS. *See* ANTIQUE CLOCK CASE TERMS.

ENCAUSTIC. *See* ANTIQUE CLOCK CASE TERMS.

ENDIVE SCROLL. *See* ANTIQUE CLOCK CASE TERMS.

ENDSHAKE. Endwise freedom of movement of a staff, arbor, spindle, etc.

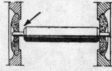

ENDSHAKE.

ENDSTONE. The jewel disc fitted to form the end of a hole, so that the end of the pivot can work upon it whereas without it, the shoulder of the pivot would take the weight or thrust. Sometimes referred to as Jewel Cap or Endpiece. *See* WATCH PART NOMENCLATURE.

ENDSTONE.

ENERGY. The total quantity of work a person, machine, etc., is capable of doing without any reference to the time taken. (Electrical.) Measured in Joules (*q.v.*) or Watt-seconds, a function of power and time during which the power is exercised.

ENGAGING CONTACT. *See* Approach Contact and Receding Contact.

ENGAGING FRICTION. The type of resistance set up when an inclined stick is pushed over a surface point forwards.

ENGAGING FRICTION.

ENGINE TURNING. A system of engraving a repetitive design by a machine. *See* Guilloché, ANTIQUE CLOCK CASE TERMS.

ENGLISH EMPIRE. *See* ENGLISH PERIOD STYLES, page 38.

ENGLISH LEVER. Refers to a lever watch of English manufacture; but more generally meant to define the ratchet-toothed escape wheel and the conventional type of English lever escapement.

ENGLISH LEVER.

See Lever Escapement. It will be noted that the impulse is on the pallets only and not divided between the escape wheel teeth and pallets as with the Club Tooth Escapement.

ENGLISH PERIOD STYLES. *See* page 38.

ENGLISH SCREWS. There is no standard English watch Thread. There are various makers of screw plates, *e.g.* Stubs, Thewlis, etc., the threads are coarser that the Swiss. They also differ among themselves. For clock screws B.A. (*q.v.*) Standard Screws are obtainable.

ENRICHMENT. *See* ANTIQUE CLOCK CASE TERMS.

ENTABLATURE. *See* ANTIQUE CLOCK CASE TERMS.

ENTERING FILE. *See* Files.

ENTRY PALLET. The pallet on that side of an escapement first reached by an advancing tooth of the escape wheel. In the lever escapement it is sometimes referred to as the "Right" stone or "Straight" stone. *See* WATCH PART NOMENCLATURE. *Illus. opposite.*

ENTRY PALLET.

EPACT. The age of the moon on January 1st.

EPHEMEROUS TIME. A standard of time based on the tropical year at 1900 which is used in the legal definition by the Comité Permanent des Poids et Mesures. A tropical year is the time required for the sun to increase its mean longitude by 360° in relation to the true equinox. (Sidereal time is referred to a fixed equinox).

EPICYCLIC TRAINS. A train of wheels in which one wheel or pinion travels round a fixed wheel, such as is found in the Tourbillon (*q.v.*) and Karrusel escapements and also in some systems of " up and down " going barrel keyless mechanisms. (A) Drives A1; B is a stationary wheel. The pinion A travels round the wheel B. *See* Sun and Planet Gears.

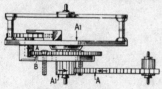

EPICYCLIC TRAINS.

EPICYCLOID. A curve traced by a point in the circumference of a circle, known as the generating circle, as it rolls upon another circle. It is the curve used in the formation of wheel teeth in horology and known as Epicycloidal gearing working in conjunction with the Hypocycloidal gear (*q.v.*).

EPICYCLOID.

EPIDIASCOPE. A projection lantern which can be used for projecting pictures of transparencies (as slides) or of solid or opaque objects. In the latter case the screen image is not laterally inverted and a watch movement can be seen working exactly as if it were being views normally.

EPILAME. A system of oiling in which the bearing surfaces, *i.e.*, pivots, are coated with a film of Epilame before the oil is applied. It was claimed that the process prevented creeping. Introduced by Paul Ditisheim.

EPISCOPE. A simpler form of Epidiascope without provision for showing transparencies and usually throwing a laterally inverted image. Sometimes known as a Mirrorscope although no mirror is actually employed.

EQUATION OF TIME. The difference between apparent Solar Time and Mean Solar Time. With the aid of an Equation of Time Table it is possible to arrive at Mean Time by reading the time as shown by a sun dial and adding the Equation figure. Solar Time agrees with Mean Time on April 15th, June 15th, August 31st and December 24th. The date varies slightly as the year does not contain an exact number of days. The duration of the Solar Year is 365 days, 5 hours, 48 mins., 48 secs. The Mean Time year is 365 days which involves reckoning an extra day per

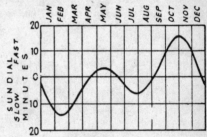

EQUATION OF TIME.

year every fourth year (Leap Year) and a further adjustment by omitting a Leap Year three times in every four centuries. Leap Year was thus " missed " in 1900. Clocks are made which show Solar and Mean Time and it is the difference between the two which is the Equation of Time. Tables are available in the " Nautical Almanac," " Whitaker's Almanack " and " Watch and Clock Yearbook " (N.A.G. Press Ltd.) showing the Equation of Time for each day of the current year.

EQUIDISTANT ESCAPEMENT. A design of lever escapement wherein the locking corners of both pallet stones are placed at equal distances from the pallet arbor. *See* also Circular Lockings.

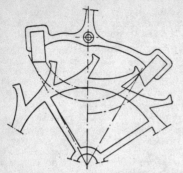

EQUIDISTANT ESCAPEMENT.

Unlocking the escape wheel is more favourable that with Circular Pallets (*q.v.*) but the impulse face of the exit pallet needs to be cut at a greater angle, because the action of impulse takes place further from the point of tangency. Equidistant pallets therefore need greater accuracy in manufacture. *See* Semitangental.

EQUILIBRIUM. Said of a body when it is in a state of rest or when forces acting on it do not alter its rate of movement.

ERG. A unit of work or energy. Equal in magnitude to the work done when the operating point of a force of one Dyne is allowed to move one centimetre in the direction of the force.

ERMETO WATCH. The name given to a form of folding watch. Made by the Movado Watch Co., Switzerland.

ESCAPEMENT. That part of the mechanism of a clock or watch which allows the power driving the mechanism to Escape. The escapement consists of the mechanism from and including the escape wheel, *e.g.*, in the " lever ": Escape wheel and pinion, lever, and balance complete with its spring; of a pendulum clock: Escape wheel and pinion; pallets with crutch, etc., pendulum complete with its suspension. The escapement is the controller, measurer, or governor. Those in use today are:— Chronometer (Detent), Lever, Horizontal, Pin Pallet, Anchor or Recoil, Dead Beat, Pin Wheel, Brocot, Double-Three-Legged, which *see* under their headings.

ESCAPE WHEEL. The last wheel in a clock or watch train; it is the wheel which gives impulse to the controlling part of the mechanism, *i.e.*, the balance or pendulum. *See* Escapement.

ESCUTSHEON. *See* Antique Clock Case Terms.

ESSEN RING. A special quartz crystal shape developed by Dr. L. Essen, of the National Physical Laboratory, for Quartz Crystal Clocks (*q.v.*).

EUREKA CLOCK. An electric battery clock invented by Kutnow, where a large balance is employed in the place of a pendulum. Invented by Kutnow Bros., U.S.A., June 1906.

EXCENTRIC. *See* Eccentric.

EXCENTRIQUE. Chuck used in ornamental turning for producing intricate patterns by means of intersecting eccentric circles.

EXCITANT. The electrolyte of a primary cell.

EXCITATION. The magnetomotive force which produces the magnetic flux, as in an electromagnet.

EXCITING COIL. The coil or winding of an electromagnet system which carries the current producing the magnetic field.

EXIT PALLET. The last pallet to be engaged by an escape wheel tooth in its advance through the escapement. In the lever escapement it is sometimes referred to as the " Left " stone or, the " Bent " stone. *See* Watch Part Nomenclature.

EXIT PALLET.

EXPANSION. The increase in one or all dimensions of a body, especially due to a rise in temperature or decrease of pressure.

EXTERNAL CIRCUIT. The circuit to which current is supplied by a generator or other source.

EXTERNAL SCREW THREAD. A screw thread formed or cut upon the exterior of a cylinder. Also termed a Male Thread.

EXTRADOS. *See* Antique Clock Case Terms.

EXTRUSION. Forcing out by pressure. The production of filaments, wires, rods, tubes, etc., by forcing a mass of the parent material under pressure through a die of appropriate size and section.

EYE GLASS. A glass used by clock and watch makers to enable the work to be viewed closely. The eye glass is used not necessarily to magnify the object but to enable it to be brought closer to the eye. The number marked on the side of the glass indicates that the object is in focus when the glass is so many inches from the object. Also called a Loupe. Single eyeglass (left), 3 inches, and with the double eyeglass, $\frac{1}{4}$ inch focus.

EYEGLASSES (LOUPES)

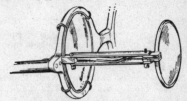

EYE GLASS FITTED TO SPECTACLES.

F

FACE. Another name for the dial of a watch or clock. The front (*see* Dial). Also, " to face," refers to skimming with a cutter, to make flat, true or clean, the surface of metal held in the lathe, etc. In gearing it refers to that part of the working surface of a tooth which lies above the pitch line.

FACE CUTTER. *See* Milling Cutter.

FACE PLATE. Refers to that part of the Mandrel (*q.v.*) on to which work is mounted to be worked and is usually provided with " dogs " or clips.

FACE PLATE.

FACE WIDTH. *See* Tooth Width.

FACING. The process of finishing the ends of pinion heads. *See* " Practical Watch Reparing."

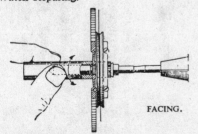

FACING.

FACILE TIME STAMP. *See* Warwick Time Stamping Clock.

FAHRENHEIT SCALE. A method of graduating a thermometer widely used in English speaking countries, the lower and upper fixed points being respectively 32° and 212°. *See* TEMPERATURE CONVERSION TABLE.

FALSE PLATE. The plate on to which a dial is fitted, usually furnished with pillars or feet which are secured to the front plate of the clock movement.

FAN-FLY. *See* Fly.

FARAD. The unit of measurement of electrostatic Capacitance (*q.v.*). It is that capacitance which, raised to a potential of one volt, carries a charge of one coulomb. For practical purposes the unit is too large and is subdivided into Micro-farads and pico-farads (*q.v.*).

FAUN. *See* ANTIQUE CLOCK CASE TERMS.

FAVAS. *See* ANTIQUE CLOCK CASE TERMS.

F.B.H.I. Fellow of the British Horological Institute (*q.v.*).

FEATHER BANDING. *See* ANTIQUE CLOCK CASE TERMS.

FEATHER EDGE. The rough edge left on metal after machining or filing. Also on fine cutting edges after sharpening on a stone. It is a burr. This term is also used to describe a file of an elongated diamond cross section shape. Also refers to a form of decoration on silverware, especially spoons and forks.

FEATHER EDGING. A form of decoration on metal work, a series of feather-like slanting lines.

FERROUS. Made of or containing iron. Material containing iron is said to be ferrous and that not containing iron is said to be non-ferrous.

FERRULE. A form of pulley, used to cause work to rotate in the lathe or turns for the purpose of turning. Sometimes referred to as a collet. Ferrules are made for various purposes; the simple ferrule consists of a brass pulley which is intended to be cemented to the object, *e.g.*, a wheel.

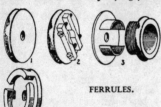

FERRULES.

The screw ferrule to attach to an arbor. The balance ferrule for attaching to a balance. There are two types, one having spring-like arms, and the other screw grip device. (1) Simple ferrule; (2) Screw ferrule; (3) Screw ferrule for balance; (4) Spring ferrule for balance.

FESTOON. *See* ANTIQUE CLOCK CASE TERMS.

FIDDLE BACK. *See* ANTIQUE CLOCK CASE TERMS.

FIELD. The region in which the influence of a force, electrical or magnetic, etc., is readily detectable. The path of the lines of force of a magnet or solenoid, especially in its immediate vicinity.

FIELDED. *See* ANTIQUE CLOCK CASE TERMS.

FIGURE OF EIGHT CALLIPER. Callipers in the shape of the figure 8; used for truing wheels, etc. *See* Calliper.

FIGURE OF EIGHT PIECE. An end-stone piece in the form of the figure 8.

END STONE

FIGURE OF EIGHT PIECE.

FILAMENT. A fine wire of high resistance heated to incandescence by an electric current as in an electric lamp bulb. A wire, forming an electrode of a thermionic valve, etc., with or without a prepared emissive surface, heated to such a point that electrons are freely liberated from it. Known as Directly Heated Cathode (*q.v.*).

FILES. For types used in horology, *see* illustration.

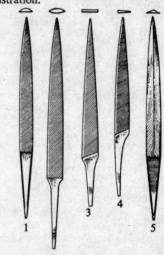

1. HALF ROUND. 2. CROSSING. 3. ENTERING.
4. KNIFE. 5. BARETTE.

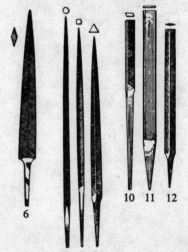

6. LOZENGE. 7. ROUND. 8. SQUARE.
9. THREE SQUARE. 10. PIVOT. 11. JOINT.
12. RACHET.

FILES TO RE-SHARPEN. *See* WORK-SHOP HINTS AND HELPS, page 300.

FILLIGREE. *See* ANTIQUE CLOCK CASE TERMS.

FILLET. *See* MOULDINGS.

FINGER PIECE. The piece used in conjunction with the star wheel of the Maltese Cross stop work (*q.v.*).

FINIAL. *See* ANTIQUE CLOCK CASE TERMS.

FINE METRIC THREAD. Bergeon of Le Locle make a screw plate with a Fine Metric Thread, made for watches and clocks; tabulated from ·3 mm. to 5 mm. Corresponds to Swiss standard No. N.H.S. 56,100 up to 2 mm., and to International Metric Thread (S1 thread) from 2 to 5 mm. Standard for most of the Swiss Ébauches (*q.v.*) of the present time.

FINISHER. The name given to the craftsman who turned in the train of a watch movement, a craft now almost extinct. His work was to finish off the barrel, turn and pivot the train wheels, cut the undercuts in the pionion heads and face them and leave the movement ready for the escapement maker.

FIVE MINUTE REPEATER. *See* Repeater.

FIXMOBIL. A detachable endstone the purpose of which is two fold; it preserves the oil and also acts as an end piece. It is not necessary for the pivots

FIXMOBIL.

to be conical, a square shouldered pivot, provided the pivot is long enough to contact the end piece, can be used. The advantage is that the friction of the train is reduced. It cannot be used for pivots which project for a purpose, *e.g.*, the lower centre wheel pivot and the seconds hand pivot. Fixmobil end pieces are of jewel or steel made by Parechoc S. A., Le Sentier, Switzerland, the makers of Kif (*q.v.*). *See* Giracap and Lubrifix.

FLAMBEAU FINIALS. *See* ANTIQUE CLOCK CASE TERMS.

FLANGE. A projecting rim or collar; that part of a glass bezel which slopes down on to the dial *See* PARTS OF THE POCKET WATCH CASE, page 79.

FLANK. That part of the working surface of a tooth which lies below the pitch line.

FLANK. That part of a wheel tooth or pinion leaf which contacts when engaging. The term is more applicable to the pinion leaf.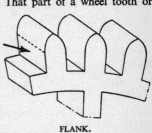

FLANK.

FLASH. *See* ANTIQUE CLOCK CASE TERMS.

FLAT BALANCE SPRING. *See* Balance Spring.

FLEMISH FOOT. *See* ANTIQUE CLOCK CASE TERMS.

FLEUR-DE-LIS. *See* ANTIQUE CLOCK CASE TERMS. *Also* STYLES OF WATCH HANDS, page 146.

FLEX. A common term for flexible cord or cable, *i.e.*, a flexible conductor comprising a number of fine wires twisted or braided together and provided with any suitable insulant covering. A common form consists of two such conductors twisted about each other and known as Twin Flex.

FLEXIBLE. Pliant. Yielding to pressure or distortion without fracture. Resilient, *e.g.*, cord, metal wires, coiled, leaf, or suspension springs.

FLEXURE. A turn or bend. The displacement of a spring under a load.

FLICK LEAF CLOCK. Also referred to as a TICKET CLOCK. Where the time of day is shown by figures, a leaf flicking over every minute and the time is read graphically *e.g.* 12.45. Known in America as " Plato " clock. Invented by E. Fitch, May 1903.

FLIRT. A device to cause sudden movement of mechanism. Such as the piece fitted to the cannon pinion of a minute repeater, just under the minute snails which is caused to " flirt " forward at each ¼ hour to ensure that the rack drops on to the top or highest step and that no blows are struck by the minute hammer until one minute past the quarter. Also the lever in chiming clocks which discharges the strike train.

FLORAL CLOCK. A clock combined with a bed of flowers. The dial and numerals are made by a pattern of flowers and plants in the ground and the hands are troughs with flowers planted in them. Such a clock is to be seen in the grounds of Edinburgh Castle. Some have striking and even cuckoo mechanisms.

FLUTED MOULDING. *See* Antique Clock Case Terms.

FLUTING. *See* Antique Clock Case Terms.

FLY. The governor or controller of the speed of a chime or strike train. It is the last piece in the train of wheels. Also, the fan used in the Gravity Escapements (*q.v.*) to control or lighten the blow of the escape tooth on the pallet.

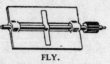

FLY.

FLY-BACK CHRONOGRAPH. *See* Chronograph.

FLY CUTTER. A wheel cutter consisting of a single cutting tool secured to a boss; used in a wheel cutting engine.

FLY CUTTER.

FLY SPRING. The spring of a watch case that causes the cover to fly open. *See* Case Spring; Also Parts of the Pocket Watch Case, page 79.

FLY WHEEL: A wheel of relatively large mass used for storing up kinetic energy. In horology a form of fly wheel is sometimes used in synchronous clocks to make the drive from the rotor smoother.

FLUX DENSITY. The measure of strength of a Magnetic Flux (*q.v.*), *i.e.*, the number of lines of force in a unit area of the field taken at 90° from the direction of the field. Symbol B.

FOB. A decorative attachment to the pocket watch used in place of the Albert (*q.v.*). The word "Fob" is the German "fuppe," a small pocket. A lady's fob watch is termed Chatelaine (*q.v.*).

FOB.

In recent years it has come to refer to a form of pendant watch used by ladies and usually worn hanging from a brooch or clip, the tendency now being towards further elaboration in the nature of a dress accessory.

FOIL. *See* Antique Clock Case Terms.

FOLIATED. *See* Antique Clock Case Terms.

FOLIOT. The predecessor of the Balance; a pivoted bar fixed to the verge and used in the verge escapement. A weight was carried on each arm to determine its time of oscillation, if the weights were moved towards the centre the clock would gain.

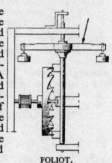

FOLIOT.

FOLLOWER. The wheel or pinion which is driven; it follows. *See* Driver and Driven. Also the adjustable hole or bearing of the verge watch. The pivot near the wheel of the verge escape wheel works in a hole drilled into a plug which is adjustable and enables the endshake of the escape wheel pinion to be adjusted. *See* Counter Potence.

FOOTBALL TIMER. *See* Timer.

FOOT POUND. A unit of work; it is equal to work done in raising a mass of 1 pound through a vertical distance of 1 foot.

FOOT WHEEL. A wheel operated by the foot to cause the lathe to operate; a form of treadle.

FOOT WHEEL.

FORCE. In mechanics, any influence acting on a body that changes or tends to change the body's state of rest or uniform motion, in a straight line. A term referring to the strength of main-springs, based on the thickness of the spring. *See* page 172 for conversion from Martin gauge to the metric size.

FORK. That part of the lever escapement into which the ruby or impulse pin engages. Also referred to as the Notch.

FORK.

FOUR HUNDRED DAY CLOCK. A clock which will run for 400 days with one winding. Usually refers to the clock fitted with a rotating pendulum of which there are several types and grades. The rotating pendulum is also used in the Atmos Clock (*q.v.*). The escape wheel and pallets are similar to the Anchor Escapement (q.v.); the difference is that the crutch operates upon

400 DAY CLOCK ESCAPEMENT.

a spring of rectangular section. The pendulum consists of a long fine wire of rectangular section, and clipped securely to this wire is a crutch, which embraces a pin projecting from the pallets. The motion of the pallets rocking from side to side sets up a tension in the suspension spring of the pendulum. When the bob or weight of the pendulum is given a twist the crutch will eventually unlock the escape wheel which will in turn twist the suspension spring, and it is the tension thus stored up in the spring which keeps the pendulum rotating backwards and forwards.

FOUR-LEGGED GRAVITY ESCAPEMENT. Similar to the Double Three-Legged Gravity Escapement (*q.v.*), differing in having only one escape wheel of four teeth or legs.

FOURTH WHEEL. Usually the wheel that drives the escape wheel (and carries the seconds hand of a normal seconds dial). In a going barrel, the barrel is counted as the 1st wheel, the centre wheel as the 2nd driving the 3rd, followed by the fourth wheel driving the escape wheel.

FRAISE. A cutter. *See* Ingold Fraise.

FRAME. The plates of a watch or clock movement, *i.e.*, the bottom and top plates of a watch or the front and back plates of a clock.

FREE ESCAPEMENT. An escapement in which the balance or pendulum has mechanical contact with, or is influenced by other parts of the mechanism during an insignificant part of its vibration or oscillation.

FREE PENDULUM. The practical Free Pendulum (or nearly free) was invented by William Hamilton Shortt, M.Inst.CE., railway engineer. In 1910, F. Hope-Jones, inventor of the Synchronome electric clock, interested W. H. Shortt in horology and worked in collaboration with him. It was established that with the pendulum " free ", *i.e.*, with no interference or work to do, near perfect timekeeping would be possible. This was achieved by using a Synchronome clock as a " slave " to perform the escapement functions. The slave counts the oscillations of the free pendulum and the free pendulum controls the pendulum of the slave clock. The action briefly is this: The free pendulum A has pivoted to it the small wheel B. At every fifteenth swing to the left (30 seconds) the gravity lever C is released by the slave clock through the electromagnet D and the jewel pallet E drops on to the wheel B and gently imparts impulse to the pendulum at the correct part of its swing. As the lever C drops off the wheel B it releases the Synchronome remontoire F which re-sets the lever C and operates the synchronising electro-magnet G of the slave clock. The slave pendulum has fitted to it a vertical leaf spring J on its left hand side. The magnet G controlled by the free pendulum draws down a horizontal armature K into the path of the leaf spring J and if the slave pendulum is slow, the leaf spring is bent, which accelerates the slave pendulum. If the slave pendulum is correct or fast, the armature K, when pulled down,

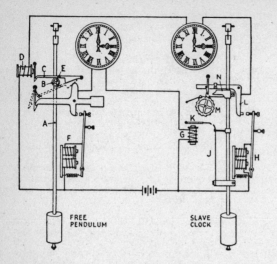

FREE PENDULUM

SLAVE CLOCK

THE FREE PENDULUM, on the left, is kept in an air exhausted cylinder mounted on a heavy base such as a large concrete block. It controls the rate of the slave clock which does the work of counting.

misses the spring J and the slave pendulum is not affected. This arrangement keeps the slave pendulum in step with the master. It is known as a " hit and miss " synchroniser. For it to function correctly the slave pendulum must be regulated to lose about 5 seconds a day or 1/500th part of a second per half minute. Thus the slave clock is held firmly in synchronisation with the master clock. The slave clock itself is impulsed by the gravity arm L which is released from its catch by a lever on wheel M at every complete rotation. The wheel M is turned one tooth by a pallet fixed to the pendulum at every swing to the right. When the gravity arm L has given its impulse to the pendulum, by means of a small wheel attached to it bearing on the impulse pallet N fixed to the pendulum, it falls and completes the circuit of the electro-magnet H, which lifts and resets it and operates the slave dial or dials. This also operates the electro-magnet D to release the gravity impulse lever of the free pendulum, as already explained. The free pendulum is mounted in an air exhausted cylinder for greater accuracy. This reduces the impulse needed to keep it swinging as well as errors due to the presence of air. The timekeeping properties are in the order of 1/10th of a second per year and the first clock, made by Shortt himself, was set up in the Edinburgh Observatory in 1921. This system of time measurement was employed in astronomical observatories throughout the world until it was superseded by the Quartz Crystal Clock (q.v.) invented by W. A. Marrison in 1929.

FRENCH CLOCK STYLES. *See* page 45.

FRENCH PLATE. A technical term referring to copper or brass plated with silver leaf and burnished.

FRENCH POLISH. *See* ANTIQUE CLOCK CASE TERMS.

FRENCH SILVERING. A method of finishing metal surfaces by manual deposition of silver on the metal. A paste compound of silver chloride, salt, and cream of tartar is rubbed on. A matt surface is thus formed. *See* WORKSHOP HINTS AND HELPS, page 300.

FREQUENCY. The number of cycles or complete oscillations per second of any periodic phenomenon. It is the reciprocal of the period or periodic time. Also named the periodicity. Electrically, refers to the frequency at which an electric current alternates and is measured in cycles or kilo-cycles per second.

FREQUENCY, AUDIO. Frequencies of the order 25 c.p.s. to 15 kc.p.s.

FREQUENCY, RADIO. Frequencies of the order 10 kc.p.s. upwards.

FREQUENCY DEMULTIPLICATION OR DIVISION. The process of producing an alternating current the frequency of which is a simple sub-multiple of another " parent " frequency. *See* Dividers.

FRET. *See* ANTIQUE CLOCK CASE TERMS.

FREQUENCY STABILISATION. The prevention of frequency drift or changes in a self-oscillating circuit due to variations in supply voltage, temperature of components, etc. Also the maintenance of a generator, *i.e.*, an alternator, at its correct working speed irrespective of the load variations.

FRICTION. Resistance to motion; it is experienced when one surface is caused to slide over another when in contact.

FRICTION CIRCLE. An imaginary circle within a shaft and journal bearing (*e.g.* pivot and hole). If a line of thrust passes within this circle, the shaft will become friction locked and fail to rotate.

FRICTION, COEFFICIENT OF. The force with which friction resists the motion of one surface over the other. The force is dependent on the coefficient of friction, which is the ratio of the limiting friction to the normal resistance between two sliding surfaces. It is constant for any constant pair of surfaces.

FRICTION JEWELS. *See* Jewels; Friction.

FRICTIONAL REST ESCAPEMENT. Where the escape wheel is constantly in contact with the balance, *i.e.*, the Horizontal; Duplex; Virgule escapements (*q.v.*). A term used to distinguish from the "detached" escapement, *i.e.*, Lever; Chronometer (*q.v.*). Clock escapements such as the Anchor, Dead Beat, etc., are frictional rest types but are not usually so termed. A detached clock escapement is usually referred to as a "Free Pendulum" (*q.v.*).

FRICTION SPRING. A spring used to cause drag. Used in some clocks to cause the cannon pinion to "carry." Also the spring to cause drag to the centre seconds pinion to take up "back lash" sometimes referred to as "Tension Spring." Friction or tension springs are used in horology for other purposes but the above instances are the most common applications.

CLOCK FRICTION SPRING.

WATCH FRICTION SPRING.

WATCH FRICTION SPRING.

FRIESLAND CLOCK, *See* Dutch Clock.

FRIEZE. *See* ANTIQUE CLOCK CASE TERMS.

FULCRUM. The point about which a lever operates. The point or pivot about which a lever turns.

FULL DEPTH. The sum of the addendum and dedendum; equivalent also to the working depth of a gear plus the clearance.

FULL PLATE. Refers to a watch movement design, the top plate of which covers the movement, the balance and balance cock being placed externally, on top of the plate; distinct from the $\frac{1}{2}$ or $\frac{3}{4}$ plate and Bar Movements (*q.v.*).

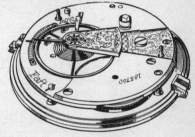

FULL PLATE.

FULLY ADJUSTED. Refers to a watch which has been adjusted for changes in temperature and five positions. *See* Adjusted.

FULLY JEWELLED. Refers to a watch having 15 or more jewels, *i.e.*, top and bottom jewel holes to the 3rd, 4th and escape wheels, pallets and balance; 2 jewel pallet stones; 2 end stones to the balance and, a jewel impulse pin.

FURNITURE STYLES. *See* next page.

FUSE. A device used to protect electrical apparatus against the effect of an excess of current. A fusible metal, connected in the circuit, which melts and interrupts the circuit when an excessive current flows.

FUSE LINK. The fusible element in a fuse. Usually a wire or strip of conductor which is so proportioned that a current above normal generates sufficient heat to melt it thus acting as an automatic overload switch.

FUSEE. The spirally grooved pulley of varying diameter used to equalise the pull of the mainspring. Attributed to Jacob Zech of Prague in 1525, but probably known before. Drawings by Leonardo Da

Vinci (b. 1452, d. 1519) show the fusee in principle. Prior to its introduction, the Stackfreed (*q.v.*) was used for the same purpose but was comparatively crude and ineffective. Clocks and watches fitted with a fusee are referred to as Fusee clocks and watches.

FUSEE CAP. The cam-shaped steel piece fitted to the fusee which forms the stop-piece. It operates with the Fusee Iron (*q.v.*).

FUSEE CAP.

FUSEE COLLET.
The collet or cap by which the fusee assembly is held together.

FUSEE COLLET.

FUSEE CHAIN. The chain which conveys the power of the mainspring from the barrel to the fusee.

Illus. on next page.

FURNITURE STYLES IN FRANCE
For English Styles see page 44.

LOUIS XIII (1610–43). Change from Baroque of Henri IV to classic grandeur of Louis XIV beginning of use of scroll and shell like forms. Strong Italian Baroque influence but interior use of painted panel promises the later developments.

LOUIS XIV (1643–1715). Classic formality at beginning with lavish modifications later. Curved headed panel shell work at top. Complicated interlaced thin acanthus scrolls. (André Charles Boulle, using Béram's " grotesques "). Beginnings of ormulu.

RÉGENCE (1715–1773). Growing love of curves ousted remains of classical dignity. Use of ormulu increased. Chinese influence.

LOUIS XV (1750–1774). N.B. overlaps with Régence. Interiors became richer and more bizaare. Curves everywhere, frequently asymmetrical. Fantasy, combined richness and delicacy and unbridled imagination.

LOUIS XVI (1774–93). Reaction set in, return to classic. Occasional pilaster framing. Broken curves died out. Similar to Louis XIV but more delicate. False pastoral influence but peak period of elegance.

DIRECTOIRE Transitional between Louis XVI (restrained classic) and Empire (Roman heavy).

EMPIRE (1799–1814) Neo-classic. Increased use of bronze appliqué ornament. Continued with modification till 1840.

VERNIS MARTIN (Four brothers).
Guillaume, died 1749.
Simon, Etienne. Julien and Robert (1706–65). Did not invent but perfected the process. At the height of their fame had three factories in Paris, one of which was still in existence in 1785.

BOULLE André Charles (1642–1732). A cabinet maker second only to Jean Macé. At age of 30 was granted lodgings in Louvre galleries. Was given Macé's lodging in 1672 by Louis XIV, the patent reading, " chaser, gilder and maker of marqueterie." Again Boulle was not the inventor but the past master improving on the Renaissance artists by inlaying brass into shell or wood.
Note: " Buhl " is a name invented by auctioneers and furniture dealers for cheap and relatively modern shell inlays or simulated imitations.

ORMULU Properly an alloy of copper and zinc with occasional addition of tin. Colour heightened by use of " gold lacquer " immersion in dilute sulphuric or by burnishing. Also used to describe gilded brass or copper and, by the unscrupulous, gilt spelter.

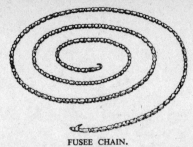

FUSEE CHAIN.

FUSEE CUP. A dust cup fitted to the winding square of the fusee.

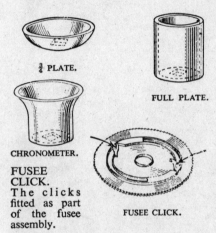

¾ PLATE.

FULL PLATE.

CHRONOMETER.

FUSEE CLICK.

FUSEE CLICK. The clicks fitted as part of the fusee assembly.

FUSEE DETENT. *See* Detent.

FUSEE ENGINE. A tool for cutting the grooves on a fusee.

FUSEE HOOKS. The hook of the fusee chain which operates on the fusee. (A) Barrel hook; (B) Fusee hook.

FUSEE HOOKS.

FUSEE HOLLOW. The hollow cut into the top of the fusee of a ¾-plate watch movement; it enables the top pivot to be sunk into the height of the fusee cone.

FUSEE HOLLOW.

FUSEE IRON. The stop fitted on to the plate of a fusee movement which intercepts the fusee stop-piece when fully wound.

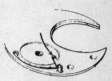

FUSEE IRON.

FUSEE MAINTAINING POWER. The maintaining power fitted as part of the fusee assembly. The maintaining power consists of a thin, steel ratchet wheel on to which the clicks are fitted, the maintaining spring fitting into the main wheel and the detent. *See* Maintaining Power.

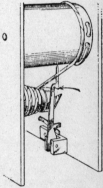

CLOCK FUSEE IRON.

FUSEE PIECE. The top pivot bearing of the fusee; usually associated with the ¾-plate movement where the bearing is held in position by screws.

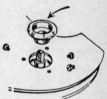

FUSEE PIECE.

G

GADROON. *See* ANTIQUE CLOCK CASE TERMS.

GALLERY. *See* ANTIQUE CLOCK CASE TERMS.

GALLOWS TOOL.
A tool used by clockmakers to hold pinions while the leaves are being shaped. The upper part fits loosely so that the pinion " gives " as it is being filed thus keeping the filed surface flat.

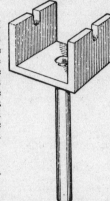

GALLOWS TOOL.

GARNET. Used for the manufacture of jewel holes and endstones, now superseded by the synthetic stones (*q.v.*). Garnet is soft and apt to discolour pivots.

GARTER BACK. Refers to the termination of engine turning employed on watch cases.

GAS CONTROLLER. A spring-driven clock movement used to operate a gas tap and principally employed in lighting and extinguishing street lamps at set times and for the control of gas furnaces in printing works and similar places.

GATE. A form of mainspring fitting; it has the advantage of holding the end coil of the spring free of the other coils and thus minimising friction.

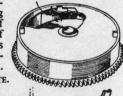

GATE.

GATHERING PALLET.
The pallet or pin that gathers up the rack of striking clocks and repeating watches. Sometimes referred to as the Tumbler.

ENGLISH STYLE GATHERING PALLET·

FRENCH STYLE GATHERING PALLET.

GAUGE. A measuring instrument. There are a number of gauges used in horology such as:—Micrometer; Pinion; Pivot; Vernier; Mainspring; Douzième; Dixième; Hand, etc. (*q.v.*).

GAUGE BLOCKS. A system of precision measurement by steel blocks. Invented by C. E. Johansson. The gauge block sets are built up of certain series of gauges which are hardened, ground and lapped steel blocks with two opposite surfaces flat and parallel to each other. The distance between these two surfaces is marked on each block or gauge, and these surfaces are made with such extraordinary care and high finish that two or three blocks when wrung together will adhere with remarkable strength. The accuracy is of such high order that practically the same measuring result is obtained with a combination of a number of blocks as with one block only of the same nominal size.

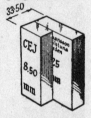

GAUGE BLOCKS.

GAUSS. The unit of density of magnetic flux, named after Karl P. Gauss, a German mathematician who defined the unit. A watch with a steel component in its escapement, *i.e.*, the lever, roller, or balance spring will not run in a magnetic field of 50 Gauss. Gauss is equal to one Line of Force (*q.v.*) per square centimetre, or one Maxwell (*q.v.*) per square centimetre.

GEARING. Refers to the intersection of a toothed wheel with another or with a pinion. A train of wheels.

GEARS. The forms of gears used in horology are:—Epicycloidal; Hypocycloidal; Involute; Circular Arc. (*See* under separate headings.)

STYLES OF GEMSTONE CUTTING

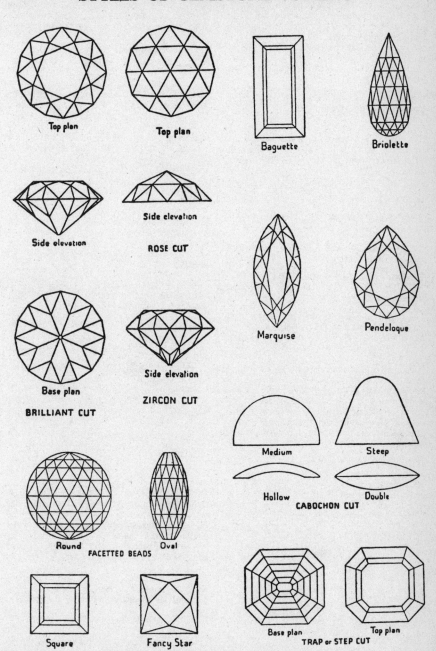

137

GEAR TOOTH. A specially formed projection on the edge of a wheel, its object is to engage with a similar tooth on another gear in order to provide positive transmission of movement from one wheel to another without slipping.

GEMSTONES. Styles of cutting. *See* previous page.

GENERATING CIRCLE. *See* Cycloid, Epicycloid, and Hypercycloid.

GENEVA MOVEMENT. Refers to the Bar type of movement in which a series of bars in a form of bridges and cocks constitutes the " top plate." *See* Bar Movement.

GENEVA OBSERVATORY TESTS. *See* WATCH TESTING STANDARDS, pages 242–8.

GENEVA STOP WORK. Another name for the Maltese Cross stop work (*q.v.*).

GEORGIAN STYLE. *See* ANTIQUE CLOCK CASE TERMS.

GERMAN WATCH TESTING SPECIFICATIONS. *See* WATCH TESTING STANDARDS, pages 242–8.

GILBERT. The unit of magnetomotive force. Definable as that total magnetising force which is produced by $4\pi/10$ ampere turns. *See* Ampere Turns.

GILT. Originally a gold coating applied to base metal such as brass by the mercuric gilding process (also called fire gilding and water gilding). Now used to describe the finish on articles lightly covered with gold or gold alloy by an electrolytic or chemical process and not up to the standard of gold plating.

GIMBALS. *See* Gymbals.

GIROCAP. Made for the same purpose as Fixmobil (*q.v.*) but the end stones are of jewel only. Made by The Universal Escapement Ltd., La Chaux-de-Fonds, Switzerland, the makers of Incabloc (*q.v.*). *See* Lubrifix.

GIROCAP.

GLASS BRUSH. A brush made from fine threads of glass; a bundle of glass threads is bound into a stick-like shape with string and, as the brush end wears

GLASS BRUSH.

down, the string is unwound, thus exposing more glass threads. It is very useful as a scratch brush and for cleaning the fine teeth of chronograph wheels. Also for surfacing silver watch dials where the figures are engraved and enamelled.

GLASSES, WATCH. *See* facing page.

GLORY. *See* ANTIQUE CLOCK CASE TERMS.

GLUCINUM. *See* METALS USED IN HOROLOGY.

GLUCYDUR. *See* METALS USED IN HOROLOGY.

GNOMON OR STYLE. That part of a sundial or similar indicator which casts the shadow to indicate solar time.

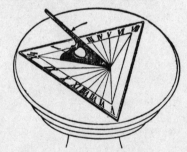

GNOMON OR STYLE.

GOING BARREL. The barrel or container of the mainspring of a clock or watch on which teeth are provided so that the mainspring power is conveyed direct to the train as distinct from the Fusee and Barrel (*q.v.*). *See* Barrel and WATCH PART NOMENCLATURE.

GOING FUSEE. A fusee (*q.v.*) provided with maintaining power. Many fusees, particularly in clocks, are not so fitted.

GOLD. *See* METALS USED IN HOROLOGY.

GOLD FILLED. Another term for rolled gold. *See* METALS USED IN HOROLOGY.

GOLD PLATED. Base metal coated by a gold alloy by electro-deposition and/or a chemical process. Sometimes an additional thermal process is used to produce hard gold plating. The minimum thickness should be 10 micron. *See* Rolled Gold, page 182.

GOLD, ROLLED. A thin sheet of gold (20 micron is recommended as the thinnest) permanently bonded to one or both sides of a backing metal such as nickel silver, nickel, stainless steel, silver, or bronze. Used for watch cases.

GOLD SPRING. The gold spring attached to the detent of the Chronometer Escapement (*q.v.*). Also referred to as the " Passing Spring " or " Discharging Spring."

GOLDEN NUMBER. Meton, in 432 B.C. observed that after a period of 19 years the new and full moons returned on the same days. If one year is added to the present year and divided by 19 the remainder is the Golden Number, *e.g.* 1960+1÷19, remainder 4. The number giving the position of any year in the Metonic Cycle.

STYLES OF WATCH GLASSES

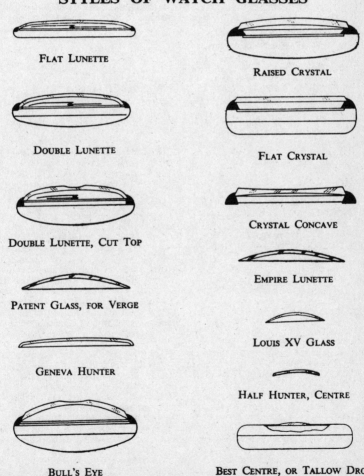

FLAT LUNETTE

RAISED CRYSTAL

DOUBLE LUNETTE

FLAT CRYSTAL

DOUBLE LUNETTE, CUT TOP

CRYSTAL CONCAVE

PATENT GLASS, FOR VERGE

EMPIRE LUNETTE

GENEVA HUNTER

LOUIS XV GLASS

HALF HUNTER, CENTRE

BULL'S EYE

BEST CENTRE, OR TALLOW DROP

GOLDSMITHS HALL. *See* Hall Mark.

GOLIATH. Refers to a large watch of from 24 to 28 lignes and used as a clock. Either a 30-hour or 8-day movement.

GOLIATH.

GONG. A length of wire which is round, square, or rectangular in section coiled in a volute, or mounted as a straight rod, used for the purpose of sounding similar to a bell. Gongs are used in clocks for both chiming and striking the hours, etc., and in repeating and alarm watches. The very flat " bell " is sometimes referred to as a gong.

GOTHIC. *See* ANTIQUE CLOCK CASE TERMS.

GRAHAM ESCAPEMENT. *See* Dead Beat Escapement.

GRAHAM'S PENDULUM. *See* Mercurial Pendulum.

GRAIN. (1) The fine lines left by filing or polishing in one direction only; hence, straight grain, circular grain. (2) In bar

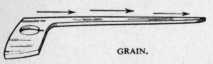

GRAIN.

and sheet metals a grain due to rolling stresses is said to run in the direction of rolling. Sometimes taken into account in manufacturing processes, particularly in the case of springs. A spring should be made so that when deflected, the stress is against and not with the grain, *i.e.*, the spring should be cut lengthwise from the rolled strip, not crosswise. (3) The size of abrasive particles; usually denoted by a number. Used also in describing the degree of coarseness of grinding wheel, emery cloth, Carborundum.

GRAND-DAUGHTER CLOCK. A style of clock of recent introduction similar to the grandfather clock but about 3 ft. 6 ins. to 4 ft. 6 ins. tall.

GRANDE SONNERIE. A full or grand strike. Refers to a clock or watch that strikes the hours and the quarters at each quarter. For instance, at 7.15 the 7 hours will be struck and then one quarter. At 7.30, the 7 hours and 2 quarters. At 7.45, the hours and 3 quarters and so on.

GRANDFATHER CLOCK. A long-case clock of about 6 ft. 6 in. or more. Usually associated with the domestic clock as distinct from the Astronomical Clock (*q.v.*) which also is a long-case clock. The term " grandfather clock " was first used in the song " My Grandfather's Clock," written in 1876. The old masters referred to such clocks as " Long Case " and these clocks would be, therefore, to the generation of about 1750 to 1800, their grandfather's clock. *See* PERIODS OF ENGLISH LONG CASE CLOCKS, page 79.

GRANDMOTHER CLOCK. A clock similar to the Grandfather clock but not so tall, usually 5 ft. 6 ins. to 6 ft. 6 ins. Grandmother clocks by the old masters are rare.

GRASSHOPPER ESCAPEMENT. For many years the invention of this escapement has been credited to John Harrison (1693–1776), but the earliest known example of a grasshopper escapement is in a turret clock made by James Harrison (1697–1766) the younger brother of John. (*See* Horological Journal, March and April, 1954). James Harrison has stated that his clocks, with this escapement, by which he rated his early timekeepers, were made in 1726 (two in number). In clocks made by James Harrison the escape wheel teeth are curved but John Harrison employed straight sided teeth in the escape wheels of three large marine timekeepers. The figure shows the type of grasshopper used by James Harrison in a long-case clock of 1728. Its action is typical and is as follows:—The pendulum is swinging to the left. The tip of tooth F is pressing into the angle of pallet B and as this pallet is pivoted at C to the frame A the latter is made to rock on its knife edges E and impulse is thereby given to the pendulum D which is fixed rigidly to frame A. The rocking motion of frame A also causes the pallet B to descend into the path of the oncoming tooth G and just before the pendulum reaches the end of its vibration to the left the tip of tooth G engages in the angle of pallet B. The final motion of the pendulum to the left causes pallet B to press against tooth G and consequently the escape wheel recoils slightly. This recoil releases the pressure contact between tooth F and pallet B and the latter immediately swings up under the influence of a weight K and is finally arrested by the buffer spring H which up to this moment has been resting on its stop J. The pendulum

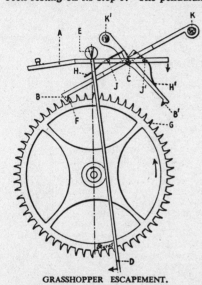

GRASSHOPPER ESCAPEMENT.

then commences the return swing to the right and a similar cycle takes place impulse being given by tooth G acting on pallet B and in due course this pallet swings up and is finally arrested by spring buffer H. No oil whatever is required in this escapement because all frictional surfaces are brass working against lignum vitae which is a naturally greasy wood.

GRAVER. A hand cutting tool used by clock and watch makers for turning in the turns or lathe. The tool is also used by engravers and is known to engineers by the term Burin.

SQUARE.
LOZENGE.   ROUND.

GRAVITY. The force which attracts all bodies towards the centre of the earth. A natural force exhibited by all masses.

GRAVITY CLOCK. A clock where the motive force is derived from the weight of the clock movement itself falling. To wind, the movement is raised, and through a rack and pinion device motive power is conveyed to the clock mechanism. The model illustrated is a modern example of a gravity clock.

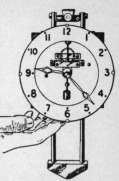

GRAVITY CLOCK.

GRAVITY ESCAPEMENT. An escapement in which gravity provides the impulse. See Double-Three-Legged Gravity Escapement.

GREAT WHEEL. The wheel attached to the fusee and also the wheel, or the teeth which form part of the barrel, of the Going Barrel (q.v.). Also the wheel to which the mainspring is attached in some low grade watches and clocks.

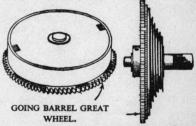

GOING BARREL GREAT WHEEL.

FUSEE GREAT WHEEL.

GREENWICH MEAN TIME. Abbreviated G.M.T. The mean of the Solar days, i.e., the mean of the time as shown by the Sun Dial. (A fuller understanding as to why the mean Solar time or G.M.T. is checked by sidereal observations will be gathered by reference to Solar time and Sidereal time.) G.M.T. was introduced by Act of Parliament in August 1880 in the " Statutes (Definition of Time) Act." The terms of the act are:—" Whenever any expression of time occurs in any Act of Parliament deed, or other legal instrument, the time referred to shall, unless specially stated, be held in the case of Great Britain to be Greenwich time, and in the case of Ireland, Dublin, mean time." In 1916 Greenwich Mean Time was, by the Time (Ireland) Act, made legal time in Ireland also.

GREENWICH OBSERVATORY, ROYAL. *See* page 217.

GREENWICH OBSERVATORY TESTS. *See* WATCH TESTING STANDARDS, page 242.

GREGORIAN CALENDAR. The calendar as used to-day in Western Europe. It is the Julian calendar as reformed by Pope Gregory The Great in 1582. In England this calendar was adopted by Act of Parliament in 1752.

GREY FINISH. The finish left on steel work as a contrast or matching to other highly polished or grained parts. It is a very fine grained, soft, matt surface.

" GREY, IN THE." " In the grey " refers to the finish *prior* to the final polishing of steel work and the *actual final* finish of brass. Thus, the top plates of English watches were left " in the grey " by the actual manufacturers, engraved with the vendors names, etc., and then gilded to match the rest of the movement when the watch was purchased by them.

GRID. The Central Electricity Board's system of power transmission lines connecting the generating stations and sub-stations of authorised suppliers of electricity in Great Britain. The control grid (or other electrode) of a thermionic valve such as a radio valve, consisting of an open-work metal lattice, mesh, spiral, or similar construction, on which a signal from a preceding source is impressed. It may thus be considered as the " input " terminal of the valve's circuit.

GRID BASE. The range of potential or voltage between which—(1) Anode current is zero, (2) Grid current commences to flow.

GRID BIAS. *See* Bias.

GRID BIAS RESISTANCE. A resistance inserted in the cathode lead of a valve which has the effect, due to anode current flow, of applying a negative, or " biasing " voltage upon the grid. *See* Bias.

GRID CIRCUIT. The circuit between the grid and cathode of a thermionic valve.

GRID CONDENSER. The condenser (capacitor) connected between the grid terminal (of a valve) and the other portion(s) of the grid circuit.

GRID CURRENT. The current which flows in the grid circuit when the grid, by reason of its potential rising positively with respect to the cathode, or only slightly

less negative than the cathode, acts as if it were an anode.

GRID LEAK. A high resistance of the order of megohms, connected across the grid condenser (capacitor) to prevent a D.C. voltage appearing on the grid by providing a path, *i.e.*, " leak." In effect, the resistance and capacitance together form a " Time constant " which may be long or short, as required.

GRID SWING. The limits about its mean value between which the grid potential swings under working conditions.

GRIDIRON PENDULUM. A form of compensated pendulum consisting of alternate steel and brass (or zinc) rods so coupled together that the coefficient of expansion of the brass or zinc, being greater than that of steel, compensates for the longitudinal or " downward " expansion of the steel. The centre of oscillation of the pendulum thus remains constant during changes in temperature. Invented by John or James Harrison about 1725. No clock has yet been found with an original pendulum by John Harrison. A clock in the Guildhall Museum, London, signed James Harrison has a gridiron pendulum, which is probably contemporary.

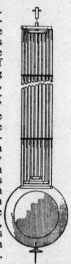

GRIDIRON PENDULUM.

GRIFFIN. *See* ANTIQUE CLOCK AND CLOCK CASE TERMS.

GRINDING. The operation of finishing metal by means of abrasive prior to polishing or bringing a shaped piece to exact size.

GROUND. The American term for Earth (*q.v.*).

GUARANTEE. This can be a vague term; usually it refers to the length of time the vendor of a watch or clock holds himself responsible, sometimes 12 months or 2 years. Repairs, etc., are undertaken free of charge with certain reservations, or sometimes unconditionally. With some manufacturers it just means that the product was made with the best materials. Sometimes the time of guarantee is related to the thickness of deposit on a gold plated watch. *See* Rolled Gold, page 182.

GUARD, INDEX. *See* Boot.

GUARD PIN. Also referred to as the Safety Pin and Dart. It is the pin fitted to the lever of the lever escapement and is the device to keep the lever in its correct position to receive the impulse pin, particularly in the event of a shake or blow overcoming the Draw (*q.v.*) on the pallets.

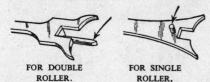

FOR DOUBLE   FOR SINGLE
ROLLER.   ROLLER.

GUARD, WATCH. Usually refers to a leather strap used in place of and for the same purpose as a chain or Albert. *See* Albert.

WATCH GUARD.

GUILLAUME BALANCE. A cut bi-metallic compensation balance, invented by Dr. Chas. Eduard Guillaume, where, instead of steel, as is used in the ordinary cut balance, nickel-steel is used. The Guillaume balance practically eliminates the Middle Temperature Error (*q.v.*).

GUILLOCHÉ. Refers to engine turned, *e.g.*, case engine turned. *See* ANTIQUE CLOCK CASE TERMS.

GUILLOCHIS. Refers to engine turning, *e.g.*, engine turning on case.

GUT. An extremely strong cord made from the intestines of sheep (best quality) or oxen: it is actually the " cured " or " tanned " intestinal muscle of the animals.

GUT PALLETS. *See* ANTIQUE CLOCK CASE TERMS.

GYMBALS or GIMBALS. A universal joint used for mounting the Marine Chronometer in its box. The purpose of gymbals is to maintain the instrument in a horizontal position during the pitching and rolling of the ship.

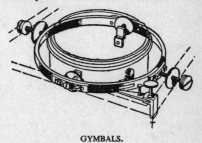

GYMBALS.

GYRATION. To revolve, *i.e.*, " To spin like a top." The act of revolving. *See* Radius of Gyration.

H

HAIR SPRING. An undesirable term for the Balance Spring (*q.v.*). It is not good horological language and is so named by the uninitiated because of its hair-like appearance. The term is also used in connection with the similar control or return springs of indicating instruments.

HALF CHRONOMETER. Usually refers to a lever escapement fitted with a bi-metallic, cut compensated balance (*q.v.*) and a steel balance spring.

HALF DEAD BEAT ESCAPEMENT. A clock escapement the action of which is a combination of the Dead Beat and Anchor escapements (*q.v.*). It is made with impulse faces similar to the Dead Beat but the " resting "

HALF DEAD BEAT ESCAPEMENT.

faces of the pallets are not concentric with the pallet arbor, being set out to give a slight degree of recoil.

HALF HUNTER. *See* Demi Hunter.

HALF PLATE. A movement in which the top plate carries the upper pivots of the barrel or fusee and barrel, centre wheel, and third wheel; the fourth wheel top pivot is carried by a separate cock. The ¾ plate carries the top pivots

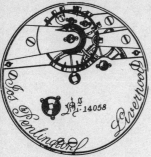

HALF PLATE.

of the barrel, centre, third *and fourth*.

HALF QUARTER REPEATER. A repeating mechanism watch or clock, that strikes one blow to denote the half quarter of an hour, *e.g.*, at five minutes to 8 o'clock: 7 blows on a low note to denote 7 hours, 3 " ting tangs " to denote ¾ to 8 o'clock, 1 blow on a higher note denoting the passing of 7¾ minutes since the last quarter.

HALF ROUND FILE. *See* Files.

HALF TIME. " Running to half time " means that a watch, without its balance spring, keeps exactly half the time it would normally do with the balance spring fitted. A watch so running records ½ hour when it has actually been going for 1 hour. The purpose of the test is to determine the correct weight of the balance. Used when adjusting fine pocket and deck watches.

HALL MARK. The Governmental control of gold and silver. In 1300 the Goldsmith's Company was formed in London to protect the public against fraudulent qualities of gold and silver, articles, etc.,

EXAMPLES OF COMPLETE HALLMARKS

British   GOLD   Imported

| Gold mark | Quality mark | Town mark | Date letter | Maker's mark | | Date mark | Quality mark | Town mark | Maker's mark |

SILVER

| Sterling Silver mark | Quality mark | Town mark | Date letter | Maker's mark | | Town mark | Silver quality mark | Date letter | Maker's mark |

| Britannia silver mark | Town mark | Date letter | Maker's mark | | Town mark | Silver quality mark | Date letter | Maker's mark |

and the privilege of assaying and marking was conferred upon the Company by Statute. Thus, with certain exceptions owing to the fragility of the article, it became illegal to offer for sale any gold or silverware, not bearing the Hall's assay mark. Old city companies operated from establishments called " Hall," hence " Hall Mark," *e.g.*, the assay mark of the Company established in the Goldsmiths' Hall, London. There are six Halls at which plate is assayed and hall-marked in Britain to-day, London, Birmingham, Sheffield, Chester, Glasgow and Edinburgh. Each has its distinguishing sign. *See* " Hall Marks," by A. Tremayne. Gold is alloyed with copper and silver to toughen and strengthen it. Equal quantities of copper and silver form a good alloy, but there are innumerable formulas used by manufacturers which include many different metals each designed to produce alloyed gold of

London   Birmingham   Sheffield   Chester   Edinburgh   Glasgow   Dublin

The Town Marks on Imported Plate in use since May 1906

·9584

Britannia

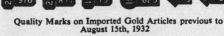

Quality Marks on Imported Gold Articles previous to August 15th, 1932

·925

Sterling

Marks on Silver

Quality Mark on Imported Gold Articles since August 15th, 1932

MARKS ON IMPORTED ARTICLES

the required character or colour. Gold can be yellow, red, or brown in many shades. It can be quite white or even green or blue. The effects are obtained by the use of alloys. But the full assayable quality of the gold must be maintained if the articles are to pass the Hall. Eighteen carat (three-quarters gold, one quarter alloy) was the legal standard between 1477 and 1575. It was raised to twenty-two carat (twenty-two parts gold two parts alloy) in 1575 and this standard has never been altered. Eighteen carat was again introduced as an additional standard in 1798, and in 1854 three additional standards of 15 ct., 12 ct. and 9 ct. were legalised. The next—and, so far, the last—change was in 1932 when the 15 ct. and 12 ct. standards were dropped and 14 ct. substituted. The gold standards now legal in Great Britain and Northern Ireland are: 22 ct. (·916); 18 ct. (·750); 14 ct. (·585); 9 ct. (·375). Silver standards are Sterling (925 parts in 1,000 pure silver) and Britannia (958·4 parts in 1,000 pure silver). Examples of London Hall Marks are shown on the previous page. All foreign articles imported are detained by the Customs and submitted to an Assay Office, *selected by the importer.* Articles of gold and silver proved to have been made more than one hundred years before the date of importation are exempt from assay and marking, as well as articles genuinely imported by the owner for private use. Also articles so finely wrought as to be liable to damage by marking are exempt at the discretion of the *Assay Offices.* Each Office has a special town mark for imported plate. This is followed by a quality mark in figures (on both Gold and Silver) and the usual Date Letter. The Swiss " Hall Mark,' known as " State controlled precious metal standards," are as illustrated below. Nine carat gold is not a recognised standard in Switzerland.

GOLD, 18 CARATS.

GOLD, 14 CARATS.

SILVER (STERLING) 0·925.

SILVER, 0·800.

PLATINUM.

HAMMER. That part which strikes the bell, gong, tube, etc., in striking, chiming, or alarm mechanisms. The familiar tool, *i.e.*, clock hammer, watch hammer, as used by horologists and other craftsmen.

HAMMER.

HAMMER HARDENING. A system of hardening by hammering. Most metals respond to this treatment, and non-ferrous metals, *i.e.*, brass particularly, hammering or rolling is the only means of hardening.

HAMMER HEAD. The weighted end that actually strikes the bell, gong, etc., (A) in illustration, (B) is the hammer rod. The striking head of the tool, as distinct from the shaft or handle on which it is mounted. There are various shapes of head suited to particular uses such as planishing, riveting, etc.

HAMMER
AND STEM.

HAMMER ROD. *See* Hammer Stem.

HAMMER STEM. The wire or rod carrying the hammer head of a strike, chime or alarm mechanism. (B) in illustration to Hammer Head.

HAMMER TAIL. The fitting usually attached to the arbor, or the rod of the hammer, upon which the hammer spring operates.

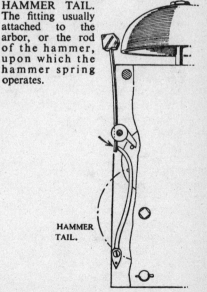

HAMMER
TAIL.

STYLES OF WATCH HANDS

1. LOUIS XVI (with counter poise).
2. LOUIS XV (with counter poise).
3. ROSKOPF (with counter poise).
4. ROSKOPF, SPADE, SWELL.
5. ROSKOPF, SPADE.
6. SPORTS.
7. POINTED SPORTS.
8. CORAL.
9. JAVELIN.
10. OVER.
11. GOLF.
12. MARS.
13. ALSACE CROSS.
14. LEAF.
15. SWALLOW.
16. SWALLOW, SKELETON.
17. HOLLOW LANCE.
18. HOLLOW LANCE, FANCY.
19. CRESCENT.
20. TURKISH.
21. HOLLOW FUCHSIA.
22. MODERN MITRE.
23. LOZENGE MITRE.
24. ALPHA.
25. ALPHA, SKELETON.
26. UPRIGHT LINE.
27. UPRIGHT LINE, SKELETON.
28. DOUBLE BOY.
29. SKELETON.
30. FANCY SKELETON.
31. LOZENGE, SKELETON.
32. BATON, SKELETON.
33. HOLLOW BATON.
34. HOLLOW TAPER BATON.
35. MODERN SKELETON.
36. TAPER BATON.
37. SERPENTINE.
38. BATON, NARROW.
39. BATON, PARALLEL.
40. BATON, POINTED.
41. LOZENGE, POINTED.
42. LOZENGE, POINTED, HOLLOW.
43. SPADE, DOUBLE SWELL.
44. SPADE, AMERICAN.
45. SPADE, LIGHT DOUBLE SWELL.
46. SPADE, HEAVY DOUBLE SWELL.
47. SPADE, PARIS.
48. SPADE, DOUBLE.
49. SPADE, POINTER.
50. SPADE, RAILWAY.
51. BREGUET, ANTIQUE.
52. BREGUET, EMPIRE.
53. BREGUET, STRAIGHT.
54. LOZENGE.
55. DISTAFF.
56. ARROW.
57. SCOTTIES.
58. MODERN.
59. CUBIST.
60. POLAR.
61. GOTHIC, TREFOIL.
62. STAG BEETLE.
63. LANCE.
64. FUCHSIA.
65. PYRAMID.
66. MIRABILE, OPEN.
67. CHEVRON.
68. DOUBLE TRIANGLE.
69. TRIANGLE OPPOSÉ.
70. FRAMEE.
71. POLUX.
72. CATHEDRAL.
73. FLEUR-DE-LIS.
74. DOUBLE ROMAN.
75. SPADE, PARALLEL.
76. CUBIST OBLIQUE.
77. MIRABILE, SOLID.
78. FLORIDA.
79. GOTHIC, WITHOUT ESCARGOT.
80. LOUIS XVI.
81. LOUIS XV.
82. ORIENTAL.
83. LOZENGE MITRE.
84. SIMPLE ROMAN.
85. GOTHIC, WITH ESCARGOT.
86. LANCE, FANCY HOLLOW.
87. CROSS-OVER.
88. TULIP.
89. LYRE.
90. LANCE, SOLID.
91. HOLLY.

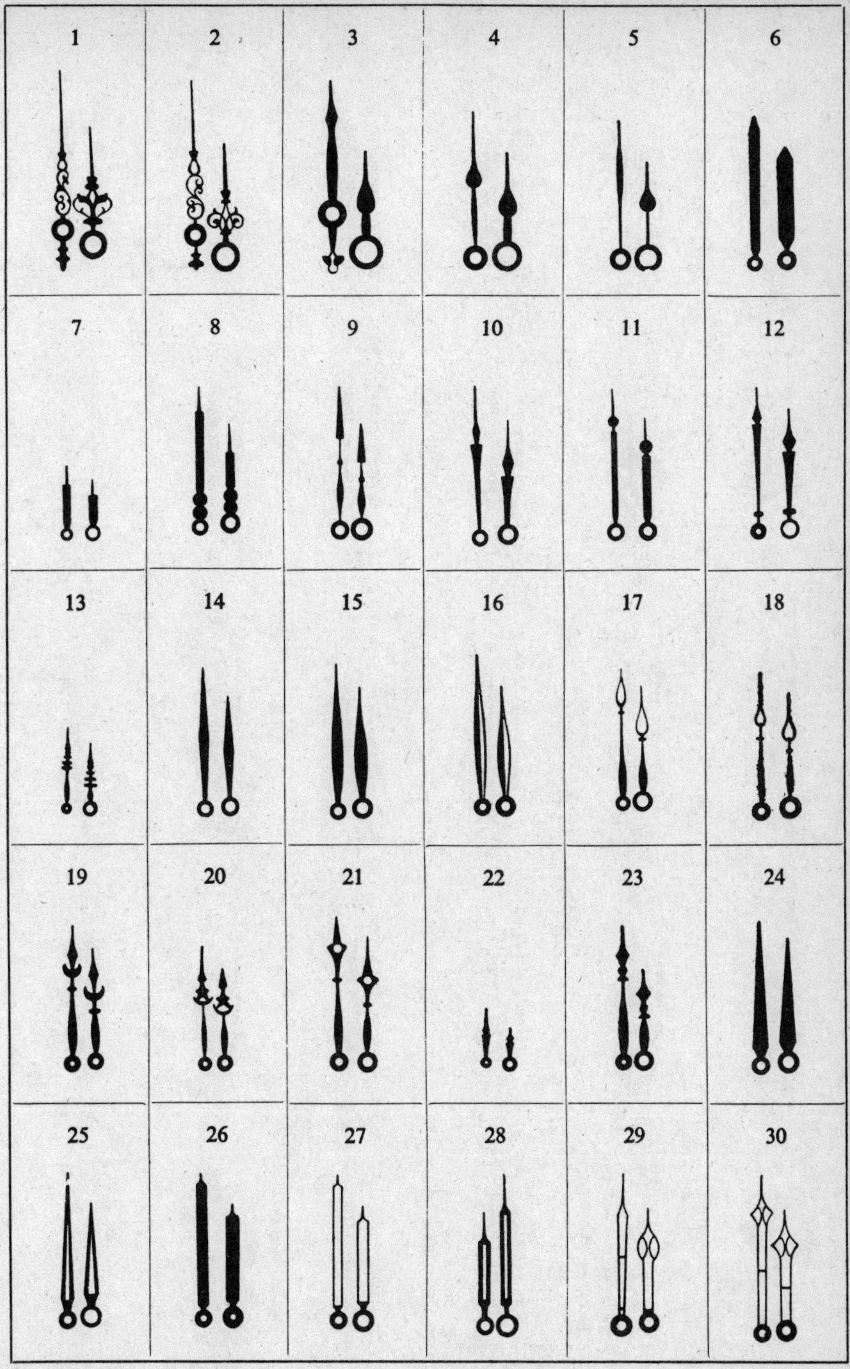
1
2
3
4
5
6
7
8
9
10
11
12
13
14
15
16
17
18
19
20
21
22
23
24
25
26
27
28
29
30

31	32	33	34	35	36
37	38	39	40	41	42
43	44	45	46	47	48
49	50	51	52	53	54
55	56	57	58	59	

60	61	62	63	64	65
66	67	68	69	70	71
72	73	74	75	76	77

78	79	80	81	82

83	84	85	86	87	88	89	90	91

HAND COLLET. *See* Collet.

HAND GAUGE. The scale across the top gives the length of the hand. The slot at the right-hand side gives the diameter of the part on to which the hand is to fit. The three tapered wires on the left give the diameter of the hole in the hand.

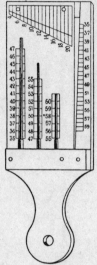

HAND GAUGE.

HAND LEVERS. A pair of levers used in removing the hands of a watch.

HAND REMOVING LEVERS.

HAND REMOVING TOOL. A tool made for the purpose of removing watch hands. There are several varieties of which the illustration here is one.

HAND REMOVING TOOL.

HAND REST. Another name for the "Tee" rest (*q.v.*) used in turning.

HAND SET. *See* Set Hand.

HANDS. The pointers of a watch or clock, indicator, etc. *See* STYLES OF WATCH HANDS, page 146. Sometimes called fingers —a lay term. The term "hand" is also used for indicating dials or instruments of larger types but, in the case of finer apparatus, the term "needle" is more common.

HAND TONGS. A type of pliers having recessed jaws to take hour pipes, bushes or other circular pieces, and provided with a sliding link to lock the jaws. *See* Sliding Tongs.

HAND TONGS.

HAND TOOLS. The tools used at the bench such as pliers, files, screwdrivers, broaches, burnishers, etc., as distinct from those employing mechanical action.

HAND VICE. A small vice, used by clock makers which is held in the hand. (*See* also Pin Vice.)

HAND WASHER. *See* Dial Washers.

HAND WHEEL. A wheel device used to drive the lathe or turns by hand.

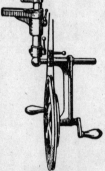

HAND VICE.

HANGING POSITION. Another term for Pendant Up (*q.v.*).

HARD CORE. A term for the hard packed dirt and rust sometimes found in pinion leaves, the corners of pin pallet escape wheel teeth, etc. They require manual cleansing, being very resistant to washing methods.

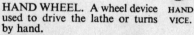

HAND WHEEL.

HARDENING. The process of making steel hard by very rapid cooling from a temperature above a critical range. Usually effected by quenching in water, oil, petroleum or air blast, etc. *See* Blueing and Tempering. Metallurgically, the action sought is the suppression of the normal change from Austentite to Pearlite and the formation of the hard form of steel, Martensite.

HARDENING MEDIA. The liquids or other substances used in quenching steel. *See* Case Hardening.

HARD PLATING. A thick layer of chromium-plating deposited directly upon the base metal without a copper or nickel intermediary. It resists friction wear but is porous and thus liable to corrosive wear.

HARD SOLDER. Silver solder. Made in 3 grades. HARD. Requires a high temperature to flux but lower than melting point (960° C.) of silver. HALF-EASY. A flux temperature lower than that of Hard. EASY. Flows at the lowest temperature. *See* WORKSHOP HINTS AND HELPS, page 300.

HARD'S BALANCE. A chronometer balance introduced by Wm. Hardy in 1804. It was claimed that it reduced the Middle Temperature Error.

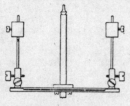

HARDY'S BALANCE.

HARMONIC. An alternating current or wave the frequency of which is a multiple of the fundamental frequency. In thermionic valve circuits the presence of harmonics is often troublesome, but is essential to the production of Square Waves which are the sum of an infinite series of sine wave Harmonics.

HARMONIC GENERATOR. *See* Frequency Multiplier.

HARMONIC MOTION. Simple Harmonic Motion. Abbreviated S.H.M. A point moves in S.H.M. when it vibrates backward and forward so that its acceleration is proportional to its distance from the central point of its excursion. As an example, imagine a wheel lying in a horizontal plane on a vertical axis, moving at a uniform speed and, having a pin projecting upwards from the periphery. Viewed at eye level, the pin will then appear to vibrate to and fro in the plane of the wheel, moving with decreasing speed as it approaches either limit of its excursion and accelerating therefrom to its greatest speed at the moment of passing across the central line, *i.e.*, coincident with the axis. This apparent movement of the pin is Simple Harmonic Motion. The vibrations of a pendulum or a balance closely approximate to S.H.M.

HARMONIC PATTERNS. Geometric patterns produced by a Harmonograph, as used in Engine turned ornamentation of watch cases and other articles.

HARRISON'S PENDULUM. Another name for the Gridiron Pendulum (*q.v.*).

HARTNUP'S BALANCE. A chronometer balance designed by Hartnup about 1845, it was claimed that it reduced the Middle Temperature Error (*q.v.*).

HARTNUP'S BALANCE.

HEAD—PINION. *See* Pinion-Head.

HEADSTOCK. The main part of a lathe containing the spindle to which the driving pulleys are fitted.

HEARTPIECE. A heart-shaped cam used in chronographs, etc., to cause the hand to fly back to zero. Invented by Adolphe Nichole in 1844 (Patent No. 10,348), but was used by Winnerl (pupil of Breguet), Paris, in 1838 who claimed the invention. Also attributed to P. F. Ingold (of Ingold-Fraise, etc.).

HEARTPIECE.

HEAT. That form of energy into which all other forms of energy finally change; measured in British Thermal Units, *i.e.*, that quantity of heat needed to raise 1 lb. water through 1° F. Or in Calories, *i.e.*, the quantity of heat required to raise 1 litre of water through 1° C.

HEATER. The heating element which raises the cathode of a valve, etc., to its operating, *i.e.*, emissive temperature. The term is usually applied to Indirectly Heated Valves.

HEATER INSULATION. The insulating sleeve, etc., between the cathode surface and the heating element in an indirectly heated valve, etc. Also known as Cathode Heater insulation.

HEAT TREATMENT. Any heating process applied to a material, especially metals, such as softening, hardening, tempering, annealing, normalising, etc.

HEEL. That part of the tooth of a Club Tooth escape wheel of the lever escapement which first acts on the pallet. *See* Toe of Tooth.

HEEL.

HELICAL GEAR. A gear having teeth cut in the form of helices or spirals. In the form known as "Hooke's Gearing" helical gears connect shafts which are parallel to one another and a gear of right hand helix engages with a mating gear of left hand helix. The amount of helical twist in the widths of gears of this type is generally made equal to slightly more than one circular pitch of the teeth, to ensure smooth running. *See* also Crossed Axis Helical Gears.

HELICAL SPRING. A spring formed by winding a wire round a cylinder. The Helical balance spring, the upright spring with its coils one above the other. Usually used in Marine chronometers. (*See* Balance Spring.)

HELIX. The shape taken by a length of material, or a long narrow body when coiled into the form which results from winding in a single layer on a cylinder or threaded rod. The Helix is contained in the Helical Spring (*q.v.*).

HENRY. The practical Unit of Inductance (*q.v.*).

HEPPLEWHITE STYLE. *See* Antique Clock Case Terms.

HEPTODE. *See* Valve.

HERRING BONE. *See* Antique Clock Case Terms.

HERSTMONCEUX CASTLE. *See* page 217.

HEXODE. *See* Valve.

H.F. PENTODE. *See* Valve.

HIGH FREQUENCY. A general term for alternating current frequencies above 10 kcs. per sec. Generally referred to as Radio frequencies. Abbreviated as H.F. or R.F.

HOB. A type of wheel-tooth and pinion-leaf milling cutter in the form of a worm. Used in a machine which drives both the hob and the blank at appropriate speeds and feeds them closer together as cutting progresses. Compared with the simple circular cutter, the advantage of the hob is that any size of wheel of a given pitch of teeth may be cut with the one hob. The process is known as hobbing.

HOCKEY TIMER. *See* Timer.

HOG'S BRISTLE. In horology, the predecessor of the balance spring. Used before the introduction of the steel balance spring to control the balance. The bristles were used as a "spring" from the early 16th

century: previous to its introduction timepieces were not entirely portable, *i.e.* could not be worn on the person. The application of the hog's bristle is interesting. The bristle acts as a buffer for the arms of the balance to bank against. The example illustrated has a long bristle drawn through two holes so that the ends project up under the balance and between its arms. As the balance vibrates first one arm banks or bounces against one bristle end and then as the balance returns the other arm bounces off the bristle end. Regulation is effected by the index and as the bristle is moved nearer to the centre of the balance its arc is curtailed, and therefore quickens its rate, and conversely, as the bristle is moved away from the centre so the arc is increased and the rate is slower. The arrows in the illustration point to the Hog's Bristle.

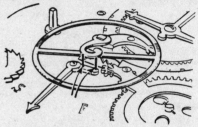

HOG'S BRISTLE.

HOLDER, WATCH. *See* Watch Holder.

HOLLOW FUSEE. *See* Fusee Hollow. The ¾-plate fusee watch was sometimes called "Hollow Fusee."

HOLLOW MOULDING. *See* Mouldings.

HOLLOW PINION. A pinion with a hole through its centre such as the centre pinion of some of the older types of watches.

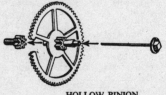

HOLLOW PINION.

HOLLOW PUNCH. A punch with its centre drilled out such as is used to rivet a balance staff to the balance. A cutting punch as used for cutting leather washers, and holes, etc.

HOLLOW PUNCH.

HOOD. *See* ANTIQUE CLOCK CASE TERMS.

HOOK, BARREL. *See* Barrel Hook.

HOOK, BARREL ARBOR. *See* Barrel Arbor Hook.

HOOK, FUSEE. *See* Fusee Hook.

HOOKE'S LAW. " Ut tensis, sic vis " (As the tension is, so is the force), *i.e.*, strain is proportional to the stress producing it. The fundamental law of springs.

HOOKING-IN. The term defining the form of hooking of the mainspring to the barrel of the older type of English fusee watch. Also of chronometers. This form of hooking has the advantage of holding the mainspring close to the inner side of the barrel and thus helps to minimise mainspring friction. Also referred to as " Square hooking."

HOOKING-IN.

HOOP WHEEL. A wheel in the striking train of the old type of clock. It has a brass edge or " hoop " attached to the side, extending for about ⅞th of the circumference, and acts as the locking device for the striking train.

HOOP WHEEL.

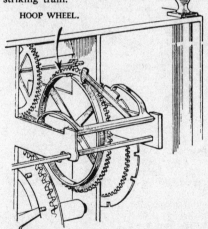

HORIZONTAL ESCAPEMENT. Another name for the Cylinder Escapement (*q.v.*).

HORNS. The part of the lever, in the lever escapement, which forms the notch. The " ears " of the notch. *See* Fork.

HORNS.

HOROLOGY. The art and science of the construction of mechanism for measuring the passage of time and indicating the time of day. The term Horological is used to distinguish between time-keepers driven by weights or springs and those operated by electricity. A person who practises Horology is called an Horologist.

" HOROLOGICAL JOURNAL." The official organ of the British Horological Institute. Established with the inception of the B.H.I. (*q.v.*) in 1858, it was the world's first " trade " journal and ever since its first issue it has appeared monthly. The journal is devoted to the science of Horology and allied subjects. Publishers: N.A.G. Press Ltd., 226, Latymer Court, Hammersmith, W.6. Editor: Eric M. Bruton, F.B.H.I., F.G.A.

HOROLOGICAL INSTITUTE, BRITISH. An organisation founded on September 6, 1858, to develop the science of horology and to foster the arts and various branches of manufacture arising out of it; to stimulate and encourage the production of the best workmanship by suitable rewards and marks of distinction—and to attain these results by the formation of a library, reading room, and a collection of tools, models and machinery; also by the delivery of lectures and the reading of original papers on subjects connected with the art of horology and the various branches of trade or manufacture connected therewith. It has sections for all interested in Horology, professionals including technicians, repairers, retailers and any others engaged in the industry, and also for amateurs, experimenters, antiquarians and others. The Institute celebrated its centenary in 1958 when its reconstructed premises were opened at 35, Northampton Square, London, E.C.1 to house a library which has become the biggest horological library in the world by the addition of the Ilbert Bequest in 1957. One of the Institute's principal activities is educational. It runs correspondence courses in technical horology and also in horological salesmanship and holds examinations in centres all over the country in co-operation with the Educational authorities. Official Journal: " Horological Journal " (*q.v.*). Secretary: F. B. Cowen, M.B.E., M.C., T.D., F.B.H.I.

EMBLEM OF THE B.H.I.

HORSE. A stand or bracket to hold a clock movement while being tested out of its case.

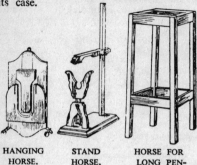

HANGING HORSE.   STAND HORSE.   HORSE FOR LONG PENDULUM CLOCK.

HORSE HAIR. Used as the string of a bow for purposes of turning in the turns, and for drilling, etc., when a ferrule is used. It is the hair from the tail of a horse and has the great advantage of not fraying.

HORSE POWER. Work done at the rate of 33,000 Foot Pounds per minute.

HOUR. An interval of 60 minutes, $\frac{1}{24}$th part of a day.

HOUR CIRCLE. The graduated circle, or dial, of a clock showing the hours. Also known as Chapter Ring; Hour Ring. In Astronomy, another name for the declination circle. The graduated circle of an equatorial telescope reading sidereal time and right ascension.

HOUR CIRCLE.

HOUR GLASS. An old form of timing instrument consisting of a waisted glass vessel containing fine sand, and used for timing the duration of a sermon or interment, etc. Also used by the Navy to mark the duration of a short period of time. Sometimes used to-day as an egg timer.

HOUR HAND. The hand of a chronometer, clock or watch that points to or indicates the hours. *See* STYLES OF WATCH HANDS, page 146.

HOUR GLASS.

HOUR PLATE. Another name for a dial marked to denote the time of day.

HOUR RACK. The rack of a striking clock or repeating watch which determines the number of hours struck. The Striking rack which regulates the number of hours in a chiming clock, to distinguish it from the chime rack.

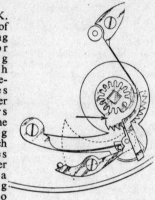

HOUR RACK OF REPEATING WATCH.

The term is most commonly used in connection with repeating watches since they have two or three such racks; in the case of a minute repeater, one for the hours, one for the quarters, and another for the minutes.

HOUR RACK OF CLOCK.

HOUR STAR. The star wheel of a striking mechanism upon which the snail is fixed, the snail determines the number of hours to be struck and the wheel is moved each hour.

HOUR STAR.

HOUR ZONE. Another name for Hour Circle (*q.v.*).

HOUR WHEEL. The wheel of the motion work to which the hour hand is attached. A general term for any wheel which revolves twice in a day or performs some hourly function. *See* NOMENCLATURE OF WATCH PARTS.

HOUR WHEEL.

HUNTER. Where the face of a watch is fully covered by a cover or lid. It is usual for the cover to fly up at will: but there are some, more particularly wrist watches, have the action reversed; when the cover is lifted, it will spring down upon release. *See* Demi Hunter. *Also* WATCH CASE STYLES.

HUSKS. *See* ANTIQUE CLOCK CASE TERMS.

HUYGENS ENDLESS ROPE. Method of providing maintaining power to drive the clock while the weight was being raised in the first pendulum clock by Christiaan Huygens, 1657. The endless cord passes over the pulley A which is attached to the great wheel and supports the driving weight B. It then passes over pulley C, which is provided with ratchet teeth and pivoted to the inside of the clock case to support the small weight D. As the part of the cord marked E is pulled down to wind the clock, the ratchet wheel H turns under its click to raise the driving weight B, which still continues to drive the clock as it applies torque to wheel A. The actual driving weight is half of weight B less half of weight D. The system was used in many 18th century longcase clocks. Sometimes the pulley with the ratchet drove the striking train also, thus employing only one weight for two trains. It is not suitable for clocks going more than 30 hours. Used

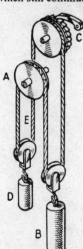

HUYGENS ENDLESS ROPE.

today in Automatic Winding (*q.v.*) for tower clocks.

HYDROGEN CLOCK. A clock made by Pasquale Andervalt, of Trieste. Presented to the Clockmakers Company, it now forms part of the collection at the Guildhall, London. The hydrogen gas is generated by the action of dilute sulphuric acid on a zinc pellet and is collected in a glass bell jar in such a manner as to provide the power for the train and pendulum controlled escapement. The replenishment of the zinc pellet and the release of the spent hydrogen is automatically arranged. Presented to the Clockmakers' Company in 1874. *See* Air Clock.

HYPOCYCLOIDAL CURVE. A line traced by a point in the circumference of a circle known as the generating circle rolling on the interior circumference of another circle. This principle is used in the design of pinion leaves; when the diameter of the rolling circle is equal to the radius of the circle in which it is rolling, the " curve " becomes a straight line.

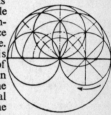

HYPOCYCLOIDAL " CURVE " AS A STRAIGHT LINE.

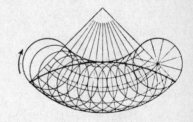

AS A CURVE.

HYPOID BEVEL GEAR. A bevel gear where the axes of the driving and driven shafts are at right angles and not in the same plane, which results in sliding action between the teeth.

HYSTERESIS (MAGNETIC). A state in magnetic materials wherein the induced flux lags behind any changes in the inducing force, resulting, in effect, in a form of energy loss.

I

ICE BOX. A low temperature chamber used for testing watches, chronometers, etc., when adjusting for changes in temperature. The ice box is now superseded by the refrigerator.

ICE HOCKEY TIMER. *See* Timers.

IDLE WHEEL. A gear wheel in a train of wheels which does not affect its ratio or speed. Its purpose may be either to make up the distance between wheels or to reverse the direction of rotation.

IMPEDANCE. The ratio of the R.M.S. (root mean square) value of the voltage applied to an electric circuit, to the current in the circuit.

IMPOST. *See* ANTIQUE CLOCK CASE TERMS.

IMPULSE CLOCK. A clock or dial driven by electrical impulses from a master clock.

IMPULSE PALLET. The pallet of the impulse roller which receives the impulse. Some of the older types of escapement were not provided with a jewelled impulse pallet. *See* Chronometer.

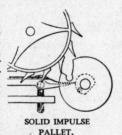

SOLID IMPULSE PALLET.

JEWELLED IMPULSE PALLET.

IMPULSE PIN. Also termed the Ruby Pin; the pin fitted to the roller of the lever escapement which

IMPULSE PIN.

receives the impulse to keep the balance vibrating. Usually made from a jewel stone. The impulse Pin unlocks the escapement. *See* WATCH PART NOMENCLATURE.

IMPULSE ROLLER. The roller of the lever escapement to which the Impulse Pin (*q.v.*) is fitted. *See* NOMENCLATURE OF WATCH PARTS, page 285. In the chronometer, the roller through which impulse is imparted to the balance either directly to the roller or through a jewel impulse pallet fitted to it. *See* Impulse Pallet.

IN BEAT. A term used to signify that the action of an escapement is even. *See* Beat.

INCABLOC. A shock resisting system, where the jewel holes and endstones of the balance " give " when the watch receives a shock. The spring like settings operate until a shoulder turned on the balance staff contacts a block and so takes the effect of a major shock.

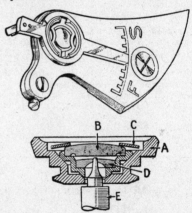

A. Plate.   C. Spring.   E. Balance Staff.
B. Endstone.   D. Jewel hole.

INCASTAR. A system of regulating a watch by lengthening or shortening the

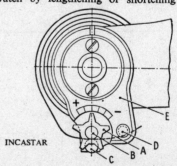

INCASTAR

balance spring. No index is employed and watches fitted with this device are " Free Sprung " (*q.v.*). To put the watch in beat after altering the length of the balance spring, the whole device is moved. Invented by the makers of Incabloc (*q.v.*). A, The index; B and C, Roller gripping balance spring; D, Stud, to guide superfluous balance spring; E, Movable plate to put watch in beat after regulation. Can also be used to obtain correct pinning point in positional timing. *See* " Practical Watch Repairing."

INCISED ORNAMENT. *See* Antique Clock Case Terms.

INCLINED PLANE CLOCK. A drum clock which, rolling down an inclined plane, provided the motive power. No mainspring is used but, usually a weighted piece is attached to the arbor of the centre wheel; to " re-wind," the whole clock is lifted to the top of the incline. Attributed to Nicholas Grollier in the latter part of the seventeenth century.

INDEPENDENT SECONDS. A seconds hand driven by a separate train but controlled by the timekeeping train. There are exceptions but, usually, the independent seconds hand beats seconds; the independent train terminates with a pinion carrying a pin or " flirt " which engages in the leaves of the escape wheel pinion and allows the secondary train and its seconds hand to jump forward each second.

INDEX. Also termed the Regulator; that part of a watch or clock to which the index pins are fitted, controlling the active length of the balance spring. *See* Nomenclature of Watch Parts, page 280.

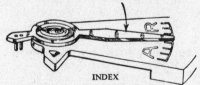

INDEX

INDEX PINS. The pins or Boot (*q.v.*) and one pin, which embrace a coil of the balance spring (*See* Index) and Curb Pins.

INDEX PLATE. The dividing plate used in the lathe for wheel cutting, etc.

INDIA OIL STONE. Artificial oilstone composed of grains of aluminium oxide cemented together to form a solid block. Made by Morton Abrasives Co., U.S.A. There are three grades, coarse, medium and fine, depending on the size of the grains. The medium grade is suitable for rough grinding of broken or very worn gravers and slide rest cutters. The fine grade is not fine enough for finishing watchmakers' gravers and other tools which require Arkansas or Turkey Stone (*q.v.*). India stones are used with oil in the ordinary way. The same type of stone, known as Aloxite is made by Carborundum Co., Manchester.

INDIAN TIME. Five and a half hours fast of G.M.T.

INDICTION. A cycle or period of 15 years, introduced by Constantine as a fiscal term.

INDUCTANCE. The property of an electrical conductor or circuit which tends momentarily to oppose the initial current flow, and the cessation, or any change of current. Also applied to apparatus as a general name. *See* Inductor.

INDUCTOR. Any electrical apparatus such as a coil, choke, or any conductor designedly possessing a high or requisite degree of inductance. Generally referred to as an Inductance (*q.v.*).

INERTIA. The inability of a body to change its state of rest or uniform motion without external influence.

INFUSIBLE. Said of any body or substance apparently impossible to melt.

INGOLD FRAISE. A form of rounding-up cutter for correcting the form of wheel teeth. Invented by Pierre Frederic Ingold (1787–1878). Now superseded by the Rounding-up or Topping Tool Cutter (*q.v.*).

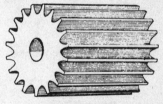

INGOLD FRAISE.

INLAYING. *See* Antique Clock Case Terms.

INNER TERMINAL. Usually refers to the inner coil of the balance spring where it is secured to the balance spring collet; especially when the shape or curve of the coil is of the theoretically correct form.

INSIDE SHAKE. The freedom of the escape wheel of the lever escapement when a tooth is locked by the exit pallet stone and the lever so placed that the tooth which has just left the Entry stone is not free to be moved backwards past the discharging corner of the entry pallet, *i.e.*, when the pallet stones embrace the full number of escape wheel teeth possible, usually three teeth. Also refers to the freedom of an escape wheel tooth inside the cylinder of the Cylinder Escapement (*q.v.*).

LEVER ESCAPEMENT.

CYLINDER ESCAPEMENT.

IN STEP. In phase; Synchronous (*q.v.*).

IN THE WHITE. *See* ANTIQUE CLOCK CASE TERMS.

IN VACUO. In a Vacuum (*q.v.*).

" INSTANTANEOUS " VELOCITY, DIRECTION, ETC. In diagrams representing the action of linkage mechanism and the like, the velocity, direction, etc., as the case may be, appertaining at a particular instant, as distinct from the average velocity, direction, etc. during an operating cycle.

INSULATOR. Any substance or material which is substantially unable to permit a flow of electric current. Also termed a Dielectric Insulant. Any device, usually of resinous or vitreous material, for the purpose of insulating an electrical conductor. Of recent years special forms of ceramic and plastic materials have been developed for this purpose.

INTARSIA. *See* ANTIQUE CLOCK CASE TERMS.

INTEGRAL BALANCE. Another name for the Guillaume balance (*q.v.*).

INTERCHANGEABLE. Usually refers to material, or spare parts, of a watch or clock which may be used without alteration. The type of watch or clock movement based on mass production of interchangeable parts.

INTERMEDIATE WHEEL. The wheel which engages with the minute wheel of a keyless watch for the purpose of setting the hands. *See* page 281.

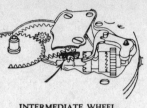

INTERMEDIATE WHEEL.

INTRADOS. *See* ANTIQUE CLOCK CASE TERMS.

INVERTED BELL TOP. *See* ANTIQUE CLOCK CASE TERMS.

INVOLUTE. The curve traced by a point on a flexible line or cord which is kept straight or taught and unwound from a circle or cylinder.

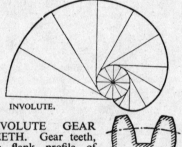

INVOLUTE.

INVOLUTE GEAR TEETH. Gear teeth, the flank profile of which, consists of an involute curve.

INVOLUTE GEAR TEETH.

ION. An atom or molecule of an element modified by having more or less than its normal or stable number of Electrons (*q.v.*).

IONISED. Conversion into an ion by the loss of an electron.

ISOCHRONOUS. " Moving in equal time," *i.e.*, when a watch keeps the same time whatever the extent of the arc of vibration of the balance. Hence, if a watch keeps accurate time when fully wound and at any period throughout its going until the mainspring is unwound, it is said to be isochronous. In practice this is almost an impossibility. In a clock, when the extent of the arc of the pendulum is constant, it is isochronous.

ISOVAL. *See* METALS USED IN HOROLOGY.

IVES' WAGON-SPRING CLOCK. *See* Wagon Spring Clock. *Also* ANTIQUE CLOCK CASE TERMS.

J

JACKS. *See* Striking Jacks.

JACOBEAN STYLE. *See* ANTIQUE CLOCK CASE TERMS.

JACOB'S CHUCK. A chuck in which the jaws are opened or closed by turning a geared key. Usually used as a drill chuck.

JACOT DRUM. An accessory used in the lathe for the purpose of polishing pivots.

JACOT TOOL. A tool used by watchmakers for burnishing pivots, etc.

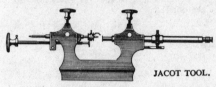

JACOT TOOL.

JARDINIERE. *See* ANTIQUE CLOCK CASE TERMS.

JAWS. Another name for Chops (*q.v.*). Also the gripping surface or part of a vice, or holding tool.

JEWEL HOLE. *See* Jewelled ; Jewels, Loose; Jewels, Friction; Jewels, Set. *Also* WATCH PART NOMENCLATURE.

JEWEL HOLE GAUGE. A steel plate having a graduated series of holes to determine the inner diameter of a hole to suit a particular pivot. Some plates are themselves fitted with jewel holes. A needle gauge is used to determine the inner diameter of the hole.

JEWELLED. A term used in horology to define bearings or holes and surfaces made from jewel stones. Until recent years the jewels were made from natural stones, *e.g.*, Ruby, Sapphire, and in lower grade work, Garnet. To-day, synthetic stones are used. The term " fully jewelled " generally refers to a movement fitted with a minimum of 15 jewels, *i.e.*, top and bottom jewel holes to the third, fourth, and escape wheels, pallet and balance staffs; endstones to the top and bottom balance pivots; two jewel pallet stones and a jewel pin.

JEWEL HOLE GAUGE.

JEWELS, LOOSE. Refers to the system of jewelling watches, etc., usually associated with English work. The jewel is " set " into a brass ring or collet, which is then held in position by screws.

JEWELS, LOOSE.

JEWELS, FRICTION. Jewel holes, etc., which are held in position by friction. They are " forced " or pressed into position as distinct from the " set " or rubbed-in jewel. *See* " Practical Watch Repairing " for method of fitting. *See* Jewel Setting Tool.

JEWELS, SET. Jewel holes, etc., which are " set " or " rubbed in " to hold them in position.

SWISS STYLE.

ENGLISH STYLE.

JEWEL SETTING TOOL. A development of the Staking Tool (*q.v.*) with punches and stakes for setting friction-held jewels.

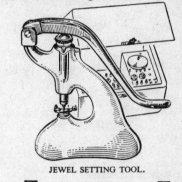

JEWEL SETTING TOOL.

HAND TOOL FOR RUBBED IN SETTINGS.

JIG. An appliance used for guiding parts into position during assembly. Also a form of tool used in producing interchangeable parts.

JIG BORER. A machine tool of very high precision, largely used in the production of prototypes. It accurately locates the position for holes and then forms the holes by Boring (*q.v.*) with practically no tolerance.

JOCKELE CLOCK. Any small Black Forest clock. The name derives from Jacob Herbstrieth of Hinterzarten, who, in about 1780 began making miniature clocks about 3 in. high, and 1¼ in. deep. Jockele is a diminutive form of Jacob. It is pronounced " yockeler."

JOCKEY PULLEY, WHEEL, OR SPRING. A device fitted to a belt drive to preserve a constant tension on the driving and driven pulleys. In the case of the spring form, also known as a Spring Tensioner. Another application aims at preventing backlash in a freely moving part by providing a friction brake in the form of an idle pulley or wheel.

JOHANSSON BLOCKS. *See* Gauge Blocks.

JOINT. The horologists' name for a hinge, *i.e.*, the joints or hinges of a watch case.

JOINT FILE. A file used by watch-case makers for filing the recess to receive the charniere forming the joint. Teeth are cut on the rounded edges only.

JOINT PUSHER. A tool used for the removal of pins from the joints of watch cases, etc.

JOINT
FILE.

JOINT PUSHER (1).

A

JOINT PUSHER (2).

This tool (2) is spring loaded; it is secured in a vice and the end A is given a sharp blow with a hammer.

JOULE. A unit of energy equivalent to 10^7 Ergs. It is the energy represented by the flow of a current of one ampere, across a potential difference of one volt, in one second.

JOULE EFFECT. The heating effect of a current passing through a conductor.

JOULE'S LAW. The heating effect of a current I, passing through a conductor of resistance R, for a period T, is directly proportional to $I^2 R T$.

JUBILEE MARK. An additional punch on silverware to the hallmarks of the years 1933–4, 1934–5, and 1935–6 of all the Assay Offices as a tribute to the Silver Jubilee of the reign of H.M. King George V. Suggested and pioneered by the late Arthur Tremayne and described fully and illustrated in " Hallmarks and Date Letters". Silverware bearing this punch is known as " Jubilee Silver " and has considerable scarcity value. *See* Hall Mark.

JULIAN CALENDAR. The civil calendar based on a tropical year of 365·25 days instituted by Julius Caesar in 45 B.C. The basis of our calendar but modified by the Gregorian reform. (*See* Gregorian Calendar.)

JUMPER. A spring so shaped that it causes a piece to jump or move suddenly. As for instance the counter wheel of a chronograph or the star wheel carrying the hour snail in a French carriage clock; the wheel with star-shaped teeth is made to advance part of the way under the

PIVOTED JUMPER.

SPRING JUMPER.

influence of direct drive and the jumper causes it to complete its action suddenly. Also refers to a spring-operated lever which performs a similar action.

JUMPING DIAL. A dial which is advanced one division at a time, or as many as may be determined, by an instantaneous or semi-instantaneous mechanism. Also the name given to a watch in which the hours, minutes, and seconds are displayed on separate circular dials. The hour and minute divisions are viewed through

JUMPING DIAL.

narrow apertures in the solid case front. By a jumping action, the hour and minute dials are advanced on the sixtieth second of the hour and minute—or as nearly as the action will allow. The seconds dial usually rotates continuously, being in fact a calibrated circular hand. It may, however, rotate anti-clockwise to preserve the correct sequence in numbering or the dial may be calibrated in reverse. Both wrist and pocket types are met with but are not generally popular at the present time.

K

KARRUSEL. A revolving escapement, more robust and slower moving than the Tourbillon (q.v.). Invented by Bonniksen in 1893–4. The whole escapement including

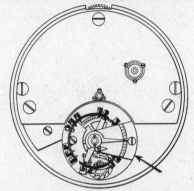

KARRUSEL.

(in the case of the lever escapement) the escape wheel, lever and balance, is arranged on a carriage which is driven by the third wheel at the rate of, in one calibre, about 1 revolution in 40 minutes. In another, the carriage is driven by the fourth wheel at the rate of 1 revolution in 39 minutes. The purpose of these escapements, as of all Tourbillon escapements, is an endeavour to solve the problem of vertical positional errors.

KEEL MOULDING. See ANTIQUE CLOCK CASE TERMS.

KERF. See ANTIQUE CLOCK CASE TERMS.

KETTLE FRONT. See ANTIQUE CLOCK CASE TERMS.

KEW. The official tests of watches were originally conducted at the Kew Observatory near Richmond, Surrey. This work is now carried out at the National Physical Laboratory, Teddington, but the name "Kew" remains in association with these tests. A Kew "A" certificate refers to a certificate issued by the N.P.L. for a watch which has passed stringent tests as specified by the laboratory. The "B" certificate permits greater tolerances of performance. Since March, 1951, the Kew "A" Certificate system has been abolished and in its place the following has been substituted. The Test is now known as "Craftsmanship Test for Time-of-Day Watches." All watches are submitted to the same tests but the tolerances are graded 1a, 1b, 1c, 1d; the grade 1a being the more severe. The specification reads, "Very few watches are expected at present to fall into grade 1a in all respects but most watches which would have been able to pass the N.P.L. (Kew) Class A test would satisfy at least the Grade 1d tolerances." See WATCH TESTING STANDARDS.

KEY. In horology, the word usually applies to the key to wind the mainspring, especially of a watch. Strictly, the term " winder " is more correct since a key is " an instrument for moving the bolt of a lock forwards or backwards " and, when speaking of clocks and chronometers the word can be confusing since some clocks and most chronometers are provided with locks needing keys.

KEYLESS. The ability to wind up the mainspring without the use of a key. Usually refers to a watch which is wound by a button or crown. Sometimes a clock which has the key permanently attached to its square is spoken of as being " keyless."

KEY-WIND. A term usually used to distinguish between watch movements of the (older) type requiring a key to wind the mainspring and those of the keyless type. There is a tendency in the lay mind to confuse Key-wind and Keyless movements with a question of quality, i.e., to the detriment of the Key-wind. As a rough and ready distinction, in the general run of watches this may serve but it should be borne well in mind by all who handle movements in any number that some of the finest examples of the watchmakers' craft extant are to be found in the Key-wind category.

KIDNEY PIECE. A cam, similar in shape to a kidney, used in clocks denoting the difference between Greenwich Mean Time and Solar Time; the difference is called the Equation of Time.

KIDNEY PIECE.

KIF. A shock resisting system; made by Parechoc S.A., Le Sentier, Switzerland.

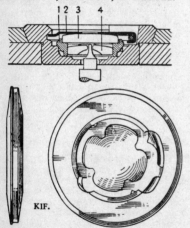

KIF.

KINETIC ENERGY. The energy possessed by a moving body by reason of its mass and the rate at which it is travelling.

KIRCHOFF'S LAWS. Two fundamental laws concerning the currents and voltages in electrical circuits. (1) At any point in a network, the sum of the currents flowing towards that point is always equal to the sum of the currents flowing away from it. Alternatively, that the sum is zero. (2) In any closed circuit or in a network, the sum of voltages dropped across each of the conductors is equal to the sum or total of the electromotive force applied to the circuit. In conjunction with Ohm's Law (q.v.) the values of currents, voltages and resistances in a complicated series and/or parallel circuit can be resolved and calculation errors, etc., quickly detected.

KNEE PUNCH. A crank-shaped punch used for removing plugs from cylinders of the horizontal escapement.

KNEE PUNCH.

KNIFE FILE. See Files.

KNOCKING THE BANKING. A term referring to the Lever and Horizontal escapements when, due to an excessive arc of vibration of the balance, the impulse pin in the Lever escapement knocks the back of the lever notch; and, in the Horizontal escapement, the banking pin on the balance knocks the banking in the balance cock. In both cases the " knocking," (also referred to as " banking ") causes a gaining rate.

KNUCKLES. The parts forming the joint of a watch case, which are soldered to the cover. In a three-knuckle joint (the minimum) two knuckles (tubes or chenier) are soldered to the cover and one chenier to the middle or main part of the case. A five-knuckle joint has three soldered to the cover and two to the middle. See PARTS OF THE POCKET WATCH CASE, page 79.

KNURLING TOOL. A tool consisting of a hardened and tempered steel wheel having serrations or a pattern on its periphery. Used for impressing serrations or a decorative pattern by holding the tool hard against the work which is revolved.

KNURLING TOOL.

KOOSEN'S CLOCK. An electric clock invented in 1862 by Koosen. Consisted of a small electric motor controlled by a sensitive governor of the centrifugal type which actuated a switch. By this means the speed of the motor was almost uniform, the circuit being alternately opened and closed; the spindle of the motor was geared to the wheel work of the clock.

KULLBERG'S BALANCE. Invented by Victor Kullberg in the latter part of the nineteenth century. An auxiliary Compensation (q.v.) Balance.

KULLBERG'S BALANCE.

L

LACQUER. A protective covering for metals. Shellac dissolved in methylated spirit is used to lacquer brass parts such as clock plates, etc. Cellulose solutions are used to lacquer watch and clock dials and silverware. Also a kind of varnish made from a resinous exudation of the " Varnish Tree " used by the lacquerers of Japan and China as a form of decoration on woodwork.

LAMINATE. *See* ANTIQUE CLOCK CASE TERMS.

LAMINATIONS. The shaped metal stampings, usually of " electrical steel " such as Stalloy, etc., from which the magnetic circuit of motors, generators, chokes, transformers, etc., is built up, with the object of reducing losses.

LAMINATED MAGNETS. (*a*) A permanent magnet consisting of a number of magnetised strips. (*b*) A laminated core used in electromagnets designed for use on A.C. supplies.

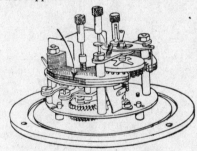

LAMINATED MAGNETS.

LANCET. *See* ANTIQUE CLOCK CASE TERMS.

LANTERN CHUCK. A device in which a screw or similar piece can be held so that its end projects through the chuck so that it can be worked upon. Used in the lathe, or by hand, as in the Screwhead Tool (*q.v.*).

LANTERN CHUCK.

WATCH LANTERN CHUCK.

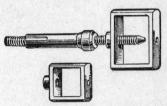

CLOCK LANTERN CHUCK.

LANTERN CLOCK. *See* ANTIQUE CLOCK CASE TERMS.

LANTERN PINION. A pinion head or " leaf " formed of wire pins—known as trundles—held between two circular plates. There are variations of the application as for instance, pins secured to the centre of a wheel with no plate or cap, the pins jutting out from the wheel surface.

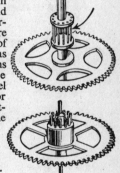

OPEN END LANTERN PINION.

LANTERN RUNNER. The runner used in the jacot tool, lathe or turns; a perforated disc is so arranged that the ends of pivots projecting through can be polished, etc. Used in conjunction with Eccentric Runner (*q.v.*).

LANTERN RUNNER.

LAP. A tool used for polishing; usually consisting of a wheel-like disc made to revolve in some form of lathe. Can be used to obtain dead flat surfaces, *e.g.*, the ends of the headsofscrews, arbors, etc., or, with a shaped lap, to form balance staff pivots, etc.

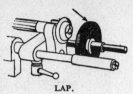

LAP.

Laps are made of metal, such as iron, or bell metal, or boxwood and charged with an abrasive or polishing powder. Laps are also used by gem stone cutters, an operative being termed a lapidary.

LATARD THREAD. *See* Martin Screw Plate.

LATCH OR LACHED PLATES. *See* ANTIQUE CLOCK CASE TERMS.

LATHE. A tool or machine devised to give circular motion to work to enable it to be fashioned or turned. The generally accepted definition refers to the machine tool such as the Boley, Webster-Whitcombe, Pultra, Lorch, etc., lathes. The watch and clockmakers' lathes are essentially precision tools. Turns operated by a bow and any tool which causes work to revolve for turning is, strictly speaking, a lather.

POLE LATHE. A type of lathe used by watch-case makers: consists of a lathe head operated by a cord passing round a driving pulley, one end being attached to a form of treadle, the other to the end of a long pole or rod secured above the lathe in a horizontal position, thus providing a spring like action allowing a backward and forward movement to the work similar to the action obtained with a bow; it also enables work to be rotated through an arc less than a full circle which facility is sometimes required in watch-case work. *See* " The Watchmaker's Lathe " published by N.A.G. Press.

LATITUDE. The imaginary lines of demarcation of the earth's surface running parallel to one another from east to west or west to east. The angular distance of a place north or south of the equator measured along the meridian. Lines (imaginary) drawn round the earth's surface parallel to the equator are called parallels of latitude.

LATTICE. *See* ANTIQUE CLOCK CASE TERMS.

LEAD (Electrical). A term used for any wire (single, twin, or multiple) carrying electric current between points. Also Phase (*q.v.*) relationship.

LEAD (Horological). The continuous action by which the tooth of a wheel impels the leaf of a pinion and causes it to turn through an arc of its rotation. In the case of a worm of helical gear, the length measured in the direction of the axis in which the helical twist is 360°.

LEAD (Mechanics). (*a*) The difference in phase or time by which one mechanical action is in advance of a second consequent or separately initiated action. (*b*) The chamfer, groove, or lip, etc., formed to assist or guide the correct mating or locating of pieces fitting or acting together, *e.g.*, die lead.

LEAD-ACID ACCUMULATOR. The widely used form of accumulator employing lead, etc., plates and an electrolyte of dilute sulphuric acid (*cf.* Hickel-Iron Accumulator).

LEAF OF PINION. The leaves are to the pinion as the teeth are to the wheel but, w h e r e a s a wheel remains a wheel without teeth, a pinion must have leaves or an equivalent such as pins. *See* Lantern Pinion.

LEAF OF PINION.

LECLANCHÉ CELL. A primary voltaic cell. A positive pole of carbon is surrounded by a packing of manganese dioxide and powdered carbon contained in a porous pot. This stands in a solution of sal-ammoniac contained in a glass jar. A zinc rod also placed in the jar forms the negative pole. The cell develops an E.M.F. of approximately 1·5 volts. In the above form, the cell is unsuited to continuous usage. In another form however—the well-known Dry Batteries which, electrically, are essentially the same—the cells are widely used for many purposes.

LEFT HAND SCREW. Where the screw is turned to the left to screw it up. Modern left hand screws usually have a slot cut on each side of the centre slot.

LEFT-HAND SCREW.

LEFT PALLET STONE. *See* Exit Pallet.

LENTICULAR BOB. *See* Bob.

LENTILLE GLASS. *See* ANTIQUE CLOCK CASE TERMS.

LENZ'S LAW. A fundamental law stating that the direction of electric currents induced in a circuit as a result of a change in the interlinkages between the circuit and a magnetic field is such as to oppose the change of interlinkages. *See* " Chambers Technical Dictionary."

LEPAUTE WATCH-BEAT RECORDER. This instrument employs the tuning fork controlling device. The performance of the watch is recorded permanently and a graph is burnt into a strip of paper by a spark. All watch beats can be observed by changing a disc.

LEPAUTE'S ESCAPEMENT. A " pin wheel " escapement for clocks invented by Lepaute about 1752.

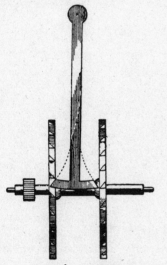

LEPAUTE'S ESCAPEMENT.

LEVER. A rigid bar, rod, or beam supported at one point called the fulcrum about which the rod can be turned. There are 3 orders or systems of the lever:—
(1) The fulcrum between effort and load.
(2) The load placed between fulcrum and effort.

1ST ORDER.

2ND ORDER.

(3) The effort applied between fulcrum and load.

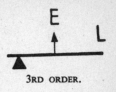

3RD ORDER.

In horology the term " lever " is used in a general sense to denote the various forms of lever escapement. Of the escapement, it is that part conveying the impulse from the pallets to the balance and conversely the unlocking action from the impulse pin to the pallets.

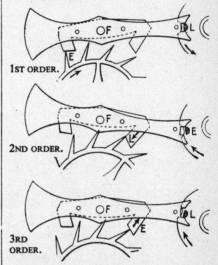

1ST ORDER.

2ND ORDER.

3RD ORDER.

The English type lever employs mechanically the 3 orders of the lever:—First order —impulse on entry stone; Second order— unlocking on exit stone. Third order— impulse on exit stone. With the straight line lever escapement the first order only is employed,

LEVER ESCAPEMENT. The escapement invented by Thos. Mudge in 1759. Deriving its name from one of the component parts which acts as a lever. It is claimed by some authorities that the lever escapement was invented by Hautefeuille in 1722 (*see* Rack Lever Escapement) and that Mudge invented a " roller and lever " action. The action of the escapement is as follows: The escape wheel rotates in direction as arrow; the escape wheel tooth A is locked on the pallet B. The ruby pin C, fixed to the roller D, which is rotating in the direction as arrow, engages in the notch E and moves the lever F to the right. The tooth A is unlocked and the wheel slides

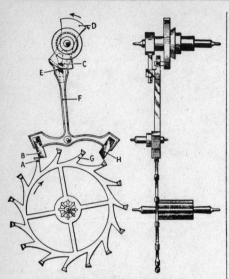

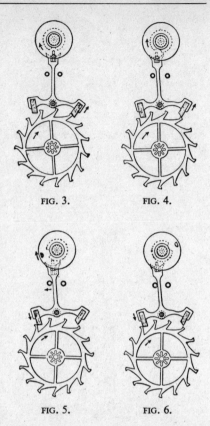

FIG. 3.   FIG. 4.

FIG. 5.   FIG. 6.

DOUBLE ROLLER CLUB TOOTH LEVER
ESCAPEMENT (STRAIGHT LINE).

along the impulse face of the pallet B and
so gives impulse to the balance through the
impulse pin, the roller D is fixed to the
staff to which the balance is also fixed. The
tooth G drops on to the pallet H and the
escape wheel is thus arrested. Upon the
return journey of the balance the tooth G
is unlocked and so the cycle is repeated.
The escape wheel of this escapement has
a slight recoil. Fig. 1. Escape wheel is
locked by right hand pallet. Fig. 2. Ruby
pin unlocks escape wheel. Fig. 3. Escape
wheel gives impulse to balance. Fig. 4.
Escape tooth drops off right hand pallet.
Fig. 5. Escape wheel is locked by left hand

pallet. Fig. 6. Escape wheel draws lever
to banking pin and holds it there until it is
unlocked again. The Club Tooth lever
escapement is the form in popular use
to-day. The Ratchet Tooth form was the
immediate predecessor. *See* English Lever.

LEVER NOTCH. *See* Fork.

LIFT. Refers to the angle of the impulse
faces of the pallets
of the lever escape-
ment. Sometimes
used to designate
the impulse angle or
the angle of total
engagement, *i.e.*,
lock, run, and active
impulse.

LIFTING HOOD. *See* Hood, ANTIQUE
CLOCK CASE TERMS.

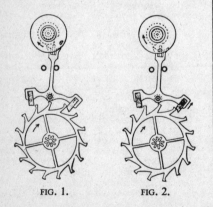

FIG. 1.   FIG. 2.

LIFTING PIECE.

The piece in striking and chiming mechanism used to release the train and allow it to operate.

LIFTING PIECE.

LIGHT CLOCK.

A clock fitted with a lever escapement and driven by a mainspring. The mainspring is wound by a motor through a train of wheels and the motor is powered by light. The system employed is the photo cell. Patented and made by Patek Philippe of Geneva, Switzerland. It is pointed out that the photo-cell, similar to the human eye, is most sensitive and its prolonged exposure to too strong (natural or artificial) light rays can injure it. The security margin is however substantial, up to 5,000 lux and 60° C. (= 140° F.). It is calculated that the clock will go for 24 hours if exposed to a mean illumination for 4 hours and when the mainspring is wound fully it will go for 3 days in full darkness.

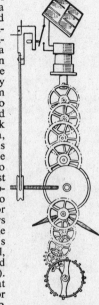

LIGHT CLOCK.

LIGHTS. A term used when referring to the freedom of the teeth of the escape wheel of the chronometer or detent escapement with the impulse roller. When the escape wheel is locked and in such a position that the edge of the impulse roller is between two teeth, the distance of the teeth from the roller should be equal. It is then said that the "lights are equal."

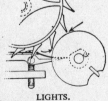

LIGHTS.

LIGNE. A unit used in the measurement of watch movements. It is 1/12 French inch *i.e.* 2·256 mm. The size of a watch movement is referred to as " so many lignes," *e.g.*, 8¾''' lady's size or 18''' gentleman's pocket size, etc. The three small strokes (''') are the accepted symbol for ligne.

LIGNUM VITÆ. *See* WOODS FOR CLOCK CASES.

LIMB. Refers to the segment of a cut balance, *i.e.*, the rim into which the timing and temperature screws are fitted.

LIME. Killed lime. Very efficacious for drying purposes, *e.g.*, after a balance has been cleaned in cyanide, washed in water, and brushed dry, it should be placed in lime for about an hour to ensure all moisture is removed. Also used in the storage of steel balance springs and highly finished steel parts. In recent years Silica Gel has been used for the purpose of storing steel-work. It is in the form of crystals, and placed in a linen bag, absorbs moisture, " the dehydration of air."

LIME, VIENNA. *See* Vienna Lime.

LIMED OAK. Oak treated with lime to give it a whitish-grey finish.

LIMIT GAUGE. A gauge so made as to afford means of checking that the dimensions of a part are within specified limits. Usually in a double ended form marked " Go " and " Not Go."

LIMIT OF ELASTICITY. When a material or substance has been stressed so that it fails to resume its original form, it is said to have been stressed beyond its limit of elasticity, or to have become " set."

LIMITING FRICTION. The frictional force between two surfaces when movement between them is just commencing. It is equal but opposite to the force applied to produce the movement. After slipping has occurred, the value reduces. Hence, to maintain slipping, a lesser force is required and this value, which just maintains the movement, is known as the Kinetic limiting friction. (*cf.* Coefficient of Friction).

LINE. In a fusee clock: the medium through which the power of the mainspring is transmitted to the fusee. In a weight-driven clock: the line by which the weights are supported. Made either of Gut (*q.v.*) or strands of wire twisted together. In regulators, the line is often made of silk or specially woven linen cord. Another term for Ligne (*q.v.*). A unit of magnetic flux measurement. One line is equivalent to one Maxwell (*q.v.*). One line per cm² is equivalent to one Gauss (*q.v.*).

LINE OF ACTION. Said of the direction or line in which a force acts.

LINE OF CENTRES. A line drawn from centre to centre, *i.e.*, of a wheel and the pinion it engages; a line drawn between the centre of the pallet staff hole and balance staff hole. The pallet is thus described as moving so many degrees upon either side of the " line of centres."

LINE OF THRUST. A straight line passing through the point of contact between a pair of mating teeth which lies upon the common normal to the two mating curves when friction is absent, and lies at an angle, whose tangent equals the coefficient of friction, to the common normal when friction is present. The term " line of action " is sometimes used for the line lying upon the common normal, so that the term " line of thrust " may be reserved for the condition in which friction is present.

LINEAR. A mathematical or functional relationship between two quantities such that one is directly proportional to the other for all values. A desirable feature in many mechanical actions, but difficult to attain without some complication. Applied to scales having equidistant divisions, particularly measuring and electrical instruments, gauges, etc.

LINEAR TIME BASE. *See* Time Base.

LION'S MASK AND RING HANDLES. *See* ANTIQUE CLOCK CASE TERMS.

LIP. The curved edge of the cylinder in the horizontal escapement on which the escape wheel teeth act giving impulse. The projection fitted to the cover of a watch case to facilitate opening.

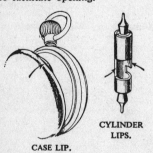

CASE LIP.   CYLINDER LIPS.

LISTEL. *See* MOULDINGS.

LITHERLAND'S ESCAPEMENT. A rack and pinion lever escapement invented by Litherland in 1792. *See* " Rack Escapement."

LITZENDRAHT WIRE. An electrical conductor built up from a number of fine wires each separately insulated and thus providing parallel paths. Used in high frequency circuits to reduce losses. Commonly spoken of as " Litz " wire.

LIVE. Refers to an electrical circuit or any conductor connected thereto in which there is a current flowing or from which, by virtue of a potential, a current would flow if a further connection or contact were made to another point of different potential. An earth or neutral point is not generally considered a " live " point but it can so become and, in Cathode Ray Tube work, may be at a high voltage above the tube's negative supply. All parts of any electrical circuit should be assumed live, especially in relation to Earth (*q.v.*), until proved otherwise.

LIVE CENTRE. Where the centre rotates, *e.g.*, the head stock of the lathe. Distinct from the " Dead Centre " (q.v.) which remains stationary.

LOBSTER CLAW ESCAPEMENT. Invented by Antoine Tavan in 1804 and so named because of its similarity to the claws of a lobster. The action of this escapement is as follows:—The balance with its spring

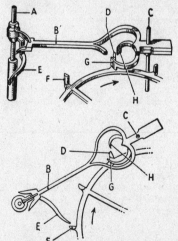

LOBSTER CLAW ESCAPEMENT.

is attached to the staff A and rotating anti-clockwise the lever B pivoted at C, is moved to one side and the tooth D is released by the claw like device, the escape wheel moves forward and the impulse pallet E is in such a position as to receive impulse from the tooth F. The tooth F then drops on to the outside of the claw at G and is locked there until the balance returns and the tooth escapes between the two claws. The face of the inner claw at H is then ready to receive the next tooth. The balance receives impulse in one direction only. This escapement has the combined action of the lever, to unlock; the cylinder, to lock; the duplex, to give impulse.

LOCAL TIME. The mean Solar Time at any particular place: the time that would be shown by observations at that place. A point 1° east of Greenwich would have a " local time " 4 minutes ahead of G.M.T. The mean solar, sidereal, or apparent solar time at an observer's position, as distinct from the Standard Time (q.v.) for the area reckoned from a meridian chosen for that area. Local apparent solar time is the time as indicated by a sundial correctly set for the latitude of its position.

LOCATING PIN. A pin or stud projecting from the surface of a part and mating with a hole, slot, etc., in another part to ensure the correct positional relationship. Sometimes, a loose rod, accurately machined, employed to locate a number of pieces during assembly or machining. It may be permanent or temporary. Pins which add rigidity to the piece such as bridges, cocks, etc., are referred to as Steady Pins (q.v.).

LOCKING. That part of the pallets of the lever escapement which arrests the progress of the escape wheel and locks or holds it there until released. The jewel stone fitted on to the detent of the chronometer escapement which holds the escape wheel until released. Locking also refers to position—when the escape wheel drops on to the face of the pallet of the Anchor and Dead Beat escapements and the cylinder of the Horizontal escapement; in these cases the term is a loose one since the escape wheel is not actually locked but merely arrested. It is sometimes called the " rest " or " resting face " in these escapements.

LOCKING PLATE. Also known as the Count Wheel. It is the wheel which determines the number of blows to be struck in striking mechanism. It has been superseded in modern domestic striking

clocks by the Striking Rack (q.v.) but is still used in turret or tower clocks and in domestic chiming clocks to determine the number of quarters to be chimed.

LOCKING SPRING. See Case Spring.

LOCUS. The path described by a point constrained to move to certain conditions.

LONGCASE CLOCK. The original and better definition of a Grandfather Clock (q.v.). The discrimination in the terms lies in the fact that, strictly, there is no particular form of longcase clock which can be described as a grandfather clock. See PERIODS OF LONGCASE CLOCKS, page 38.

LONGITUDE. The imaginary lines of demarcation of the earth's surface radiating north and south from the poles, and dividing the globe into 360°, each degree being equivalent to 4 minutes of time. The angular distance of a place east or west of Greenwich. Specifically, the angular distance of the meridian of any point east or west of the meridian of Greenwich (see Meridian). The angle is measured on a parallel to the equator, i.e., on a parallel of latitude.

LORMIER. See Corona, ANTIQUE CLOCK CASE TERMS.

LOSSES. A term referring to the percentage of energy in mechanical, electrical, and chemical transformations which is absorbed or given out without performing work or contributing to the exchange. The physical limitation preventing the complete exchange of all available energy or the building of a 100% efficient machine.

LOSSIER CURVE. The theoretical inner and outer terminals of a Breguet balance spring. Designed from a formula evolved by L. Lossier.

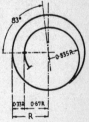

LOTUS. See ANTIQUE CLOCK CASE TERMS.

LOSSIER CURVE.

LOUPE. See Eye Glass.

LOW LOSS. A term applied to certain plastic and ceramic insulation materials used especially where high frequency currents are involved.

LOW RELIEF. See ANTIQUE CLOCK CASE TERMS.

LOZENGE FILE. *See* Files.

LUBRIFIX made for the same purpose as FIXMOBIL (*q.v.*) but the end stones are made of jewel only. Made by Seitz, Les Brenets, Switzerland, the makers of Rubyshock (*q.v.*). *See* Giracap.

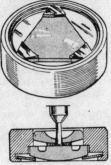

LUBRIFIX.

LUGS. The rounded extension pieces incorporated in cocks or similar fitments, often accommodating pivot or screw holes. Also the wires of "loops" attached to, or extensions integral with, the case of a wrist watch by which the strap, clip, bracelet, band or other fixing is attached.

LUMINOUS. A dial of a watch, clock or instrument in which the figures or divisions and the hands are rendered luminous by painting with a radium compound. The standard of brightness is measured in terms of Equivalent Foot Candles (E.F.C.).

LUMINOUS PAINT. In horology it refers to the radium compound, *see* Luminous.

LUNATION. A lunar or moon month. Approximately 29 days, 12 hours, 45 minutes.

LUNAR WORK. The mechanism of a watch or clock which shows the phases of the moon.

LUNETTE GLASS. *See* Styles of Watch Glasses, page 139.

LYRE CLOCK. *See* Antique Clock Case Terms.

M

MACHINE. In mechanics, any arrangement which enables force to be transmitted which will either overcome a greater resisting force or will allow the force to be applied in a more convenient way.

MACHINE CLEANING. *See* Cleaning Machines.

MAGNET. A part or an essembly of parts which exhibits magnetism in one form or another. A mass of steel or special alloys in bar, horse-shoe, or circular form which has been magnetised. Called a Permanent Magnet.

MAGNETIC. Any material which is capable of exhibiting or reacting to magnetism.

MAGNETIC ALLOYS. Alloys of metals, capable of accepting a very high degree of magnetism. Such as Permalloy, Mu-metal, Silicon-Iron, Nickel Alloys, Cobalt.

MAGNETIC ESCAPEMENT. An escapement employing magnetic, etc., materials, in which impulse and locking are effected solely by the magnetic coupling between the components. Patents have been taken out by Baker (America), Straumann (Swiss, in Germany). In 1948 a patent was granted to C. F. Clifford, of Bath, for a magnetic escapement as illustrated here. It is silent, very efficient, and may be constructed in various forms. Essentially, the action is based upon the sinusoidal locus or path traced by any point " P " in an oscillating system (such as a pendulum), projected upon the surface of a uniformly rotating cylinder lying horizontally behind the pendulum in the same plane, or level, as " P " (Fig. 1). The escape wheel may consist of a disc of high permittivity material such as Mumetal (*q.v.*) having its circumference pressed into sine-wave form. This is driven normally by weight or spring, the power being low enough to avoid " breaking " of the magnetic lock. This escape wheel is positioned in the same plane as an annular magnet in the form of a yoke or stirrup, to which the normal suspension spring and pendulum rod are attached. (*See* Fig. 2.) The escape wheel thus turns within the " tunnel " swept by the magnet ring as the pendulum vibrates. Two internal

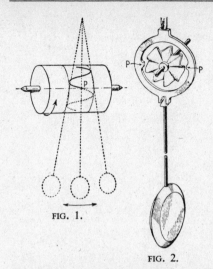

FIG. 1.

FIG. 2.

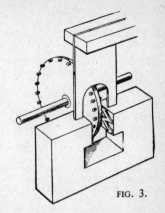

FIG. 3.

and diametrically opposite poles (P) are formed in the magnetic ring and are thus presented to the escape disc's edge, with a suitable clearance space. The Mumetal disc thus affords a ready " return " path for the magnetic flux between the poles, and if stationary, acts much as a keeper, tending to restrain any movement of the pendulum. Alternatively, if the escape wheel turns, the magnet poles will be influenced to follow the path of the escape wheel edge as it moves across the pole faces. At the limit of vibration the pendulum pauses before reversal and momentarily " locks " the escape wheel, as in the stationary position. The escape wheel, however, being under a drive, slightly leads the pendulum. Thus the return vibration of the poles follows the succeeding wave edge rather than " recalling " the edge already traversed. The escape wheel thus advances beat by beat, locking at each vibration limit but impulsing the pendulum during the whole of the remaining action. Another and very efficient form of the escapement is illustrated, a discontinuous sine wave being here formed on the pole faces of a " U " shaped magnet and the escape disc replaced by a non-magnetic wheel carrying short Mumetal rods which complete the magnetic circuit and follow the sine wave track in a similar manner to that described above (Fig. 3). A reed of predetermined periodicity may replace the pendulum. This applies to the latest portable forms, but its efficiency is not high compared with the pendulum version. A feature of the escapement is that strong external fields have no apparent effect

upon it and that it may be dismantled without serious magnetic losses. Due to the absence of any mechanical contact in the escapement itself, lubrication and frictional losses are eliminated.

MAGNETIC FIELD. The region in space around any kind of magnet within which its influence may be detected. Particularly the region (usually limited) in which the field affects other apparatus, sometimes undesirably.

MAGNETIC FLUX. Quantitatively determined as the product of:—(a) The density of the field in imaginary Lines-of-force (q.v.); (b) The area, taken at 90° from the direction of the field, over which the field acts. See Gauss.

MAGNETISED. A general term applied to a watch excapement, etc., in which the steel parts such as lever, roller, balance cross arm, balance spring, have been subjected to magnetism affecting the escapement action.

MAGNETISM. A term denoting the presence of a magnetic field.

MAGNETISING FORCE. Another term for Magnetic Force. It is the measure of the force exerted at a point in a magnetic flux. Symbol H.

MAGNETOMOTIVE FORCE. A magnetic flux in a magnetic circuit produced by a current carrying coil.

MAINS CLOCK. A term sometimes used to denote the " Synchronous Motor Clock " (q.v.). The term is coined from the fact that the clock is driven and controlled by power from the mains. Alternating current supplies in Britain are controlled at 50 cycles (50∿) per second and, by reason of its construction, the motion of the clock is synchronised with the frequency of the A.C. mains.

MAINSPRING. The main or principal spring of a watch or clock or other spring driven mechanism; the driving force, as distinct from any other springs, such as operate levers, etc. A reliable method of determining the thickness of the spring of a watch mainspring for a particular barrel, is to divide the diameter of the barrel arbor by 32 for a high grade movement; by 30 for a medium grade, and by 28 for a low grade. Another method is to divide the inside diameter of the barrel by 100, that is, the thickness of the mainspring should be $\frac{1}{100}$th part of the inside diameter of the barrel. The $\frac{1}{100}$ is an approximate measurement and is a little too large. This rule is based on (1) the $\frac{1}{32}$ of barrel arbor, and (2) arbor $\frac{1}{3}$ inside diameter of barrel (approximately). Therefore $\frac{1}{32} \times \frac{1}{3} = \frac{1}{96}$, i.e., spring is $\frac{1}{96}$ of inside diameter of barrel. It will be observed that $\frac{1}{96}$ is for a fine quality movement, so to take $\frac{1}{100}$ is to fit a spring a little too weak. A useful method to determine the length of the spring is as follows:—for the average 30 hour watch where 5½ to 6 turns of the barrel arbor are required, the inside diameter of the barrel can be divided into three parts; one (C) to be occupied by the barrel arbor, one (B) empty spare (when the spring is unwound), and the third (A) by the mainspring. The mainspring should occupy a little less than $\frac{1}{3}$ as the illustration shows. Both these methods apply to watch movements only, they do not necessarily apply to clock movements. Americans term it the " Motor Spring." For table of mainsprings, see below, also see page 276.

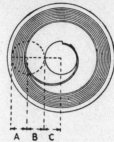

MAINSPRING PROPORTION
IN BARREL.

MAINSPRING GAUGE. A gauge used to measure the height of mainsprings and known as the Martin gauge. The measurements are purely arbitrary. For conversion table showing Martin gauge to mm. See table. Another mainspring gauge is one used to measure the thickness or strength. A Pivot Gauge (q.v.) is usually used for this purpose. The Micrometer Gauge (q.v.) is also a useful gauge to measure both the height and strength of mainsprings.

MAINSPRING GAUGE.

MAINSPRING GAUGE HEIGHTS AND METRIC EQUIVALENTS			
Martin or Geneva Height	mm.	Martin or Geneva Height	mm.
4/0	0·85	12	2·15
3/0	0·95	13	2·20
2/0	1·05	14	2·30
0	1·15	15	2·40
1	1·25	16	2·50
2	1·35	17	2·55
3	1·40	18	2·60
4	1·50	19	2·70
5	1·60	20	2·80
6	1·65	21	2·90
7	1·70	22	2·95
8	1·80	23	3·00
9	1·90	24	3·10
10	1·95	25	3·20
11	2·05		

MAINSPRING GAUGE FORCES AND METRIC EQUIVALENTS			
Martin or Geneva Force	mm.	Martin or Geneva Force	mm.
21	0·06	6	0·21
20	0·07	5	0·22
19	0·08	4	0·23
18	0·09	3	0·24
17	0·10	2	0·25
16	0·11	1	0·26
15	0·12	0	0·27
14	0·13	2/0	0·28
13	0·14	3/0	0·29
12	0·15	4/0	0·30
11	0·16		
10	0·17		
9	0·18		
8	0·19		
7	0·20		

MAINSPRING PUNCH. *Top.* To punch holes in mainsprings. *Lower.* To punch the hook in watch barrels and to punch holes in mainsprings.

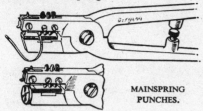

MAINSPRING
PUNCHES.

MAINSPRING, UNBREAKABLE. *See* Vimetal.

MAINSPRING WINDER. A tool made for the purpose of winding the mainspring into its barrel. Made for both clocks and watches.

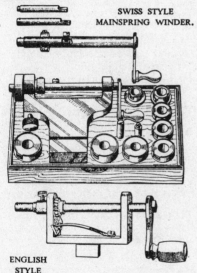

SWISS STYLE
MAINSPRING WINDER.

ENGLISH
STYLE

MAINTAINING POWER. The mechanism to maintain the driving power while the weight or mainspring with fusee is being

WATCH MAINTAINING
POWER.

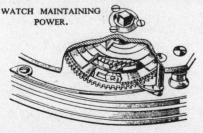

rewound (in which operation the main power is off). The mechanism of a fusee watch or clock which keeps the mechanism going during rewinding. There are spring and weight operated forms. Without maintaining power, the train of a fusee or weight driven mechanism reverses when the power of the mainspring or weight is taken off during winding. *See* Bolt and Shutter, also Huygens Endless Rope.

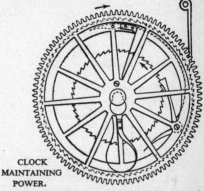

CLOCK
MAINTAINING
POWER.

MAIN WHEEL. The first wheel in a watch or clock. Of a fusee mechanism, the wheel attached to the fusee, also referred to as the " Great Wheel." In a going barrel it is the wheel attached to and forming part of the barrel, *i.e.*, the barrel is the main wheel. *See* Great Wheel.

MAKE BEFORE BREAK SWITCH. A multi-way switch so designed that any circuit change through it is made before an existing circuit is opened.

MALLEABILITY. The quality of a material which allows it to be hammered or rolled out into thin sheets or plates.

MALTESE CROSS. *See* Stop Work.

MANDREL OR MANDRIL. A face-plate fitted with " dogs " or clips to hold work during turning, fitted to a lathe, or as a separate self-contained tool. In engineering a mandrel is a bar set between centres to mount tools or work.

MANDREL
OR
MANDRIL

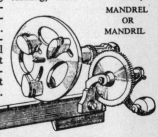

MANIVELLE ESCAPEMENT. A form of Virgule escapement (*q.v.*), invented by Lepaute (1720–1789).

MARBLES AND ORNAMENTAL STONES

SUITABLE FOR THE MANUFACTURE OF CLOCK CASES

ADNETER ROT LIENBACHER. A pink marble with deep red patches fringed with black. (Austria.)

AGATE. A type of quartz having a micro-crystalline structure and with the general name of Chalcedony; the term *agate* is usually used for the banded varieties. Used as a form of decoration and also as a bearing or friction surface, *e.g.* V bearings as used in compasses, pallet stones in clocks, etc.

ALABASTER. A massive variety of the mineral *gypsum* (calcium sulphate). Usually white with veins of darker colours, but may be yellow, orange, brown, grey, or if heavily mottled, black. Rather soft but may harden with age. Unlike true marble this material does not effervesce if touched with acid. The most common sources are Derbyshire and Tuscany in Italy. Much employed for the cheaper ornamental stone clock cases.

" ALGERIAN ONYX." A translucent stalagmitic calcite with mahogany ribbon-like markings. It is not a true onyx, which is a variety of quartz. (Algeria.)

ALSTON. A deep black marble spotted with light grey patches. It is not a true marble but is a coralline limestone. (England.)

AMARANTHE D'OSSERAIN. A dark violet marble with dark green and brown patches. (France.)

" APUAN ONYX." A coloured semi-translucent marble. Not a true onyx. (Italy.)

ASHBURTON DARK. A dark grey marble with red and white patches. It is a fossil limestone, not a true marble, and takes a high polish. (England.)

BALLACHULISH. A white marble with dark grey mottled patches. (Scotland.)

BARDILLA. One of the Italian coloured marbles. Dove-coloured with slightly darker parallel veins running through the mass.

BELGIAN BLACK. A deep black limestone taking a high polish, which is found in the Ardennes district of Belgium. From this material are made the cheaper black marble clock cases.

BIRD'S EYE. A dark grey to medium brown marble with grey fragments of fossil crinoids, the sections sometimes resembling a bird's eye. It is a fossil limestone and takes a high polish. (England.)

BLACK MARBLES. *See* Alston; Belgian Black; Dent Black; Galway Black; Irish Black; Noir de Sable; Plymouth Black; Radford.

" BRAZILIAN ONYX." A white semi-translucent stalagmitic calcite with faint gold-coloured veinings. Some varieties are a green colour. (Argentina.)

BRÈCHE MÉDOUX. A rich deep orange marble with black, white, grey, yellow and brown markings. (France.)

BROWN MARBLES. *See* Bird's eye; Rosewood.

BYZANTINE. A rose-coloured marble, sometimes showing broad green bands. (Canada.)

CAMPAN ROSE. A variegated marble largely built up of calcareous nodules, giving an almond-shaped mottling. It is pink and white in colour and shows green and white veinings. CAMPAN ROUGE and CAMPAN VERT are similar marbles with a red or green general colour respectively. (France.)

CANADIAN BLUE STONE. *See* Sodalite.

CARRARA. A white crystalline marble, some of which has a few grey lines running through it. (Italy.)

CIPOLLINO. A green marble of varying shades with wavy bands of white and pale green markings. The name was early applied to material found in Greece, but the name is now used for similar material from Italy; Canada; Switzerland and the United States.

CONNEMARA. A serpentinous marble variegated with white and various shades of green. (Ireland.)

CONVENT SIENA. A rich orange marble

MARBLES—Cont.

with purple and black veins. Used for period work. (Italy.)

CREAM MARBLES. *See* Hopton Wood; Skyros.

DENT BLACK. A deep black marble. Occasionally fossil shells and corals are found in it. Not a true marble but a fossil limestone. (England.)

DERBY FOSSIL. A medium-grey colour marble with longitudinal and transverse markings. It is a fossil limestone which takes a high polish. Also known as Monyash Marble. (England.)

DUKE'S RED. A deep blood-red marble of great beauty. Taking a high polish it is one of the handsomest, and one of the rarest of English marbles. The red colour is due to iron oxide. (England.)

ENGELSBERGER. A bright red marble with white patches. (Austria.)

FAWN MARBLES. *See* Grey Ipplepen; Orsera.

GALWAY BLACK. A deep black marble. (Ireland.)

GIALLO DI MORI. A bright yellow-orange marble with light and dark sinuous veinings. It is a compact limestone taking a high polish. (Austria.)

GIBRALTAR STONE. A stalagmitic calcite found in the limestone caves at Gibraltar. It is brown with amber coloured sinuous veinings which give it an attractive appearance when polished.

GREEN MARBLES. *See* Campan vert; Cipollino; Connemara; Green Poppenberg.

GREEN POPPENBERG. A fawn-coloured marble tinted with green and marked with a network of dark green veins and red threadlike markings. Sometimes known as ALLAGEN MARBLE. (Germany.)

GREY IPPLEPEN. A light grey to fawn marble with white veins and slender red markings. (England.)

GREY MARBLES. *See* Ashburton; Bird's eye; Derby Fossil; Hopton Wood; Kingsteignton; Little Belton; Skye.

HOPTON WOOD. A marble (Fossil limestone) varying in colour from light cream to dove grey containing fossil shells and encrinites. Takes a high polish. (England.)

INCA ROSE. *See* Rhodochrosite.

IONA STONE. A serpentinous marble, usually of green colour, but may be yellow or white with indigo veins. The material is similar to Connemara marble by varies more in shade. (Scotland.)

IRISH BLACK. A pure black marble. (Ireland.)

IRISH WHITE. *See* Pinka Grenna.

JADE. The term jade is used for two well-defined minerals which may have a similar shade of green colour. Nephrite, from Turkestan, Siberia, New Zealand and the United States, varies in shade from dark green, through spinach green to a greenish white, the latter being termed mutton fat jade. The dark green New Zealand material is the so-called Maori jade or New Zealand greenstone. The more highly prized jadeite, mostly from Upper Burma, varies from an emerald green to white, the latter often showing patches of green. Jadeite is often found in shades of lilac, brown, bluish, mauve, black and tomato red. These colours are rarer. The jades are simulated by a number of other natural minerals, such as some serpentine; and the massive varieties of green garnet and idocrase.

JASPER. Correctly an impure quartz which is usually of a brown colour, but may be green, red or yellow. Often has the colour variegated or in bands. Much harder than the marbles and does not effervesce with acids. The name JASPER is also misapplied to a red limestone from Vermont, U.S.A.

JASPER STONE (JASPER MARBLE). A rich crimson marble with veins of a darker shade. A stone of great beauty. (Wales.)

JAUNE ST. BEAUME. A mottled white and yellow marble with red thread-like markings. (France.)

" JAVA ONYX." Stalagmitic carbonate o lime which may be dull white in colour or variegated with wavy and ribboned amber-coloured bands. (Java.)

KINGSTEIGNTON. A light pinkish-grey fossiliferous limestone which is profusely marked. (England.)

LAASER. A white crystalline marble. (Austria.)

LABRADORITE. A variety of feldspar which shows, when polished in certain directions, broad flashes of colour, which

MARBLES—Cont.

may be green, purple, orange, blue and red. The colours being due to reflective interference of light.

LANGUEDOC. A fiery red marble with red markings. (France.)

LAPIS LAZULI. A hard compact rock of various shades of blue, some being azure while others are darker. Owing to its rarity it is classed as a gemstone. Usually used as a veneer on a base of some other stone, such as slate. Found in Central Asia and Chile. Often contains spangles of iron pyrites which look like specks of gold.

LITTLE BELTON. A pink and grey marble mottled with slender red markings, also another variety, yellow, pink and grey, mottled with white veins. (England.)

MALACHITE. A beautiful green mineral, carbonate of copper, resembling agate in texture. It owes its name to the Greek word *mallow*, the colour of the mineral being similar to that of the mallow leaf. The material is rather fragile and is usually employed as an inlay or as a veneer. Owing to its contrasting colour it is often used as an inlay in conjunction with " Brazilian onyx " in ornamental clock cases. Malachite is found in copper mines of Russia, South Australia, The Belgian Congo, Rhodesia and the U.S.A.

MALLORCA. A red marble with white and green markings. (Spain.)

MARBLE. Strictly, marble is a crystalline rock consisting of granular crystals of calcite; *e.g.*, the white statuary marbles of Carrara. The term is used, however, for those limestone rocks which take a high polish and are attractively veined and coloured. A third group, *onyx marble*, is a micro-crystalline calcite deposited from waters heavily charged with lime, forming stalagmitic and stalagtitic deposits. They form some of the most beautiful of the marbles; *e.g.*, " Brazilian onyx." All marbles effervesce when touched with acid.

MONYASH MARBLE. *See* Derby Fossil.

" MOROCCAN ONYX." A stalagmitic calcite. The body colour may be deep red; white with golden-coloured veins; blue-grey with green ribboned veinings, or with a delicate pink ground. (Morocco).

NOIR DE SABLE. A handsome black marble with white veins. (France.)

ONYX. A banded variety of chalcedony (agate). It is a crypto-crystalline variety of quartz.

ONYX MARBLE. A stalagmitic calcite (marble) often showing banding and coloured veinings. Unlike alabaster, some of which can appear similar, onyx marble is harder and also effervesces when acid is put on it. Examples of onyx marble are the so-called " Brazilian onyx "; " Algerian onyx "; etc., and Gibraltar stone.

" ONYX NUAGL." An onyx marble of a light amber colour with white cloudy patches. (Algeria.)

OPHICALCITE. A green or yellow serpentinous calcite; *e.g.*, Connemara marble and Iona stone.

ORANGE MARBLES. *See* Convent Siena and Brèche Médoux.

ORSERA. A light fawn-coloured marble. (Austria.)

PARIAN. A lustrous, delicate, sub-translucent true crystalline marble, whitish in colour. It is the famous Grecian statuary marble. (Greece).

PINKA GRENNA. An almost white marble of Connemara type in which the green patches are also tinged with pink. It is a variety of Ophicalcite. (Ireland.)

PINK MARBLES. *See* Adneter; Byzantine; Campan Rose; Kingsteignton; Little Belton; Red Petitor, Skye.

PLYMOUTH BLACK. A deep black marble with white veins. (England.)

POJIZONAZZO. A bright red marble with brown and white markings. (Germany.)

PORPHYRY. A rock of volcanic origin which contains large crystals of feldspar. There are two distinct kinds—the green and the red. The green porphyry from Greece has a dark olive-green ground-mass, with light green feldspathic crystals sprinkled abundantly through it. The red porphyry from Egypt is similar except that the ground mass is red and the feldspar crystals are light pink or white in colour.

PURBECK MARBLE. (Paludina limestone). A fossiliferous limestone containing myriads of fossil shells of a fresh water snail. It is brown or grey in colour. (England.)

RADFORD. A nearly black marble with white veins. (England.)

MARBLES—Cont.

RED IPPLEPEN. A red and grey marble with light pink veinings. (England.)

RED MARBLES. *See* Duke's red; Engelsberger; Jasper stone; Languedoc; Mallorca; Pojizonazzo; Red Ipplepen; Red Ogwell.

RED OGWELL. A marble varying from light to dark red with grey and white veins and marking. Takes a high polish. Handsome in appearance. (England.)

RED PETITOR. A mottled red and pink marble. (England.)

RHODOCHROSITE. A rose red manganese carbonate mineral showing banding in browns, pinks and white, due to its stalagmitic formation. Used for inlays to give contrasting colour effects with the white onyx marbles. Trade names are " Rosinca " or " Inca Rose." Effervesces with acid.

RHODONITE. A rose-red coloured manganese silicate. Unlike the carbonate (rhodochrosite) it is not banded and also often shows black markings of manganese oxide which are not seen in rhodochrosite.

ROSÉ DES ALPES. A light yellow marble with thin red markings. (France.)

ROSÉ ST. GEORGE. A light yellow semi-crystalline marble with floral rose-pink markings. (France.)

ROSÉ VIF. A reddish-brown marble with pink and white patches. (France.)

ROSEWOOD. A dark brown marble with parallel reddish veins. Takes a high polish and is similar in appearance to the wood—rosewood. Of great beauty and rarity. (England.)

ROSINCA. A trade name for rhodochrosite.

" ROUGE AGATE " A rich crimson onyx marble with white, pink, amber and purple present to form a mottled appearance. (Algeria.)

ROUGE GRIOTTE. A brilliant red marble. (Belgium.)

ROUGE JASPÉ ANTIQUE. A brilliant red marble with broad orange streaks. (France.)

SARDONYX. A red and white banded chalcedony (quartz) consisting of layers of red cornelian or sard and white chalcedony

SERPENTINE. A green magnesium silicate mineral, some varieties of which simulate the jades. The material most commonly met with in the larger ornamental stone work is the impure rock serpentine which occurs so extensively at the Lizard, Cornwall. This rock serpentine is usually mottled in different shades of green, may display veinings of brownish-red, white, purple, and black. Some varieties are mainly red with the other colours as veinings or patches. When serpentine is disseminated in crystalline limestone, ophicalcite results; *e.g.*, The Connemara marbles.

SKYE. Various marbles of this name; greyish-violet with white veins; pure white; delicate pink; dove colour. (Scotland.)

SKYROS. A semi-translucent cream marble with dark cream to brown veins. (Greece.)

SODALITE. A mottled bright-blue rock-like mineral similar in appearance to lapis lazuli, to which it is closely related. Unlike true lapis lazuli, sodalite never shows bright gold-like specks of pyrites. It is used as an inlay in conjunction with the light coloured onyx marbles, or even by itself, in clock cases. In the clock case trade the material is often known as Canadian blue stone. (Canada.)

THULITE. A rose-pink variety of the mineral zoisite which makes a handsome ornamental stone. The pink ground colour is marked with white patches and veins of dark grey. It is used as an inlay to give a contrasting colour. (Norway.)

" UTAH ONYX." A translucent onyx marble with a bright lemon yellow colour with orange veins. (Utah, U.S.A.).

VEINÉ DORÉ. A light orange crystalline marble. (Italy.)

VERDE ANTICO (Verde antique). A brecciated serpentine with small patches of calcite. It is debated whether the material is a true serpentine or an ophicalcite. In appearance it may be likened to Connemara marble. (Greece.)

VERDE MOULIN. A violet and pink marble with light green and white veins. (Spain.)

VERDITE. A rich green stone often marked with yellow or orange spots or patches. Although rather soft it is used as a contrasting material in conjunction with

MARBLES—Cont.

light-coloured marbles such as " Brazilian onyx." (S. Africa.)

VERT D'ESTOUR. A white marble with the ground almost covered with light green markings. (France.)

VILLAFRANCHE VIOLET. A number of violet or reddish-violet coloured marbles are found in the Villafranche quarries, Pyrénées-Orientales, France. They have a violet ground through which run white calcite veins.

VIOLET MARBLES. *See* Amaranthe d'Osserain; Villafranche Violet.

VIOLETTO DI BROCAT. A white marble with dark purple veins. (Italy.)

WHITE MARBLES. *See* Carrara; Laaser; Parian; Skye; Violetto di Brocat.

WHITE PENTELIC. A white crystalline marble with faint grey veins. (Greece.)

" YAVA ONYX." A green coloured onyx marble often with amber-coloured veinings. (U.S.A.).

YELLOW CLOUDED PETITOR. A yellow marble with numerous small pink veins giving a mottled appearance. (England.)

YELLOW MARBLES. *See* Giallo di Mori; Rosé des Alpes; Rosé St. George.

YELLOW SIENA. A light yellow marble with transparent veins. (Italy.)

MARINE CHRONOMETER. *See* Chronometer.

MARTIN MAINSPRING GAUGE. *See* Mainspring Gauge.

MARTIN SCREW PLATE. Martin is the original name of the manufacturer of the screw plate and in no way indicates the pitch of the thread. Old threads still met with are Bourgeaux, and Latard, the Latard thread being the finer of the two. Bourgeaux has 26 numbers, ranging from 00–24 and Latard 21 numbers from 0–20. They cover a range from approximately 2·25 mm. down to ·3 mm. Original plates marked Latard or Bourgeaux still extant. Modern Swiss plates are usually Perrelet et Martin, or Martin Fils, and plates by these makers marked " B " correspond to Bourgeaux and marked " L " to the Latard thread. Plates marked " S " have very fine threads intended for Swiss barrel arbors. Left-hand thread plates by all makers are marked " G " (Gauche). Sizes of these old Swiss threads are not standardised or tabulated. *See* Progress Thread.

MARQUETRY. *See* ANTIQUE CLOCK CASE TERMS.

MASK. *See* ANTIQUE CLOCK CASE TERMS.

MASS. The amount of matter in a body.

MASTER CLOCK. A term usually referring to the main clock of an electrical impulse time-keeping system.

MASTER OSCILLATOR. An oscillator, usually fork or crystal controlled, which determines the operation of all other circuits and apparatus associated with it, especially control of frequencies.

MATCHING. A term used by the old English lever watch escapement makers to define the operation of selecting a pair of pallets to suit the escape wheel.

MATERIAL. A term used for the spare parts of a watch or clock. A " Material Dealer " is a vendor of spare parts. *See* facing page for Swiss Standardisation of Supplies.

MATRIX. *See* MARBLES AND ORNAMENTAL STONES.

MATT FINISH. Where the surface of metal is finished with a matted or " grey " surface; such as would be left after using oilstone dust and oil or sand-blasting.

MATTING. *See* ANTIQUE CLOCK CASE TERMS.

MAXWELL. The unit of magnetic flux (*q.v.*). 1 Maxwell = 1 line of force (*q.v.*).

MEAN DAILY RATE. The sum of the daily rates for a given period divided by the number of days in the period.

MEAN VARIATION OF DAILY RATE. This is calculated as follows. The mean daily rate is first determined for each of the periods of a watch or chronometer test. The differences between the mean rate and the actual rate are then found for each period. Finally, these differences are added together and the sum divided by the total number of days in the test. The quotient is the mean variation of daily rate.

STANDARDISATION OF SUPPLIES OF WATCH
MATERIAL

(*See* also WATCH PART NOMENCLATURE, page 275.)

Swiss manufacturers vary in their schemes of standardisation of identification numbers for convenience of ordering spare parts, but the most comprehensive has been introduced by the " Watch Makers of Switzerland ". The numbers given with the illustrations in the following pages, Nomenclature of Watch Parts, and Nomenclature of Chronograph Parts, are the official numbers for those particular parts.

The first figure of a number indicates the section of a watch to which the part belongs, *i.e.*,

100 onwards:	Frame and barrel.
200 ,, :	Wheels and pinions.
300 ,, :	Regulating device and plates.
400 ,, :	Winding and setting mechanisms.
550 ,, :	Special material for date and calendar mechanisms.
600 ,, :	Jewels and end stones.
650 ,, :	Bushings.
700 ,, :	Lever escapement.
780 ,, :	Cylinder escapement.
790 ,, :	Pin pallet escapement.

Screws for any part have the number of that part preceded by the figure 5, *e.g.*, pull-out piece 443; pull-out piece screw 5443.

Special material for alarm watches and clocks has four figure numbers beginning at 7000.

Chronographs and stop watch parts begin at 8000, recording chronograph with hour recorder parts at 8600, and recording chronograph with split seconds at 8800.

Parts of automatic watches are not considered to be special and are included under the ordinary three figure numbers.

◆

MEAN TIME. *See* Greenwich Mean Time.

MEASURING MACHINE. A machine similar to the Jig Borer (*q.v.*) but " pin points " a measurement accurately. To ensure absolute accuracy such machines are sometimes kept in rooms of an even temperature. Sometimes called a Pointing Machine.

MECHANICAL ADVANTAGE. The ratio between work performed by a machine and the force required to work the machine.

MEDALLION. *See* ANTIQUE CLOCK CASE TERMS.

MEGOHM. Unit of high resistance. Equivalent to 1,000,000 Ω. Values of 500,000 and 250,000 are usually spoken of as " $\frac{1}{2}$ meg," " $\frac{1}{4}$ meg."

MERCER'S BALANCE. An auxiliary compensation balance invented by Thomas Mercer (1822–1900).

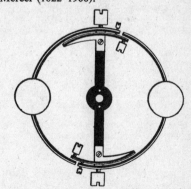

MERCER'S BALANCE.

MERCURY. *See* METALS USED IN HOROLOGY.

MERCURY SWITCH. A switch where the fixed contacts are mercury cups into which the moving contacts dip. Also, where mercury is contained in a tube which can be tilted causing the mercury to bridge the contacts, as employed in the Craig Free Pendulum (*q.v.*).

MERCURIAL PENDULUM. In broad terms, a pendulum the bob of which consists of a glass jar or some metal container holding a quantity of mercury which compensates the elongation of the pendulum rod due to changes in temperature. Invented by Geo. Graham in 1721.

MERIDIAN. The imaginary longitudinal lines drawn on the earth's surface intersecting at the poles. It is from the Greenwich meridian that all meridians calculations are made. *See* Latitude and Longitude.

MESH. A term used to denote the intersection or engagement of gear wheels.

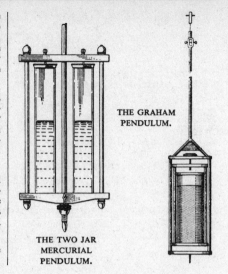

THE GRAHAM
PENDULUM.

THE TWO JAR
MERCURIAL
PENDULUM.

METALS USED IN HOROLOGY

ALLOY. A mixture or compound of a metallic element with one, or more, metallic (or sometimes non-metallic), elements, *e.g.*, Brass is an alloy of the metals copper and zinc; Steel is an alloy of the metal iron with the non-metal carbon.

ALLUVIAL GOLD. Gold found in sand or gravel, etc., as distinct from the gold found in ore. Usually present in the form of granules or scales, sometimes referred to as gold dust.

ALUMINIUM. A metallic element. This metal is little used in horology other than as containers for the transport of watch movements, and other boxes. *See* Elinvar.

AMERICAN GOLD. This metal has a higher percentage of copper in its alloyed state when compared with the English gold alloys. The presence of copper accounts for the red colour, much appreciated in S. America. Also known as red gold.

ANTIMONY. A metallic element. Little used in horology other than as a washer or gasket in waterproof watch cases. Also used for making cheap clock cases.

ARGENTAN. Nickel or German Silver, sometimes used in the manufacture of watch cases.

BELL METAL (or Hard Bronze). An alloy of copper and tin. Used as the bearings for turret clocks and also useful as a polishing medium when used with diamantine.

BERYLLIUM ALLOYS. The metal beryllium is white in colour and is one of the lightest metals known. When alloyed with other metals it is one of the most valuable alloys for the manufacture of balance springs introduced into horology. Under the trade name of Nivarox beryllium is alloyed with iron, cobalt, copper, etc., and from this alloy balance springs are made which give astounding results. It is harder than Elinvar (*q.v.*) and enjoys the same physical properties; it is non-magnetic, non-rusting; elasticity is little affected by changes in temperature. *See* page 60 for table giving data concerning Nivarox.

BI-METALLIC. When two dissimilar metals are either fused or riveted together. Used, among other purposes, to make watch and chronometer balances, where brass is fused to steel or nickel-steel.

BLUE STEEL. The name given to steel which has been hardened and tempered to a blue colour. Blue steel is usually worked in its tempered state; it is not first softened and then hardened and tempered after fashioning.

BRASS. An alloy of copper and zinc. Common brass consists of 2 parts copper and 1 part zinc.

METALS—Cont.

BRAZING. Soldering with brass instead of say, soft, or gold, or silver solders. Sometimes used by clock repairers when repairing a steel part.

BRONZE. A similar metal to brass with the addition of a small percentage of tin in its alloy. Used in the manufacture of clock case, and ornaments. *See* Phosphor Bronze.

CARBON STEEL. Steel is an alloy of iron and carbon, so the term carbon steel is another name for steel.

CHROMIUM. Metallic element of steely grey colour; largely used as a plating metal.

CHROME STEEL. By the addition of chromium to steel during manufacture, the steel is given a quality enabling it to be made extremely hard. Used in horology by manufacturers for machine tool cutters.

COPPER. A metallic element. Used in horology as the base for enamelled dials; the co-efficient of expansion of copper and vitreous enamel are similar, so the risk of the enamel cracking during cooling is minimised.

ELINVAR. An alloy of 36% nickel, 12% chromium, plus small quantities of carbon, manganese and tungsten and the remainder iron. Elinvar was invented by Dr. Chas. Guillaume in 1913. The name is derived from " Elasticity Invariable." It has the inestimable quality of possessing a practically invariable elastic modulus in ordinary temperatures. Used in horology for the manufacture of balance springs. Melior, Melius, Parelinvar, Metelinvar, Durinval, and X.A.M., are the proprietary names of grades of Elinvar with the addition of other metals, not disclosed, but including one or more of the following:—

MOLYBDENUM—Metallic element; does not readily oxidise and when alloyed with iron or steel renders it hard without being brittle.

TITANIUM—Metallic element; toughens steel when alloyed with it.

VANADIUM—Metallic element; alloyed with steel it increases its hardness and malleability.

ALUMINIUM—Metallic element; alloyed with steel it has deoxidising powers and in certain conditions confers non-magnetic properties.

GERMAN SILVER. An alloy of copper 60%, zinc 20% nickel 20%. Also known as Nickel Silver.

GILDING METAL. An alloy of copper and zinc, similar in appearance to gold. Used for low priced watch cases, etc. Originally known as Pinchbeck, named after its clockmaker inventor.

GLUCEDOR (GLUCYDUR). The French name for Beryllium Alloy (*q.v.*).

GLUCINUM. The original name for the metal BERYLLIUM. The name Glucina was given to the oxide of beryllium by Vauquelin in 1797 owing to the sweet taste of some of its salts—and glucinum for the metal, which was not isolated until 1828 (by Wöhler). The term beryllia and beryllium, for the oxide and the element (metal) respectively are now used almost exclusively. *See* Beryllium Alloy.

GOLD. Metallic element. Used in horology in an alloyed state. The standard of pure gold is 24 carats. Alloyed with other metals to standards of 22, 18, 14 and 9 carats, the four standards recognised by law in England, *i.e.*, of the 24 carats, 18 carats are pure gold and 6 carats other metal and this constitutes 18 carat gold. Used in horology principally for the cases of watches, etc., subject to Hall Mark (*q.v.*). The Continental method of marking gold is: 18ct. ·750, 14ct. ·585, 9ct. ·375, *i.e.*, ·750 pure gold and ·250 other metal, etc.

GUNMETAL. An alloy of copper and tin. Used in horology as bearings for turret clocks. " Gunmetal " watch cases (so called) are made from steel, chemically treated to make black, blue or brown. They are not, as a rule, made of gunmetal.

INVAR. An alloy of nickel and steel. Preceded Elinvar (*q.v.*), and invented by the same man. Similar properties to Elinvar, but is much softer. Derives its name from Invariable.

IRON. Metallic element. Little used in horology in its unalloyed state. Useful as a medium with oilstone dust for grinding steel work and as a polishing medium when used with diamantine.

ISOVAL. The chief defect of the " self-compensating " balance springs hitherto in use is that they all tend to make watches lose considerably in the short arcs as compared with the longer vibrations. M. Dubois has succeeded in developing an alloy which he has named Isoval; it is free from this defect, and claims that by the use of springs of this alloy, isochron-

METALS—Cont.

ism can be realised over much wider variations of arc than has been possible before. The thermal compensation is claimed to be as good or better than that obtained with any other type of spring. Isoval springs are non-magnetic and inoxidisable. Their normal colour is white, but they can be blued so as to resemble tempered steel.

LEAD. Metallic element. Used in horology as the filling of weights for weight-driven clocks and as filling of some pendulum bobs.

MAZAK. An alloy of zinc, copper, aluminium and magnesium. Used in horology as a Hot Pressing, for the barrels, including the gear teeth, of clocks. Although comparatively soft it possesses good wearing qualities.

MELIOR. See Elinvar.

MELIUS. See Elinvar.

MERCURY. Metallic element. Used in horology as a means of compensating the pendulum for changes in the temperature. Also used in gilding, known as mercurial gilding.

METELINVAR. A grade of Elinvar (*q.v.*) an alloy of:—

Carbon	0·6%	Tungsten	3%
Manganese	2%	Molybdenum	1·5%
Nickel	40%	Iron	46·9%
Chromium	6%		

In addition to the properties of Elinvar, it has the quality of giving similar results over a wider range of temperatures. (*See* page 60 for table of properties.) Used in horology for balance springs.

MOLYBDENUM. See Elinvar.

MONOMETAL. One metal. In horology it usually refers to the balance when made of one metal only, as distinct from the balance made of steel and brass: even if a balance is made of steel and brass but uncut it is referred to as a monometal balance. Balances which in themselves do not compensate for changes in temperature, are in effect, monometal. *See* Balance.

MUMETAL. An alloy of nickel, iron and copper; of high magnetic permeability.

NICKEL. Metallic element. Used in horology mainly in alloys for the manufacture of watch cases.

NICKEL STEEL. *See* Invar.

NIVAROX. A proprietary name given to an alloy of iron, beryllium (*q.v.*), etc., used in the manufacture of balance springs. *See* page 60 for table giving properties.

PALLADIUM. Metallic element, of the platinum group. Now little used in horology. Formerly, before the introduction of the new non-magnetic metals, was employed for the manufacture of balance springs in conjunction with the cut compensation balance in non-magnetic watches. Also used for chronometer balance springs owing to its corrosion resistance.

PARELINVAR. *See* Elinvar.

PERMALLOY. An alloy of nickel and iron. After suitable heat treatment develops a high magnetic permeability. *See* Supermalloy.

PHOSPHOR BRONZE. An alloy of copper, tin and a small percentage of phosphorus. A hard, fine-grain metal. similar in appearance to brass and used in horology to make escape wheels, levers and rollers. Especially suitable for non-magnetic watches.

PINCHBECK. *See* Gilding Metal.

PLATINUM. Metallic element. Principally used in horology for the manufacture of watch cases, when it is alloyed with iridium to make it hard. Minute quantities also used to make timing screws for watch balances.

RADIUM. Metallic element. Used in horology in the manufacture of luminous compounds.

RED GOLD. *See* American Gold.

RHODIUM. Metallic element. Used in horology as a form of plating, principally for plating diamond set watch cases; owing to its peculiar whiteness it adds lustre to diamonds; untarnishable.

ROLLED GOLD. A thin layer of gold rolled on to a base metal, *i.e.*, a plate of base metal with a layer of gold on each side. Used in horology for the manufacture of watch cases; usually marked 5, 10, 15 or 20 years, meaning that the gold on the case should wear for the number of years marked. In Switzerland there is a federal law which enforces the description and quality of rolled gold, also the use of the words " rolled gold " or " plaqué or " the letter L attached to the term, if the article is made from laminated gold sheet

METALS—Cont.

and the letter G if a galvanic or gilding process is employed. The vital portions of the Swiss Act are contained in the following extracts:—Watch cases and other manufactured articles bearing the description Gold Plated or Rolled Gold, or simply Plated or Rolled, or any other similar description in any language, with or without a guarantee of the duration of the plating, must be covered with a gold leaf resisting the action of nitric acid at 25° Baume, used at a temperature of 15° to 20° (minimum standard of gold—10 carats). The same to apply to watch cases and other goods bearing a guarantee, such as " Guaranteed for 20 years," or simply bearing the words " 5 years," " 10 years," or " 20 years," or their translation in another language. In order to fulfil the conditions of Clause I, Gold Plated goods must have a minimum thickness of gold of 12 microns for goods produced by rolling, and of 6 microns for goods produced by electro-depositing. (1 micron = 0·000039 inch.) When such goods bear a guarantee of their duration as mentioned, the gold surface shall have the following thickness.

Duration of Guarantee	Rolled microns	Electro- Deposited	Equivalent mm.
5 years	12	6	0·012
10 „	24	12	0·024
15 „	36	18	0·036
20 „	48	24	0·048
25 „	60	30	0·060

Vide ' The Dial ' by DENNISON WATCH CASE Co., July, 1926.

SILVER. Metallic element. Used in horology, when alloyed with other metal to make hard, for the manufacture of watch and clock cases. Subject to " Hall Mark " (q.v.). Standards are: Britannia ·9584, Sterling ·925, i.e., ·925 fine silver and ·075 other metal.

SPELTER. Crude zinc. Used in horology as castings for low priced clock cases, gilt finish, etc. Also used in the manufacture of some clock movements, e.g., plates and the heads of lantern pinions, etc.

STAINLESS STEEL. Steel containing chromium and sometimes a small percentage of silicon and nickel. Used in horology for the manufacture of watch cases, etc.

STEEL. An alloy of iron and carbon.
Hard steel . . ·9% to 1·5% carbon
Mild steel . . up to ·5% „

Ordinary steel . . ·5% to 1·5% „
Silver steel . . 1% to 1·2% „
Soft steel . . . ·1% „

SUPERMALLOY. An improved form of Permalloy (q.v.).

TIN. Metallic element. Little used in horology other than as a medium for polishing the softer metals, e.g. brass or gold.

TITANIUM. See Elinvar.

VANADIUM. See Elinvar.

VIMETAL. An alloy made by Heraeus Vacuum Schmelze, Hanau, Germany. Supplied to the Swiss mainspring manufacturers in the form of rolled strip, not heat treated. The Swiss makers further roll down and slit the strip and punch the holes, form the ends, etc. and give the final heat treatment. The virtue of this metal is that it is non-rusting and does not suffer fatigue to the same extent as hardened and tempered steel. Tests have been made which prove that it is unaffected by acid and fatigue. Tests show that its form is unchanged by being wound up in a barrel for 20,000 times, equivalent to over 54 years of normal wear. The metal cannot be drilled with an ordinary steel drill but a hole can be pierced by punching. An alloy of this type was first developed by The Elgin Watch Company of America for use in mainsprings, but similar alloys had been used for other purposes in Europe for some years previously. Vimetal springs are marketed by the Swiss mainspring makers under the names Vimetal, Nivaflex, Ytire, Stabilor.

WHITE GOLD. An alloy of yellow gold and palladium; one part palladium and six parts gold. Standards are 18ct., 14ct. and 9ct. Subject to Hall Mark (q.v.). Some of the lower grades of white gold do not contain palladium, nickel is used as the whitener.

WROUGHT IRON. The first commercial form of iron; practically free from carbon.

X.A.M. See Elinvar.

ZINC. Metallic element. Used in horology as a means of compensating the pendulum for changes in temperature. See Gridiron Pendulum. Also used as a medium, with diamantine, for polishing steel work.

METAL RECTIFIER. A device for the production of unidirectional current from an alternating supply. Based on the rectifying property of a layer of oxide on a metal surface. Much used in charging accumulators, radio, etc.

METALLISED VALVE. A thermionic valve the glass envelope of which is sprayed or otherwise coated with a conducting metallic film, usually connected to the cathode terminal or earth. The metallic screen thus formed provides an electrostatic shield against external influences.

METHYLATED SPIRIT. A methyl alcohol. A volatile, colourless fluid. Used by horologists as a solvent of shellac, its action being accelerated when heated. Also used as a fuel in the spirit lamp because of its heating qualities and cleanliness of the flame. Commercial ethyl alcohol 90% about 8% wood spirit and smaller quantities of paraffin. It contains pyradine and purple dye to make it non-drinkable. A highly volatile fluid.

METONIC CYCLE. A period of 19 years, after which new and full moon occur again on approximately the same days of the month. *See* Golden Number.

METRONOME. An instrument used by musicians for marking time by means of an inverted pendulum. The pendulum is supported at the reverse end to that usual in clocks. Also in the form of a pocket watch, where a hand, connected to a train of wheels terminating in a rack and balance, swings backwards and forwards.

MICRO-FARAD. The practical unit of measurement of capacitance (*q.v.*). It is 1/1,000,000 of a Farad. Abbreviated mF, μF.

MICRO - MICRO - FARAD. *See* Pico-Farad.

MICROMETER GAUGE. Usually a " U " shaped gauge in which the gap is regulated by an accurate screw thread which forms one of the measuring faces. The distance between the contact surfaces is read off a scale un- covered by a thimble carried by the adjustable screw and

MICROMETER GAUGE.

by a circular scale engraved on the thimble. Micrometer gauges are calibrated to measure in fractions of an inch, usually up to 0·001 in., or millimetres, usually up to 0·01 mm. The micrometer device is applied also to other standard gauges.

MICRON. One thousandth of a millimetre.

MIDDLE TEMPERATURE ERROR. The change in rate of a watch or chronometer, or any timekeeper fitted with a balance (and usually associated with the cut bi-metallic balance) observed at temperatures lying between two fixed temperatures at which, by adjustment, the rate is the same, *e.g.*, a watch is adjusted at 42° F. and 90° F. the rates being then identical or as nearly so as possible. At any temperature or range of temperature between these fixed points say, 64°–66° the rate is found to vary. Such variation is the " Middle Temperature Error." The error is calculated by the following formula:—

$$\left(\frac{Rc+RH}{2}\right) - RM = \text{Middle Temperature Error.}$$

Where Rc = rate in cold temperature.
RH = rate in warm temperature.
RM = rate in middle temperature.

MILLIAMPERE. A sub-unit of the measure of flow of an electric current. It is 1/1000 of an Ampere (*q.v.*).

MILLING CUTTER. A wheel with teeth shaped for cutting materials when the wheel is rotated in a milling machine. A wheel with teeth on the periphery only, is known as a Face Cutter; and on the side, as a Side Cutter. The illustration shows a side and face cutter combined. Narrow face cutters are called Slitting Saws. A cutter used for milling; *i.e.* cutting grooves, etc.

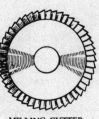

MILLING CUTTER.

MINUTE COUNTER. The hand of a chronograph or timer indicating the minutes, *i.e.*, usually, each revolution of the chronograph, or timer seconds hand (as a rule, a centre seconds) is recorded by the minute counter hand moving one space or division or as nearly so as possible.

MINUTE COUNTER.

MINUTE HAND. The hand of a time-keeper which indicates the minutes. *See* WATCH PART NOMENCLATURE. Also STYLES OF HANDS, page 146.

MINUTE NUT OR PINION. The pinion attached to the Minute Wheel (*q.v.*).

MINUTE NUT OR PINION.

MINUTE REPEATER. A watch or clock which strikes the minutes at will. Usually, the hours, quarters and then the minutes are sounded, *e.g.*, one minute to twelve as shown by the hands would be sounded by 11 blows on the hour gong or bell, then 3 quarters in the form of a ting-tang (one high note, one lower note) and then the 14 minutes on the high note.

MINUTE WHEEL. The wheel which is driven by the cannon pinion and which in turn drives the hour wheel through its pinion called the " minute nut." *See* ANTIQUE CLOCK CASE TERMS.

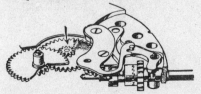

MINUTE WHEEL.

MINUTE WHEEL STUD. The pin, stud, or post on which the minute wheel rotates.

MINUTE WHEEL STUD.

MOCK PENDULUM. *See* ANTIQUE CLOCK CASE TERMS.

MODILLIONS. *See* ANTIQUE CLOCK CASE TERMS.

MODULE. The pitch circle diameter per tooth of a gear. The module is obtained by dividing the pitch diameter by the number of teeth in the gear: The module also equals the circular pitch in millimetres divided by

$$M = \frac{\pi . \text{Pitch diameter}}{\text{Number of teeth}}$$

It is the reciprocal of the diametral pitch. (*See* Diametral Pitch.)

MOLECULE. The smallest particle of an element or compound, possessing all that element's or compound's chemical properties, which can normally exist in a free state. The molecule may comprise only one atom or a great many atoms. Owing to recent research and development enabling special conditions to be created at will it should be kept in mind that the above definition is strictly general and subject to modification.

MOLYNEUX BALANCE. An auxiliary compensation balance invented by Robt. Molyneux in 1840.

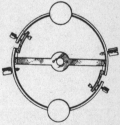

MOLYNEUX BALANCE.

MOMENTUM. The property possessed by a moving body by virtue of its mass and velocity.

MOMENT OF INERTIA. A measure of resistance that a body offers to rotation, or to any change in its velocity of rotation, is called its " moment of inertia," usually denoted by the letter I.

MONOMETAL BALANCE. This term denotes a balance made from one metal as distinct from a bi-metallic cut balance. An uncut bi-metallic balance is, from an horological viewpoint, a monometal balance to which it is in effect equivalent.

MONTGOMERIESTONE. A fine, greyish blue stone, similar to slate, for finishing brass. It is used with water: it is a fine grade of Water-of-Ayr Stone (*q.v.*).

MOON DIAL. The dial carrying representations of the moon (usually two) by which, in conjunction with an aperture in the main dial, the moon's phases are indicated. Usually associated with clocks and calendar watches. A lunation is considered to be $29\frac{1}{2}$ days; to simplify gearing, the moon dial is half covered, and is made to rotate once in 59 days (59 teeth stepped one tooth each day).

MOON DIAL.

MOON WORK. The mechanism incorporated in a clock or watch movement for actuating the moon dial or otherwise indicating the phases of the moon. *See* " Complicated Watches " (N.A.G. Press Ltd.).

MORBIER CLOCKS. Clocks made in the village of Morbier, near St. Claude, France from about 1750 until 1900. They were usually of the longcase variety and also the lantern type of wall clock with long pendulum. Originally fitted with a long pendulum verge escapement, subsequently with the anchor escapement. One of the characteristic features is the

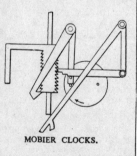

MOBIER CLOCKS.

straight or upright rack to the striking

mechanism. Also known as Comtoise clocks, taken from the district or county of Franche-Comté in which Morbier is situated. Often to be seen in Eastern France and Switzerland marked with the name and address of the vendor, rarely seen with the name Morbier or Morez, a nearby town.

MOSAIC. *See* ANTIQUE CLOCK CASE TERMS.

MOTION WORK. The train of wheels of a watch or clock, etc., directly connected with the hour and minute hands. The train usually consists of: cannon pinion, minute wheel and nut, and the hour wheel. *See* Wheels. *Also* WATCH PART NOMENCLATURE.

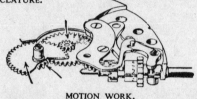

MOTION WORK.

MOTOR. An American term for the barrel and mainspring. Sometimes used to define a synchronous electric clock, *i.e.*, the mechanism consisting of the rotor and stator (*q.v.*).

MOTTLED. *See* ANTIQUE CLOCK CASE TERMS.

MOULDINGS

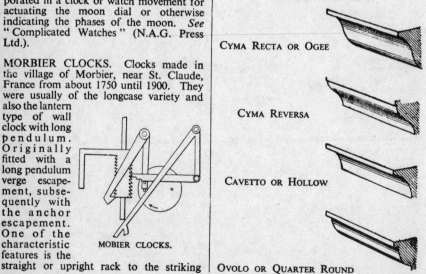

CYMA RECTA OR OGEE

CYMA REVERSA

CAVETTO OR HOLLOW

OVOLO OR QUARTER ROUND

MOULDINGS—cont.

FILLET, LISTEL OR BAND

BOLECTION

TORUS

ASTRAGAL OR BEAD

BIRD'S BEAK, ROLL OR SCROLL

FLUTES

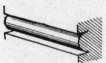

FLUSH OR SUNK BEAD

EDGE ROLL

POINTED BOWTELL

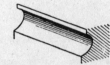

SCOTIA OR TROCHILUS

PLAIN BOWTELL

KEEL MOULDING

MOUNTAIN STANDARD TIME. Seven hours slow of G.M.T. (*q.v.*).

MOVEMENT. A term used to denote the mechanism only of a watch, clock, chronometer, etc.

MOVEMENT HOLDER. A tool for holding a watch movement while it is being assembled or adjusted. The illustration shows the tool from the underside.

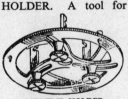

MOVEMENT HOLDER.

MUDGE'S ESCAPEMENT. This escapement, the first detached lever escapement made, was invented by Thomas Mudge in 1754. The action is similar to that of the Lever Escapement (*q.v.*) with the exception that there is no draw, as already mentioned. As the escapement had no Draw (*q.v.*) special provision was made to minimise the effects of friction of the lever bearing against and interfering with the free vibration of the balance. The illustration is taken from "The Marine Chronometer" by R. T. Gould.

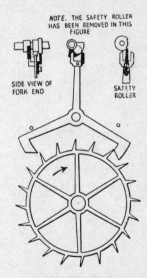

NOTE. THE SAFETY ROLLER HAS BEEN REMOVED IN THIS FIGURE

SIDE VIEW OF FORK END

SAFETY ROLLER

MUDGE'S ESCAPEMENT.

MULTIVIBRATOR. A form of valve oscillator usually comprising two resistance-capacity coupled valves which conduct alternately, producing an irregular wave form rich in harmonics. The operation is automatic and lends itself to control by a stable frequency driver stage. The oscillator is used in Divider Circuits (q.v.) and to provide synchronising impulses for the operation of apparatus or other circuits associated with its master frequency controller where accurate timing is essential. Also used in square-wave production. Some applications are: close one switch and open another; cause a valve or valves to operate (conduct) and render inoperative (cut off) others; initiate a signal, visual or aural, and blank out or suppress another etc.

MUMETAL. *See* METALS USED IN HOROLOGY.

MUNTINS. *See* ANTIQUE CLOCK CASE TERMS.

MURAL CLOCK. Refers to a clock made to hang on the wall; in horology the term usually refers to a decorative wall clock, *e.g.*, Cartel, " Act of Parliament Clock " (q.v.).

MUSHROOMED. A term referring to the flattened ends of balance staff pivots due to a blow or fall, etc. A plain arbor pivot sometimes presents a similar appearance but is due to " waisting " or cutting of the pivot by the hole.

MUSICAL ALARM CLOCK. Where a musical box mechanism is fitted which is released at a predetermined time and music takes the place of a bell.

MUSICAL CLOCK. A term usually applied to a clock which plays a tune, automatically, at each hour or other pre-determined time.

MUSICAL WATCH OR CLOCK. A clock or watch fitted with mechanism similar to a musical box which is released at each hour or can be played at will.

MUTUAL CONDUCTANCE. A term used in radio referring to the change in anode current per change of grid voltage causing it. Commonly spoken of as the Slope of the valve and expresses the efficiency of the valve as an amplifier in normal circuit use. The measure is expressed in milliamperes per volt. Symbol Gm.

MUTUAL INDUCTANCE. The property of two electrical circuits by virtue of which energy is transferred between them. Measured in terms of the rate of change of linkage in the one when there is a unit rate of change of current in the other. Also termed Coefficient of Mutual Induction.

MUTUAL INDUCTION. The transference of energy between two circuits, especially between coils in which a change of current in one induces an electromotive force in the other. It occurs only when there is a change and during that change.

N

NACRE. Mother-of-pearl. Often used in inlay work.

NAPOLEON. *See* Demi-Hunter.

NATIONAL PHYSICAL LABORATORY The National Laboratory at Teddington, Middlesex where among other activities the " Kew " watch tests are conducted. Commonly spoken of in the abbreviated form " N.P.L." The original " Kew " tests are now superseded by the new tests known as " Craftsmanship Watch Test " and conducted at the N.P.L. The conditions as laid down by the N.P.L. are

given on page 243. *See* Kew.

NATURAL FREQUENCY. The frequency of vibrations of a freely vibrating body.

NAUTICAL ALMANAC. An official annual publication giving exhaustive details and information concerning astronomical matters, Equation of Time tables, etc. Published by H.M. Stationery Office.

NAUTICAL TIME. *See* Ship's Bell Clock.

NAVIGATOR WATCH. A watch giving

the time in various cities of the world. Operated by manipulation of moveable dials, made by Tissot Watch Co., Switzerland.

NAVIGATOR WATCH.

NECK. A short length of a spindle, tube, etc., reduced to a smaller diameter than those sections immediately adjacent upon either side, *i.e.*, resembling a human neck.

NECKING. *See* ANTIQUE CLOCK CASE TERMS.

NEEDLE. A term sometimes applied to the Compass Needle. The indicating " hand " of a fine instrument, especially an electrical measuring meter, etc.

NEEDLE FILE. A file having a round, steel handle solid with it and presenting a needle-like appearance; made in various section, round, half-round, square, triangular. Sometimes known as Swiss files, although this term also embraces non-tapering shapes which are not included under needle files.

NEEDLE GAUGE. A fine needle-like gauge used in determining the interior diameter of a hole. *See* Friction Jewel Hole.

NEGATIVE. The opposite pole or electrode to the Positive (*q.v.*). Any point in a circuit at a relatively lower potential to another point. Conventionally, the pole or electrode to which the current is considered to flow from the

NEEDLE FILES.

Positive side of the supply. This convention is now considered incorrect the flow being actually in the reverse direction. In many cases the Negative and Earth potentials are common, *i.e.*, the Negative is returned to Earth. It is possible, however, to arrange that part of a circuit or power supply is at a potential considerably lower or " Negative " to Earth.

NEGATIVE SET. A form of keyless mechanism in which the control to set the hands or to wind the mainspring, is fitted in the pendant of the watch case and operates a spring-loaded automatic selector mechanism as distinct from the " Positive " Setting Mechanism (*q.v.*).

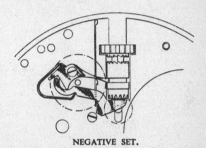

NEGATIVE SET.

NEUTRAL AXIS. The longitudinal section lying midway between the two outside faces, *e.g.*, the neutral axis of a piece of mainspring is that part which remains the same length after the spring has been bent into a curve. The dotted line in the illustrations indicate the Neutral Axis. The top, normal; centre, under stress; bottom, the modulus of elasticity

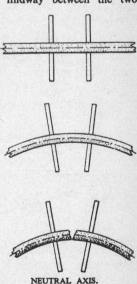

NEUTRAL AXIS.

has been exceeded and the spring breaks.

NEUTRAL POINT. That portion or point in a cut bi-metallic balance rim not materially affected by changes in temperature. The "Neutral point" is situated near to the fixed ends of the limbs. The centre bar expands outwards in heat, the limbs inward. Therefore, there must be a point which

NEUTRAL POINT.

neither approaches or recedes from the centre about which the balance turns. This point is the neutral point.

NEW ZEALAND TIME. Twelve hours fast of Greenwich Mean Time (*q.v.*).

NICKEL-IRON ACCUMULATOR. An accumulator similar to the Lead-Acid type (*q.v.*) but employing plates of nickel hydroxide and iron or cadmium, the electrolyte being potassium hydrate.

NICKEL PLATING. A bright finish much used a few years ago. An electro deposition of nickel which nowadays is generally a step in further plating processes.

NIELLO. A form of semi-hard black decoration used on watch cases usually of silver. The design is deeply engraved and filled with lead-oxide compound which provides a block pattern similar to inlay work. Also known as Tulla-work from Tulla, a Russian town where the work originated.

NIPPERS. Cutting pliers.

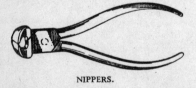

NIPPERS.

NI-SPAN. An alloy for balance springs, made by Henry Wiggin & Co. Ltd., Birmingham. The nominal composition is 42% nickel, 5·5% chromium, 2·50% titanium, balance iron. Ferro magnetic at room temperature and in the highly cold

worked condition will have a thermoelastic coefficient of approximately -5×10^{-6} per °F. but by suitable ageing treatment this can be varied through zero to slightly positive if desirable.

NITRIC ACID. A powerful corrosive and oxidising agent. Symbol $H N O^3$. Used by jewellers, etc., for testing platinum, gold, silver and palladium, and as a cleaning agent in dilute form. Is a constituent of Aqua-Regia (*q.v.*) and is also known as Aqua-Fortis (*q.v.*).

NITRIDING. A special process of case-hardening. A special type of steel is heated in gaseous ammonia. Practicable only on an industrial scale.

NITRO-CELLULOSE. A cellulose nitrate. The chief plastic form is Celluloid formerly used in making "unbreakable" watch glasses.

NIVAFLEX. Trade name given to an unbreakable mainspring. *See* Vimetal, METALS USED in HOROLOGY.

NIVAROX. *See* METALS USED IN HOROLOGY.

NOBLE METALS. The metals Gold, Silver, Platinum, so called by reason of their resistance to chemical combination with non-metals, and also in part to their beauty and permanence and comparative rarity.

NOCTURNALS. Night dials; instruments for ascertaining the time at night by the positions of certain fixed stars—usually the "pointers" of the "Great Bear" or "Plough," *i.e.*, α and β Ursæ Majoris.

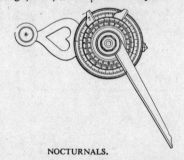

NOCTURNALS.

NODES. The point of intersection of the orbit of the moon with the Ecliptic (*q.v.*).

NOMENCLATURE OF WATCH PARTS. *See* pages 275–289.

NON-FERROUS ALLOY. Any alloy not based on iron, *e.g.*, alloys based on copper, lead, zinc, nickel, magnesium, aluminium, etc. *See* Ferrous.

NON-MAGNETIC. A term denoting that a material or object is impervious to or unaffected by magnetism.

NON-MAGNETIC STEEL. A special steel containing a percentage of manganese which does not exhibit magnetic properties.

NON-MAGNETIC WATCH. A watch in which parts normally liable to the effect of magnetism are made of non-magnetic materials, *e.g.*, the balance spring, roller, and lever.

NORMAL PITCH. The pitch of the teeth of a worm, spiral or helical gear measured to the tooth helix along the surface of the pitch cylinder.

NORMALISING. The system of heating metals so to bring them back to their normal state. After hammering brass, for instance, during fashioning, it can be returned to its normal hardness by heating.

NOMENCLATURE OF WATCH PARTS. *See* page 275.

NOTCH. The lever notch or Fork (*q.v.*).

NUREMBERG EGG. *See* Egg Watch.

NURL. *See* Knurling tool.

NUTATION. A short-period fluctuation in the precessional movement of the earth's pole about the pole of the ecliptic. A slight error of approximately $+$ 1 second in 19 years due to nutation is experienced in the oscillation of a pendulum.

O

OBELISK. *See* ANTIQUE CLOCK CASE TERMS.

OFF-SET SECONDS. Where the seconds hand is to one side in the conventional manner as distinct from the Centre Seconds (*q.v.*).

OFF-SET SECONDS.

OGEE MOULDING. *See* ANTIQUE CLOCK AND CLOCK CASE TERMS. Also, a term referring to the turning on the wheels of watches, clocks and chronometers,—a form of finish.

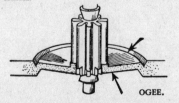

OGEE.

OGIVE. An old term for the tip on a gear tooth. *See* Addendum.

OHM. The unit of electrical resistance. The international ohm is given by a conductor which is a column of mercury 106·30 cm. long, of mass 14·4521 gram and of uniform cross-sectional area, at a temperature of 0° Centigrade.

OHM'S LAW. Ohm's law states that the voltage drop across a conductor (resistance) is directly proportional to the current flowing. The law governs the flow of a steady current in a circuit. It is usually expressed in symbols as follows:—
Letter I = Current in amperes.
  ,,   E = Voltage drop across R in volts.
  ,,   R = Resistance in ohms.
Then: $I = E/R$, or $R = E/I$, or $E = I \times R$. *See* Kirchoff Laws.

OIL.
ANIMAL. Oil obtained from animals, as sperm from the whale, porpoise jaw oil from the porpoise and neats foot oil from foot bones of sheep and oxen.
MINERAL. Oil derived from minerals, as petroleum and hydrocarbon oils obtained from mineral sources.
SYNTHETIC. A manufactured oil as Silicones.
VEGETABLE. Oil obtained from plants, seeds, etc.

OIL CUP. The Sink or Chamfer (*q.v.*) to hold oil.

OIL POT. A receptacle to hold oil conveniently while being used.

CLOCK OIL POT.

WATCH OIL POT.

OILER. A tool used for conveying oil to the pivots, etc., of clocks, watches, etc. It consists of a piece of wire with a flattened end, usually mounted in a holder, and is used in much the same way as a dipper.

OIL FINISH. *See* ANTIQUE CLOCK CASE TERMS.

OIL SINK. The counter-sink at pivot holes to retain or store oil; a reservoir.

OIL STONE. A slip of Arkansas, Turkey, or India stone used with oil to sharpen cutting tools. May be used loose or mounted in a box-like platform with a cover.

OIL STONE DUST OR POWDER. Turkey stone ground to a fine powder; mixed with oil to a paste it is used in grinding steel work.

OLIVETTE. The bush or guide of the push-piece of the side set watch. *See* PARTS OF POCKET WATCH CASE, page 79.

OLIVETTE.

OLIVE JEWEL HOLE. A jewel hole in which the axial bearing surfaces on which the pivot runs are curved instead of being straight and parallel.

OLIVE JEWEL HOLE.

OPEN FACE. Refers to a watch not fitted with a Hunter or Half Hunter (*q.v.*) cover over the dial.

ORMOLU. *See* ANTIQUE CLOCK CASE TERMS.

ORMSKIRK ESCAPEMENT. A form of Verge Escapement (*q.v.*), where two escape wheels are employed. The name is taken from the village of Ormskirk, near Liverpool, where watches with this escapement were made.

ORRERY. A mechanical device, or contrivance, consisting of a number of spheres mounted on rods, each sphere representing one of the heavenly bodies, and operated by wheel work. The spheres perform an orbit round a common centre at which is placed a representation of the sun. The device illustrates the relative sizes, positions and motions (but not distances) of heavenly bodies. The name is taken from the 4th Earl of Orrery for whom one of the earliest was made in 1715. An orrery is a mechanical planetarium. The illustration is taken from " Astronomical Dialogues," by J. Harris, F.R.S., published 1719 and is the first Orrery to be made. The Earl of Orrery was the patron of JOHN ROWLEY the famous scientific instrument maker of Fleet Street and a close neighbour of Thos. Tompion.

ORRERY.

OSCILLATION. A complete cycle or period or repeatable alternation of a reciprocating effect, *e.g.*:—(1) A swing from zero to left, back and beyond zero to right, returning to zero is a mechanical oscillation. (2) A cycle of alternating current from zero value to a maximum positive value reducing to zero and passing to a maximum negative value returning again to zero is one oscillation. The time of oscillation of a balance or pendulum is thus twice that of a single beat.

OSCILLATION, CENTRE OF. *See* Centre of Oscillation.

OSCILLATING CURRENT. Alternating currents of frequencies of the order of several hundred or more cycles per second. These frequencies are met in radio work, sound amplification, etc. An important distinction is that unlike a true alternating current the amplitude per cycle of an oscillating current may vary rapidly, the frequency remaining constant. These currents are generated in resonating circuits comprising inductance and capacitance, usually by means of thermionic valves, which may be likened to a generator energising yet controlled by, its own circuit, and thus maintaining a constant cycle of operation.

OSCILLATOR. A device usually comprising one or more thermionic valves and resonant circuits for the production of oscillating currents and which is usually self running, *i.e.*, maintains itself in oscillation. There are several forms of oscillator in general use either singly, as in test apparatus and radio receivers, or combined as in the Quartz Crystal clock, etc.

OSCILLATOR DRIFT. A term denoting frequency drift or variation due to the effects of supply voltage variations, temperature changes and gradual alteration of circuit component values, in a system producing oscillating currents. The Quartz Crystal form of oscillator is noted for its stability. Hence its use as a master or controller, *e.g.*, Quartz Crystal clock.

OUTSIDE DIAMETER. In gearing it refers to the diameter over the tips of the teeth. The diameter of the addendum circle.

OUTSIDE SHAKE. The necessary freedom of the escape wheel teeth of the Lever escapement, relative to the exit pallet, in a correctly proportioned escapement. Part of the test applied to determine the correct size of escape wheel for a given pair of pallets. The lever is so placed

O.S. ON LEVER ESCAPEMENT.

and held, that a tooth resting on the entry pallet locking face is about to unlock. The escape wheel is now made to reverse; whereupon the heel of the tooth which has passed beyond the exit pallet will butt on to the back of it. The degree or extent of this movement is known as the outside shake. Outside shake of the Cylinder

escapement, refers to the freedom of the escape wheel, when so placed that the point of one tooth and the heel of another embrace the shell of the cylinder. *See* Inside Shake.

O.S. ON CYLINDER ESCAPEMENT.

OUT OF BEAT. *See* Beat.

OUT-OF-PHASE. The relationship obtaining between bodies or quantities alternating or oscillating at the same frequency but reaching their respective maxima or minima at different instants of time. Conveniently expressed in degrees. Thus, 180° (*i.e.*, Anti-Phase), 90°, 10°, etc., it being understood that 360° represents one full cycle of oscillation.

OUTPUT TRANSFORMER. A transformer, coupling the last stage of a thermionic valve device (*e.g.*, amplifier) with its load such as a relay or electrical machine, or loud speaker.

OUTPUT VALVE. A valve designed expressly to deliver alternating current power in contradistinction to the voltage amplifying characteristics of other valve types. Also termed a Power valve.

OVEN. A heated chamber used in testing watches, etc., when rating for temperature changes. A temperature control and indicator may be " built in." The usual practice is to test at temperatures of 42° F., 67° F., and 92° F. In some instances such as for special tropical use, watches, are tested in a temperature as high as 120° F.

OVERBANK.
LEVER ESCAPEMENT. When the ruby pin passes to the wrong side of the lever notch thus causing the watch to stop.
CYLINDER ESCAPEMENT. When the banking pin on the balance passes on to the wrong side of the fixed banking. This particular fault is uncommon. More generally, it happens that due to the position of the stationary banking, or the position of the cylinder shell relative to the balance banking pin, the cylinder becomes locked by the escape wheel teeth. This condition is also known as " Overbanked." CHRONOMETER ESCAPEMENT. When, owing to an excessive arc of vibration of the balance, the escape wheel is unlocked a second time during one vibration, causing

considerable gaining in rate. This fault is also known as " Tripping."

DUPLEX ESCAPEMENT. A similar circumstance to the chronometer overbank. *See* Banking.

OVERCOIL. Another name for the Breguet Balance Spring (*q.v.*).

OVER-COMPENSATION. Normally a balance fitted with a steel balance spring will lose in heat. To compensate this effect, a cut, bi-metallic balance is used, the limbs of which move inwards with rising temperature. Screws or weights on these limbs are arranged so that an accurate compensatory action is obtained. It can so happen, however, that the screws or weights are given such a position that the balance causes a gain in heat. It is then said to be over compensated. A similar condition can arise in pendulum clocks, when the clock gains in heat.

OVER-SPRUNG. The fitting or attaching of the balance spring above the balance relative to the cock. In many of the old full-plate watches the balance spring is fitted between the balance and the top plate, *i.e.*, under the balance relative to the cock. The conventional position of the spring to-day is over-sprung.

OVOLO MOULDING. *See* ANTIQUE CLOCK CASE TERMS.

OYSTER WATCH. The name given to a waterproof watch made by the Rolex Watch Co. Switzerland.

OYSTER or OYSTERED. *See* ANTIQUE CLOCK CASE TERMS.

OYSTER WATCH.

P

PACIFIC STANDARD TIME. Eight hours slow of G.M.T. (*q.v.*).

PAD. The acting surface of the Anchor or Recoil escapement (*q.v.*).

PAD FEET. *See* ANTIQUE CLOCK CASE TERMS.

PAD.

PAIR CASE. Two watch cases: the movement is fitted into one case and the whole watch is then fitted into an outer case. Common in the seventeenth and eighteenth centuries.

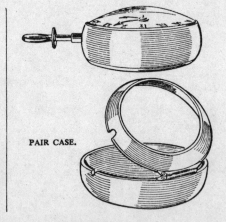

PAIR CASE.

PALLET. That part of the escapement upon which the escape wheel teeth operate and transmit impulse to the Balance or the Pendulum. The term " Pallets " or " Pair of Pallets " usually refers to the pallets complete, as illustrated. Also *see* Impulse Pallet, Discharge Pallet.

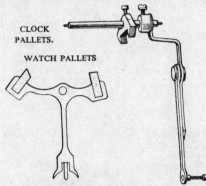

CLOCK PALLETS.

WATCH PALLETS

PALLET ARBOR. The arbor upon which the pallets of a pendulum clock are fitted; sometimes referred to as the Verge. The pallet arbor of the pallets of a watch is usually referred to as the Pallet Staff (*q.v.*). *See* WATCH PART NOMENCLATURE.

PALLET ARMS. The metal body into which the pallet stones are set; that part of a pair of pallets to which the locking and impulse parts are attached of which they form a part.

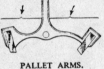

PALLET ARMS.

PALLET STAFF. The staff or arbor which carries the pallets; it usually refers to the staff of the lever escapement only; when speaking of the arbor upon which the pallets of a pendulum clock are mounted, it is usual to employ the term " Pallet Arbor " and not " Pallet Staff." *See* WATCH PART NOMENCLATURE.

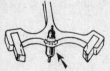

PALLET STAFF.

PALLET STONE. A pallet made of jewel stone or a jewel stone is inset into the pallet to provide a good wearing surface. Usually, the term

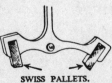

SWISS PALLETS.

refers to the lever escapement only. The pallets of some pendulum clocks are fitted with jewel stones

ENGLISH PALLETS.

and are referred to as jewelled pallets. *See* WATCH PART NOMENCLATURE.

PALMER'S MASTER CLOCK. A system of a master electric clock controlling slave dials. Invented in 1902.

PAPER DIAL. A clock or watch dial printed on a paper or cardboard ground and sometimes backed by thin metal. Commonly employed on cheap alarms in the past but now generally superseded by improved processes of metal printing and transfers.

PAPERED. A term used by jewellers and watch-case makers to define the finish of work immediately preceding polishing. A method of removing file, hammer, and other marks with emery paper. A term also used by clockmakers to define the finish to brass work by imparting a grain, either straight or circular, by the use of emery paper.

PARACHUTE INDEX. Refers to an endstone fitted into a spring. An early form of " Shock-proofing." Introduced by A. Breguet. The modern shock resisting devices are forms of the Parachute.

PARACHUTE INDEX.

PARALLEL. Electrically; two or more separate circuits or components in a circuit so connected that a current flow divides between them. Particularly, when a circuit or component draws its correct current supply be being so connected. Machines, batteries, etc., are " in parallel " when their terminals of the same polarity are connected together.

PARCEL GILT. *See* ANTIQUE CLOCK CASE TERMS.

PARECHOC. A system of shock resisting

where the jewel holes and endstones of the balance " give " when the watch receives a shock. The spring-like settings of the jewels operate until a shoulder turned on the balance staff contacts a block and so takes the effect of a major shock.

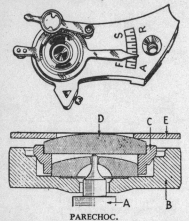

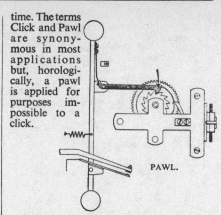

PAWL.

PARECHOC.

A. Balance staff. B. Shock resisting block. C. Jewel hole setting. D. Endstone. E. Spring to hold the assembly in position.

PARELINVAR BALANCE SPRING. *See* Metals Used in Horology.

PARLIAMENT CLOCK. *See* Antique Clock and Clock Case Terms and Act of Parliament Clock.

PARQUETRY. *See* Antique Clock Case Terms.

PARTING. The operation of cutting off a length from a piece of work or material while it is revolving in the lathe or turns.

PASSING HOLLOW. The indentation in the circumference of the safety roller, to permit the passage of the guard pin (*see* Crescent) in the lever escapement.

PASSING SPRING. *See* Gold Spring.

PATERAE. *See* Antique Clock Case Terms.

PATH OF CONTACT. The locus of the point of contact between a pair of gear teeth, during the phase of engagement.

PATINA. *See* Antique Clock Case Terms.

PAWL. A form of click which not only prevents the reversal of motion of the wheel with which it engages but, is also used to move the wheel either forwards or backwards, usually the space of one tooth at a time. The terms Click and Pawl are synonymous in most applications but, horologically, a pawl is applied for purposes impossible to a click.

PEAN. The flattened end of a hammer head; used for stretching metal. To ''Pean'' a piece of metal is to stretch it in a certain place to cause it to curl, for purposes of straightening it or to form a bend. In general engineering spelt *peen*.

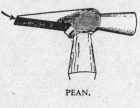

PEAN.

PEDIMENT. *See* Antique Clock Case Terms.

PEDIMENT BAROMETER. *See* Antique Clock Case Terms.

PEDOMETER WATCH. *See* Automatic Winding.

PEGWOOD. The round sticks of Dogwood used for cleaning purposes. Obtained from France.

PENDANT. That part of the watch case to which the " bow " or ring is fitted. The position of the winding button is generally referred to as the Pendant especially for timing purposes, *e.g.*, for a wrist watch, pendant down, right, or left, refers to the position of the watch determined by

PENDANT.

reference to the winding button. *See* PARTS OF THE POCKET WATCH CASE, page 79.

PENDANT SLEEVE. The steel spring clutch device screwed into the pendant of watch cases fitted for Negative Setting (*q.v.*). Its purpose is control of the stem in operating the winding and hand setting mechanism. *See* Sleeve.

PENDANT SLEEVE TOOL.

PENDELOQUE CUT. *See* GEMSTONE CUTTING STYLES.

PENDULETTE. Refers to a "Calotte" (*q.v.*) or "Goliath watch" (*q.v.*) type of clock which is not used as a portable timepiece.

PENDULUM. In horology, the time controlling element of a pendulum clock. The theoretical length of a pendulum in inches is given by $L = 39.14 \times t^2$ where t = time of swing in seconds; 39.14 = length of a pendulum beating seconds in London. The length of a pendulum is based on the formula:

$$T = 2\pi\sqrt{\frac{1}{g}}$$

where T = time of one complete vibration (one cycle) in seconds, 1 = length, and g = acceleration of gravity. For a single beat the formula is:

$$\pi\sqrt{\frac{1}{g}}$$

the pendulum was invented by Christiaan Huygens in 1656. A simple pendulum consists of a single heavy particle or mass suspended by a flexible weightless thread. This conception is applied in theoretical considerations but is, physically, an impossibility. A compound pendulum appertains to those used in clocks especially when designed to obtain a compensatory effect. To some degree every physical, actual pendulum may be said to be a compound pendulum. *See* Compensation Pendulum, Centre of Oscillation.

PENDULUM APERTURE GLAZED. *See* ANTIQUE CLOCK CASE TERMS.

PENDULUM MOCK. *See* Mock Pendulum, ANTIQUE CLOCK CASE TERMS.

PENTAGRID. *See* Valve.

PENTODE. *See* Valve.

PERIMETER. The total length of the boundary or edges of a plane figure of any shape, *i.e.*, the four sides of a square. The circumference of a circle.

PERIOD. The time occupied in one complete cycle or alternation of any recurring effect. Electrically: tle time of one complete cycle of an alternating current. Horologically: one complete forward and return swing of a pendulum, *i.e.*, the Period of a seconds pendulum is Two seconds. *See* Frequency.

PERIOD OF STYLES. *See* page 38 onwards.

PERIPHERY. The circumference of a circle. The peri- phery of a gear wheel is that part on which the teeth are cut. The term gives definition to the sur- face in another plane at the circumference of a wheel, *e.g.*, radial holes may be

PERIPHERY.

drilled into a solid wheel *from the periphery* without breaking the *circumference*.

PERMALLOY. *See* METALS USED IN HOROLOGY.

PERMANENT MAGNET. Any piece of steel or metallic alloy which, having a high degree of Remanance (*q.v.*), continues to exhibit magnetic properties for a considerable time after the cessation of the initial excitant influence.

PERMEABILITY. The property of "conduction" and concentration of magnetic lines of force possessed to a varying degree by magnetisable substances. The ratio of the magnetic flux density produced in a medium to force producing same.

PERPENDICULAR STYLE. *See* ANTIQUE CLOCK CASE TERMS.

PERPETUAL CALENDAR. A calendar mechanism which automatically sets to the correct day of the month, etc., adjusts itself for the varying number of days per month and, is self-correcting for the leap years. *See* Moon Dial for illustration.

PERPETUAL WATCH. *See* Automatic Winding.

PERSPEX. A type of transparent plastic material closely resembling glass in appearance. Also obtainable in clear and opaque colourings. Widely used in modern clock mounts and unbreakable watch glasses.

PHASE. The relationship between two or more individual quantities, actions, etc., particularly when like degrees occur at substantially or precisely the same instant. An alternating current is in phase with an alternating voltage when both reach their maxima and minima together and at the same frequency.

PHILLIPS CURVE. Usually refers to one particular curve of the overcoil of the balance spring. The curve is shaped to conform to a formula devised by Professor M. Phillips, the French mining engineer.

PHILLIPS CURVE.

PHOTO-ELECTRIC WOUND CLOCK. *See* Light Clock.

PICO-FARAD. A sub-unit of the measurement of Capacitance; 1/1,000,000 of a micro-Farad (*q.v.*). Symbol $\mu.\mu f$. Also known as Micro-Micro-Farad.

PIE CRUST EDGING. *See* Antique Clock Case Terms.

PIETRA DURA. *See* Antique Clock Case Terms.

PIEZO-ELECTRIC EFFECT. The phenomenon, whereby certain crystals, such as quartz, undergo strain in an electric field or produce charges on different faces when undergoing mechanical strain (*see* Quartz).

PIGEON CLOCK. A clock device to time the homing of pigeons. The device consists of a drum into which fit a number of capsules, each capsule allotted its separate division. The capsules are provided with caps and either numbers or names can be placed inside and the capsule fastened to the leg of the pigeon. Suppose that a number of birds are to be timed. The capsules are issued and then the case of the machine is locked, by an official of the club. As the birds arrive home the capsules are removed and placed in the machine through a hole. The drum is then made to rotate and it is this movement which records the time of placing the capsule in the machine and, at the same time an empty division is brought into place to receive the next capsule. The divisions are numbered 1 to 12 (or more, according to the size of the drum), and the drum set so that the first capsule to arrive drops into No. 1 division. The time is recorded on a paper roll by a rubber stamping device similar to the Warwick Time Stamping Clock (*q.v.*).

PILASTER. *See* Antique Clock Case Terms.

PILLAR. The distance pieces separating the plates of a clock, chronometer, or watch.

PILLAR FILE. A flat, narrow file, from about $3\frac{1}{2}$ in. to 6 in. in length.

PILLAR PLATE. The plate of a clock, chronometer, or watch to which the pillars are attached. In a watch it is usually the "lower" or "bottom" plate. In a clock, the front plate. *See* Bottom Plate.

PILLAR FILE.

PILOT HOLE. A small diameter hole drilled as exactly as possible to act as a guide for a large drill or broach.

PIN BARREL. A cylinder carrying short steel pins which actuate the musical " Comb " of a musical clock or " box."

PINCHBECK. *See* Metals Used in Horology.

PIN CHUCK. *See* Pin Tongs.

PINION. A small, toothed wheel or "cog." Excepting in Motion Work (*q.v.*) the pinion is usually the driven member of a pair of gears, a wheel driving the pinion. The teeth of a pinion are termed " leaves " and, for horological use, they are normally of the Hypocycloidal form (*q.v.*).

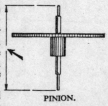

PINION.

PINION GAUGE. A gauge for the

measurement of pinions. There are two in common use. One, a form of caliper; the other, a form of wire gauge—a steel plate having a series of graduated holes.

COMPARATIVE PINION GAUGE.

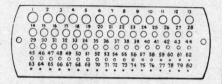

WIRE GAUGE TYPE PINION GAUGE.

PINION HEAD. That section or part of the pinion forming the leaves. Usually, when referring to a pinion the term includes the leaves complete with arbor, Strictly, the pinion comprises two parts, the arbor and the head.

PINION HEAD.

PINION HOLLOW. *See* Undercut.

PINION LEAF. A term used to denote the " tooth " of a pinion as distinct from the tooth of a wheel.

PINION POLISHING MACHINE. A machine used in a factory for polishing the leaves of pinions. The pinion rests in two vees. A thin revolving wooden disk, set *very* slightly at an angle, *i.e.*, not running at right angles to the pinion, is charged with a polishing medium. The disk is lowered on to the pinion while rotating and eventually the edge of the disk takes the form of the pinion leaf and because of the slight cant of the disk the pinion is caused to rotate by it. Thus all the leaves are polished and the form of the leaves is not altered. Once the disk has been formed by the pinion it will last a considerable time, provided the same type of pinions are being polished.

PINION SAFETY. *See* Safety Pinion.

PINION WIRE. Extruded wire drawn to the shape of the pinion leaves. Sold by material dealers in lengths of about 12 ins. From this the arbor is turned, leaving the Pinion Head (*q.v.*). In manufacture to-day the pinion head is cut from the solid.

PINION WIRE.

PIN PALLET. A design in which the escapement pallets are in the form of pins. Usually associated with the Roskopf movement. The action of this escapement is similar to that of the Lever Escapement (*q.v.*) with the exception that the impulse is all on the escape wheel and is not divided between the escape teeth and the pallets as with the club tooth lever escapement. Also, the half-round pins of agate or steel used in the pendulum clock escapement invented by Brocot (*q.v.*).

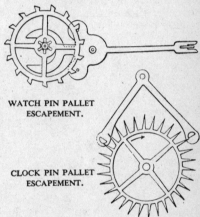

WATCH PIN PALLET ESCAPEMENT.

CLOCK PIN PALLET ESCAPEMENT.

PIN TONGS. A tool consisting of a split chuck which is drawn into a hollow handle by a screw collet bearing upon the end of the chuck which is conically shaped. Used for holding wire and the like. Also called a Pin Chuck.

PIN TONGS.

PIN VICE. A very small hand vice fitted to a long handle.

PIN VICE.

PIN WHEEL. The wheel of a striking clock to which pins are fitted to lift the hammer. Some striking clocks are fitted with cams to the wheel in the form of a star when it is known variously as the " Pin " wheel, or " Star " wheel.

PIN WHEEL ESCAPEMENT. An escapement in which the teeth of the escape wheel are in the form of pins projecting at right angles from the wheel; found in many French clocks of good quality. The escapement is also used in turret clocks on the Continent. An advantage is, that if the pallet holes wear, the action of the escapement is not materially affected. The action is as follows:—The escape wheel rotates in the direction as arrow. The pallets are fixed to the pallet arbor to which the crutch is also fixed. The pendulum is embraced by the crutch and as the pendulum swings to the left the escape wheel pin A slides down the impulse face B of the left hand pallet and so impulse is imparted to the pendulum. As the pin A drops off the pallet it will drop on to the pallet D and when the pendulum swings to the right impulse will eventually be given to it through the right hand pallet and so the cycle is repeated. Fig. 1.—Pendulum about to receive impulse. Fig. 2.— Escape wheel imparting impulse. Fig. 3.— Escape wheel arrested by pallet D.

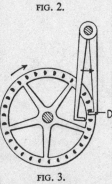

FIG. 1.

FIG. 2.

FIG. 3.

PIN WHEEL ESCAPEMENT.

PIP. The slight protrusion or " narrowing " inside the cannon pinion bore, formed to cause it to snap on to its arbor.

PIPE. A tubular projection or boss, *e.g.*, that part of the minute hand which is pressed on to the cannon pinion and that part of the hour hand which is pressed on to the pipe of the hour wheel.

PITCH. Of a wheel: the distance between the centre of one tooth and the centre of next tooth, or, the measurement of a space and a tooth, measured on the pitch circle or pitch line, more correctly " circular pitch." Of a screw: the distance between the centre of a thread to the centre of the next thread. Usually given in the number of threads per inch. *See* Diametrical Pitch and Module.

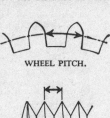

WHEEL PITCH.

THREAD PITCH.

PITCH CIRCLE. The circle drawn from the centre of a toothed wheel and upon which the construction or curve of the tooth is formed. In the case of a pinion it is the circle drawn from the centre of the pinion and determines the termination of the active part of the pinion leaf. For a depth to be correct these two circles should touch as shown in the illustration.

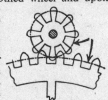

PITCH CIRCLE.

PITCH CONE. The pitch surface of a bevel gear.

PITCH CYLINDER. The pitch surface of a spur or helical gear. The pitch surface is imaginary, such that if gears with parallel axes consisted of smooth Pitch Cylinders (*q.v.*) and drove one another by friction at the line of contact between them the relative velocities of rotation would be correct.

PITCH DIAMETER. The effective diameter of wheels and pinions. The diameter of the " Pitch Circle."

PITCH LINE. A line between the face and flank of a tooth, lying down, the pitch surface in the direction of the width of the gear. Pitch Line may also mean part of a pitch circle of infinite radius, *i.e.* of a rack.

PITCHING. The operation of correctly positioning wheels and pinions so that their " depths " (or meshing; gearing; engagement) is correct.

PITCH POINT. The point at which the two pitch circle of wheels or pinions intersect when in gear.

PITCH RADIUS. The distance from the centre of a wheel to the Pitch Circle (*q.v.*).

PITH. The soft centre part of the branches of the Elder tree: used in horology for cleaning purposes.

PIVOT. The horological name for the reduced or turned down end of an arbor, etc. Generally, three main forms are used : (A) The "Square shoulder;" (B) The " Conical pivot;" (C) The " Cone " pivot.

PIVOTED DETENT. A term applying to the detent of the chronometer escapement (*q.v.*) which is pivoted and controlled by a spring similar to a balance spring; in contradistinction to the Spring Detent The action is exactly similar to the Chronometer Escapement (*q.v.*) with the difference that instead of the detent to which the locking pallet is fixed being a long spring, it is pivoted at A and the coiled spring B (wound up or set) returns the detent, after it has been moved to unlock the escape wheel. The piece C is a counter weight.

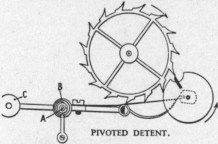

PIVOTED DETENT.

PIVOT FILE. *See* Files.

PIVOT GAUGE. A gauge originally intended for use in determining the size of pivots but most frequently used as a mainspring gauge.

PIVOT GAUGE.

PIVOT HOLE. The hole or bearing in which a pivot works or runs.

PIVOTED HOOK OR BRACE. The hook of a mainspring which pivots round, thus allowing full development of the mainspring. *See* " T " Piece.

PIVOTING. A loose term meaning the work of the " Finisher " (*q.v.*).
Also, the operation of drilling up an arbor or pinion to fit a new pivot. *See* Pivoting Tool and " Practical Watch Repairing."

PIVOTING TOOL. A simple form of lathe used in drilling up arbors, *i.e.*, balance staffs, pinions, etc., when fitting new pivots.

PIVOTING TOOL.

PLANE. In geometry, a flat surface considered without the third dimension of thickness.

PLANETARIUM. A representation of the heavenly bodies in the form of spheres and stars. *See* Orrery. Also a room having a domed, semi-circular roof on which, by means of special apparatus, a representation of the heavens may be projected, *e.g.*, the London Planetarium.

PLAIN BOWTELL MOULDING. *See* ANTIQUE CLOCK CASE TERMS.

PLANISHING. The operation of working a metal surface flat. Usually a soft metal such as silver or brass. It is first hammered by a special hammer having a polished face and then worked over with a wide-edged tool similar to a chisel with the cutting edge squared off—a form of scraper.

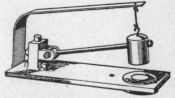

HAND PLANISHER.

PLANISHING HAMMER.

PLANTED. *See* ANTIQUE CLOCK CASE TERMS.

PLANTING. The setting out of the centres for the pivot holes, etc., in the plates of a watch or clock. The location and disposition, etc., of the bearing, etc., of any mechanical piece in watch or clockwork, etc.

PLAQUE. *See* ANTIQUE CLOCK CASE TERMS.

PLASTICS. A generic term for a wide range of materials, some natural but most produced synthetically by controlled chemical processes of great complexity. The substances may be shaped under heat and pressure, or, assume their final form actually in the mould when so treated, or may be in readily usable forms after completion of manufacture. There are two main branches: Thermo-Setting and Thermo-Plastic. Raw materials used include coal tar, skimmed milk, wood flour, cotton linters, molasses, etc. So far clock cases, mounts, etc., are the chief uses for plastics in horology. Also " unbreakable " watch glasses and " exhibition " clock plates. *Examples*—Natural: Shellac. Semi-synthetic: Erinoid. Synthetic: Nylon.

PLATE. The frame of a watch or clock is usually formed by two plates separated

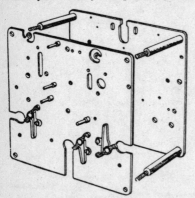

CLOCK FRAME WITH TWO PLATES.

by pillars. The " train," etc., is pivoted between them. (Electrically.) The active internal positive and negative electrodes of an accumulator or secondary cell. An old term for the Anode of a valve.

PLATFORM ESCAPEMENT. An escapement mounted on a separate self-contained plate. Used on carriage clocks, etc., and in some modern designs of clocks for considerations of mass production and repair. The term refers to an escapement having a balance and balance spring, *i.e.*, Chronometer, Lever, Cylinder, Duplex, etc.

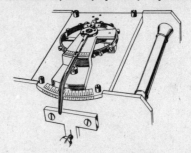

PLATFORM ESCAPEMENT.

PLATO CLOCK. *See* Flick Leaf Clock.

PLAY. Freedom, such as " end shake " or " side shake " of a pivot in its holes. Generally, the freedom of any working part.

PLIERS. A form of tongs with various shaped jaws, *e.g.*, flat, round, etc.

PLIERS.

PLINTH. *See* ANTIQUE CLOCK CASE TERMS.

PLUG. In horology, refers to stopping a hole to make it solid. Also the stoppings or plugs fitting into the cylinder of the Horizontal Escapement (*q.v.*) upon which the pivots are formed.

PLUNGER. The pump action of a repeating watch ; where the pendant is pressed in to cause the watch to repeat.

POCKET CHRONOMETER. A pocket watch fitted with the Chronometer Escapement (*q.v.*). The term is applied, however, on the Continent to any high grade precision pocket watch.

POCKET WATCH. A watch made to be worn or carried in the pocket as distinct from a wristlet, fob, or other style.

POINT OF ATTACHMENT (POINT D'ATTACHE). Refers to the pinning of the balance spring to the balance spring collet. To obtain the best results when timing in the vertical positions, the spring must develop up from a line drawn passing through the centre of the balance jewel hole and at right angles to a parallel line drawn from the pendant and passing through 6 o'clock. This requirement refers to pocket watches. With wrist watches, which when worn are more in the pendant down position, the rule is that the spring develops up when in the pendant down position. When these conditions are present, it is known as " Correct point of attachment " and when absent as " Point of Attachment Error." The discovery of the Correct Point of Attachment is attributed to Jules Crossman in the latter part of the last century. Fig. 1—Showing the correct point of attachment for a pocket watch. Fig. 2—The correct position for a wrist watch. In both instances the spring can develop up from the left or right. With the wrist watch particularly, the theoretically correct pinning point, as Fig. 2, cannot always be observed and each calibre of movement dictates its own pinning point. *See* " Practical Watch Repairing " (N.A.G. Press Ltd.).

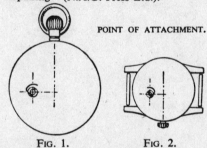

POINT OF ATTACHMENT.

FIG. 1.   FIG. 2.

POINTED BOWTELL MOULDING. *See* ANTIQUE CLOCK CASE TERMS.

POISE. In equal balance; in horology the term refers usually to the lever of the lever escapement and to balances generally. When a balance has no " dead point " it is said to be " in poise."

POISING TOOL. A tool having parallel

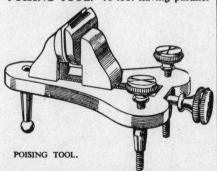

POISING TOOL.

double knife edges set horizontally used to test the Poise (*q.v.*). The knife edges are adjustable for variable lengths of staff and may be of ground steel highly polished or agate.

POLARITY. The distinction applied to north and south poles of a magnet, etc., or of the positive and negative terminals of a cell or generator or the supply therefrom.

POLE. The location where a magnetic flux enters or leaves a surface. A distinguishing term applying to the ends of a magnet or the areas from which lines of flux emerge, North Pole, or to which they converge, South Pole. Similarly, a term applied to D.C. supplies, *e.g.*, a dynamo, cell, accumulator, in respect of the terminals, current being said to flow from the Positive Pole and to return to the Negative Pole. (This is known as the Conventional Flow of electricity.) The blade or contact of a switch. Also, that diameter of a sphere or body, about which it rotates. Especially one end of the diameter.

POLE LATHE. *See* Lathe.

POLE PIECE. A special facing cap of magnetic material applied to magnets to assist or control the effect.

POLISHER. Strips of material such as steel, iron, bell metal, tin, zinc, boxwood, etc., used in polishing work. They may be of square section or shaped to suit the work in hand.

POLISHING BLOCK. A block of metal used for polishing, *i.e.*, bell metal, tin, zinc.

POLISHING STAKE. A flat platform of polished metal on which polishing material, red stuff, diamantine, etc., is mixed. Generally enclosed in a boxwood case for

POLISHING STAKE.

dust protection and sometimes arranged in a tier of two or three.

POLLARD. *See* ANTIQUE CLOCK CASE TERMS.

PORTFOLIO. A leather folding clock. *See* Calotte.

PORTICO TOP. *See* Pediment, page 30.

POSITIONS. A term used referring to the positional adjustments of watches. Such as, timing a watch dial up (D.U.), dial down (D.D.), pendant right (P.R.), pendant left (P.L.), pendant up (P.U.). The signs, T pendant up, ⊢ pendant left, ⊣ pendant right, are also used.

POSITIONAL ERRORS. Changes of rate with changes of position. Calculated by the mean rates in all these 5 positions—D.U., D.D., P.R., P.L., P.U. (in pocket watches) or P.D. (in wrist watches); then finding the difference between the rate in each separate position, and the Mean Daily Rate (*q.v.*).

POSITIVE SETTING. Where the hands of a keyless watch are set directly by the winding shaft, as distinct from the Negative Setting (*q.v.*).

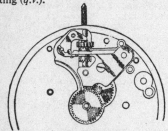

POSITIVE SETTING.

POST. A pillar secured at one end only; such as the posts or pegs upon which parts of the chronograph, repeating, strike and chime, etc., mechanisms function. Sometimes called a Stud.

POSTMAN'S ALARM CLOCK. *See* page 31.

POST MERIDIEM. Denotes the hours after Noon. Abbreviated P.M. *See* Ante Meridiem.

POTANCE or PO-TENCE. Also spelt POTTANCE. A lower cock or bracket such as the lower support for the balance staff in a "Full plate" Movement (*q.v.*).

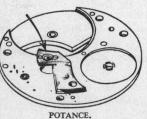

POTANCE.

POTENCE FILE. Similar to a Pillar File

(*q.v.*) but wider, and from about 4 to 6 inches in length.

POTASSIUM ACID BITARTRATE. Known as Cream of Tartar and is used in cleaning silver; its action being very efficacious in obtaining a good white colour. Used in its dry state it is a safe medium for cleaning silvered watch and clock dials.

POTENTIAL (Electrical). An electrical pressure or condition between one point, generally a conducting medium, and another point, said to be at a lower potential, such as Earth (*q.v.*). Potential difference between such points is measured in Voltage and expressed in Volts.

POTENTIAL ENERGY. The amount of work a body can do by reason of its position.

POTENTIOMETER. Generally a graduated resistance connected across a supply source and from which a required (variable) voltage may be tapped. A system of resistances or other components may also be arranged as a Potentiometer for the correct supply to a sub-circuit.

POUNCED. Ornamentation by embossing or Chasing (*q.v.*).

POUNDAL. The force which gives to a mass of 1 pound an acceleration of 1 foot per second per second.

POWER. The rate at which work is done.

POWER CURVE. A curve indicating graphically the decline or increase in power, *i.e.*, the power of a mainspring between winding and unwinding.

POWER VALVE. The (final) valve in a thermionic amplifier, capable of passing an appreciable current and from which the energy is derived to drive associated circuits or apparatus, *e.g.*, loudspeakers, relays, etc. *See* Valve.

PRECISION CLOCK. *See* Adjusted.

PRECISION WATCH. Refers to an Adjusted Watch (*q.v.*).

PRESS TOOLS. The dies used in a press tool. The products of the press tool are referred to as stampings.

PRESSURE. A force acting upon a surface or exerted upon a surface.

PRESSURE ANGLE. The angle between the common normal of the mating tooth surfaces and the common tangent plane of the pitch cylinders (*q.v.*). The term is applicable to involute gearing.

PRESSURE OF WATER. *See* Atmosphere.

PRIMARY. The winding of a transformer connected to the input side considered from the view point of the SECONDARY or output side.

PRIMARY CELL. A voltaic cell which delivers a current to a circuit connected to it by self-generation arising from the exchange of chemical to electrical energy. The action is non-reversible.

PRINCEPS ELECTRIC CLOCK SYSTEM. A system of a master electric clock controlling slave dials. Invented by Major C. E. Prince, in 1924.

PRISE OR PRIZE. To force up or off by leverage, *e.g.*, removal of a barrel cover.

PROCESS TIMER. Clock for timing industrial processes. Usually scaled in seconds or minutes and continuous or with stop and start mechanism.

PRODUCTION TIMER. *See* Timers.

PROGRESS SCREW PLATE. The most popular modern Swiss screw thread; made in a wide range of sizes for both watches and clocks. The numbers of Progress threads indicate outside diameter of screw in 1/10 mm.; *e.g.*, No. 18 = 1·8 mm. This thread is standardised and tabulated and details can be found in " Machinery's Screw Thread Book." The Progress Screw Plate was originally intended for gauging screws sold under this name. Progress thread is somewhat coarser than either " B " or " L " of the Martin Plate (*q.v.*).

PROJECTION COMPARATOR. An instrument which projects a solid object on to a screen: an accurate magnified shadow of the part is thrown on a transparent drawing magnified to the same scale enabling accurate comparison to be made.

PULLEY. A grooved wheel of any size turned or driven by a cord, flexible rope, etc. In horology, small pulleys such as are employed for driving work in turns, etc., are known as Ferrules. Pulleys are used with weights in driving some clocks. Mechanically, a single pulley offers no advantage excepting convenience. Two or more pulleys, known as a system of pulleys, confer mechanical advantage, especially in lifting weights.

PULLEY, SAFETY. The double pulley used as an accessory to the lathe. The line driving the work passes round one pulley and is allowed to touch lightly upon a second pulley which is directly coupled to the work. Thus, providing a form of friction clutch. The system is also employed to provide a close regulation of driving cord tension in dealing with delicate work.

SAFETY PULLEY.

PULL-OUT-PIECE. The small lever of the " Stem Set " watch. It depresses a further lever, so engaging the hand-setting mechanism when the winding button is withdrawn. *See* WATCH PART NOMENCLATURE. Also termed " Bolt " and " Tirette."

PULL-QUARTER. *See* ANTIQUE CLOCK CASE TERMS.

PULSATING CURRENT. A Direct Current (*q.v.*) which periodically changes in magnitude.

PULSE. Energy released in a short, sharp discharge. Said especially of interrupted or spaced flowings, of direct current or radio transmission, etc., such as in Radar.

PULSEMETER. The dial of a Chronograph (*q.v.*) or Timer (*q.v.*) calibrated to denote the rate of the pulse per minute. *See* Timers.

PUL-SYN-ETIC. A system of a master electric clock controlling slave dials; made by Gent and Co. Ltd.

PUMP CENTRE. The spring-loaded centring rod of the mandrel. A workpiece with a true hole through it is centred about the hole by the tapered end of the pump centre.

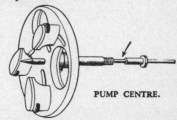

PUMP CENTRE.

PUMP REPEATER. *See* Plunger.

PUMP WIND. A form of keyless mechanism in which a plunger, fitted usually to the watch pendant, is pumped in and out to wind the mainspring.

PUNCH. (1) A steel or brass rod and used to convey a blow to a required point. (2) A tool for cutting out holes, shapes, etc., at one blow. (3) A tool for making centres. In horological use the shape and purposes are too numerous to specify. There are pointed, flat, rounded, conical, hemispherical, etc., ended punches, and some are solid, some " hollow," *i.e.*, having a hole drilled axially in the end. For many purposes, the punches are held in a guide accurately placed in relation to an anvil or Stake (*q.v.*). *See* Staking Tool.

PUSH PIECE. That part of the watch case, locket, etc., which is pushed to release the lock and so open the case. Also, the pin which is depressed to set the hands of a " side set " watch. Also, the piece to actuate the chronograph mechanism.

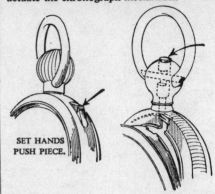

SET HANDS
PUSH PIECE.

CASE PUSH PIECE.

PUTTO. *See* WATCH PART NOMENCLATURE.

Q

QUAIL CLOCK. A clock similar to the cuckoo clock (*q.v.*) but with a bellows imitating the sound of the quail.

QUARTER CLOCK OR CHIME. A clock that chimes at each quarter of the hour, *i.e.*, quarter past, half past, and quarter to the hour and at the hour. It is generally understood that a chime clock chimes at the quarters.

QUARTER ROUND MOULDING. *See* ANTIQUE CLOCK CASE TERMS.

QUARTER RACK. The rack of a repeating watch or clock which releases the train, counts the quarters to be sounded and relocks the train.

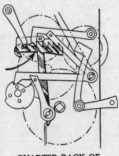

QUARTER RACK OF
A CLOCK.

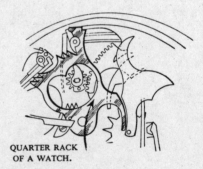

QUARTER RACK
OF A WATCH.

QUARTER REPEATER. *See* Repeater.

QUARTER SCREWS. The four screws fitted to the balance of an escapement for the purpose of mean time adjustment. To permit their advance to, or withdrawal from, the balance centre, they have longer stems than the temperature adjustment screws. They are usually fitted one at or near each end of the balance cross arm and

QUARTER SCREWS.

midway along each limb of the balance. Some balances have only two timing screws but they are still known as " Quarter Screws."

QUARTER SNAIL.

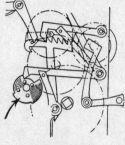

The snail of a repeating watch or chiming clock, etc., that determines the fall or drop of the rack and regulates the number of quarters to be struck. *See* Quarter Rack.

QUARTER SNAIL.

QUARTZ. Crystalline silica occurring widely throughout natural rocks. A variety possessing Piezo Electric properties is widely used in Radio and Electronic work and in the Crystal Clock (*q.v.*).

QUARTZ CRYSTAL. A piezo-electric variety of quartz usually cut in the form of a disc, square, or rod, in such a way that its natural frequency when subjected to an electrical field is at a required frequency, *e.g.*, 100 kilocycles per second. It has the great advantage of extreme stability and is widely used in Radio Frequency control. *See* Quartz Crystal Clock.

QUARTZ CRYSTAL CLOCK. A quartz crystal controlled synchronous motor clock. The most accurate timekeeper known to science at present in general use. The properties of quartz crystal were first applied to horology by Warren A. Marrison in 1929. The crystals oscillate at a frequency of the order of 100,000 per second and can be compared with each other to 1 part in 10^{10}. Physically and electrically they are exceedingly stable. The " natural " frequency being too high for convenient time measurement, it is reduced by a system of frequency division or Demultiplication (*q.v.*) to 1,000 per second. At this frequency electrical linkage is readily provided to drive a motion train. The whole process is controlled by the quartz crystal acting as a Master Oscillator (*q.v.*).

QUARTZ OSCILLATOR. Another term for Crystal Oscillator.

QUATREFOILS. *See* ANTIQUE CLOCK CASE TERMS.

QUEEN ANNE STYLE. *See* ANTIQUE CLOCK CASE TERMS.

QUENCHING. The process of plunging heated metal into a liquid such as water, oil, petrol, mercury, etc., employed in hardening and tempering (*q.v.*).

QUICKSILVER. Another name for Murcury (*q.v.*).

QUIRK. *See* ANTIQUE CLOCK CASE TERMS.

R

RACK. A segment of a circle or a straight bar having teeth cut along one edge or both. The shape of the teeth may be of a gear pattern or Ratchet shape (*q.v.*). The rack in a clock or watch is that part controlling the number of blows to be struck or quarters to be chimed. *See* Quarter Rack and Hour Rack. In a watch, it regulates the striking of the hours, quarters, or minutes, etc. *See* Repeating Rack. Rack for timing watches. *See* Watch Rack.

RACK.

RACK HOOK. The lever of a strike or chime clock mechanism which engages in the teeth of the rack and holds it in position during the process of striking, preventing the rack from falling back while it is being gathered up by the " Gathering Pallet " (*q.v.*).

RACK HOOK

RACK LEVER ESCAPEMENT. A lever escapement employing a toothed rack in place of the Notch (*q.v.*) gearing with a pinion which replaces the normal balance staff. First invented by Hautefeville in 1722, and by Peter Litherland in 1791.

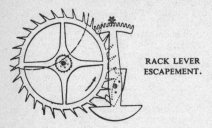

RACK LEVER ESCAPEMENT.

The action of this escapement is similar to the Lever Escapement (*q.v.*) with the difference that there is no roller and impulse pin, and it is not free.

RACK TAIL. The arm attached to the rack of strike and chime clocks; its purpose is to determine the extent of the drop of the rack on to the snail, thus regulating the number of blows to be struck.

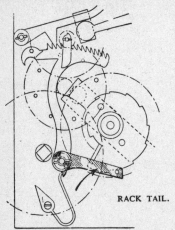

RACK TAIL.

RADIO CLOCK. A master clock monitored or impulsed by time transmission pulses broadcast by radio.

RADIUS CUTTER. A cutter of various shapes used for cutting sinks or routing out.

RADIUS CUTTER.

RADIUS OF GYRATION. The distance from the centre of rotation of a pendulum or balance to the centre of oscillation of the pendulum bob or balance rim. *See* Gyration.

RAILWAY TIME. Another term for Greenwich Mean Time (*q.v.*).

RATCHET FILE. *See* Files.

RATCHET TOOTH. A saw-like tooth of a ratchet wheel. Ratchet wheels are also made with gear-shaped teeth, *e.g.*, in watches; although the teeth of such wheels are in fact ratchet teeth, they are not generally understood to be " Ratchet tooth " shape. *See* Ratchet Wheel. The term also refers to the escape wheel of the lever escapement where the teeth are pointed in contradistinction to the Club Tooth form (*q.v.*).

RATCHET TOOTH.

RATCHET WHEEL. A toothed wheel into which a click engages permitting the wheel to revolve in one direction only. The wheel can be provided with teeth of normal or ratchet shape. *See* Watch Part Nomenclature.

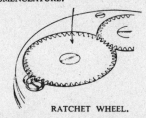

RATCHET WHEEL.

RATE. The term defines " steady time-keeping." An instrument which registers an error, either gaining or losing 1 second per day and does not vary from that error, is said to have a " good rate." If the instrument has an error say, either gaining or losing 10 seconds per day and does not vary from that 10 seconds it is said to have a " good rate " but is " wide " If the error fluctuates from day to day or is inconsistent, then the instrument is said to have a " poor rate." A " rated " instrument is one that has been " Adjusted " (*q.v.*). The expression " a close rate " implies that the rate of an instrument is not only good but the divergence from true running very small.

RATING. The operation and procedure of adjusting a timepiece to close limits of timekeeping. The term is usually associated with precision work, *i.e.*, adjusting a time-piece in different positions and for changes in temperature. *See* TESTING STANDARDS FOR WATCHES.

RATING NUT. The nut at-tached to the pendulum rod to raise or lower the pen-dulum bob.

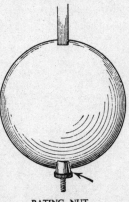

RATING NUT.

RATIO. When applied to gearing it refers to the proportional size of two gears which operate to-gether. If for instance, one gear is half the size of the other, it will rotate at twice the speed of its companion and it is then said to have a " two to one " ratio.

RAT-TAIL FILE. A tapering round file.

REACTANCE. The quality of an induct-ance or capacitance in the presence of an A.C. That portion of the total impedance or " resistance " of an A.C. circuit due to inductance and capacitance. Measured in Ohms.

REAMER. A tool used for enlarging holes; similar to a Broach (*q.v.*), but having longitudinal or spiral flutes to form the cutting edges.

RE-BUSH. To fit a new " bush," *i.e.*, to fit a new hole. A hole that has worn oval or wide is renewed by fitting a tube which is then opened out to suit the pivot.

RECEDING CONTACT, or recess contact or disengaging contact. That part of the phase of engagement between a pair of teeth which takes place after the point of contact has passed the line of centres.

RECEIVING PALLET. Another name for the Entry Pallet (*q.v.*).

RECESSING MACHINE. A jewel bearing recessing machine used for pro-ducing a cup shaped depression, the Oil

Sink (*q.v.*) in a jewel. Also called a cupping machine. Also, a milling machine using end mills, *i.e.* cutters which have their cutting edges on the ends, for recessing watch plates, etc.

RECOIL. To move backwards. A slight reversal of the normal run of the " train " (*q.v.*) caused by certain types of escape-ments, *e.g.*, Recoil escapement (*q.v.*). *See* Recoiling Click.

RECOIL ESCAPEMENT. An escape-ment where the escape wheel recoils after locking. Usually the term refers to the Anchor Escapement (*q.v.*).

RECOILING CLICK. A click which recoils and allows the ratchet wheel to reverse slightly when the winding force (as in a watch) is re-moved. The purpose is to prevent the mainspring being wound too tightly, straining the hooking and causing it to exert tempor-arily a force beyond its nor-mal strength which in turn might cause

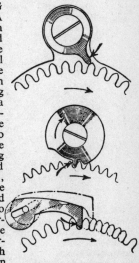

RECOILING CLICK.

striking the banking and a disturbance of the rate of the timepiece. In the top illustration the click banks against the left-hand corner of the plate. In the middle illustration the click banks against the teeth of the ratchet and in the lower illustration the click runs back and banks on its pivot.

RECORDERS. *See* Timers, Time Re-corders, Timing Machines.

RED STUFF. A form of Rouge (*q.v.*) for polishing brass. Used in a manner similar to that of Diamantine (*q.v.*) with a polisher of tin.

REEDING. *See* ANTIQUE CLOCK CASE TERMS.

REGENCY PERIOD. *See* ANTIQUE CLOCK CASE TERMS.

REGULATOR. The name given to a precision, weight-driven timepiece clock. Usually fitted with the Dead Beat escapement (*q.v.*) and provided with some form of compensation pendulum. Regulators are also made with other forms of escapement, *i.e.*, the Pin Wheel (*q.v.*) (especially the Continental makes), and the Double Three-Legged escapement (*q.v.*). The dial of a Regulator is usually arranged with the minute hand in the centre, the seconds hand above and the hour hand below the centre. Another type of clock in this category for general work is known as the Vienna Regulator (*q.v.*). *See* Astronomical Clock. The term Regulator applies also to the index of a balance escapement. (*See* Index).

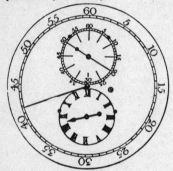

REGULATOR.

REID'S ESCAPEMENT. Invented, as a modification of Mudge's escapement (*q.v.*), by Thomas Reid of Edinburgh (1746–1831) for use in Astronomical Regulator (*q.v.*) clocks. The action of the escapement is as follows:— The tooth A is locked by the pallet B. The pendulum as it vibrates to the right will unlock A from B. When the escape wheel rotates, the tooth C will pass along the impulse face of the pallet D, raising it and opposing the pallet spring E until C is arrested on the locking face of the pallet D. When C is in turn unlocked from D, the pallet B is raised. The pendulum during vibration is opposed during its Supple-

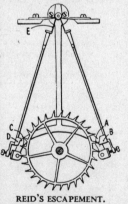

REID'S ESCAPEMENT.

mentary Arc (*q.v.*) by the pallet springs and by gravity. It is assisted in returning by the pallet springs and by gravity from the limits of the supplementary arc, until the pallets reach their repose positions and are again raised. The small difference between its opposed and assisted passage maintains the vibration of the pendulum.

RELUCTANCE. The quality of a magnetic circuit in resisting magnetisation. The ratio of the magnetomotive force to the magnetic force or flux produced.

RELUCTIVITY. The reciprocal or inverse ratio of Permeability (*q.v.*). It is a measure of the magnetic conductivity of a material.

REMANANCE. The quality of retention of magnetic properties after initial excitation. The flux density remaining after subjection to a magnetomotive force. Very high in steel (and other alloys), but low in soft iron.

REMONTOIRE. Usually refers to a device whereby the main source of power periodically winds a spring or lifts a weight to drive the actual mechanism. The purpose is the provision of a constant force, *e.g.*, a spring-driven clock winds up a weight. The weight then transmits the power to the escapement. There are many versions of the same principle.

RENAISSANCE. *See* page 32.

REPEATER. Refers to a clock or watch where the last hour and the quarters and minutes can be sounded at will.
QUARTER REPEATER. The last hour as shown on the dial and the quarters are sounded, *e.g.*, at 10 minutes to 8 o'clock, 7 blows are struck, followed by 3 ting-tangs to indicate the quarters.
MINUTE REPEATER. The last hour, then the quarters, then the minutes are sounded, *e.g.*, at 10 minutes to 8 o'clock, 7 blows are struck, followed by 3 ting-tangs, then 5 single blows to indicate the minutes.
HALF QUARTER REPEATER. The last hour, the quarters, and the nearest half quarter are sounded, *e.g.*, at 5 minutes to 8 o'clock, 7 blows are struck, then 3 ting-tangs, followed by 1 single blow to indicate $7\frac{1}{2}$ minutes past the last quarter.
FIVE MINUTE REPEATER. The last hour, the quarters, and one blow for each 5 minutes past the last quarter are sounded, *e.g.*, at 5 minutes to 8, 7 blows are struck, then 3 ting-tangs, followed by 2 single blows indicate the 10 minutes past the last quarter. Some repeating clocks and watches employ the Westminster or other chimes, but the same principle prevails. *See* Dumb Repeater.

REPEATING RACK. The rack of a repeating watch which winds up the repeating mainspring. Separate racks are provided to sound the hours, quarters, minutes, half quarters and the 5 minute periods of the respective types of repeater watches.

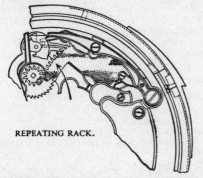

REPEATING RACK.

REPEATING SLIDE. The slide fitted to the side of the case of a repeating watch by which, when it is drawn round, the repeating mainspring is wound up and the mechanism set in motion.

REPEATING SLIDE.

REPELLENT ESCAPEMENT. A form of the lever escapement in which, instead of "Draw" (*q.v.*), the escape wheel repels the pallets so that the lever end is in constant contact with the roller. Invented by J. F. Cole.

RE-PIVOTING. The operation of re-

making or replacing a broken pivot. *See* Pivoting.

REPOUSSÉ. A decorative treatment of metal. The metal is hammered or punched up from the reverse side to form a decoration or design when viewed from the face or "front." Used on watch cases, especially in the seventeenth and eighteenth centuries.

REPUBLICAN TIME. *See* ANTIQUE CLOCK CASE TERMS.

REPULSION. A movement of a body away from a force acting upon it. The force exerted mutually between two magnetic or electrical poles of the same sign.

RESILIENT ESCAPEMENT. A form of the Lever Escapement in which the tail of the lever is narrowed down to form a spring; the tail operates on the banking pins so that if, due to excessive vibration of the balance, the ruby pin strikes upon the back of the lever notch the lever will "give," absorbing the blow and protecting the ruby pin and pallet staff pivots. There are other forms of resilient escapements where no banking pins are provided; the resilience is obtained either by dispensing with the "draw" of the pallets or by the

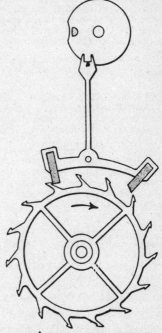

COLE'S RESILIENT ESCAPEMENT.

pallets contacting the stem of the escape wheel teeth and forcing the wheel backwards. All systems are now obsolete, the spring-tailed lever being the most popular when in favour.

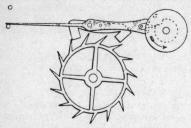

SPRING-TAIL LEVER ESCAPEMENT.

RESILIENT HOOK. A form of hooking of the mainspring to the barrel. A short piece of spring is attached to the mainspring, forming a flexible anchorage.

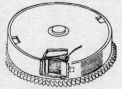

RESILIENT HOOK.

RESILIENT MAINSPRING. Usually refers to a mainspring, which when unwound, prior to use, is in the shape of the letter " S." Also known as a Reverse Mainspring or Reverse Curve spring.

RESIN. A product from the secretion of the sap of certain plants and trees. *See* Rosin.

RESISTANCE. The quality of offering opposition. The characteristic, to a greater or lesser degree of every electrical conductor. The resistance of a conductor is measured in Ohms (*q.v.*) and is given by the Voltage divided by the current in amperes. The conductor may be part or the whole of a circuit. Components known as Resistors as used in radio and similar circuits are resistances of specified values of Ohms ranging from 50 to several million (Megohms).

RESISTANCE-CAPACITY COUPLING A form of coupling employed to link two valve circuits. A resistance and a condenser (capacitor) are so used that of the steady and alternating voltages appearing across the resistor, only the alternating voltages are applied to the grid of the second valve.

RESISTOR. An electrical component, part, or special conductor possessing a specified, comparable, or appreciable value

of resistance. May be made of carbon, composite materials, or resistance wire.

RESTING BARREL. A type of barrel fitted to some of the earlier Fusee movements. The barrel does not rotate but remains stationary and is fixed to the bottom plate. The outer end of the mainspring is attached to this barrel, the inner end to an arbor upon which is mounted the barrel for the fusee chain. Invented by Harrison. A similar contrivance was also made by L. Donne.

REST, SLIDE. *See* Slide Rest.

REST " T." *See* Tee Rest.

RETARD. To make slow. Symbol " R ."

RETURN BAR. The lever or bar of the keyless mechanism which operates on the castle wheel. It returns or thrusts the castle wheel into mesh with the crown wheel.

REVERSE FUSEE. Refers to the arrangement whereby the normal planting of fusee and barrel is reversed. The advantage is that the pull of the fusee chain comes between the fusee arbor, and the centre pinion, thus minimising friction. Also known as Right-hand Fusee.

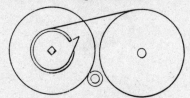

ORDINARY FUSEE.

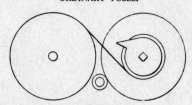

REVERSE FUSEE.

REVERSE MAINSPRING. *See* Resilient Mainspring.

REVERSO WATCH. The name given to

REVERSO WATCH.

a wrist watch where the watch can be reversed. Made by LeCoultre Co., Switzerland.

REVOLUTION CLOCKS. *See* ANTIQUE CLOCK CASE TERMS.

RIBAND DECORATION. *See* ANTIQUE CLOCK CASE TERMS.

RIBBON STICK. *See* ANTIQUE CLOCK CASE TERMS.

RIDGED-BACK FILE. A tapered file with a ridge running along the back and having cutting teeth on the flat surface only.

RIEFLER ESCAPEMENT. An escapement, invented by Sigmund Riefler, 1893, in which impulse is conveyed to the pendulum through the flexing of the suspension spring. The actual escapement is the Brocot Dead Beat (*q.v.*) employing two escape wheels, one for locking and the other for impulse. It is generally assumed to be Riefler's invention (he patented it in 1893), but a clock made by A. Breguet in 1823, and now in Buckingham Palace, has a pin wheel escapement and impulse is transmitted to the pendulum through the flexing of the suspension spring.

RIEFLER PENDULUM. A pendulum having a rod of nickel steel, the bob resting on a short tube of aluminium. An earlier Riefler pendulum had mercurial compensation.

RIEFLER WATCH ESCAPEMENT. Where the balance spring is fitted beneath the balance arm; and the balance spring stud is attached to the end of the lever, where the notch is normally situated. Impulse is given to the balance through the winding up of the balance spring. Practically a " free balance " escapement.

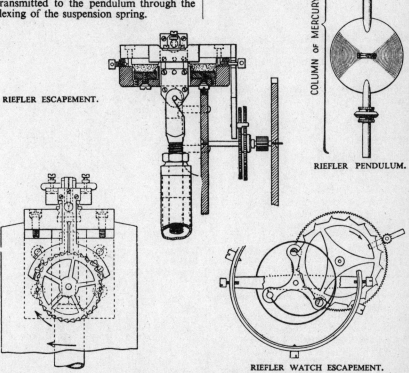

RIEFLER ESCAPEMENT.

COLUMN OF MERCURY

RIEFLER PENDULUM.

RIEFLER WATCH ESCAPEMENT.

RIGHT ANGLE ESCAPEME T. The lever escapement in which the line of centres of the lever and balance staff are at right angles to one another. In contra-distinction to the "Straight line" Level Escapement (*q.v.*).

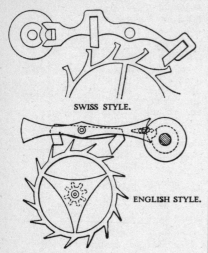

SWISS STYLE.

ENGLISH STYLE.

RIGHT ASCENSION. Hour-angle of a star or other heavenly body measured along celestial equator from the first point of Aries.

RIGHT HAND FUSEE. *See* Reverse Fusee.

RIGHT HAND STONE. Another name for the Exit Pallet Stone (*q.v.*) of the lever escapement.

RING CHUCK. A split chuck for use in the lathe, to hold rings, *i.e.* bezil.

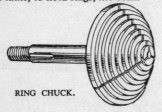

RING CHUCK.

RISE AND FALL. A device consisting of a snail upon which rests a lever; the pendulum is attached to the other end of the lever and, by making the snail revolve the active length of the pendulum is adjusted, so regulating the clock by making the pendulum to rise or fall between the "chops" of the suspension.

RISING HOOD. *See* ANTIQUE CLOCK CASE TERMS.

RITCHIE'S SYNCHRONISER. An electrical system of synchronisation whereby a clock is arranged to have a gaining rate and, at a pre-determined time, the minute hand is arrested and then released as the synchonising is effected.

RIVET. A form of "burring" formed by hammering. Also refers to a short pin with a head; a brad.

RIVETING HAMMER. A hammer head having a rounded striking surface. A ball-pean hammer.

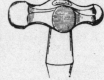

RIVETING HAMMER.

ROCKING BAR. The plate or bar of a form of keyless mechanism which carries the winding wheels and so named by reason of the rocking motion by which the winding is effected.

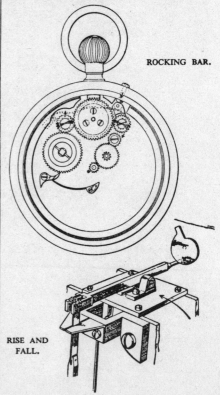

ROCKING BAR.

RISE AND FALL.

ROCOCO. *See* ANTIQUE CLOCK CASE TERMS.

ROE. *See* ANTIQUE CLOCK CASE TERMS.

ROLLED GOLD. *See* page 138.

ROLLER. Lever Escapement. The disc or platform, with the impulse pin attached, which is fitted to the balance staff. *See* Lever Escapement, Double Roller, Single Roller.

SINGLE ROLLER.

DOUBLE ROLLER.

CHRONOMETER (*q.v.*). The disc to which the impulse pallet is attached or to which the discharge pallet is attached, and fitted to the balance staff.

CHRONO-METER ROLLERS.

DUPLEX (*q.v.*). The cylindrical " collar " with a " V " shaped vertical slot, fitted to the balance staff, which acts as a rest and impulse medium; usually made of ruby.

DUPLEX ROLLER.

ROLLER ABSTRACTOR. A tool for removing the roller from the balance staff of the lever escapement; there are numerous patterns of this tool. The one shown illustrates the principle.

ROLLER JEWEL. An American term for the Impulse Pin (*q.v.*).

ROLLER REMOVER. *See* Roller Abstractor.

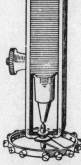

ROLLER ABSTRACTOR.

ROLLER REST. An accessory of the lathe; a roller, pivoted between centres, to take the place of the " T " rest. Used in filing work when fitted up in the lathe. A similar fitment is employed on the Screw Head Polishing Tool.

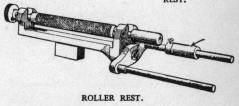

ROLLER REST.

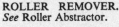

ROLLER REST.

ROLLER TABLE. An American term for the Roller (*q.v.*).

ROLLING FRICTION. The friction experienced when a round body is rolled over another. It is the least detrimental form of friction. Since friction cannot be entirely eliminated, horologists in common with other engineers seek to employ " rolling " friction in preference to " engaging " or " disengaging " Friction (*q.v.*), *i.e.*, rubbing or sliding friction.

ROLLING LEAF PINION. Refers to a " Lantern Pinion " (*q.v.*) where the pins or trundles are in the form of a roller, so that they rotate.

ROMAN CALENDAR. The calendar used by the Romans and on which the modern calendar is based. Firstly there were 10 months; Martius (March), Aprillis (April), Maius (May), Junius (June), Quintillis (fifth month), Sextillis (sixth month), September (seventh month), October (eighth month), November (ninth month, December (tenth month). A total of 304 days. Numa added two months: Januarius (January) and Februarius (February) making a total of 355 days. The Julian calendar (*q.v.*) replaced the early Roman calendar. *See* also Gregorian calendar and Calendar.

ROMAN DIAL. A dial the figuring of which is in Roman characters. Thus:—

1	2	3	4	5	6	7	8	9	10
I	II	III	IV	V	VI	VII	VIII	IX	X

11	12	50	100	1000
XI	XII	L	C	M.

ROMAN STRIKING. A system of sounding the time using the principle of Roman numerals or numbering. Invented by Joseph Knibb and employed in clocks.

The clock is provided with two bells, one low tone (indicated by the large dot) and the other, a higher pitch (indicated by the smaller dot in the illustration). The sequence is thus:—

Hours.	1	2	3	4	5	6	7	8	9	10	11	12
STRIKING	•	•	•	•	●	●	●	●	●	●	●	●
		•		●		•	•		●	●	●	●
			•					●				●
								●				●

RONDELLING. Making jewels circular after sawing, usually done by Centreless Grinding (*q.v.*).

ROOT CIRCLE. A circle drawn round a Wheel or Pinion (*q.v.*) at the bottom of the teeth spaces.

ROOT CIRCLE.

ROSE CUTTERS. A circular cutter having the cutting teeth formed upon the end of the tool. Used in sinking, recessing, etc. A " pivot " or " pilot " can be fitted into the cutter, to act as a guide, when a hole is to be sunk, such as to increase endshake.

ROSE CUTTER.

ROSIN. The residue from the distillation of turpentine. Used in horology as a soldering flux. *See* Resin.

ROSKOPF WATCH. Refers to a watch made by Roskopf of La Chaux-de-Fonds, Switzerland which has a lay-out or calibre peculiar to its own. Georges Roskopf, a German, started a factory in Switzerland about 1866 and produced the first cheap rugged watch. The word Roskopf has become synonymous with a cheap pin pallet watch, implying that all pin pallet watches are Roskopf, but such is not the case.

A. Intermediate wheel.
B. Barrel.
B'. Minute wheel, spring friction tight on the barrel which enables it to rotate to set the hands.
C. Hour wheel.
D. Idle cannon pinion.
E. Third wheel.
F. Fourth wheel.

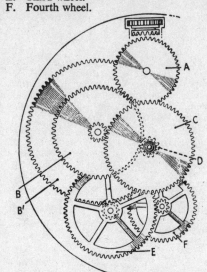

ROSKOPF WATCH.

ROTARY FILE. A form of cutter used for enlarging holes.

ROTARY FILE.

ROTOR. Part of an electrical apparatus, generally an Armature (*q.v.*) which is caused to rotate. In an electric (synchronous) clock it is the revolution of the Rotor under the influence of the electro-magnetic Stator (*q.v.*) which drives the reduction gearing or train and motion work to indicate the time. The term Rotor is applied usually to alternating current machines. Also the pedometer-like weight of the automatic winding watch (*q.v.*). *See* page 55.

ROTTEN-STONE. Natural mineral. A form of Tripolite found in Derbyshire. A powerful abrasive. Sold by material dealers in blocks and used either in crushed form mixed with oil to form a paste, or, by dipping a brush in oil and wiping it over the block. It is thus used in cleaning parts of clock movements. It imparts a dull polish to brass and steel. A brighter polish can be obtained by mixing rouge in a paste of crushed rottenstone and oil.

ROUGE. A refined form of oxide of iron

used for polishing purposes, especially for Gold and Silver. Also used with silver solder to prevent solder running to where it is not wanted.

ROUGHING. The first stage in making a new part; preceding finishing, polishing, etc. The initial stages in cutting or shaping up blank material.

ROUGH MOVEMENT. Another name for Ébauche (q.v.).

ROUGH STAFF, PINION MATERIAL. The partly completed or shaped parts as obtained for general use from " Material " dealers. Generally, these are not intended for named or specified movements and the quality, tempering, etc., may vary widely. (Compare with Interchangeable Material.)

ROUND FILE. See Files.

ROUND NOSE PLIERS. See Pliers.

ROUNDEL. See ANTIQUE CLOCK CASE TERMS.

ROUNDING-UP FILE. A thin file with cutting teeth on one side and a polished, rounded back. Used for shaping the leaves of pinions of clocks. Hand-made pinions sre formed from Pinion Wire (q.v.) the leaves being filed by hand to suit the teeth of the wheel with which it is to work.

ROUNDING-UP FILE.

ROUNDING-UP TOOL. A tool used for recutting or re-shaping wheel teeth. Also termed a Topping Tool.

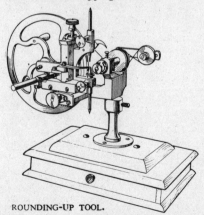

ROUNDING-UP TOOL.

ROWING TIMER. See Timers.

ROYAL GREENWICH OBSERVA-TORY. The Royal Observatory, Greenwich, situated in the south-east of London, was established by Charles II in 1675. When international agreement on the selection of a zero or prime meridian from which the longitudes of all places should be measured was sought in 1884, the choice of the meridian through the transit circle of the Royal Observatory was a recognition of the importance of the contributions of the Observatory to astronomical and nautical science. With the growth of London there has been a progressive deterioration in the conditions for astronomical observations at Greenwich, and the installation of brighter street lighting made the skies at night too bright for long exposure photography. The Observatory was, therefore, moved to Herstmonceux, Sussex, and was officially announced by the Admiralty on April 12, 1946. The removal has not changed the position of the prime meridian of longitude. The Observatory occupies the building, Herstmonceux Castle, which was built in 1446 by Sir Roger de Fiennes, Treasurer of the household of Henry VI. In 1777 the interior was pulled down, but the outer walls and towers have remained intact with 20th century restoration. The interior has been modernised. Although positioned at Herstmonceux, the Observatory is still known as the Royal Greenwich Observatory.

ROYAL PENDULUM. Another name for the Seconds Pendulum (q.v.).

RUBY. Jewel holes, endstones, pallet stones and impulse pins were made of the natural mineral. The Impulse Pin still retains the name " Ruby Pin." The same chemical composition and structure is found in the Synthetic Stone (q.v.) now used.

RUBY CYLINDER. The cylinder of the Horizontal escapement made of ruby.

RUBY FILE. A very fine file made of ruby and used for the slight filing of hardened and tempered steel.

RUBY PIN. The Impulse Pin of the lever escapement, also known as the Impulse Pin (q.v.).

RUBY ROLLER. The jewel roller of the Duplex escapement (q.v.).

RUBYTINE. A powder used in polishing steel work; applied in a method similar to that of Diamantine (q.v.). It has the same chemical composition as the latter but is mixed with a little rouge, or red oxide of iron, during manufacture. Generally it is sharper than the diamantine of the corresponding grade.

RUDD'S CLOCK. The first " free pendulum " invented by R. J. Rudd. It may be seen at the Science Museum, London.

RUMBLING—*See* Tumbling.

RUN. Another term for freedom and usually applied in respect to a sliding " action " as distinct from " end shake " or " Side Shake " (*q.v.*) Also used in the sense of the term " Warn " (*q.v.*).

RUN OF LEVER. An American term for the " Run to the banking " (*q.v.*)

RUN TO THE BANKING. In the lever escapement, it is the movement of the lever to the banking as the escape wheel tooth slides up the locking face of the pallet stone, immediately after Locking(*q.v.*). The movement should not be confused with the Draw (*q.v.*). It is sometimes referred to as the Slide-Locking (American).

RUN TO THE BANKING.

RUNNER. An accessory to the Lathe, Turns, or Jacot tool (*q.v.*). Used as a centre to hold work while being turned or as a " bed " when polishing pivots or as a means of holding work while its ends are polished, *e.g.*, a balance staff pivot(s). (*See* also Squire's Runner, Safety Runner, Eccentric Runner.)

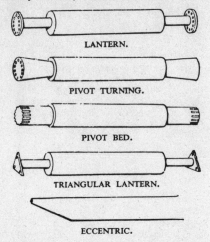

LANTERN.

PIVOT TURNING.

PIVOT BED.

TRIANGULAR LANTERN.

ECCENTRIC.

RUN OUT. *See* ANTIQUE CLOCK CASE TERMS.

RHYTHMIC TIME SIGNALS. Time signals emitted by high-powered radio stations for navigational and other purposes. The signals differ from the exact second. These signals are spaced 61 to the minute enabling the error of a chronometer, or other time measuring instrument, to be accurately determined by observing the instance of coincidence between the signals and the ticks of the time measuring instrument.

S

SADDLE. The bearer or fitting attached to a lathe bed on which the slide rest is mounted.

SADDLE COIL. A form of deflection coil, wound as a rectangle and bent to fit over the neck of a Cathode Ray Tube (*q.v.*).

SAFE-EDGED FILE. A file having one edge or side blank, *i.e.*, with no cutting teeth. It enables a step or shoulder to be filed without damage to the surface at right angles to that being cut. A combination burnisher and file is similarly arranged.

SAFE-EDGED FILE.

SAFETY ACTION. Refers to the action of the guard pin with relation to the roller of the lever escapement. More correctly a general term describing the related sequence of operation and positions of the lever, guard pin, roller and impulse pin and " draw " of the lever escapement.

SAFETY BARREL. Where the barrel is composed of two parts: a steel barrel without teeth into which the mainspring is wound; the great wheel with barrel arbor attached. Its purpose is to protect the barrel teeth and centre pinion, etc. Should the mainspring break, the steel barrel containing the mainspring is free to revolve and thus absorbs the recoil. (A) The barrel; (B) Great Wheel; (C) Barrel arbor; (D) Ratchet wheel.

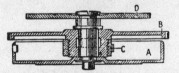

SAFETY BARREL.

SAFETY FINGER OR PIN. Another name for the Guard Pin (*q.v.*).

SAFETY PULLEY. *See* Pulley, Safety.

SAFETY PIN. *See* Guard Pin.

SAFETY PINION. Refers to the centre pinion, the pinion head of which is made to screw or thread on to its arbor. In the event of mainspring breakage, the recoil shock of the spring causes the pinion

head to unscrew thus relieving the strain on the barrel teeth and third-wheel pivots. The comparatively stout centre wheel construction normally transmits the shock to the third wheel pivot without itself being damaged.

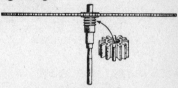

SAFETY PINION.

SAFETY ROLLER. Another name for the Roller (*q.v.*) (Single or Double) of the lever escapement.

SAFETY ROLLER.

SAFETY RUNNER. A safety runner as used in the turns is illustrated. The end face is provided with a conical hole which thus supports the shoulder of a pivot introduced into it during working operation upon the pivot, etc., at the opposite end of an arbor, staff, etc., upon which pressure may be exerted without undue risk to the pivot. A similar runner is used in the Pivoting Tool (*q.v.*).

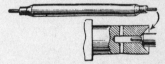

SAFETY RUNNER.

SAL AMMONIAC. Ammonium Chloride. Used as a flux, more especially as a " bit " cleaner; also as the electrolyte in Leclanche cells and dry batteries, etc.

SAND BLAST FINISH. A process of cleaning metals by means of a high velocity blast of sand, steel shot, or grit. Gives a pitted, dull, matt surface especially good as a " key " for paints, enamels, etc., and some forms of plating.

SAPPHIRE. A natural mineral. In horology the pale sapphire was used for jewel holes, end stones and pallet stones; now superseded by the Synthetic Stone (*q.v.*).

SAPPHIRINE. A polishing material for steel; used in a manner similar to that of

Diamantine (*q.v.*). Consists chiefly of aluminium oxide with addition of small quantity of blue colouring matter. Is coarser in grain and sharper than Diamantine. Also, a naturally occurring and rare alumino-silicate of magnesium found in Greenland.

SATIN FINISH. A term relating to the finish given to metal work, especially, Gold, Silver, Platinum, and Stainless Steel. It is a very fine straight " grain," imparting a form of matt surface and is used as a final finish to watch cases, etc. *See* ANTIQUE CLOCK CASE TERMS.

SATURATION. The condition or property of a magnetic material whereby increase of a magneto-motive force beyond a point of maximum flux density, results in a decrement of flux. The term has several applications in Electrical and Thermionic engineering, *e.g.*, transformers, valves, solenoids, etc. Also refers to a solution in which the solvent is incapable of absorbing a further quantity of the substance—a Saturated Solution.

SAVAGE'S TWO-PIN ESCAPEMENT. A variation of the Lever escapement having two gold pins in the place of the single Impulse Pin (*q.v.*), the pins acting as unlocking pins only, the impulse being imparted to the balance by a pin on the lever which also acts as the " guard " pin. The advantage claimed is that unlocking takes place on the line of centres, and impulse fairly close to it.

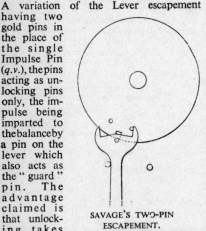

SAVAGE'S TWO-PIN ESCAPEMENT.

SAW-TOOTH GENERATOR. The name given to the circuit (or other means), by which a saw-toothed wave form is produced. Applied most commonly to cathode-ray tubes (oscilloscopes, etc.), as a Linear Time base.

SCALLOP. *See* ANTIQUE CLOCK CASE TERMS.

SCANNING. The repetitive traverse of the screen of a cathode-ray tube by the electron beam. In oscilloscope work, the visible " picture " is known as a " Trace " or " Figure." The term is more closely applied to Television.

SCAPE. An abbreviated reference to the Escape Wheel. Also " Scapement " for Escapement; 'Scape Action, etc.

SCOTIA. *See* MOULDINGS.

SCRAPER. A sharp edged tool used for surface cutting; a form of metal shaver.

SCRATCH BRUSH. A harsh brush, employing metal wires—usually fine brass wire —instead of bristles. Used in cleaning and imparting a frosted surface to gilding and plating. Also used to remove the burrs thrown up by the wheel cutter, etc. *See* Glass Brush.

SCREEN. The coated, fluorescent surface of a cathode-ray tube. An electrode of a thermionic valve, interposed between the Anode (*q.v.*) and other electrodes. *See* Valve.

SCREENED GRID. *See* Valve.

SCRAPER.

SCREWS. Said to have come into use for watches in Germany about 1540 and 50 years later in England. Screws were used much earlier for other trades. *See* American Screws, English Screws, Progress Screws, Fine Metric Threads, and Martin Screws.

SCREW FERRULE. A form of pulley which is secured to the work for turning, polishing, etc., by a bar which tightens on to the work by two screws. Another type consists of a split pulley, the two parts screwing together to grip the work.

SCREW FERRULE.

SCREW-HEAD FILE. *See* Slitting File.

SCREW-HEAD TOOL. A form of lathe used in finishing the heads of screws, etc., and for reducing the length of the tapped shank, etc.

SCREW-HEAD TOOL.

SCREW PITCH. *See* Screws and Pitch.

SCREW PLATE. A steel plate having a number of graduated tapped holes for making screw threads. Unlike the engineers' die which cuts the thread, the horologists' screw plate usually burrs up a thread by pressure. Some plates, however, are obtainable with cutting edges and clearing holes. *See* also Martin Plate, Progress Plate, Die.

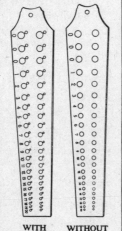

WITH CLEARANCE.   WITHOUT CLEARANCE.

SCREW THREAD. The spirally cut or burred-up grooves which essentially form a screw.

SCREWS, QUARTER. *See* Quarter Screws.

SCREWS, RATING. *See* Rating Screws.

SCREWS, TEMPERATURE. *See* Temperature Screws.

SCREWS, TIMING. *See* Timing Screws.

SCROLL CHUCK. A form of self-centring chuck. *See* Universal Chuck.

SCROLL ORNAMENT. *See* ANTIQUE CLOCK CASE TERMS.

SCULLING TIMER. *See* Timers.

SEAT BOARD. *See* ANTIQUE CLOCK CASE TERMS.

SEAWEED MARQUETRY. *See* ANTIQUE CLOCK CASE TERMS.

SECONDARY. A shortened form of Secondary Winding (*q.v.*).

SECONDARY CELL. A voltaic cell the electro-chemical action of which is reversible thus enabling the cell to be " charged " from an external source, *e.g.*, an accumulator.

SECONDARY COMPENSATION. Another term for " Auxiliary compensation " (*q.v.*).

SECONDARY ELECTRONS. Electrons emitted from a surface as a result of bombardment by primary (*i.e.* initiating) electrons.

SECONDARY EMISSION. The emission of secondary electrons from a surface.

SECONDARY ERROR. The same as Middle Temperature Error (*q.v.*).

SECONDARY VOLTAGE. The voltage appearing at the output terminals of, and described generally as being " across," the secondary winding.

SECONDARY WINDING. A coil, loop, or winding linking with the flux produced by an electric current in a Primary winding. The coil of a transformer from which the Output is obtained. *See* also Tertiary.

SECOND TAP. The tap used, after the Taper tap to carry the full thread through a hole or, farther down into a blind hole.

SECONDS HAND. The hand of a chronometer, clock, or watch, or timing instrument, which indicates seconds.

SECONDS, INDEPENDENT. *See* " Independent Seconds," and compare with Centre Seconds.

SECONDS PENDULUM. A pendulum beating seconds. Sometimes referred to as " Royal Pendulum." The theoretical length at sea level is 39·14 inches in London.

SECONDS PIVOT. The extended pivot to which the seconds hand is fitted. Usually it is on the Fourth Pinion (*q.v.*) of the off-set seconds watch movement and the escape pinion of the seconds pendulum clock movement. In the case of the centre seconds the pivot is referred to as " the centre seconds pivot."

SECTOR. A simple proportional gauge. used to ascertain the correct proportions between a wheel diameter and the pinion gearing with it. There are limitations as to the accuracy of the gauge above and below certain dimensions. *See* " Practical Watch Repairing." Also, a portion of a circle bounded by two radii and the arc they enclose.

SECTOR.

SEDAN CLOCK.

SEDAN CLOCK. A small hanging clock usually associated with the period of the Sedan Chair.

SEIZURE. An extreme form of Binding (*q.v.*) between sliding or moving surfaces due to lack of lubricant, expansion, inadequate clearance, etc.

SELENIUM CELL. A photo-electric cell based upon the electrical behaviour and light sensitivity of Selenium.

SELF-CENTRING CHUCK. *See* Universal Chuck.

SELF INDUCTION. The phenomenon and property of an electrical circuit whereby any change of current flow is resisted, the circuit attempting to maintain the current at a constant value.

SELF-STARTING SYNCHRONOUS CLOCK MOTOR. A type of Synchronous Clock Motor (*q.v.*), having a shaded pole (*q.v.*) or other means whereby the rotor is automatically started and synchronised upon the application of an A.C. supply.

SELF-WINDING WATCH. *See* Automatic Winding.

SELLERS (OR U.S.S.) THREAD. The United States Standard thread which has flat roots and crests. Now standardised for certain British products also.

SEMI-HUNTER. *See* Demi-Hunter.

SEMITANGENTAL ESCAPEMENT. Refers to the Lever escapement having the entry pallet stone planted 31° from the line of centres and the exit pallet stone 29° therefrom. It is claimed that locking and impulse actions are more nearly equal on each stone than is the case with the Circular (*q.v.*) and Equidistant (*q.v.*) escapements. The semitangental escapement is claimed by designers of escapements to be the best yet conceived.

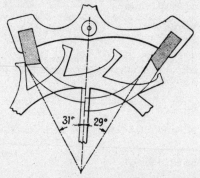

SEMITANGENTAL ESCAPEMENT.

SEPARATOR. The thin sheet of wood, perforated celluloid, glass, or other material used to separate the plates of secondary cells such as an accumulator.

SERIES. A method of connecting two or more electrical circuits or components, etc., so that one and the same current flows through them all. [*Note.*—If a component so inserted in a circuit has a sub-circuit of its own not " in series," it is disregarded in considering the main circuit as a whole, the various sections thereof being said to be wired " in series."]

SERIES WINDING. A term indicating that, in an electrical machine, one coil (such as a solenoid, armature, etc.) is " in series " with another coil or part of the apparatus. Commonly applied to motors.

SERPENTINE. *See* MARBLES AND ORNAMENTAL STONES.

SET. A term used in connection with the escapement when fitted with a balance. The escapement is said to " set " when, the balance having been stopped with the driving power on, it is possible for the balance to remain stationary after the removal of the interrupting medium. Also describes the fit or relative positions of parts.

SET HANDS ARBOR. The arbor of a watch or clock by which the hands are set. Usually comprises an arbor fitting friction tight through a hollow pinion having a square at one end and the cannon pinion fitting tightly at the other. *See* Hollow Centre Pinion. Some synchronous clocks employ a wheel or pinion gearing with the motion work and mounted upon an arbor projecting rearwards through the plates and actuated by a milled knob at the rear of the case. This assembly revolves with the motion work.

SET HANDS DIAL. A small dial, conveniently placed, which repeats the time shown by the main dial(s) of a turret clock; used in regulating or setting to time, etc.

SET HANDS SQUARE. The square of a keywind watch or clock where it is necessary to use a key or squared button to set the hands.

SETTING UP. Refers to the part winding of the mainspring, where a fusee is employed, before the chain or line is wound on to the fusee, or, before the stop finger of stop work is placed in position on a going barrel. Also refers to the fitting up or placing in position, of work in the lathe or cutters in an automatic machine.

SEXTANT. An instrument used at sea for ascertaining the altitude of heavenly bodies.

SHADED POLE. A term applied to electro magnetic systems having one pole piece " shaded " by a non-magnetic metal such as a copper ring. The effect is to produce a momentary lack of balance in the pole strengths when the supply is switched on. Used in the self-starting synchronous motor clocks. Also termed Shielded pole.

SHAFT. In engineering, a shaft refers to a long axis of rotation, but in horology it refers only to the Winding Shaft. *See* Stem.

SHAGREEN. *See* ANTIQUE CLOCK CASE TERMS.

SHAKE. A term denoting working clearance, *i.e.*, End-Shake (*q.v.*) and Side-Shake (*q.v.*) of a pivot in its hole.

SHEAR STEEL. Steel " corrected " during manufacture by " shearing." The bar is heated and hammered then folded several times upon itself and again heated, hammered and rolled. This process is repeated a number of times until the whole bar is of the same density, hardness, and malleability, etc.

SHEEP'S HEAD CLOCK. *See* ANTIQUE CLOCK CASE TERMS.

SHEFFIELD PLATE. Articles made of copper upon which sheets of silver have been welded. Distinct from electro-plate.

SHELLAC. A resinous substance used to secure pallet stones, ruby pins, etc., in their settings. Also used, diluted with methylated spirits, to lacquer plates, etc., of clocks, instruments, etc. A natural Plastic (*q.v.*). A purified form of Lac and obtained mostly from India.

SHERATON PERIOD. *See* ANTIQUE CLOCK CASE TERMS.

SHIFT. The movement of the trace or image, as a whole, upon the screen of a cathode-ray tube for purposes of centralising, etc. Effected by variation of the standing voltages applied to the deflector plates or, the steady current passing in the deflector coils.

SEXTANT

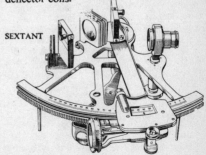

SHIM. A thin packing piece, washer, etc. Used in adjusting a clearance or an exact height, etc. Also used in magnetic systems to adjust pole gaps, etc.

SHIPPER. An American term defining the Pull-out-Piece (*q.v.*) of the negative setting keyless mechanism. The word "Shipper" is also used preceding those parts comprising the mechanism, *e.g.*, "Shipper spring," "Shipper lever," etc. (A) Shipper spring; (B) The Shipper.

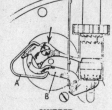

SHIPPER.

SHIP'S BELL CLOCK. In horology the term refers to a clock which strikes according to a system similar to that used on board ship where a bell is struck manually to denote "watches" or a period of duty. A Ship's Bell Clock may not necessarily agree with the nautical time since the majority of "domestic" ship's bell clocks strike the series of blows up to eight, starting at 12.30 p.m. with one bell and adding a blow at each half hour up to 4 p.m. when eight bells are sounded. Then the same sequence is repeated, whereas true nautical time strikes one bell at 6.30 p.m. to denote the Dog Watches (where the domestic clock would strike five bells) 7 p.m. two bells, 7.30 p.m., three bells and 8 p.m. eight bells, as noted in the table of nautical times. Some ship's bell clocks are made to strike true nautical time but the majority strike as the table in pairs, *i.e.* ding to denote one bell, ding, ding to denote two bells, and ding, ding, ding, to denote three bells *and so on*. It will be noted that the hours are as on board ship.

a.m.	p.m.	bells
12.30	12.30	1 bell
1.00	1.00	2 bells
1.30	1.30	3 "
2.00	2.00	4 "
2.30	2.30	5 "
3.00	3.00	6 "
3.30	3.30	7 "
4.00	4.00	8 "
4.30	4.30	1 "
5.00	5.00	2 "
5.30	5.30	3 "
6.00	6.00	4 "
6.30	6.30	5 "
7.00	7.00	6 "
7.30	7.30	7 "
8.00	8.00	8 "
8.30	8.30	1 "
9.00	9.00	2 "
9.30	9.30	3 "
10.00	10.00	4 "
10.30	10.30	5 "
11.00	11.00	6 "
11.30	11.30	7 "
12.00	12.00	8 "

Nautical Time is as follows:—

The 24 hours is divided into 7 watches.

Midnight to 4 a.m.	Middle Watch
4 a.m. to 8 a.m.	Morning Watch
8 a.m. to Noon	Forenoon Watch
Noon to 4 p.m.	Afternoon Watch
4 p.m. to 6 p.m.	First Dog Watch
6 p.m. to 8 p.m.	Last Dog Watch
8 p.m. to Midnight	First Watch

The purpose of the two day watches is to make an odd number of watches in the 24 hours thus giving the men different watches each day. Table of Nautical Times follows:—

1 Bell

12.30 p.m.	4.30 p.m.	6.30 p.m.	8.30 a.m.
12.30 a.m.	4.30 a.m.	8.30 a.m.	

2 Bells

1.00 p.m.	5.00 p.m.	7.00 p.m.	9.00 p.m.
1.00 a.m.	5.00 a.m.	9.00 a.m.	

3 Bells

1.30 p.m.	5.30 p.m.	7.30 p.m.	9.30 p.m.
1.30 a.m.	5.30 a.m.	9.30 a.m.	

4 Bells

2.00 p.m.	6.00 p.m.	10.00 p.m.
2.00 a.m.	6.00 a.m.	10.00 a.m.

5 Bells

2.30 p.m.	10.30 p.m.	10.30 a.m.
2.30 a.m.	6.30 a.m.	

6 Bells

3.00 p.m.	11.00 p.m.	
3.00 a.m.	7.00 a.m.	11.30 a.m.

7 Bells

3.30 p.m.	11.30 p.m.	
3.30 a.m.	7.30 a.m.	11.30 a.m.

8 Bells

12.00 Noon	4.00 p.m.	8.00 p.m.
12.00 Midnight	4.00 a.m.	8.00 a.m.
	(Nautical Time.)	

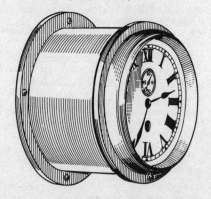

SHIP'S CLOCK.

SHIP'S CLOCK. A lever timepiece usually fitted into a round brass case. (*See* Ship's-Bell Clock). Illus. on facing page.

SHOCK ABSORBER. A resilient system. *See* Shock Resisting Watch.

SHOCKPROOF WATCH. An undesirable term for Shock Resisting Watch (*q.v.*).

SHOCK RESISTING WATCH. A watch in which the endstones, or, the endstones and the jewel holes of the balance staff are sprung so that they " give " when the watch is subjected to a shock. For particulars of systems *see* " Practical Watch Repairing," and Incabloc, Parechoc, Shockresist, Wyler Balance, Fixmobil, Girocap, Lubrifix. Various systems are identified below:

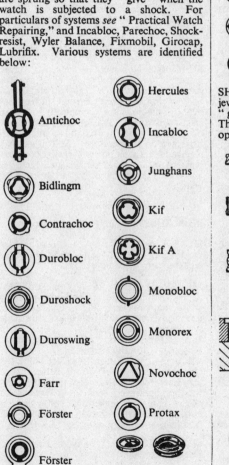

Antichoc

Bidlingm

Contrachoc

Durobloc

Duroshock

Duroswing

Farr

Förster

Förster

Hercules

Incabloc

Junghans

Kif

Kif A

Monobloc

Monorex

Novochoc

Protax

Resomatic

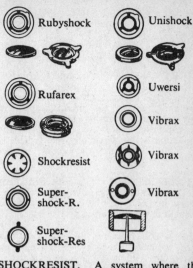

Rubyshock

Rufarex

Shockresist

Super-shock-R.

Super-shock-Res

Unishock

Uwersi

Vibrax

Vibrax

Vibrax

SHOCKRESIST. A system where the jewel holes and endstones of the balance " give " when the watch receives a shock. The spring-like settings of the jewels operate until a shoulder on the balance staff

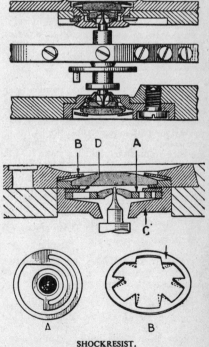

B   D   A

C

A   B

SHOCKRESIST.

contacts a block and so takes the effect of a major shock. A. Spring setting of jewel holes. B. Spring to hold assembly in position. C. Shock resisting block. D. Ring to secure spring setting of jewel.

SHORT CIRCUIT. The introduction of a comparatively low resistance path in an electrical circuit such as to render the whole or part of the circuit inoperative and sometimes causing the passage of an excessive, disruptive current in the remaining path. Generally referred to as a " Short " especially when occurring as a fault.

SHORTT CLOCK. The Free Pendulum (*q.v.*) observatory clock designed by H. W. Shortt in 1922. The first was installed in Edinburgh Observatory.

SHROUDS. The caps or ends of the lantern pinion into which the pins or trundles are fitted.

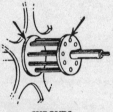

SHROUDS.

SHOULDER. The vertical surface exposed in a shaft, arbor, etc., by reason of a reduction from one diameter to a lesser. The working thrust face of a pivot other than the balance staff pivots, or pivots running on Endstones (*q.v.*).

SHUNT. Another term for Parallel (*q.v.*) but frequently employed when speaking of components forming a unit or particular parts of a circuit and in connection with the winding of motor coils, etc. Circuits connected " in shunt " or " in parallel " are then so arranged that the same E.M.F. is applied to them. (Compare Series.) Also a resistance placed in parallel with a meter, *e.g.*, ammeter, enabling the range of the instrument to be proportionally increased, the scale being duplicated or adapted accordingly, *e.g.*, Normal: 0–5 amps; With shunts: (1) 0–10 amps; (2) 0–50 amps.

SIDEREAL DAY. The time between two successive transits of the first point of Aries across the Meridiam.

SIDEREAL TIME. Time between two successive meridianal transits of a fixed star. A sidereal day is approximately 3 minutes 56 seconds longer than a mean solar day.

SIDE SHAKE. The freedom or " play " of a pivot in its hole: as distinct from end-shake.

SIGNAL. Refers to an aural or visual public time signal such as a Minute Gun, etc. Also, a term referring to the electrical impulse transmitted by a time-keeping system or, the similar impulse (electrically) at the grid of a valve in thermionic work. Hence term Signal Voltage—being the voltage, from any source, purposely generated and applied to a circuit or component on which it has a desired material effect.

SIGNS OF THE ZODIAC. *See* Zodiac.

SILICA. Silicon dioxide. Occurs naturally in crystalline form as Quartz, etc.

SILICA GEL. *See* Lime.

SILICON. Non-metallic element. Used extensively in manufacture of alloys for magnetic purposes. Silicon is manufactured by reducing silica with carbon under great heat. Silicones are, chemically, a close relation of glass. It is claimed for silicon oil that it remains in good condition in extremes of temperature. Silicon oil has received little attention in horology. It has been tested by some Swiss watch factories and found unsatisfactory as a lubricant for watches.

SILICONES. *See* Silicon.

SILK SUSPENSION. *See* Suspension.

SILVER SOLDER. A form of solder or brazing spelter containing silver or nickel silver. (*See* Solder.)

SILVERED DIAL. A very finely divided deposition of silver producing a pleasing white matt or very fine grained surface, used for clock, watch and instrument dials in metal. *See* WORKSHOP HINTS AND HELPS for method of silvering dials. Nowadays, usually protected by a colourless lacquer or varnish, a defect being the tarnishing action of atmospheric fumes, dust borne chemicals, moisture, etc. Many watches, however, are fitted with solid silver dials the appearance of which is quite distinct from the silvered dial which is sometimes described as a " silver dial."

SILVERING. *See* WORKSHOP HINTS AND HELPS, page 300.

SIMPLE HARMONIC MOTION. *See* Harmonic Motion.

SIMPLE PENDULUM. *See* Pendulum.

SINE WAVE. A wave form of a simple harmonic type of transverse vibration. The graphical representation of one complete cycle of such a vibration, commonly applied to alternating and oscillating currents.

SINGING BIRD BOX. *See* Bird Box.

SINGLE BEAT ESCAPEMENT. An escapement which beats or gives impulse to the balance or pendulum in one direction only, *e.g.*, Chronometer (*q.v.*) and Duplex (*q.v.*).

SINGLE ROLLER ESCAPEMENT. Refers to the lever escapement wherein the impulse roller acts also as the safety roller. (Compare with Double Roller.)

SINK. A recess, *e.g.*, the recess cut into the plate of a watch to receive the ratchet transmission wheels of a keyless watch. Also the recess to hold oil, a Chamfer (*q.v.*). The oil sink of a clock or watch, etc.

SKELETON DIAL. *See* WORKSHOP HINTS AND HELPS, page 300.

SKELETON MOVEMENT. A movement of a watch or clock having the plates cut away, or pierced, so as to render the train, etc., visible.

SKELETON MOVEMENT.

SLAVE CLOCK. The second master clock used to provide impulse release and so on in a Shortt or similar type of free pendulum precision clock. Also wrongly applied, sometimes, to a dial driven from a master clock, which is actually an impulse or repeater dial.

SLEEVE. A tube; more particularly, the spring clutch device fitted to the pendant of a Negative Setting watch case (*q.v.*).

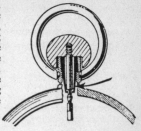

SLEEVE.

SLIDE. An American term for " Run to the Banking " (*q.v.*).

SLIDE-UP ROOF. *See* ANTIQUE CLOCK CASE TERMS.

SLIDE REST. A rest or holder for a cutting tool used in conjunction with the lathe. The tool is fixed to the "rest" which can be propelled longitudinally and laterally by means of a screw drive giving a firm sliding action across or along and, in many cases, at an angle to the work.

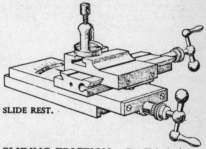

SLIDE REST.

SLIDING FRICTION. *See* Friction.

SLIDING GAUGE. Another name for the Vernier Guage (*q.v.*).

SLIDING PINION. Another name for the Castle Wheel of the Keyless Mechanism (*q.v.*).

SLIDING TONGS. A form of pliers with a sliding link embracing the handle(s) so that work may be held securely in the jaws without continuous pressure of the fingers.

SLIDING TONGS.

SLITTING OR SLOTTING FILE. A double-edged thin, blade-like file, having teeth upon the edges only: used in cutting

the slots in screw heads, etc. Also termed
" Screw Head " file.

SLITTING OR SLOTTING FILE.

SMOOTHING. Refers to the eradication
of the " ripple " or unidirectional D.C.
pulses, resulting from the " rectification "
of alternating current to direct current by
metal or valve rectifiers.

SMOOTHING CHOKE. The choke,
inserted in conjunction with a capacitor
(condenser), by means of which the raw
D.C. obtained from a rectifier is " filtered "
to a steady potential. Further chokes may
be fitted either in the supply unit or
elsewhere in the circuit.

SMOOTHING CONDENSER. The cap-
acitor(s) used in conjunction with a choke
which filter or " level out " the ripple of
the D.C. normally delivered by a rectifier
from an A.C. supply. Usually two
capacitors are employed, one known as
the reservoir, the other as the smoothing
condenser. Approximately of 4 to 16 mfd.
capacity, respectively.

SNAIL. A form of
cam; used in horo-
logy to determine the
number of blows to be
struck, in striking and
chime clocks and re-
peating watches, etc.
See Rise and Fall.

SNAIL.

SNAILED HOOK. The
hook in the barrel arbor
former by the body of the
arbor being turned eccen-
trically and allowing the
first coil of the mainspring
to wrap round the arbor
without distortion.

SNAILED HOOK.

SNAILING. A form of finish of metal
work; consisting of a series of fine, curved
lines radiating from
a common centre.
In American work
the lines may be
straight or nearly
so. Examples are
commonly to be
found on keyless
wheels of watches.
SNAILING.
Sometimes employed, particularly in English work, on watch barrels.

SNAP. A term referring to the fitting,
or securing, of two parts by springing
one over or into another. Thus: snap-on
bezil or back of a watch case; snap-in
barrel cover.

SOLAR CYCLE. A period of 28 years,
after which the days of the week fall on the
same days of the month.

SOLAR DIAL. A special type of operating
dial used on time switches and Gas Con-
trollers (q.v.) to adjust automatically the
" on " and " off " times of operation to
suit seasonal changes in the length of the
hours of darkness. The construction is
modified to suit various latitudes and dials
suitable for any part of the world can be
made.

SOLAR TIME. Time as determined by
the Sun. Time as indicated by a sundial.

SOLDER. A fusible alloy used in joining
metals. The solders commonly employed
in horology are hard and silver solder;
soft or lead solder; spelter or brazing solder.
Silver solder is obtainable in 3 hardnesses
(i.e., 3 fusion points):
(1) Hard. 10 parts silver, 5 parts pin-wire
    brass, 1 part pure zinc.
(2) Half Hard. 5 parts silver, 1 part pin-
    wire brass.
(3) Easy. 2 parts silver, 1 part pin-wire
    brass.
The flux used is borax. Soft solder: Approx.
2 parts tin 1 part lead. Resin, " killed "
hydrochloric acid, or one of a number of
patent pastes are employed as a flux.
Phosphoric acid (untreated) is used for
stainless steel. All acid fluxes require very
careful after-cleaning by washing with water.

SOLDERING IRON. A copper " bit "
or head used in soldering work usually
mounted on an iron stem or, as in an
electric iron, within or around a heating
jacket. Of various shapes, the bit is gauged
by its weight in ounces.

SOLENOID. Originally a Coil (q.v.) of
wire—especially a coil having one helical
layer only. Now particularly used as a
term for any coil designed or adapted to
effect an axial displacement of an armature
within the coil.

SOUTHING OF THE MOON. The time
at which the moon crosses the meridan.

SPADE FOOT. See ANTIQUE CLOCK CASE
TERMS.

SPADE HAND. See page 146.

SPANDREL OR SPANDRIL. See AN-
TIQUE CLOCK CASE TERMS.

SPELTER. *See* Solder. Also WORKSHOP HINTS AND HELPS, page 300.

SPELTER OR BRAZING SOLDER. Copper and zinc in varying proportions are used, the fusible point reducing in temperature as the proportion of zinc is increased. The flux used is borax. The essential requirement of a solder is that its fusion point must be lower than that of either of the metals being soldered.

" S " SPRING. The " Reverse " (*q.v.*), or " Resilient " (*q.v.*) mainspring is sometimes referred to as an " S " spring.

SPECIFIC GRAVITY. A comparison between the weight of a certain given volume of a material or substance and of an equal volume of pure water at 4° C. [The temperature of 4° C. is important for accuracy but a close approximation may be obtained if required for general comparison at a higher temperature.]

SPEED. The rate of change of position. The number of revolutions per minute. *See* Synchronous Motor.

SPEED CONTROL. A variable resistance, foot or hand controlled, used to vary the speed of a motor driving a lathe, buffing wheel, or drill, etc.

SPEEDOMETER. *See* Timers.

SPINNING. *See* Spun.

SPIRAL GEAR. *See* Crossed Axis Helical Gear.

SPIRIT. Specifically, a solution of ethyl alcohol, but generally referring to Methylated Spirit (*q.v.*).

SPIRIT STAIN. A wood stain of colouring matter dissolved in spirit or methylated spirit.

SPIRITS OF SALTS. A general name for hydrochloric acid especially the crude form.

SPIRITS OF WINE. Undiluted ethyl alcohol.

SPLIT CHUCK. A wire chuck used in the lathe to hold cylindrical rod shafting, arbors, etc. Also termed a collet, or wire chuck. Several wire-holding hand tools, small drill holders, etc., employ a similar pattern of chuck, but in general, these forms are not made to such limits of precision as the lathe split chuck.

SPLIT CHUCK.

SPLIT SECONDS. A Chronograph (*q.v.*) or Timer (*q.v.*) in which two second hands are fitted. One is usually exactly superimposed upon the other. The instrument is of special construction so that two readings may be recorded.

SPLIT SECONDS.

The term is a misnomer in so far as the second of time is not " split " or subdivided beyond the 1/5th or 1/10th of a second allowed by the " train " but the hand(s) " split," or appear so to divide, as follows:—From zero, the superimposed seconds hands appear as one and, when started, the chronograph action sets both hands in motion in absolute phase. By depressing the side button one had is made to stop, the other continuing. On depressing the chronograph starting button, *i.e.*, the winding button, the still moving hand is stopped. Thus two recordings are registered. Depression of the side button will now return the first mentioned hand smartly to the other hand; depression of the chronograph starter returns both hands to zero, from which position the sequence may be repeated *ad infinitum*. Further, the split hand, stopped, can be made to catch up to the other hand; useful when timing long races, to check lap times, unit distances, etc.

SPOON FITTING. *See* ANTIQUE CLOCK CASE TERMS.

SPORTS TIMERS. *See* Timers.

SPOTTING. A form of finish or decoration given to metal work; consisting of a series of circular spots or rings. The chronometer plates are traditionally " spotted."

SPRING CLICK. A click and spring combined.

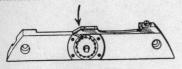

SPRING CLICK.

SPRING DETENT ESCAPEMENT. A term used to differentiate between the " pivoted detent "—favoured on the Continent—and the conventional English spring detent of the Chronometer Escapement (q.v.).

SPRING LUGS. Where the lugs or bars of a wrist watch are sprung into position.These lugs are detachable.

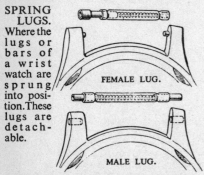

FEMALE LUG.

MALE LUG.

SPRINGER. The name applied to the craftsman responsible for the fitting of balance springs to the finished balances.

SPRINGING. The operation of selecting, shaping and fitting of a balance spring to a balance.

SPRUNG MOULDING. See ANTIQUE CLOCK CASE TERMS.

SPUN. A term referring to a method of working metal into shape where the work, usually sheet metal, is made to revolve and is " pressed " or " bent " into a required shape while revolving, e.g., a " spun " bezel is a bezel formed from thin sheet metal by the above process as distinct from a " turned " bezel which is turned from the solid.

SPUR GEARING. Toothed gearing between pairs of wheels having radially projecting teeth. Forms of spur gearing are: Epicycloidal, Hypocycloidal, Involute, (to which refer under respective sections).

SQUARE CUT. See GEMSTONE CUTTING STYLES.

SQUARE FILE. See Files.

SQUARE HOOKING. See Hooking-In.

SQUEEZE. Refers to the method of obtaining an impression, i.e., a mould of an article by means of warmed wax.

SQUEGGER. A term used in referring to the squegging oscillator which is a particular or general form of blocking oscillator (q.v.). The general form may be designed to be self-running. A particular form may require a " triggering " or initiating signal or impulse which has to be repeated to maintain the action. May be used as a Time Base (q.v.) or in Divider Circuits (q.v.).

STABILISER. A term referring to any device (such as a neon tube) applied to a source of supply for the purpose of maintaining a constancy of voltage and/or current within a stated range irrespective of variations in load or supply. Of importance in supplies to divider circuits and other oscillator circuits.

STABILITY. A property desirable in an oscillatory circuit such that its frequency remains constant without tendency to Drift (q.v.).

STABILOR. Trade name given to an unbreakable mainspring. See Vimetal.

STABLE EQUILIBRIUM. The state or position of a body such that a slight displacement is followed by a return to its original position. Or in which a slight displacement increases its potential energy.

STACKFREED. An early contrivance, prior to the Fusee (q.v.), used to equalise the force of the mainspring of a timepiece; an antique device.

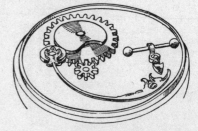

STACKFREED.

STAFF. An arbor or axis; in horology the term refers only to the axis of the balance and the pallets. (A) Balance staff; (B) Pallet staff. *See* WATCH PART NOMENCLATURE.

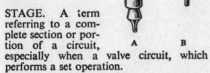

A   B

STAGE. A term referring to a complete section or portion of a circuit, especially when a valve circuit, which performs a set operation.

STALK. The wire or rod carrying the hammer of a striking or chiming clock.

STAMPING. A lamination as used for building up the core of a transformer, armature, etc.

STANDARD. *See* Bell Standard.

STANDARD FREQUENCY. The 50 or 60 cycle frequency for A.C. mains.

STANDARD TIME. Refers to G.M.T. (Greenwich Mean Time) (*q.v.*) and also referred to as " Domestic Time " and " Civilian Time." *See* Local Standard Time.

STANDARD TIME ZONES. *See* page 251–2.

STANDARD ZONE TIMES. *See* page 251–2.

STAINLESS STEEL BALANCE. A balance made by The Hamilton Watch Co. and used by them in chronometers. It consists of a rim of stainless steel and the centre arm of Invar. In heat the centre arm does not expand and the rim of the balance takes an eliptical form, at right angles to the arm. thus becoming effectively larger and losing. The balance spring used with this type of balance is a special grade Elinvar of 32% nickel (instead of 36% as in ordinary Elinvar) which gains in heat. Thus the gaining of the spring in heat is compensated by the losing of the balance. The dotted lines in the illustration show, somewhat exaggerated, the position of the adjustable weights in heat. In principle the system is similar to the Volet Balance (*q.v.*).

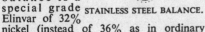

STAINLESS STEEL BALANCE.

STAKE. A form of anvil: in horology it usually takes the form of a small tool such as can be held in the vice. There are several patterns, however, and self-contained tools incorporating a revolving anvil, etc., known as Staking tools are available. Used in riveting arbors to wheels, etc.

STAKE.

STAKING TOOL. A tool providing a variety of stakes and punches accurately machined to graded sizes and complete interchangeability.

STAKING TOOL.

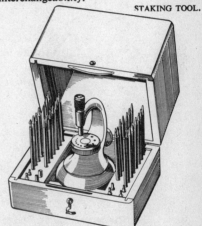

Some modern patterns are quite exhaustive in the range of pieces supplied and the work or uses to which they can be put.

STAMPINGS. *See* Press Tool.

STAR WHEEL. A wheel with pointed, straight-sided teeth such as the conventional drawing or representation of a star, *e.g.*, the star wheel of 12 teeth, to which the Snail (*q.v.*) is fitted, of a striking mechanism. A Jumper (*q.v.*) usually operates in conjunction

STAR WHEEL.

with the star wheel, as in calendar work. A star wheel is also used as a hammer lifting wheel in some striking clocks, but this is more correctly called a Cam Wheel.

STARTER. The lever or detent fitted to non-self-starting synchronous clock motors to enable the motor to be set in motion. Some gas controller clocks also have starters for their balances.

STATOR. The fixed or stationary portion of an electrical machine especially of an A.C. machine. Thus, the tunnel like arrangement of pole pieces of a syrchronous clock motor in which the Rotor revolves.

STEADY. A support for delicate work when in position in the lathe.

STEADY PINS. The locating pins of such parts as cocks, bars, and springs, etc

STEADY PINS.

STEEPLE CLOCK. Another name for Turret Clock (q.v.).

STEM. The winding shaft or stem of the keyless mechanism to which the winding button is fitted. See NOMENCLATURE OF WATCH PARTS.

STEM.

STEM SET. The method of setting the hands by partial withdrawal of the winding button fitted to the "stem" or winding shaft. See Negative Set and Positive Set.

STEP CHUCK. An accessory to the lathe. A split chuck having a series of recesses or "steps" to hold flat pieces such as wheels. See Spring Chuck.

STEP CHUCK.

STEP-DOWN TRANSFORMER. A transformer for changing an A.C. supply to a lower voltage.

STEP-UP TRANSFORMER. A transformer for changing an A.C. supply to a higher voltage.

STICK BAROMETER. See ANTIQUE CLOCK CASE TERMS.

STIRRUP. The frame supporting the jar(s) (containing mercury) of the Mercurial Pendulum (q.v.).

STOP FINGER. The finger piece of the Stop Work (q.v.).

STOP IRON. See Stop Work.

STOP SLIDE. See "All or Nothing Piece."

STOPPER. A term describing a watch, etc., which runs intermittently. A troublesome piece. A resistance usually mounted close to the grid or other connection of a valve to prevent undesirable effects in its circuit.

STOP WATCH. Strictly, the term applies to an ordinary time of day watch provided with a seconds hand and a stopping device to the balance. Sometimes referred to as a "doctor's watch." The term is used also to describe a Timer and a Chronograph (q.v.), which are distinctive mechanisms possessing particular features and usually more finely made than the stop watch.

STOP WORK. A device controlling the extent to which the mainspring can be wound also the number of turns of the barrel or fusee. In "going barrel" watches there are several systems employed. The most commonly met with consist of a star wheel and finger piece—also termed Maltese cross system. In fusee watches, etc., it refers to the Stop Iron attached

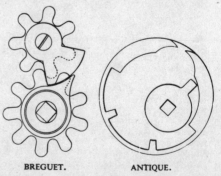

BREGUET. ANTIQUE.

to the plate and the stop piece or hook fitted to the fusee. In weight-driven clocks the term refers to a system whereby the line supporting the weights contacts a stud and causes a piece to project so preventing the barrel being wound beyond a certain point.

MALTESE CROSS.

STORAGE BATTERY. *See* Accumulator.

STRAIGHT GRAIN. A finish to the surface of metal where the surface is left with a straight grain (straight lines), *i.e.*, straight grained silvered dial, refers to a silvered dial with the surface finished with fine, straight lines.

STRAIGHT LINE LEVER ESCAPEMENT. The arrangement of the lever escapement having the escape wheel, pallets, and balance planted in a straight

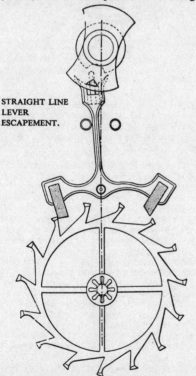

STRAIGHT LINE LEVER ESCAPEMENT.

line. Most Swiss and American escapements are of this type. The term is used to distinguish the arrangement from the Right-angle Escapement (*q.v.*). *See* Lever Escapement for a description of its action.

STRAP. Refers to the strap-like piece which holds the winding shaft (or stem) secure in a side-set keyless watch. Also, the means of securing a wrist watch to the wrist. Usually made of leather. If plastic material is used it is termed a plastic strap to differentiate, the term " strap " being practically synonymous with leather. Also, the strips of metal by which the movement of some French clocks is held in position in its case.

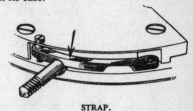

STRAP.

STRAP HINGES. *See* Antique Clock Case Terms.

STRAP WORK. *See* Antique Clock Case Terms.

STRAUMANN BALANCE. A monometallic balance made of a zinc alloy, pure zinc being impracticable. It is made in such a way that the bar or arm is in line with the direction of rolling of the metal. Consequently the arm increases in length when heated and its compensation action is similar to the Volet Balance (*q.v.*).

STRAY CAPACITY. The undesirable but inherent capacitance associated with circuit wiring. Of considerable importance at high frequencies.

STRAY FIELD. The electro magnetic field set up by machines or conductors, of an interfering character and sometimes difficult to neutralise.

STRENGTH. A term referring to the thickness only of a mainspring by which the " force " is graded.

STRIKING JACKS. Models of human or near human figures provided with hammer or club which strike bells to sound the hours or hours and quarters. It is authoritatively stated that " Jacks " were used to indicate the time of day in public clocks before the introduction of dials. A famous example of Striking Jacks is

Gog and Magog of St. Dunstan's in the West, Fleet Street, London, now removed to a residence near Regent's Park, London. Jacks are to be seen in many parts of the country, and some are employed within churches, striking before the sermon, as at Southwold, Suffolk. Domestic clocks are also found fitted with Jacks.

STRIKING RACK. *See* Rack.

STRIKING WORK. The striking mechanism of a striking clock.

STRINGING. *See* ANTIQUE CLOCK CASE TERMS.

STROBOSCOPE. A speed measuring device consisting of a slotted disc driven at a constant speed. In horology it is used as a Timing Machine (*q.v.*). A beam of light passing through the slots flashes on to the vibrating balance of the instrument under test. If the balance is vibrating at the correct speed it appears to be stationary.

STRUT. The easel-like support of a clock or watch. A " strut clock " is one having a support or strut at the back to enable the clock to stand at an angle.

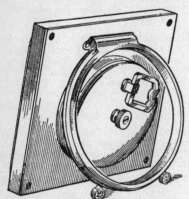

STRUT CLOCK.

STUBS SCREWS. *See* English Screws.

STUD. A short post, *e.g.*, for the minute wheel, for the striking rack, etc., in clock work. The term also refers to the balance spring stud, *i.e.*, the small pin or block to which the outer terminal of the spring is attached.

STYLE. *See* Gnomon.

SUBSCRIPTION WATCH A system introduced by Breguet of Paris, where prospective clients were invited to place an order before the watches were made.

SULPHATION. The formation of sulphate of lead in the plates of an accumulator due to disuse or lack of attention. Also the corrosion of terminals, conductors, etc., connected thereto. If prolonged, results in destruction of the cell.

SUMMER TIME. *See* Daylight Saving.

SUNK PANEL. *See* ANTIQUE CLOCK CASE TERMS.

SUNK SECONDS. A seconds dial recessed or sunk below the surface of the main dial. Its purpose is to provide a lower fitting for the seconds hand and thus greater freedom to the hour hand which normally passes over it.

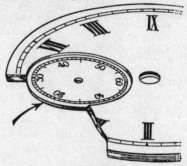

SUNK SECONDS.

SUN DIAL. A device employing a Gnomon (*q.v.*) or style casting a shadow upon a graduated circle as the sun progresses throughout the day showing Apparent Solar Time (*q.v.*).

SUN AND PLANET GEARS: or epicyclic gears. A system where one gear (or more) travels round the outside or inside of another fixed gear. Astronomical trains, in particular, when aiming at somewhat higher accuracies, usually require very high prime numbers into which the transmission ratio can be factorised. Practical reasons, however, restrict tooth numbers to figures below 100, although cases of wheels with 1000 and even more teeth are known. So, in general, astronomical trains for high accuracy are built up by a series of intermediate wheels. By appropriate selection of the teeth numbers approximations, but never the accurate prime numbers required, can be obtained. Sun and planet gears are suited to yield prime numbers many times greater than the teeth numbers of the wheels employed. This property is utilized profusely in the many astronomical clocks with mechanical astrolabes in the Renaissance period. Nothing, so far, is known about the inventor or origin of the idea. For modern straightforward clock work, sun and planet gears are not of importance. A common modern use is in the differential gear of a motor car. This action corresponds to the performance of those equation clocks where one had indicates mean and another true solar time. Joseph Williamson, 1742, in London, was the first to build a differential gear for that purpose.

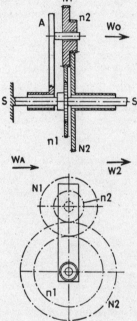

SUN AND PLANET GEARING.

SUN-RAY CLOCK. A clock case in the form of the conventional conception of the rays from the sun.

SUPPLEMENTARY ARC. Refers to the arc of vibration of the pendulum. After an escape wheel tooth has dropped on to the pallet in the recoil and dead beat escapements, the pendulum continues its oscillation, causing the pallet to engage the dropped tooth more deeply. This additional movement of the pendulum after the drop is known as the " supplementary arc."

SUPPLY. A general term referring to any source of electrical energy. Further particularised as D.C. or A.C., *i.e.*, direct current or alternating current respectively.

SURPRISE PIECE. The loose piece fitted to the cannon pinion of the minute repeater. It is flirted forward at each quarter hour to ensure that the rack cannot drop to strike 14 minutes when no minutes at all should be struck.

SURPRISE PIECE IN OPERATION.

SURPRISE PIECE UNDER CANNON PINION.

SUN-RAY WALL CLOCK.

SUSPENSION. Refers to the means by which the pendulum is hung, *i.e.*, "suspension spring" or "silk suspension." Also "knife edge" which is to be found in some antique bracket clocks and the more modern French Lyre clocks (*q.v.*).

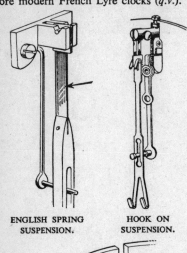

ENGLISH SPRING   HOOK ON
SUSPENSION.   SUSPENSION.

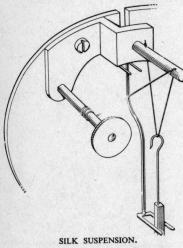

SILK SUSPENSION.

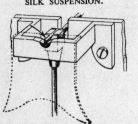

KNIFE-EDGE SUSPENSION.

SUSPENSION BLOCK. The rigid (and sometimes massive) plates, bars, or other structure from which the pendulum depends upon its suspension.

SUSPENSION BRACKET. A bracket for the purpose of suspending the pendulum separate from the Back Cock (*q.v.*). Usually employed in Regulator Clocks (*q.v.*) and Turret Clocks (*q.v.*).

SUSPENSION SPRING. The spring by which the pendulum of a clock is suspended. The long spring used in the 400-day clock is also termed suspension spring. It forms part of the pendulum. *See* Four Hundred-Day Clock.

SWAG. *See* ANTIQUE CLOCK CASE TERMS.

SWARF. The metal cuttings or chips produced in turning, drilling, etc.

SWEATING. The condensation or expulsion of water on or from a surface. Sometimes seen in airtight watch cases. Also a term used to mean heating, as when "sweating a joint" or making the solder run by applying heat.

SWEEP SECONDS. The American term for the Centre Seconds Hands (*q.v.*). Sometimes known as a cursor hand when applied to large dials, especially of synchronous clocks, the hand advancing continuously and not indicating second intervals.

SWING. The arc described by a pendulum. The excursions from a positive to a negative peak of an A.C. supply or wave form. Also the largest diameter that may be accommodated in a lathe.

SWING TOOL. A tool used in polishing; it swings between centres and so facilitates flat polishing.

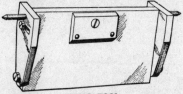

SWING TOOL.

SWISS LAPIS LAZULI. An imitation of Lapis Lazuli (*q.v.*). Sometimes known as German lapis.

SWITCH. An automatic or manual device to complete or break a circuit, especially to a supply. There are many forms, simple and multiple, usually designated by the number of poles and number of positions or " throws " to which the " poles " may be connected, *e.g.*, Single pole, single throw, double throw, three way, etc.; Double pole, single throw, etc. *See* also " Break Before Make " and " Make Before Break." A recently developed form of circular switch much used in radio and similar work consists of circular discs of insulating material carrying contacts radially disposed over which a similarly mounted contact(s) pass, actuated by a central rod. Known as wafer switches. A battery of single, double, three way, etc., switches can be assembled in tandem in this fashion, all operated by the one central rod.

SWIVEL. A form of spring catch usually associated with a watch chain or similar attachment. The word swivel means " a connection between two parts enabling one of them to revolve without the other."

SWIVEL.

SYNCHRONOUS. Literally, " with time." In step with, at the same rate or speed as. Electrically, of an A.C. motor, speed or revolution in conformity with the frequency of the supply current.

SYNCHRONOUS MOTOR CLOCK. The electric synchronous motor clock. Also called the Mains Clock (*q.v.*). Strictly, the Quartz Clock (*q.v.*) is a synchronous clock, its accuracy being derived from an incorporated master frequency standard. *See* " Electric Timekeeping."

SYNCHRONOUS MOTOR. A motor of which the rate of revolutions per unit of time is determined by the number of poles and frequency of the alternating current supplied to it. Such a motor runs in step or in phase with the current. Number of revolutions is given by formula.

$$\text{Revs. per minute} = 60 \times \frac{\text{Frequency of supply in cycles per second}}{\text{Number of pairs of poles.}}$$

SYNTHETIC STONES. One of the most important advancements in horology has been the introduction of the synthetic sapphire, as it is more commonly known, for the production of jewel holes, end stones, impulse pins, pallet stones, etc. Synthetic stones are so named since they represent the artificial reproduction of compounds previously occurring only in natural deposits. Briefly the production process is as follows:—The basic material in general is ammonia alum, a sulphate of aluminium and ammonia. It is especially manufactured to obtain a high degree of purity. The alum is first calcined in a furnace at a temperature exceeding 1,000° C. to drive off the water of crystallisation and sulphuric acid and ammonia which is also present. Pure alumina, Al_2O_3 in the form of a light, white powder, extremely finely sub-divided, remains. This product is known as Diamantine (*q.v.*). The powder is melted in a furnace at a very high temperature when it eventually fuses, forming an elongated, pearshaped globule, known as a " boule." This " boule " is cut and divided and forms the material from which the " stones " are made. An important physical difference between the natural and the synthetic stone is the ability of the latter to withstand pressure. Thus allowing the development of the Press-In jewelling technique which has been developed to a high degree of accuracy both in fitting and working.

T

"T" PIECE. A mainspring brace in the form of the letter "T."

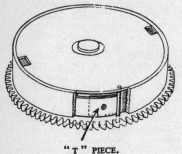

"T" PIECE.

"T" REST. The T shaped accessory to the lathe and turns; it forms a resting place to support the tool when working.

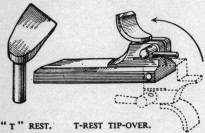

"T" REST.   T-REST TIP-OVER.

There is a T-rest tip-over where the T-rest can be tipped away from the work.

TABLE CLOCK. Usually refers to a horizontal clock with the dial at the top as illustrated. At a little later period when the vertical wood clocks were introduced, they also were known as table clocks. Some of these clocks were used on brackets and were known as bracket clocks.

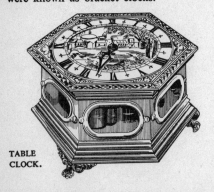

TABLE CLOCK.

TABLE ROLLER. Another name for Single Roller (*q.v.*).

TABLE TOOL. Another name for Uprighting Tool (*q.v.*).

TACHOMETER. A revolution counter, usually graduated in revolutions per minute, used for indicating the speed of rotation of shafting, motors, etc., driving machinery: an instrument such as a chronograph or timer calibrated to measure velocity, usually miles or kilometres per hour. Another version of different application is calibrated to act as a production meter. *See* pages 255-256.

TACHYMETER OR TACHOMETER. A surveying instrument not connected with horology; the word tachymeter however has been adopted to mean tachometer in horology. *See* also Telemeter.

TACT WATCH. A blind man's watch having a hand or pointer on the outside of the case which can be rotated to a stop to indicate the time of day. More properly "àtact."

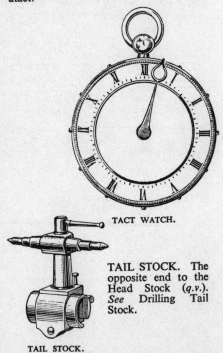

TACT WATCH.

TAIL STOCK. The opposite end to the Head Stock (*q.v.*). *See* Drilling Tail Stock.

TAIL STOCK.

TALC. A mineral. In horology the term refers to an unbreakable glass, even though not made of talc. Thus celluloid, Perspex, or other similar materials are spoken of as talc glasses. The term "unbreakable" however, is more widely used nowadays.
Note.—The term at one time also referred to Mica, a mineral of similar characteristics to Talc, but greater transparency. Since celluloid, upon its introduction, was (and still is) erroneously spoken of as "mica," it may be that the term talc in its connection with unbreakable glasses arose from this double relationship.

TALLOW DROP. An old term for the "best centre" glass as fitted to the outer case of the half hunter. It describes a glass which has a slight magnifying effect like a lens, being thick in the centre and thinning down towards the outer edges. *See* STYLES OF WATCH GLASSES. Also refers to the special shape of ends of screw heads used in English work. These are as flat as can be obtained by hand, the shape resembling the drops of grease from a tallow candle from which the name is taken.

TAMBOUR. In horology it usually refers to a type of keywind calotte, where the case of drum of the movement is secured to the outer case by screws or other means, as distinct from the conventional calotte, where either the bezel or a separate ring screws on to the body of the case or drum of the movement, so to hold it to the Outer Case (*q.v.*).

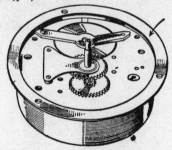

TAMBOUR.

TANG. The tapering end of a hand tool on which a handle is driven (as a file). An old file tang, suitably ground, hardened and tempered makes a good cutter for turning purposes.

TANGENT. A line touching a curve at one point only, *i.e.*, without cutting the curve when produced.

TAP. A screw thread; the term as generally used, refers to the cutting of a thread, either male or female, as on a rod or through a hole or tube. More precisely, the term refers to the tool for cutting a thread internally and the operation is known as tapping. An external thread is cut by a die and this operation, as in lathe screw cutting, is known as "threading." The tap consists of a threaded rod, its cutting surfaces being formed by longitudinal grooves which also assist in swarf clearing. For any given thread pitch and diameter three taps are usually available—first (also known as taper), second, and plug. The first is reduced by a marked taper towards the entry end, facilitating the cutting action of successive cutting edges. First and second taps usually suffice for a full thread in through holes. The plug is used to run the full thread to the bottom of a blind hole. They are also referred to as "cuts," first, second and third respectively.

TAP.

TAPER. A gradual continuous reduction of diameter, thickness, or section.

TAPERED MAINSPRING. A mainspring as used in a certain type of ball watch, in which the spring is gradually thickened towards the end, so that it acts as a slipping spring. Tapered springs were used in chronometers and fusee watches, the object being to reduce mainspring coil friction.

TEDDINGTON. The town which, in horological as in many other circles, is practically synonymous with the National Physical Laboratory which is situated there. The Kew tests are carried out there. *See* Kew.

TELEMETRE. An electrical term for a remote voltage, current, or power indicator. Also *see* page 256.

TELL-TALE CLOCK. A form of clock carried by a watchman. It is carried to pre-determined positions where keys are secured which, upon insertion in the clock, cause an impression to be made upon a chart or, by some similar device, provides proof of the man's visit and records the time of the visit.

TEMPERATURE. The degree of heat measured in relation to a chosen zero, or point such as the Centigrade and Fahrenheit temperature scales. *See* next page for conversion tables.

TEMPERATURE CONVERSION TABLE

NOTE.—Find the known temperature to be converted in the *centre column*. Then read the Centrigrade conversion to the left and Fahrenheit to right, *e.g.*, –2·8   27   80·6

27°C. = 80·6°F.
27°F. = –2·8°C.

°C.		°F.	°C.		°F.	°C.		°F.	°C.		°F.
–40·6	**–41**	–41·8	–10·6	**13**	55·4	6·7	**44**	111·2	23·9	**75**	167·0
–40·0	**–40**	–40·0	–10·0	**14**	57·2	7·2	**45**	113·0	24·4	**76**	168·8
–39·4	**–39**	–38·2	–9·4	**15**	59·0	7·8	**46**	114·8	25·0	**77**	170·6
–38·9	**–38**	–36·4	–8·9	**16**	60·8	8·3	**47**	116·6	25·6	**78**	172·4
–38·3	**–37**	–34·6	–8·3	**17**	62·6	8·9	**48**	118·4	26·1	**79**	174·2
–37·8	**–36**	–32·8	–7·8	**18**	64·4	9·4	**49**	120·2	26·7	**80**	176·0
–37·2	**–35**	–31·0	–7·2	**19**	66·2	10·0	**50**	122·0	27·2	**81**	177·8
–36·7	**–34**	–29·2	–6·7	**20**	68·0	10·6	**51**	123·8	27·8	**82**	179·6
–36·1	**–33**	–27·4	–6·1	**21**	69·8	11·1	**52**	125·6	28·3	**83**	181·4
–35·6	**–32**	–25·6	–5·6	**22**	71·6	11·7	**53**	127·4	28·9	**84**	183·2
–35·0	**–31**	–23·8	–5·0	**23**	73·4	12·2	**54**	129·2	29·4	**85**	185·0
–34·4	**–30**	–22·0	–4·4	**24**	75·2	12·8	**55**	131·0	30·0	**86**	186·8
–33·9	**–29**	–20·2	–3·9	**25**	77·0	13·3	**56**	132·8	30·6	**87**	188·6
–33·3	**–28**	–18·4	–3·3	**26**	78·8	13·9	**57**	134·6	31·1	**88**	190·4
–32·8	**–27**	–16·6	–2·8	**27**	80·6	14·4	**58**	136·4	31·7	**89**	192·2
–32·2	**–26**	–14·8	–2·2	**28**	82·4	15·0	**59**	138·2	32·2	**90**	194·0
–31·7	**–25**	–13·0	–1·7	**29**	84·2	15·6	**60**	140·0	32·8	**91**	195·8
–31·1	**–24**	–11·2	–1·1	**30**	86·0	16·1	**61**	141·8	33·3	**92**	197·6
–30·6	**–23**	–9·4	–0·6	**31**	87·8	16·7	**62**	143·6	33·9	**93**	199·4
–30·0	**–22**	–7·6	0	**32**	89·6	17·2	**63**	145·4	34·4	**94**	201·2
–29·4	**–21**	–5·8	0·6	**33**	91·4	17·8	**64**	147·2	35·0	**95**	203·0
–28·9	**–20**	–4·0	1·1	**34**	93·2	18·3	**65**	149·0	35·6	**96**	204·8
–28·3	**–19**	–2·2	1·7	**35**	95·0	18·9	**66**	150·8	36·1	**97**	206·6
–27·8	**–18**	–0·4	2·2	**36**	96·8	19·4	**67**	152·6	36·7	**98**	208·4
–27·2	**–17**	1·4	2·8	**37**	98·6	20·0	**68**	154·4	37·2	**99**	210·2
–26·7	**–16**	3·2	3·3	**38**	100·4	20·6	**69**	156·2	37·8	**100**	212·0
–26·1	**–15**	5·0	3·9	**39**	102·2	21·1	**70**	158·0	38·3	**101**	213·8
–25·6	**–14**	6·8	4·4	**40**	104·0	21·7	**71**	159·8	38·9	**102**	215·6
–25·0	**–13**	8·6	5·0	**41**	105·8	22·2	**72**	161·6	39·4	**103**	217·4
–24·4	**–12**	10·4	5·6	**42**	107·6	22·8	**73**	163·4	40·0	**104**	219·2
–23·9	**–11**	12·2	6·1	**43**	109·4	23·3	**74**	165·2	40·6	**105**	221·0
–23·3	**–10**	14·0									
–22·8	**–9**	15·8									
–22·2	**–8**	17·6									
–21·7	**–7**	19·4									
–21·1	**–6**	21·2									
–20·6	**–5**	23·0									
–20·0	**–4**	24·8									
–19·4	**–3**	26·6									
–18·9	**–2**	28·4									
–18·3	**–1**	30·2									
–17·8	**0**	32·0									
–17·2	**1**	33·8									
–16·7	**2**	35·6									
–16·1	**3**	37·4									
–15·6	**4**	39·2									
–15·0	**5**	41·0									
–14·4	**6**	42·8									
–13·9	**7**	44·6									
–13·3	**8**	46·4									
–12·8	**9**	48·2									
–12·2	**10**	50·0									
–11·7	**11**	51·8									
–11·1	**12**	53·6									

VALUES OF SINGLE DEGREES

°C	°F.		°F.	°C.
1 =	1·8		1 =	0·56
2 =	3·6		2 =	1·11
3 =	5·4		3 =	1·67
4 =	7·2		4 =	2·22
5 =	9·0		5 =	2·78
6 =	10·8		6 =	3·33
7 =	12·6		7 =	3·89
8 =	14·4		8 =	4·44
9 =	16·2		9 =	5·0

$$°C. = \tfrac{5}{9}(°F. - 32°) \qquad °F. = (\tfrac{9}{5}°C.) + 32°$$

By courtesy of:—
THE BRITISH THERMOSTAT COMPANY LTD.,
Sunbury-on-Thames, Middlesex.

TEMPERATURE COEFFICIENT. The small change in physical characteristics of materials, gases, etc., per degree rise in temperature. The variation in daily rate of a timekeeper for a change of temperature of 1° C. Usually determined by dividing the difference in the rates at 36° C. and 4° C. by the number of degrees in the temperature range i.e. 36−4 = 32.

TEMPERATURE ERROR AND COMPENSATION. The error in timekeeping due to temperature changes; the means by which compensation or correction of the error is effected. Thus, in the balance and spring, maintaining a constant period oscillation. In the case of the pendulum, the maintaining of the centre of oscillation constant. In practice these requirements are usually effected by the application of differential expansion, or, using a metal with little or no coefficient of expansion.

TEMPERATURE SCALES AND TEMPERATURE CONVERSION TABLES. *See* page TEMPERATURE CONVERSION TABLE.

TEMPERATURE SCREWS. The screws (between brackets in the illustration) of a cut Compensation Balance (*q.v.*) used for adjusting a balance to compensate for changes of temperature. The four screws (not under brackets) are the Quarter Screws (*q.v.*).

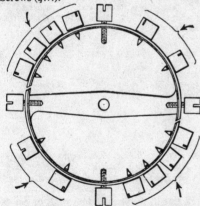

TEMPERATURE SCREWS.

TEMPERING. The process of reducing the hardness or brittleness of a metal or alloy. Sometimes described as " lowering " or " drawing " the temper, especially when the existing temper is high. *See* Blueing for temper colours of carbon steel.

TEMPER HARDENING. Refers to certain alloys which reverse the normal action and increase in hardness when heated after initial quenching.

TEMPORAL HOURS. Refers to the division of the period between sunrise and sunset into twelve equal parts; when delineating the plate of a sun-dial, certain calculations are made to correct this so that although the markings are unequally spaced, the time intervals are equal.

TEMPORARY MAGNET. An electro magnet or other magnet which loses its magnetism when the exciting influence ceases. Most electro magnets are, in this sense, temporary. A bar of soft iron will exhibit strong magnetism under the influence of a powerful magnet but cease to do so when removed from such influence.

TENACITY. Resistance to a force tending to pull particles asunder. In metallurgy, it refers specifically to the ultimate tensile stress.

TENSION. A force tending to cause extension. The opposite of compression or pressure. A state of extension—as a spring.

TENSION SPRING. Another name for the Friction Spring (*q.v.*). Also, a spring device in which the spring operates under tension, *i.e.*, extended, as opposed to a system wherein the spring is compressed, *e.g.*, certain lower grade chronographs employing spiral springs in tension to operate parts of the mechanism.

TERMINAL. A post, block, bar, etc., of metal or any point in an electrical apparatus or circuit to which or from which other conductors such as the supply leads are connected. Usually contact is made by the gripping action of screws, finger nuts or sprung blades, but soldered tags are also used. Two or more such connecting points mounted upon an insulant panel, board, etc., are termed a terminal board, terminal block or tag board. *See* ANTIQUE CLOCK AND CLOCK CASE TERMS.

TERMINAL, POSITIVE. The carbon pole of a Léclanché or dry cell. The pole or terminal of a battery, cell, dynamo, etc., from which current is conventionally considered to flow. Usually indicated by a " plus " sign and a red visual indicator.

TERMINAL, NEGATIVE. The zinc pole of a Léclanché or dry cell. The pole or terminal, etc. (as above), to which current is conventionally considered to flow. Indicated by a " minus " sign and a blue visual indicator.

TERMINAL, NEUTRAL. An earth or zero potential connection. The term must always be considered in relation to its associated circuit. The Neutral of a three-line system for instance may be at a voltage considerably above earth.

TERMINAL CURVE. The curve of the overcoil of the balance spring which is pinned to the balance spring stud. The curve from the volute to the balance spring collet *at the centre* is termed the "inner terminal curve." In general, when speaking of terminal curves it is implied that they are mathematically correct, *i.e.*, Lossier or Phillips Curves (*q.v.*).

TERN FEET. *See* ANTIQUE CLOCK CASE TERMS.

TERRESTIAL EQUATOR. *See* Equator.

TERRESTIAL MAGNETISM. The magnetic field and general phenomena observed in, on, and above the earth's surface. The magnetic poles approximate to the true geographic poles but show periodic and marked fluctuations. When kept in the same position in the earth's magnetic field, steel and other magnetic materials slowly become magnetised, especially when under vibration.

TERTIARY WINDING. A third winding in addition to the Primary and Secondary windings of a transformer as used in intervalve circuits; such as a Blocking Oscillator Divider (*q.v.*).

TESTING STANDARDS FOR WATCHES
ROYAL GREENWICH OBSERVATORY, ENGLAND
CHRONOMETER WATCHES (Centre seconds)

These watches are to be of robust construction and modern design, with a movement of approximately 50 mm. diameter. Barrel to be sufficiently deep to take a mainspring of 3 mm. height and 36 hours going. Strong keyless work, high numbered train, lever escapement, high grade bi-metallic balance of 20 mm. diameter fitted with a pair of timing screws, Breguet hairspring, 18,000 v.h. and fitted with regulator. Centre seconds transmission wheel mounted on top pivot of third pinion and engaging seconds pinion passing through hollow centre pinion. 18 ruby jewels, plus one extra jewel for top seconds pinion pivot.

Enamel dial with Arabic figures graduated in one-fifth minutes, seconds marked 5 to 60, blue steel hands, Silver or heavy nickel case with screw back, and snap-on bezil without glass. Watch to be fitted in brass mounting in mahogany box.

All watches will be tested as follows:—

In the room (18° C.)	dial up	...	...	7 days
In the oven (29° C.)	dial up	...	...	7 „
„ „ „ „	pendant up	...	5 „
„ „ „ „	pendant right	...	5 „
„ „ „ „	pendant left	...	4 „
„ „ „ „	dial up	...	7 „
In the room (18° C.)	dial up	...	...	7 „

Rating tolerances:—

Rate in room shall not exceed 3 seconds per day.

Change of mean daily rate determined in any two consecutive weeks dial up, and covering the full temperature range given above, shall not exceed 3 seconds per day.

Change of rate between the dial up and pendant up positions shall not exceed 6 seconds per day.

Change of rate between the dial up and side positions, *i.e.*, pendant right or pendant left, shall not exceed 8½ seconds per day.

ALTERNATIVE. A modern type auto-compensation balance and balance spring unit of a quality capable of complying with this rating specification may be fitted in lieu of the bi-metallic balance specified.

DECK WATCHES (Centre seconds)

These watches are to be of robust construction and modern design, with a movement of 43 to 45 mms. diameter. Barrel to be sufficiently deep to take a mainspring of 2·6 mms. height and 36 hours going. Strong keyless work, lever escapement, cut compensating balance of not less than 17 mm. diameter and 1·4 mm. depth, fitted with two timing screws. Breguet hairspring 18,000 v.h. and fitted with regulator. Centre seconds transmission wheel mounted on top pivot of third pinion and engaging seconds pinion passing through hollow centre pinion. 15 to 17 jewels plus one extra jewel for top seconds pinion pivot.

Enamel dial with Arabic figures graduated in half minutes; seconds marked 5 to 60, blue steel hands. Stainless steel (staybrite) or nickel case with screw back and bezil, fitted with best quality unbreakable glass.

All the watches will be tested as follows:—

In the room at 18° C.	dial up	...	7 days
In the oven at 29° C.	dial up	...	5 „
„ ,, „ „ 29° C.	pendant up	...	4 „
„ „ „ „ 29° C.	dial up	...	5 „
In the room at 18° C.	dial up	...	7 „

Rating tolerances:—

Rate in the room not to exceed 5 seconds per day.

Change of rate between any two periods dial up, covering the above mentioned temperature range, not to exceed 8½ seconds per day.

Change of rate between dial up and pendant up periods in the same temperature not to exceed 8½ seconds per day.

ALTERNATIVE. A modern type auto-compensation balance and balance spring unit of a quality capable of complying with this rating specification may be fitted in lieu of the bi-metallic balance specified.

NATIONAL PHYSICAL LABORATORY, ENGLAND

METROLOGY DIVISION (TIME SECTION)
CRAFTSMANSHIP WATCH TEST
Craftsmanship Test for Time-of-Day Watches

This is the highest class of watch test undertaken by the National Physical Laboratory; its standard is in many respects superior, and is in no way inferior, to that of the N.P.L. (Kew) Class A test which it supersedes. It is intended for high quality time-of-day watches of all types submitted by manufacturers, professional watch adjusters and horological students, and will only in exceptional circumstances be made available to those outside these categories.

In common with other tests provided by the N.P.L., entry to the test is not restricted on the basis of nationality. The results of the test on any watch will be regarded as confidential to the consignor of the watch. No list of results will be published by the N.P.L.

The test occupies about 6 weeks. The main observations extend into 38 days, during which the rate of the watch, its day to day consistency and its overall drift, the effect of position and temperature, and the uniformity of rate during the day are all tested. Since the day-to-day performance of a watch is slightly affected by variations of atmospheric pressure, the tests will either be carried out at constant pressure or the effect of variations of atmospheric pressure will be allowed for on the basis of determinations of the rate/pressure coefficient made subsequently to the test. A watch incorporating a chronograph mechanism must satisfy the requirements given before being submitted to the main test set out under " Arrangement of Test."

A certificate will be issued for a watch which at least complies with the widest (viz. Grade 1d) limits set out under " Tolerances ". The performance of the watch, day by day, will be given on the certificate, and the quality of performance will be separately assessed in each of the six main items of test according to the grade of tolerance complied with in that item. No certificate will be issued for a watch which fails in any one item to reach the standard of Grade 1d.

Very few watches are expected at present to fall into Grade 1a in all respects, but most watches which would have been able to pass the N.P.L. (Kew) Class A test would satisfy at least the Grade 1d tolerances.

TESTING STANDARDS—Cont.

ARRANGEMENT OF TEST

Period	Number of 24-hour intervals	Temperature	Position of Watch
1	3	20° C.	Horizontal, dial up
2	3	,,	Vertical, 12 up*
3	3	,,	,, 12 left*
4	3	,,	,, 12 right*
5	3	,,	Horizontal, dial down
6	3	,,	,, dial up
7	4†	4° C.	,, ,, ,,
8	4†	20° C.	,, ,, ,,
9	4†	36° C.	,, ,, ,,
10	4†	20° C.	,, ,, ,,
11	3	20° C.	Vertical, 12 up*

* The corresponding positions for small movements having the winding button adjacent to the 3-hour mark are vertical, 6 up; vertical, 6 left; vertical, 6 right; and vertical, 6 up, respectively.

† Where a change of temperature occurs at the beginning of a period the rate over the first 24-hour interval will be ignored.

The watch is wound and observed daily at the same time throughout the test. The watch is also observed during a selected 24-hour interval in Period 11 to determine the hour-to-hour uniformity of rate. The departure from uniformity of rate during the day is defined as the difference between the error of the watch as observed at any time during the 24-hour interval and the corresponding error computed by linear interpolation between the errors at the beginning and the end of the interval.

TOLERANCES

	Grade 1a s/day	Grade 1b s/day	Grade 1c s/day	Grade 1d s/day
Consistency of Rate. In each period, no two daily rates shall differ by more than	0·50*	1·0	2·0	3·0
Mean Rate per Period at 20° C. In each period at 20° C. the mean rate shall not exceed	±3·00	±4·0	±6·0	±8·0
Positional Adjustment. The difference between the mean rate in Periods 1 and 6 (dial up), and the mean rate in any of the Periods 2, 3, 4 and 5, shall not exceed ...	±1·00	±2·0	±6·0	±10·0
Temperature Compensation. (a) The mean rate in Periods 6 and 8 (20° C.) *minus* the mean rate in Period 7 (4° C.) shall not exceed ... ... (b) The mean rate in Period 9 (36° C.) *minus* the mean of the rates in Periods 8 and 10 (20° C.) shall not exceed ... ... (c) If "A" and "B" are the differences referred to in (a) and (b) above, then A+B shall not exceed	±0·50	±0·7	±1·5	±4·0

TOLERANCES—Cont.

	Grade 1a s/day	Grade 1b s/day	Grade 1c s/day	Grade 1d s/day
Drift of Rate. (a) No two of the four mean rates in Periods 1, 6, 8 and 10 (dial up) shall differ by more than ... ... (b) The mean rates in Periods 2 and 11 shall not differ by more than	1·00	1·5	2·5	3·5
Uniformity of Rate during the Day. When observed in Period 11 the departure from uniformity of rate during the day shall not exceed	second ±0·30	second ±0·5	second ±0·8	second ±1·2

When applying the above tolerances the rate over the first 24-hour interval in each of periods 7, 8, 9 and 10 will be ignored.

* Applicable to rates at constant pressure.

GENEVA OBSERVATORY, SWITZERLAND

Test for deck watches (Category A) and for pocket watches (categories B and C)—

(Cat. A 43 to 70 mm. dial)
(,,   B 30 to 43 mm. dial)
(,,   C 30 to 38 mm. dial)

ART. 20. The tests of 44 days' duration are divided into nine periods in the following order:—

Period	Number of days		
1	4	Normal vertical (= P.U.)	20°C.
2	4	Vertical, turn 90° clockwise from the normal (= P.R.)	20°C.
3	4	Vertical, turn 90° anti-clockwise from the normal (= P.R.)	20°C.
4	4	Horizontal, dial down	20°C.
5	4	Horizontal, dial up	20°C.
6	*1+5	Horizontal, dial up	4°C.
7	*1+5	Horizontal, dial up	20°C.
8	*1+5	Horizontal, dial up	36°C.
9	2+5	Normal vertical (= P.U.)	20°C.

* The first day of the periods 6, 7 and 8 and the first two days of the period 9 are termed " Intermediate Days " and the rates are not taken into account when calculating.

ART. 22. The mean difference resulting from a change of position (designated P1) is determined from the mean rates of the periods 1 to 5 inclusive.

For the value of the compensation the coefficients E and F* are calculated from the mean rates of the periods 6, 7 and 8.

(* where $E = \dfrac{\text{Rate at 36°C} - \text{Rate at 4°C.}}{36 - 4}$

$F = \text{Rate at 20°C.} - \dfrac{\text{Rate at 36°C.} + \text{Rate at 4°C.}}{2}$

ART. 23. The limits to obtain a certificate for deck watches and large pocket watches (categories A and B) are as follows:—

1. The mean rate of any period must not exceed 5·00 sec.

2. For the same period, the mean difference of rate must not exceed 1·00 sec.

TESTING STANDARDS—Cont.

3. The mean variation of the daily rate must not exceed 0·40 sec. in Cat. A and 0·48 sec. in Cat. B.

4. The difference between the mean rates of any two periods at a temperature of 20°C. (periods 1, 2, 3, 4, 5, 7, 9) must not exceed 7·00 sec.

5. The difference of rate from horizontal to vertical must not exceed 4·00 sec. It is calculated by comparison of the mean rate of periods 1 and 9.

6. The difference of rate between the two horizontal positions must not exceed 4·00 sec. It is calculated by comparison of the mean rates of periods 4 and 5.

7. Resumption of rate must not exceed 2·50 sec.

8. The mean variation resulting from change of position must not exceed 2·00 sec.

9. The primary error E of compensation must not exceed 0·12 sec.

10. The secondary error F of compensation must not exceed 2·00 sec.

ART. 24. The limits to obtain a certificate for pocket watches of small size (category C) (30 to 38 mm. dial) are as follows:—
The calculations are the same as ART. 23.

1. Mean rate of any period	8·00 sec.
2. Mean difference of any of the periods	1·50 sec.
3. Mean variation of daily rate	0·60 sec.
4. Differences between the mean rates of the periods at the temperature of 20°C.	9·00 sec.
5. Difference of rate between horizontal and vertical	5·00 sec.
6. Difference of rate between the two horizontal positions	5·00 sec.
7. Resumption of rate	3·00 sec.
8. Mean difference resulting from a change of position	2·40 sec.
9. Primary error E of compensation	0·16 sec.
10. Secondary error F of compensation	3·00 sec.

ART. 35. Test for watches of small size (category D). (Up to 30 mm. dial). The tests are of 44 days duration, divided into nine periods they are the same in order and duration as the tests for deck watches (ART. 20).

ART. 26. To obtain a certificate of rating in addition to the tests indicated in ART. 24 a watch of small size must satisfy the 10 following conditions:—

1. The mean rate of any period must not exceed 8·00 sec.

2. For the same period, the mean difference of rates must not exceed 1·50 sec.

3. Mean variation of the daily rate must not exceed 0·75 sec.

4. The difference between the mean rates of any two of the periods 1, 2, 3, 4, 5, 7, and 9 must not exceed 9·00 sec.

5. The difference of rate between horizontal and vertical must not exceed 5·00 sec. It is calculated by comparison of the mean rate of period 5 with the mean of the rates of periods 1 and 9.

6. The difference of rate between the two horizontal positions must not exceed 5·00 sec. It is calculated by comparison of the mean rates of periods 4 and 5.

7. The resumption of rate or difference of the mean rates of periods 1 and 9 must not exceed 3·60 sec.

8. The mean difference resulting from a change of position must not exceed 3·00 sec.

9. The primary error E or compensation must not exceed 0·20 sec.

10. The secondary error F of compensation must not exceed 4·00 sec.

OFFICIAL BUREAUX FOR TESTING WATCHES

INSTITUTED IN THE TOWNS OF BIENNE, LA CHAUX-DE-FONDS, LE LOCLE, LE SENTIER, ST. IMIER, GENEVA

EXTRACTS FROM THE REGULATIONS

ART. 1. The official bureaux of Control instituted in the towns of Bienne, La Chaux-de-Fonds, Le Locle, Le Sentier, and St. Imier receive in deposit watches sent to them for their undergoing different trials and their recording the rates.

ART. 5. The rate of each watch is compared every 24 hours with a clock checked each day with the signal of the astronomical and chronometrical Observatory of Neuchâtel.

ART. 7. Meaning of the symbols and indication of the results. The sign + means gaining, the sign — means losing.

PU	Pendant up	PD	Pendant down
PL	Pendant left	DU	Dial up
PR	Pendant right	DD	Pendant down.

T. means temperature in degrees centigrade.

DURATION AND METHOD OF TRAILS.

ART. 9–14.

POCKET WATCHES			8 DAY WATCHES			WRISLET WATCHES		
Duration	Position	Temp.	Duration	Position	Temp.	Duration	Position	Temp.
2 days	PU	room	7 days	PU	room	2 days	PL	room
2 days	PL	room	1 day	PL	room	2 days	PU	room
2 days	PR	room	1 day	PR	room	2 days	PD	room
2 days	DD	room	1 day	DD	room	2 days	DD	room
2 days	DU	room	7 days	DU	room	2 days	DU	room
1 day	DU	refrigerator	1 day	DU	refrigerator	1 day	DU	refrigerator
1 day	DU	room	1 day	DU	room	1 day	DU	room
1 day	DU	oven	1 day	DU	oven	1 day	DU	oven
2 days	PU	room	2 days	PU	room	2 days	PL	room

TOLERANCES

	POCKET WATCHES				8 DAY WATCHES		WRISTLET WATCHES	
	without mention	with mention	special* without mention	special* with mention	without mention	with mention	without mention	with mention
Mean daily rate in the five positions	−4 +10	−2 +5	−4 +12	−2 +6	−5 +5 V.H. & H.H.	−2·5 +5	0 +15	0 +15
Mean daily variation in the five positions	3	1·5	4	2	7 V.H. & H.H.	3·5 V.H. & H.H.	7	4
Maximum variation between two daily rates in the same position	5	2·5	6	3	10	5	12	8
Difference between horizontal and vertical	±10	±5	±12	±6	±10	±5	—	—
Greatest difference between the mean daily rate and any individual rate	±12	±7	±15	±9	±20	±12	±26	±16
Variation of rate per 1° Centigrade	±0·5	±0·25	±0·7	±0·35	±0·5	±0·25	±1·4	±0·8
Secondary error	±9	±4·5	±11	±5·5	±9	±4·5	—	±8
Rate resuming	±5	±2·5	±8	±4	±10	±5	±14	±8

*Complicated watches or of reduced height.

For the Swiss definition of *Wrist Chronometre*, see page 98.

TESTING STANDARDS—Cont.

GERMAN HYDROGRAPHIC INSTITUTE, HAMBURG

WATCH RATE CERTIFICATE
SPECIFICATIONS

		s I s	s II s
a.	Mean daily rate in five positions	0 to —15	0 to —15
b.	Mean variation of the daily rate in the five positions ...	7^s	4^s
c.	Greatest difference (variation of rate) between two consecutive rates in the same position	12^s	8^s
d	Greatest difference between mean daily rate and one of the rates in the five positions	±26^s	±16^s
e.	Variation of rate for each degree Centigrade...	±1·4^s	±0·8^s
f.	Resumption of rate	±14^s	±8

— = Fast $\big\}$ The — sign = fast, since it is calculated that the error is taken away
+ = Slow $\big\}$ thus:—

	H.	M.	S.
Watch set at	12	0	0
24 hr. reading	12	0	2 *i.e.*, gained 2^s.
but			—2
=	12	0	0

Conversely + = slow.

PHYSICAL-TECHNICAL LABORATORY BRUNSWICK – GERMANY

WATCH RATE CERTIFICATE FOR WRISTLET WATCHES—SPECIFICATION

In order to obtain a watch rate certificate for wristlet-watches with degree of performance AI " Good performance of wristlet watches " or AII " Especially good performance of wristlet watches," the detailed results of the test must be within the undermentioned tolerances:—

	DETAILED RESULTS	AI	AII
A.	Average variation of rate in five positions ar 20°C. before the temperature test ...	7·0 s/d^2	4·0 s/d^2
B.	Maximum variation of rate in one of the five positions at 20°C. before the temperature test.	12·0 s/d^2	8·0 s/d^2
D.	Average rate in the five positions at 20°C. before the temperature test	0·0 s/d to —15·0 s/d	0·0 s/d to —15·0 s/d
E.	Maximum difference between the average rate D and one rate in any one of the five positions at 20°C. before the temperature test	26·0 s/d	16·0 s/d
J.	Bulk alteration of rate per °C. between 5°C. and 35°C. in the position dial up	±1·40 s/d°C.	±0·8 s/d°C.
L.	Resumption of rate in the position 6 up after temperature test	±14·0 s/d	±8·0 s/d
— = Fast $\big\}$ see footnote to Hamburg test + = Slow $\big\}$		s/d = seconds per day. s/d ^{2}= two consecutive days' test.	

TETRODE. *See* Valve.

THERM. *See* Antique Clock Case Terms.

THERMIONICS. The study of the emission of electrons from heated surfaces. In general the term is now applied to the behaviour, control, and application of electron emission and to the wide range of devices developed for industrial, commercial and scientific usage.

THERMIONIC VALVE. An evacuated envelope of glass or metal containing two or more electrodes for the purpose of collecting or controlling the electron flow from a heated cathode sealed within the same or a contiguous chamber. Electrical connections are made externally via metal wires sealed into the walls or through a pinch at the base and are usually led out to a stout connector. The most common form is the ordinary radio valve. *See* Valve.

THERMOMETER. A temperature measuring instrument.

THERMOMETER SCALES. *See* Temperature Scales and Tables.

THERMOPLASTICS. Plastic substances which can be repeatedly softened or melted by heat and setting hard or stable in form when cool, without great change in their properties. *See* Plastics.

THERMOSETTING PLASTICS. Plastic substances which undergo a permanent irreversible chemical change when subjected to heat and thus assuming their final form. *See* Plastics.

THEWLIS SCREWS. *See* English Screws.

THIMBLE. A finger attachment for holding a punch so that the disengaged fingers may steady the work.

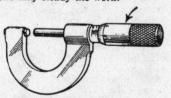

MICROMETER THIMBLE.

THIMBLE.

The rotating portion of a micrometer gauge which traverses the sleeve laterally thus exposing the sleeve scale and indicating the measurement between jaws or anvils. One revolution of the thimble corresponds to one division of the scale. Graduations similarly engraved upon the surface of the thimble enable fractional readings of the sleeve divisions to be read with great accuracy.

THIRD PINION. In a watch, the pinion on the same arbor as the third wheel which usually engages with the centre wheel.

THIRD WHEEL. The third wheel of a watch movement counting the barrel as the first and the centre wheel as the second. Or, in the instance of a fusee watch, the great wheel as the first wheel and the centre as the second. *See* Nomenclature of Watch Parts.

THREE-LEGGED GRAVITY ESCAPEMENT. Similar in action to the double three-legged gravity escapement (*q.v.*) invented by Lord Grimthorpe for use in turret clocks and regulator clocks. The action of this escapement is similar to that of the Double Three-legged Escapement (*q.v.*).

THREE-LEGGED GRAVITY ESCAPEMENT.

THREE-PART CLOCK. A chiming clock with three trains—one each for the time, strike, and chime. Chime clocks are also made with two trains.

THREE-QUARTER PLATE. A term denoting a certain design of watch movement in which the barrel, centre, third and fourth wheels (and fusee) are all under one plate. This top plate is cut away to allow the balance to be planted at the side and thus at a lower level than in the full-plate movement. *See* also Full- and Half-Plate and Bar Movements. *Illus. on next page.*

THREE-QUARTER PLATE.

THREE SQUARE FILE. *See* Files.

THREE-TRAIN CLOCK. *See* Three-Part Clock.

THROW. A form of " Turns " (*q.v.*) operated by a hand wheel. A gut line is usually employed to rotate the work, used chiefly by clockmakers.

THROW.

THYRATRON. *See* Valve.

TIC-TAC CLOCK. A French drum clock fitted with a type of recoil escapement and bob pendulum. The escapement is also to be found in some of the early English bracket clocks.

TIC-TAC ESCAPEMENT.

Sometimes referred to as " drum escapement."

TICKET CLOCK. *See* Flick Leaf Clock.

TIM. The Post Office " Speaking Clock " available at all times by telephone. The announcer's voice is recorded in such a way that the time at any given instant throughout the day is automatically transmitted to the enquirer (*i.e.*, subscriber). A master clock controls the apparatus. For further information about TIM *see* " British Time " published by Crosby Lockwood Co.

TIME. From the horologists' point of view the definition of Time is the same as for astronomy: " The fundamental unit of Time measurement is ascertained by the earth's rotation on its axis." *See* Greenwich Mean Time, Sidereal Time, Solar Time.

TIME BALL. A time signal, essentially visual. A ball, previously raised, is caused to fall at a predetermined moment to indicate the time at that moment, *e.g.*, 12 o'clock noon. Greenwich Observatory has a time ball originally intended for observation by shipping lying in the Thames off Greenwich.

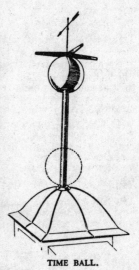

TIME BALL.

TIME BASE. A term referring to the apparatus in general and the effect in particular whereby the spot of light on a cathode-ray tube screen (*i.e.*, the electron beam) is caused to sweep across the tube face in a horizontal, vertical or circular manner at a uniform rate. The action is repetitive and the return or " fly back " sweep is arranged to occur very rapidly and may be " blacked out," *i.e.*, invisible. The time base may further be synchronised with the signals or impulses applied to the tube.

TIMES IN STANDARD ZONES*

The following list indicates the amounts by which the Zone Standard times in foreign territories are fast or slow, as compared with Greenwich Mean Time. Corrections must be made when necessary for Summer Time or Double Summer Time. *See* next page.

ARGENTINA	Buenos Aires	4 hrs. slow	
AUSTRALIA	Adelaide	9½	fast
	Brisbane	10	,,
	Melbourne	10	,,
	Newcastle	10	,,
	Perth	8	,,
	Sydney	10	,,
BRAZIL	Rio de Janeiro	3	slow
	São Paulo	3	,,
CANADA AND U.S.A... ..	Eastern Zone	5	,,
	Central Zone	6	,,
	Western Zone	7	,,
CHINA	Shanghai	8	fast
DUTCH EAST INDIES ..	Java	7½	,,
EAST AFRICA..	Mombasa	3	,,
	Zanzibar	3	,,
EGYPT	Cairo	2	,,
INDIA	Bangalore	5½	,,
	Bombay	5½	,,
	Calcutta	6	,,
	Cawnpore	5½	,,
	Madras	5½	,,
JAPAN..	Tokyo	9	,,
MEXICO	Mexico City	6	slow
NEW ZEALAND	Auckland	12	fast
	Christchurch	12	,,
	Dunedin	12	,,
	Wellington	12	,,
PERU	Lima	5	slow
SOUTH AFRICA	Bulawayo	2	,,
	Cape Town	2	fast
	Durban	2	,,
	Johannesburg	2	,,
	Salisbury	2	,,
TASMANIA	Hobart	10	,,
	Launceston	10	,,
URUGUAY	Montevideo	3½	slow

In some cases the local Mean Solar Time may be a few minutes fast or slow as compared with the Zone Standard Time.

251

TIME ZONES

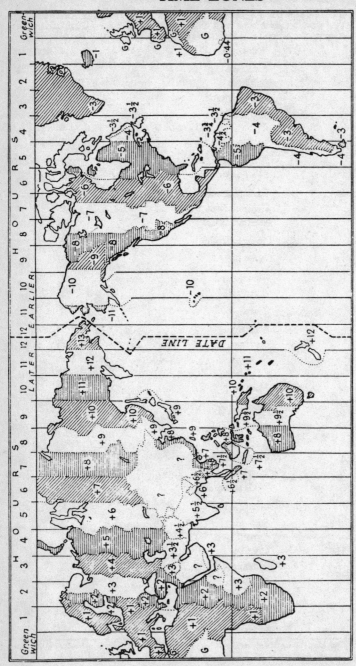

The Standard Time Zones are shown above, as adapted to suit different countries. The + and − signs give the local times in relation to Greenwich Mean Time. In navigational charts the signs are reversed to make it convenient to convert local time to G.M.T., e.g. time in Newfoundland is shown as −3½ above (3½ hours earlier than Greenwich) but on a navigation chart it would be +3½ because GMT = Newfoundland time +3½ hours.

TIME RECORDER. A specialised clock which records in printed figures on a card or paper roll the time of arrival and departure of workers or the duration of processes in a factory on the insertion of a suitable record card or depression of a lever. Another version is used for recording the periods of motion and rest of commercial motor vehicles. In these a record disk is rotated by a clock movement and marked by the oscillations of an unbalanced pendulum while the vehicle is in motion.

BOXING TIMER. Three minute rounds with 1 minute interval are indicated on the minute counter dial.

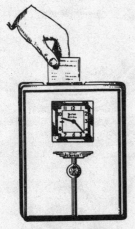

TIME RECORDER.

TIMEKEEPER. Refers to any instrument that indicates the time of day.

TIMEPIECE. A watch or clock that shows the time of day only. The term distinguishes such a piece from a striking or chiming mechanism.

TIMER. A stop watch used in timing a period such as is used at sporting events and by engineers, etc. Timers are made to beat and record 1/5th, 1/10th, 1/20th, 1/50th, and 1/100th of a second, with minute recording of 30, 60, and so on, up to 12 hours or more. Timers are distinct from Chronographs (*q.v.*). The following illustrations are of timers with dials calibrated for various purposes. The word " Timer " is also used for a person who times watches (*see* page 257). A watch timing machine (*q.v.*) is also loosely called a " timer."

DECIMAL COUNTER. The dial is divided into decimal parts of a minute, one complete revolution equals one minute, or 1·00 minutes. The 60 minute counter is divided into 60 minutes. The reading of the timer illustrated is ·25 minutes.

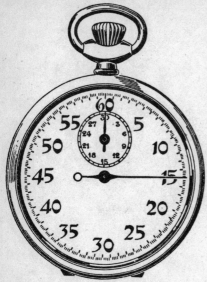

FIFTH-OF-SECOND TIMER. With minute counter up to 30 minutes.

ICE HOCKEY TIMER. The duration of play is 20 minutes each way. The minute counter dial is shaded to show the duration of 20 minutes readily. Land hockey is similar, but the duration of play is 35 minutes.

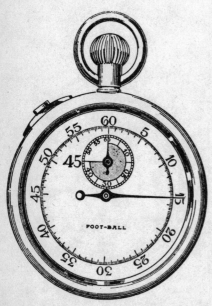

FOOTBALL TIMER. The duration of play is ¾ hour each way. The minute counter dial is shaded to show the duration of 45 minutes readily.

PRODUCTION TIMER. The dial is calibrated to show at a glance the hourly production.

If, for instance, it takes 40 seconds to produce 1 then that is equal to 90 per hour; or 9 seconds to produce 1 = 400 per hour.

glance. For instance, 30 seconds for 10 strokes = 20 per minute: or 20 seconds for 10 strokes = 30 per minute.

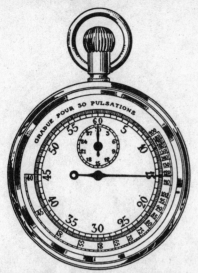

PULSE METER. The dial is calibrated so that the pulse beats per minute are shown after starting the timer and stopping at the expiration of 30 pulsations.

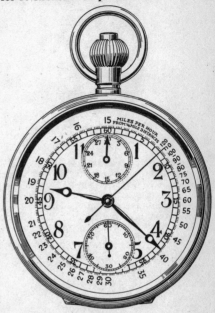

TACHYMETER CHRONOGRAPH, or SPEEDO-METER. The dial is calibrated so that the miles per hour can be seen at a glance. With the dial illustrated the calculations are made over a measured $\frac{1}{4}$ mile. For instance, $\frac{1}{4}$ mile in 15 seconds = 60 miles per hour: or $\frac{1}{4}$ mile in 10 second = 90 miles per hour.

SCULLING TIMER. The dial is so calibrated that the number of strokes per minute, counting 10 strokes, can be seen at a

An example of chronograph dial calibrated to show the tachymeter and the telemetre combined.

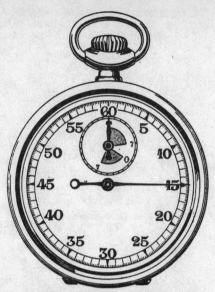

TACHYMETER CHRONOGRAPH. This dial is calibrated similar to the tachymeter already illustrated with the exception that the spiral in the centre indicates the miles per hour over a measured mile. Therefore one revolution of the seconds hand indicates 60 m.p.h., 2 revolutions 30 m.p.h. and 3 revolutions 20 m.p.h.

WATER POLO TIMER. The duration of play is 7 minutes each way with an interval of 5 minutes. The shaded portion of the minute counter dial makes the lapse of time readily observable.

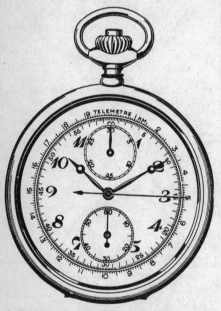

TELEMETRE, CHRONOGRAPH. The dial is calibrated so that the speed or sound and the distance can be seen at a glance. For instance, when the flash from a gun is observed the button is depressed and when the sound of the firing is heard the chronograph hand is stopped and the reading gives the distance away of the gun.

YACHTING TIMER. Yachts are given 5 minutes to toe the line for a race. This dial is calibrated so that the passing of the time limit can be seen at a glance. A gun is fired indicating that the 5 minute warning has started, the button of the timer is immediately depressed. The minute counter successively passes from 5 to 1 and when the seconds hand reaches the 60 the second gun is fired, the yacht should then be on the line and the race is on.

TIMER. A specialist in timing watches, etc. The full description is " Springer and Timer " and such a person is usually one of high technical ability. The duties comprise fitting the balance spring and adjusting for changes in temperature and carrying out positional adjustments, etc.

TIME SIGNAL. Any visual or aural signal such as the Time Ball (*q.v.*) or Minute Gun to denote a particular time of day. The term, by common usage, refers nowadays almost exclusively to the six " pips " radiated by the B.B.C. and which represent the last six seconds of the hour; a system suggested and introduced by Mr. Hope Jones. Similar signals, especially for nautical use, are radiated from this country and throughout the world.

TIME SWITCH. A mechanism the primary function of which is to operate one or more electric switches periodically at and/or for pre-determined times or intervals, *e.g.*, x-ray exposure (fractional second); street lighting (periodic interval).

TIME VERNIER. The rhythmic time signals where sixty-one beats are transmitted in each minute—usually for five minutes—mainly for navigational and surveying purposes, particularly determination of longitude.

TIMING. The regulation or Rating (*q.v.*) of a watch, clock or chronometer.

TIMING COLLETS. *See* Timing Washers.

TIMING IN POSITIONS. Regulating or " rating " a watch in various positions. A pocket watch is " rated " dial up (D.U.); dial down (D.D.); pendant up (P.U.); pendant right (P.R.); pendant left (P.L.); A wrist watch is rated similarly excepting that the pendant down position is taken instead of the pendant up.

TIMING IN REVERSE. An operation or method employed in positional adjusting. Normally, and considering the vertical position only, when a balance (not perfectly poised) is at rest and has the heaviest

portion coincident with the lowest point of the balance or, lying in the " lower " circumference, the watch will have a gaining rate. If, however, the balance vibration exceeds $1\frac{1}{2}$ turns the circumstance is reversed and the watch has a losing rate. Thus, reverting to the normal case, to effect a gaining rate in the vertical position the balance is made heaviest at the point opposite to the lowest point at rest. This form of adjustment in positional timing is termed " Timing in reverse." For further information *see* " Practical Watch Repairing." (N.A.G. Press, Ltd.)

TIMING MACHINE. A comparison machine used for testing the timekeeping properties of watches. It compares the vibrations or beats of the watch escapement under test with another series of vibrations based on a standard frequency. For the frequency standard, a quartz crystal oscillator or a temperature-controlled tuning fork is commonly used. The record of the machine may be printed on paper or shown in some other manner such as on a cathode tube. The timer can also be used for diagnosing watch faults and for this purpose the watch tick is usually amplified to give audible aid to the operator. In the hands of skilled repairers, certain types are said to indicate definite escapement conditions. It is possible to estimate the rate of loss or gain of a watch in a matter of seconds. *See* Dawe, Furzhill, Lepaute, Western Electric, etc.

TIMING NUTS. The steel nuts fitted to the ends of the quarter screws of a high grade cut balance.

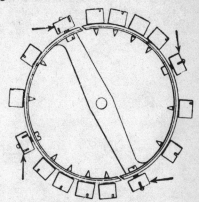

TIMING NUTS.

TIMING RACK. *See* Watch Rack.

TIMING SCREWS. Usually, the four

screws of a cut balance placed at the arms and at a quarter circumference therefrom. Also known as "quarter screws" and "mean time screws." The screws on a plain uncut balance are also used for timing purposes but are not usually referred to as "Timing Screws." The screws embraced by the brackets are the temperature screws and the four screws on each limb near the cut end are the more effective. The four screws outside the brackets are the quarter screws.

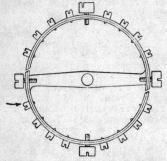

TIMING SCREWS (The small screws)

TIMING WASHERS. Small washers or collets placed under the heads of balance screws to adjust the balance weight. Obtainable in sizes and weights, the effects of which, however, are indicated in very general terms.

TIMING WEIGHTS. Refers to the sliding weights fitted to the balance, usually of a chronometer (detent escapement), and used in temperature adjusting. Strictly, they are compensation weights, the timing being effected by the Quarter Screws or nuts (*q.v.*).

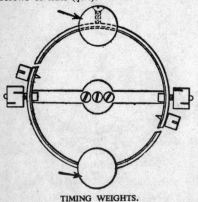

TIMING WEIGHTS.

TING-TANG CLOCK. A clock that sounds on two gongs or bells (one of lower tone than the first as a rule) in ding-dong fashion at the quarters and at the hours. Two blows indicate the first quarter; four the half-hour; six the quarter to the hour and eight at the hours, followed by the number of hours struck in the usual manner of a striking clock. *See* CHIMES.

TIP CIRCLE. A circle drawn round the tips of the teeth of a wheel or the leaves of a pinion, *i.e.*, outside the "pitch circle."

TIP CIRCLE.

TIP RELIEF. A slight rounding of the tips of gear teeth to ensure smooth engagement.

TIPSY KEY. *See* Breguet Key.

TIPPED TOOLS. Turning cutters tipped with working surfaces or edges of very hard carbide steels. *See* Carbide Tools.

TIRETTE. French for Pull-Out-Piece (*q.v.*).

TOE OF TOOTH. Refers to the teeth of the Club-Tooth Escape wheel. It is the end of a tooth opposite to the Locking Face or "heel" (*q.v.*).

TOE OF TOOTH.

TOLERANCE. The total permissible variation from theoretical size(s) of a part or parts intended to fit or work together. Usually given in thousandths of an inch. Also known as allowance or limits.

TOOL POST. A clamp resembling a post for holding the cutting tool on the slide rest of a lathe.

TOOL STEEL. A quality of steel especially suitable for tool making, particularly cutting tools.

TOOTH THICKNESS. The dimension between the working surfaces on opposite sides of a tooth, measured along the pitch circle (*q.v.*). The normal tooth thickness of helical teeth is measured along the pitch surface of the cylinder in a direction normal to the tooth helix.

TOOTH WIDTH. Tooth width of spur gears is the width measured parallel to the axis. Also known as "Face Width."

TOPPING. The operation of re-cutting the teeth in a wheel. The work is carried out by a Topping or Rounding-up tool (*q.v.*). To " top " a wheel is not the same as cutting a wheel. The rounding-up tool reshapes the teeth but does not divide the wheel equally into teeth and spaces.

TOPPING TOOL. Another name for Rounding-up Tool (*q.v.*).

TOP PLATE. The plate opposite to the Bottom Plate (*q.v.*). The plate upon which the vendor's or maker's name is usually engraved. From the general viewpoint, it may be considered as the back or rear plate of a clock, but such a distinction is lost in a watch. Hence the natural seeming description top plate, as normally viewed and dismantled.

TORCHILUS. *See* ANTIQUE CLOCK CASE TERMS.

TORQUE. A force tending to produce rotation; that which tends to produce rotation; a twist. Expressed in lb./ft., or gram/millimetres. It is measured by the weight, equivalent to the force, acting at a given radius, *e.g.*, a torque of 5 gm./mm. is a turning force such that it is exactly balanced by a weight of 5 gm. acting at a radius of 1 mm. The Adjusting Rod (*q.v.*) is a form of torque measurer.

TORSION. The stress set up in a part or a body by twisting. The term is used in a general way to indicate twisting rather than in its specific sense.

TORSION PENDULUM. A pendulum system analogous to the balance. A bob oscillates in a horizontal plane (*i.e.*, at right angles) to the line of suspension, which consists physically of a steel or alloy ribbon. The oscillation about the perpendicular results in the twisting and untwisting of the suspension which, in turn, impulses the pendulum bob via the suspension ribbon. Applied where long vibrations of a slow rate are required, giving a long run. The system is commonly employed in 400-day clocks. Also used in the Atmos Clock (*q.v.*).

TORTOISESHELL. *See* ANTIQUE CLOCK CASE TERMS.

TORUS. *See* MOULDINGS.

TOTAL LOCK. An American term referring to the combined Locking (*q.v.*) and the Run to the Banking (*q.v.*) of the lever escapement.

TOUCHSTONE (LYDIAN STONE). A dense hard, black stone used by jewellers to determine the quality of gold. The metal is rubbed upon the stone and aquafortis applied to the metal so deposited. The colour and general appearance of the streak enable the operator to judge the quality of the specimen tested. Standard pieces of gold can be used at the same time to provide a more direct comparison, the two streaks being made side by side.

TOURBILLON. A watch in which the entire escapement is fitted into a cage or carriage and the complete assembly revolving. An extended lower pivot is usually fitted to the Tourbillon carriage and on to this the seconds hand is fitted. The carriage rotates once in 60 seconds. The construction of the tourbillon needs great care and skill in manufacture and is somewhat delicate, the karrusel (*q.v.*) is more robust. While an outstanding horological achievement the necessity for it does not justify the expense, since positional errors are adjusted by means of the balance spring, etc. Invented by A. L. Breguet, its purpose is to overcome the various vertical positional errors. *See* also Karrusel and Carriage.

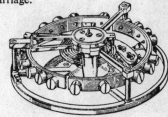

TOURBILLON.

TOWER CLOCK. *See* Turret Clock.

TRACERY. *See* ANTIQUE CLOCK CASE TERMS.

TRAIN. A succession of wheels and pinions gearing together such as the wheels and pinions of a watch or clock. The count or speed of a train in horology is determined by the number of vibrations of the balance in one hour, *e.g.*, 14,400, 16,200, 18,000, etc. The number identifies the train which is known as a " 14,400 train," " 18,000 train," etc. It is sometimes referred to as the " count " in the same manner. In clocks, the terms " high train " and " low train " refer to a train of wheels and pinions with a great or low number of teeth to the wheels and leaves to the pinions, respectively, *i.e.*, a regulator clock (*q.v.*) has a high train. The tables following give the trains of wheels commonly found in clocks and watches.

CLOCK TRAINS WITH LENGTHS OF PENDULUM

Centre Wheel	Third Wheel	Third Wheel Pinion	Escape Wheel	Escape Wheel Pinion	Vibrations of Pendulum per min.	Length of Pendulum in inches
128	120	16	30	16	60	39·14
112	105	14	30	14	60	39·14
96	90	12	30	12	60	39·14
80	75	10	30	10	60	39·14
64	60	8	30	8	60	39·14
68	64	8	30	8	68	30·49
70	64	8	30	8	70	28·75
72	64	8	30	8	72	27·17
75	60	8	32	8	75	25·05
72	65	8	32	8	78	23·15
75	64	8	32	8	80	22·01
84	64	8	30	8	84	19·97
86	64	8	30	8	86	19·06
88	64	8	30	8	88	18·19
84	78	7	20	7	89·1	17·72
80	72	8	30	8	90	17·39
84	78	7	21	7	93·6	16·08
94	64	8	30	8	94	15·94
84	78	8	28	8	95·5	15·45
108	100	12	32	10	96	15·28
84	84	9	30	8	98	14·66
84	78	7	22	7	98	14·66
84	78	8	29	8	98·9	14·41
80	80	8	30	8	100	14·09
85	72	8	32	8	102	13·54
84	78	8	30	8	102·4	13·44
84	78	7	23	7	102·5	13·4
105	100	10	30	10	105	12·78
84	78	8	31	8	105·8	12·59
84	78	7	24	7	107	12·3
96	72	8	30	8	108	12·08
84	78	8	32	8	109·2	11·82
88	80	8	30	8	110	11·64
84	77	7	25	7	110	11·64
84	78	7	25	7	111·4	11·35
84	80	8	32	8	112	11·22
84	78	8	33	8	112·2	11·15
96	76	8	30	8	114	10·82
115	100	10	30	10	115	10·65
84	78	7	26	7	115·9	10·49
96	80	8	30	8	120	9·78
84	70	7	30	7	120	9·78
84	78	7	27	7	120·3	9·73
90	84	8	31	8	122	9·46
84	78	7	28	7	124·8	9·02
100	80	8	30	8	125	9·01
90	84	8	32	8	126	8·87
100	96	10	40	10	128	8·59
84	78	7	29	7	129·3	8·42
100	78	8	32	8	130	8·34
84	77	7	30	7	132	8·08
84	78	7	30	7	133·7	7·9
90	90	8	32	8	135	7·73
84	78	7	31	7	138·2	7·38

CLOCK TRAINS WITH LENGTHS OF PENDULUM

Centre Wheel	Third Wheel	Third Wheel Pinion	Escape Wheel	Escape Wheel Pinion	Vibrations of Pendulum per min.	Length of Pendulum in inches
84	80	8	40	8	140	7·18
120	71	8	32	8	142	6·99
84	78	7	32	7	142·6	6·93
100	87	8	32	8	145	6·95
84	78	7	33	7	147·1	6·5
100	96	8	30	8	150	6·26
84	78	7	34	7	151·6	6·1
96	95	8	32	8	152	6·09
84	77	7	35	7	154	5·94
104	96	8	30	8·	156	5·78
84	78	7	35	7	156	5·78
120	96	9	30	8	160	5·5
84	78	7	36	7	160·5	5·47
84	78	7	37	7	164·9	5·15
132	100	9	27	8	165	5·17
84	78	7	38	7	169·4	4·88
128	102	8	25	8	170	4·87
84	78	7	39	7	173·8	4·65
84	77	7	40	7	175	4·55
84	78	7	40	7	176	4·43

WATCH TRAINS

NUMBER OF TEETH IN WHEELS OF WATCHES WITH 18,000 TRAINS

Centre Wheel	...	...	...	100	96	96	80	80	80	80	80	80	80	80	75
Third Wheel Pinion	...	...		12	12	12	10	10	10	10	10	10	10	10	10
Third Wheel	...	...	...	96	90	75	75	75	75	75	70	60	60	60	70
Fourth Wheel Pinion	...	...		12	12	10	10	10	10	8	8	8	8	8	8
Fourth Wheel	...	...		90	80	70	80	70	60	60	60	80	70	60	64
Escape Wheel Pinion	...	...		10	8	7	8	7	6	7	7	8	7	6	7
Escape Wheel	...	...		15	15	15	15	15	15	14	15	15	15	15	15
Centre Wheel	...	...		75	75	72	72	64	64	64	64	63	60	60	54
Third Wheel Pinion	...	...		8	8	9	9	8	8	8	8	7	8	7	6
Third Wheel	...	..	...	56	60	60	60	70	63	60	60	60	60	54	50
Fourth Wheel Pinion	...	...		7	7	8	8	8	7	8	8	7	6	6	6
Fourth Wheel	...	...		48	48	70	60	60	50	70	60	50	48	50	48
Escape Wheel Pinion	...	...		6	6	7	6	7	6	7	6	6	6	6	6
Escape Wheel	...	...	...	15	14	15	15	15	15	15	15	14	15	14	15

Because the seconds hand makes 60 turns while the minute hand makes 1, the following formula relating to the number of teeth must apply:

$$60 = \frac{\text{centre wheel} \times \text{third wheel}}{\text{third wheel pinion} \times \text{fourth wheel}}.$$

WATCH TRAINS—Cont.

NUMBER OF TEETH IN WHEELS OF WATCHES WITH TRAINS BETWEEN 14,000 AND 21,600

Trains: 14,000 | 15,600 | 16,800 | 17,550 | 18,850 | 18,900 | 19,600 | 19,800 | 19,825 | 20,020 | 21,450 | 21,600

Centre Wheel	80	64	80	64	54	58	64	80	80	66	56	61	56	66	64	60
Third Wheel Pinion	12	8	10	8	6	6	8	10	10	8	6	6	6	8	8	6
Third Wheel	70	60	70	60	54	54	63	70	72	64	54	54	55	60	60	54
Fourth Wheel Pinion	10	8	10	8	6	6	8	10	8	8	6	6	6	6	6	6
Fourth Wheel	70	60	70	60	50	50	60	70	55	60	48	50	54	60	54	48
Escape Wheel Pinion	7	6	7	7	6	6	6	6	6	6	6	6	6	6	6	6
Escape Wheel	15	13	15	14	13	13	15	15	15	15	15	13	13	13	15	15

NUMBER OF TEETH IN WHEELS OF WATCHES WITH 14,400 AND 16,200 TRAINS

	14,400							16,200				
Centre Wheel	112	96	90	80	64	64	64	90	90	72	64	64
Third Wheel Pinion	14	12	12	10	8	8	8	12	10	10	8	8
Third Wheel	105	90	80	75	64	60	60	80	75	70	60	60
Fourth Wheel Pinion	14	12	10	10	8	8	8	10	10	8	8	8
Fourth Wheel	96	80	80	64	45	60	56	72	64	60	63	54
Escape Wheel Pinion	12	10	10	8	6	6	7	8	8	7	7	6
Escape Wheel	15	15	15	15	15	12	15	15	15	15	15	15

MOTION WORK

12-HOUR DIALS

Hour Pipe	Hour Wheel	Minute Wheel Pinion	Minute Wheel	Hour Pipe	Hour Wheel	Minute Wheel Pinion	Minute Wheel
6	24	6	18	9	32	8	27
6	72	6	6	10	30	6	24
7	28	6	18	10	72	6	10
7	28	7	21	10	30	7	28
8	24	6	24	10	32	8	30
8	72	6	8	10	40	8	24
8	28	7	24	10	48	8	20
8	32	8	24	10	96	8	10
8	96	8	8	10	36	9	30
9	27	6	24	10	40	9	27
9	28	7	27	10	40	10	30
9	36	8	24	10	48	10	25

MOTION WORK—Cont.
12-HOURS DIALS—Cont.

Hour Pipe	Hour Wheel	Minute Wheel Pinion	Minute Wheel	Hour Pipe	Hour Wheel	Minute Wheel Pinion	Minute Wheel
10	120	10	10	16	48	12	48
12	36	6	24	16	64	12	36
12	42	7	24	16	96	12	24
12	36	8	32	16	72	12	32
12	48	8	24	16	64	14	42
12	40	10	36	16	56	14	48
12	48	10	30	16	84	14	32
12	60	10	24	17	68	22	66
12	48	12	36	18	72	10	30
14	42	8	32	18	54	12	48
14	48	8	28	18	72	12	36
14	42	10	40	18	64	16	54
14	48	10	35	18	72	16	48
14	70	10	24	18	72	22	66
14	56	10	30	20	60	10	40
14	48	12	42	20	80	16	48
14	56	12	36	20	72	18	60
14	63	12	32	20	80	18	54
14	72	12	28	22	72	18	66
14	84	12	24	24	60	10	48
15	48	8	30	24	72	8	32
15	45	10	40	28	64	8	42
15	60	10	30	30	40	6	54
15	48	12	45	30	72	6	30
16	48	8	32	30	40	8	72
16	64	10	30	30	90	8	32
16	48	10	40	30	60	10	60
16	60	10	32	30	72	12	60
16	80	10	24	30	120	24	72

12-HOUR DIAL MOTION WORK TRAINS

Cannon Pinion	Minute Wheel	Minute Wheel Pinion	Hour Wheel
10	30	10	40
12	36	10	40
14	40	10	42
16	40	10	48
12	36	12	48
14	42	12	48
16	48	12	48
18	48	12	54
14	42	14	56
16	48	14	56
18	54	14	56
16	48	16	64
18	54	16	64
20	60	18	72

Watch Trains from Formulaire Technique Papers.

Page 220—18,000 train
221—16,200 ,,
222—18,850 ,, 18,900, 19,600, 19,800, 19,825, 20,020, 21,450, 21,600.
224-225 12 hour dial motion work trains.

TRANSFORMER. An electrical appliance by means of which energy from one circuit may be transferred to another by magnetic induction. Strictly, of application only to alternating current circuits. Generally a change of voltage is made and a transformer may be thus defined as a machine of appliance by which the voltage from a source may be increased or decreased as desired, provided always that the total energy at the output terminals cannot be greater than the energy available at the input side. Transformers are among the most efficient apparatus known, the ratio of "power out" to "power in" approaching unity. There are many forms of transformer used ranging from high voltage types to heavy current types, power supplies for radio and television and the inter-valve types used in Divider Circuits (q.v.). A rotary transformer is used where A.C. is required from D.C. mains. It is a conversion combination of D.C. motor and A.C. alternator and not a transformer.

TRANSFORMER CORE. The laminated steel or alloy " frame " which provides the magnetic circuit of a transformer. Usually, it carries (in part at least) the windings.

TRANSIT. Passage of a celestial body across a meridian. See also Transit Instrument.

TRANSIT INSTRUMENT. A special form of telescope, mounted in such a manner and so equipped that the passage of sun and stars across a meridian (i.e., their transit), can be very accurately observed.

TRANSIT INSTRUMENT.

TRANSMISSION WHEEL. The wheel next to the ratchet wheel of a keyless watch. It usually carries the drive from the stem mechanism to the ratchet wheel. See Watch Part Nomenclature.

TRANSMISSION WHEEL.

TRAVELLING CLOCK. Refers to any type of small portable clock that can be packed without injury to the clock ; or affecting its timekeeping. The term usually refers nowadays to one of the many types of folding clock (see Calotte). All travelling clocks are fitted with a balance, not a pendulum.

TRAVERSING GEAR. A gear so arranged as to cause movement longitudinally, e.g., where a pen or marker is required to traverse a drum as in some forms of chronograph. Similarly, the cross-fed action of a slide rest on a lathe.

TREFOIL. See Antique Clock Case Terms.

TREILLAGE. See Antique Clock Case Terms.

TRIA IN UNO. See Balance Spring.

TRIAL NUMBER. A system employed to indicate the accuracy of a chronometer based upon the monthly rates. The number, thus computed determined the chronometer's position in order of merit. This system was used only at Greenwich, and was based on the weekly sums of the daily rates. Formula was "$a + 2b$" where a = the difference between greatest and least weekly sums over 29 weeks, and b = the greatest difference between one week and the next. The record was held by Kullberg, trial number $9 \cdot 1$. Hence the smaller the number the higher the position in the order of merit.

TRICKLE CHARGE. A system of continuously charging at a very low rate applied to accumulators; particularly advantageous where periods on and off load alternate, provided that normal maintenance inspection is not overlooked.

TRIGGER PIECE. Another name for the Pull-out-Piece (q.v.). Also refers or the small piece that moves the "All-or-Nothing-Piece " (q.v.).

TRIODE. See Valve.

TRIODE HEXODE. See Valve.

TRIPLE COMPLICATION. Refers to a watch provided with Chronograph Work (q.v.), Repeating Work (q.v.), and calendar (q.v.). Usually, the calendar work is of the perpetual type, i.e., automatically changes to the first of each month and indicates leap year. See Moon Dial for illustration of a triple complicated watch.

TRIPOLI. An abrasive used for cleaning clock movements and for polishing brass. A variety of "rotten stone "—a natural product, chiefly composed of fine particles of silica.

TRIPPING. A term defining the action of the chronometer and duplex escapements when, through excessive arc of vibration, the balance receives a double impulse during one excursion, causing a rapid gaining rate. Sometimes the fault in the chronometer is due to locking failure, and in the duplex escape wheel wear. *See* also Chronometer, Duplex and Banking.

TRUMPETER CLOCK. A clock where a trumpet or trumpets sound at the hours and sometimes the quarters. Such clocks are to be found which operate drums in addition to trumpets. The trumpets are operated with bellows similar to the Cuckoo Clock (*q.v.*).

TRUNDLES. The wire "leaves" of a Lantern Pinion (*q.v.*).

TRUNK. *See* ANTIQUE CLOCK CASE TERMS.

TRUNK DIAL. *See* Drop Dial.

TRUNNION. A journal or bearing disposed at right angles to the axis of the body or object supported. Usually there are two and they are co-axial. The term is applied in horology to the strong pin or rod by which the whole pendulum system of a heavy pendulum clock is hung upon the suspension bracket.

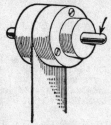

TRUNNION.

TUBE. An American term for Valve (*q.v.*).

TUBE CLOCK, *see* Tubular Clock.

TUBULAR CLOCK. Refers to a longcase clock (*q.v.*) of the chiming type in which tubes are used for the chimes instead of and as distinct from rods, bells, or gongs. Also known as Tube Clocks or Tubular Chimes.

TUDOR STYLE. *See* ENGLISH PERIOD STYLES, page 38.

TUMBLER. Another name for Gathering Pallet (*q.v.*).

TUMBLER SWITCH. A quick-break action switch, commonly used for lighting or low voltage circuits and mounted upon

a wall or panel as distinct from the "flush fitting" type which, however, may have the same action.

TUMBLING. A system employed to polish the pivots of balance staffs with Cone Pivots (*q.v.*). After the sharp cone-shaped ends have been formed, the staffs are placed in a canvas bag with cotton waste (torn to small pieces) and dry fine emery or carborundum powder. The end of the bag is then tied up and held by this end and the bottom and shaken backward and forward many times. The process is normally carried out mechanically, the polishing material with which leather chips are also commonly used for some work, and the items to be tumbled being placed in a rotating barrel, or drum, which sometimes has six or more flat sides to ensure adequate movement of the contents. By this means the staff and the pivots are polished and a certain and desirable roundness or radius is imparted to the ends of the pivots. Also known as rumbling.

TURKEY STONE. A sharp cutting stone used for whetting tools. Extremely fine grained. Also known as T/slate.

TURNING. The process of forming work or fashioning material by cutting away or removal while rotating—as in the lathe or turns or mandrel, etc., either between centres, or projecting from a chuck, face plate, etc.

TURNING ARBOR. A tapered arbor with cone pivots, fitted with a pulley or ferrule or some form of carrier. Used in turning work concentric to an existing hole (such as collets, etc.) by means of which the work is mounted upon the arbor or which serves, with the arbor, as a means of locating the true desired axis.

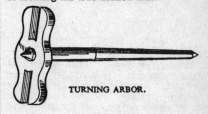

TURNING ARBOR.

TURNS. A simple form of dead centre lathe in which the work is rotated—usually by means of a bow and Ferrule (*q.v.*). *See* Dead Centre and Live Centre. English and Swiss patterns, made of brass and steel, are available for either watch or clock work and are still used by many craftsmen for special purposes.

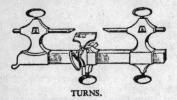

TURNS.

TURRET CLOCK. A large clock erected in a tower or church steeple. Also termed tower clock. The movement of a turret clock is normally built as a " flat bed " and is very different from a domestic clock.

TURRET LATHE. A form of lathe (a large capstan lathe) associated with manufacturing in which successive operations on work can be carried out, after preliminary setting up, by means of several tools mounted in a " turret " or special tool holder, so that each can be applied in sequence, and in repetition.

TURRET WHEEL. Another name for Column Wheel (*q.v.*).

TWEEZERS. Spring, tong-shaped tools of various shapes; used for handling small parts, cutting, shaping balance springs,

BALANCE SPRING FORMING.

CUTTING.

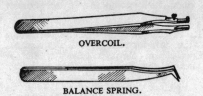

OVERCOIL.

BALANCE SPRING.

TWIST DRILL. A drill in which the cutting edges are formed at the end of the drill in the conventional manner and the twist or helical flutes are formed to clear swarf. Sized in numbers, letters, metric, decimal parts of an inch, or inch fractions, advancing 1/64th, etc. Of recent years the range has been extended well into the small sizes suitable for watch work, but great care is required in operation if a true hole is to result.

TWIST DRILL.

TWIST PILLARS. *See* ANTIQUE CLOCK CASE TERMS.

TWO-PIN ESCAPEMENT. A lever escapement having two pins fitted in the roller instead of the Ruby pin (*q.v.*). One pin unlocks, and the other receives impulse alternately. The advantage claimed is the giving of impulse on and after the lever reaching the line of centres. *See* Savage's Two-Pin Escapement.

TYMPANUM. *See* ANTIQUE CLOCK CASE TERMS.

U

UNADJUSTED. The word " Unadjusted " is stamped on some watch movements entering America. This enables them to enter at a lower rate of duty; it does not necessarily mean that the movements themselves are not adjusted for changes in temperatures and positions.

UNBREAKABLE GLASS. A term, usually abbreviated to " Unbreakable," defining the " glass " of a watch or clock made of plastic material, *e.g.*, Perspex or

Celluloid (also known as talc), etc. The best form of plastic for watch " glasses " is fully shrunk unplasticised Perspex.

UNBREAKABLE MAINSPRING. When certain stainless steel alloys are used for main springs instead of the usual carbon steel, they are claimed to be unbreakable. The torque of an alloy spring is sometimes 5 to 15% higher than a carbon spring and may *increase* with age. A typical alloy is iron, carbon, chromium, nickel, cobalt, manganese, molybdenum, and beryllium.

UNCUT BALANCE. Another name for a plain, solid, or monometal balance of a watch or clock. In general, an uncut balance provides no compensation for changes in temperature (the Volet (*q.v.*) and Straumann (*q.v.*) types are exceptions) and for an instrument so fitted some " self-compensating" metal must be used for the balance spring if a reasonable or practical degree of immunity to temperature change is required. *See* Balance Spring.

UNDERCUT. Refers to the practice in turning of cutting into or below the normal surface as in pinion heads, staffs, etc. In the case of a balance staff, it is also known as " back-slope," and in a pinion as " pinion hollow." Primarily the purpose was and is to prevent creeping of oil, but it developed almost to a fine art greatly enhancing the finish of the work. Beautiful examples are found in both chronometer and watch work wherein the pinion heads are deeply undercut.

UNDERCUT INTO BALANCE STAFF.

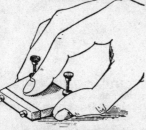

UNDERCUT INTO PINION HEAD.

UNDERHAND POLISHING. A method of polishing metal dead flat. The piece to be polished is held against the polishing lap or block either directly by hand or cemented to a tool as illustrated. There are several applications of the method including mechanically operated tools, but the principle is as illustrated. *See* Bolt Tool, also" Practical Watch Repairing." (N.A.G. Press Ltd.)

UNDERHAND POLISHING.

UNDERSLUNG. Refers to the chime rods of a chiming clock which are fitted under the movement resulting in a shallower case, the space between the back plate of the movement and the case being much reduced.

UNDERSLUNG.

UNDERSPRUNG. Refers to the arrangement where the balance spring is fitted below the balance (in relation to the cock), as is frequently found in the older English full-plate watches.

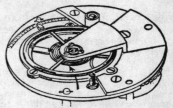

UNDERSPRUNG.

UNIFORM LEAD. A term used in connection with gearing, to define the constant speed of a wheel geared to another wheel or pinion moving at constant speed. Thus, if the ratio of angular velocities of the wheel and pinion is constant, uniform lead is said to exist. It is equal angular lead, or constant angular velocity ratio.

UNIFORM TIME. A time system corrected for variation of the Earth's rotation, and in the positions of the Poles, used by the Royal Greenwich Observatory as the basis for transmitted time signals and the Time Service Bulletins.

UNIVERSAL CHUCK. A self-centring chuck; an accessory to the lathe. Also known as self-centring chuck. Such chucks are always provided with three jaws to facilitate centring.

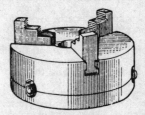

UNIVERSAL CHUCK.

UNIVERSAL KEY. A key for winding

key-wind watches, adaptable to differing sizes of winding square. *See* Birch Key.

UNIVERSAL TIME. A system of time calculation adopted by international agreement, as Greenwich Mean Time (*q.v.*) it is noted from 0 hours at Greenwich Mean Midnight.

UNLOCKING. The act of releasing. A term used in horology to define the release of a part or mechanism previously locked or inoperative. Particularly applied to the unlocking of the escape wheel, in connection with which—especially chronometer escapements—it is sometimes termed " discharging."

UNLOCKING PALLET OR STONE. Another name for the Discharge Pallet (*q.v.*) of the chronometer escapement. (Compare Exit Pallet.)

UP AND DOWN DIAL. A small subsidiary dial or separate indicator showing the extent to which a mainspring has been wound up or has run down. The zero position is " down," the maximum wind position " up."

UP AND DOWN DIAL.

UP AND DOWN WORK. The mechanism or device by which an indication is obtained (as by the up and down dial) of the extent to which a mainspring driven instrument is wound or has run down. When fitted to a fusee watch (as in some of the older English watches), the workmanship is generally of a very high order, superbly executed.

UPRIGHTING. To bring into alignment, *i.e.*, to make the arbors, wheels, pinions, etc., of a watch or clock, etc., in true disposition, at right angles to their plates or bearings. In normal practice the plates or cocks, etc., are laid horizontally for convenience. Hence the term "uprighting" in the sense of rising vertically therefrom.

UPRIGHTING TOOL. A tool, resembling a table or platform, having integral guides such that a hole can be drilled exactly at right angles to a plate or precisely in alignment with another existing hole, or its position marked by means of a pump centre.

UPRIGHTING TOOL.

URN FINIALS. *See* ANTIQUE CLOCK CASE TERMS.

V

VACUUM. Literally, a completely empty space. Physically, this is impossible of attainment and the term is, therefore, understood and applied as indicating a space wherein the air or other gas has been reduced to a very low pressure. To distinguish between the " degrees " of vacuum obtainable by the simpler pumps and the more complicated methods, the terms " high " and " low " vacuum are often applied. Thus, a pressure of 1 to 0·05 millimetres (mercury) is considered a " low " vacuum; a pressure of 0·0001 and less, a " high " vacuum. The lowest pressure so far obtainable is of the order of 10^{-1} mm.

VACUUM TUBE. A general term designating an electron tube or any similar apparatus associated with an electron flow *in vacuo*. *See* Valve.

VALVE. A thermionic or gas-discharge device which, in general, permits the passage of a current in one direction only, *i.e.*, cathode to anode. The American term is tube. Collectively the term is now applied to many forms of such a device particularly the radio valve consisting of an exhausted glass or metal or combination envelope, enclosing a system of electrodes the electrical connections of which are brought out through a " seal " or " pinch " and usually grouped in an insulating mounting or foot known as the Valve Base (*q.v.*). In horology such valves may be encountered in: Relays, Chargers, Amplifiers, Timing Machines, Quartz Clocks, " TIM," etc.

VALVE BASE. The foot or insulating mounting supporting the valve body and carrying the external electrode (and heater) contacts. These contacts or " Pins " (*q.v.*) mate in a corresponding socket suitably arranged to provide circuit connections; the valve is thus instantly detachable. To prevent incorrect insertion and electrical damage the contacts are arranged either concentrically about a keyway or spigot formed integrally with the base, or in a self-locating " pattern " mating with a correspondingly patterned socket. In another system employed particularly in the range of smaller dimensioned valves, stout wires are used, accurately positioned, sealed directly into the reinforced glass construction. Valve and base are thus integral. To afford identification of the electrode connections, a conventional numbering sequence is followed which is

read looking directly at the base, contacts uppermost. Excluding special types there are 8 patterns of base in general use. They are not interchangeable, but certain of the American and British Octal *patterns* will fit the same valve holder. In certain instances, however, the base fitted to a valve is optional.

BRITISH. Pattern location; 4, 5, 7 and 9 contacts (*a*).

SIDE CONTACTS. Pattern location; 5, 8, contacts. Obsolete.

INTERNATIONAL OCTAL. Keyway location; 8 contacts (*b*). B8B (B89), Loctol.

MAZDA OCTAL. Similar to I./O. " Mazda " valves only.

LOCTAL. Similar to I./O.

AMERICAN U.X. Pattern location; 4, 5, 6, 7, contacts (Heater/Cathode contacts larger) (*c*).

CONTINENTAL. Similar to British; 7 contacts.

FOOTLESS. Keyway location; 8 contacts (*d*). B8A. One of the smaller bases having a central spigot and equi-spaced pins sealed directly into the glass. Located by a boss and socket—a form of bayonet catch. (*e*). In the instance of a valve having fewer electrodes than the contacts of the base employed, the unused contacts are blank, or one or more may be removed.

VALVE CHARACTERISTICS. The data by which the performance and suitability of a valve is determined. Refer to appropriate technical literature for further information.

VALVE PINS. The external metal projections to which the internal electrode connections are made and to which the circuit connections are made by means of the socket.

VALVE SYMBOLS. A standard graphical representation of the electrode arrangements of valves; used in circuit drawing.

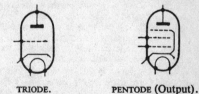

TRIODE.   PENTODE (Output).

VALVE TOP CAP. Refers to the connection(s) placed at the upper or opposite end to the foot. Usually an anode or grid connection.

VALVE TYPES (CLASSIFICATION). Manufacturers' type numbers and letters

BR5

2, 3, 5, 4, 1

(*a*)

BR7

7, 1, 2, 6, 3, 5, 4

(*a*)

UX6

3, 4, 2, 5, 1, 6

(*c*)

IO8

4, 5, 3, 6, 2, 7, 1, 8

(*b*)

B8A

4, 5, 3, 6, 2, 7, 1, 8

(*e*)

FO8

8, 1, 2, 7, 3, 6, 5, 4

(*d*)

are very extensive owing to the wide range covered and there is little conformity in the markings employed. On broader lines, classification is related to the number of electrodes and hence the particular type of work for which a valve is suited. The following types may be met in connection with horological work.

DIODE. (Cathode, anode.) Detector (demodulation), rectifier ($\frac{1}{2}$ wave).

DOUBLE DIODE. (Cathode, 2 anodes.) Rectifier (full wave), detector and bias control. D.C. restorer.

TRIODE. (Cathode, grid, anode.) Detector, A.F. amplifier, voltage control, power output, oscillator.

SCREENED GRID. (Cathode, grid, screen, anode.) As Triode, and R.F. Amplifier.

PENTODE. (Cathode, grid, screen, suppressor, anode.) R.F. amplifier, A.F. amplifier, power output, oscillator.

PENTAGRID or HEPTODE. (Cathode, 5 grids, anode.) R.F. amplifier, oscillator, frequency changer.

OCTODE. (Cathode, 6 grids, anode.) Similar to Pentagrid.

TETRODE. (A special form of Screen Grid valve. Often known as beam tetrode.) Power and R.F. applications.

TRIODE HEXODE. A double valve the two sections interacting:—

(1) (Cathode (common), grid, anode.)
(2) (Cathode (common), 4 grids, anode.) R.F. amplifier, frequency changer.

THYRATRON. A gas-filled triode. Electronic switch, time base. The combination of two or more types of electrode assemblies in one envelope gives rise to the appropriate compound names such as double-diode-triode, triode-heptode, etc. In many cases there is no interaction between the adjacent assemblies, and the valve may be considered as a space-saving convenience. The expression R.F. indicates radio frequency. See Frequency. The expression A.F. indicates audio frequency. See Frequency. Valves, generally, fall into one of two further categories. Directly heated: indirectly heated. In the first named, the cathode is itself heated by a current passing through it. In the second case, the cathode is insulated from a heating element adjacent to it.

V.A.P. Refers to a clock of French manufacture fitted with either a Tic-tac Escapement (*q.v.*) and Bob Pendulum (*q.v.*), or a Lever Escapement (*q.v.*). In the latter case the lever and escape wheel are incorporated in the movement as distinct from the more conventional Platform Escapement (*q.v.*). These clocks were made by Valonge à Paris; thus V.A.P. became the trade mark.

VECTOR. A straight line representing in length and direction the magnitude of a quantity and its relation to other quantities, as in the parallelogram of forces.

VEE-BLOCK. An accurately machined block, usually made in pairs, used in marking out, testing, and clamping cylindrical work.

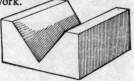

VEE-BLOCK.

VEE THREAD. Where the profile of the screw thread is V-shaped as, for example, in the Whitworth thread.

VEE THREAD.

VEIN. A fine break or crack showing in an enamelled dial as a thread-like line. Often invisible when thoroughly and properly cleaned.

VELOCITY. The rate of change of position of a body, having regard also to the direction in which it is moving. If in a straight line, usually defined as linear velocity. If about a point, angular velocity.

VENEER. See ANTIQUE CLOCK CASE TERMS.

VERGE. The pallet arbor of the verge escapement.

VERGE CLUB-FOOTED ESCAPEMENT. See Debaufre Escapement.

VERGE ESCAPEMENT. Considered to be the oldest form of escapement known in horology. (Definite proof of an earlier escapement cannot be found and allusions to "clocks" do not suggest any earlier form, but the possibility remains.) Also known as the "crown wheel" (*q.v.*) or "vertical" escapement. See Foliot.

VERNAL EQUINOX. The Spring equinox, March 21st, when the length of the day and the night are equal. It is the instant at which the sun, in its apparent annual motion, crosses the celestial equator.

VERNIER GAUGE. A gauge having a main scale the divisions of which can be further subdivided by means of a secondary movable scale divided into an equal number of intervals, but having one unit less than the main scale, *i.e.*, with a main scale divided into millimetres a space of 9 mm. on the secondary scale is divided into 10 equal parts, each division thus being less than 1 mm. by 1/10th or 0·1 mm. If the secondary scale is matched against the main scale a measurement to within 0·1 mm. can be read accurately.

VERNIER GAUGE.

Vernier gauges are made which can be read to 0·01 mm. with ease. The name is applied to several types of instrument dealing with small intervals. The principle was first applied by Pierre Vernier the inventor.

VERNIER TIME SIGNALS. *See* Rhythmic Time Signals.

VERTICAL ESCAPEMENT. Another name for the Verge Escapement (*q.v.*).

VIBRATING TOOL OR VIBRATOR. A tool comprising a standard balance and balance spring accurately adjusted to a set "count" against which the number of vibrations of another balance and spring may be compared.

VIBRATING TOOL OR VIBRATOR.

VIBRATIONS. A term very widely used to describe the motion of a body displaced from a position of equilibrium or rest. If the motion is of an even, equal, and regular character it may be described as an oscillation. In horology the term vibration is applied to the "swing" of a pendulum or balance in *one* direction only. The extent or amplitude of the displacement is measured in degrees, turns, or arc. The time or interval of one such swing is customarily used to identify the "count" of a pendulum, *e.g.*, 1 second, $\frac{3}{4}$ second, $\frac{1}{2}$ second (and hence its length), but the "count" of a balance is reckoned in vibrations per hour, *e.g.*, 22,000; 18,000; 16,200, etc. The term "period" is also applied to the "swing" but may be said to be unsuitable since the standard definition period of oscillation is accepted as the time of a complete cycle or excursion of displacement from zero to zero, and comprises *two* "swings" or "beats."

VIBRAX. A unique system of shock-

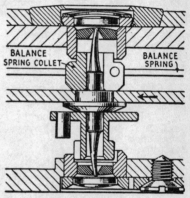

VIBRAX.

absorber where the flexure of the balance staff pivots is employed. The end stones are sprung set, to take end shocks. Radial shocks are taken by the boss of the balance staff through the balance spring collet and the roller. The amount of movement is limited; therefore the staff pivots can only be flexed a certain amount. The illustration shows the effect of a radial shock to the left. Made by EMO S.A., La Chaux-de-Fonds, Switzerland.

VICE OR VISE. A gripping or holding tool fixed to the bench and consisting of two jaws operated by a screw.

VICE or VISE.

VICE, HAND OR THUMB. *See* Hand Vice.

VICE CLAMS OR CHOPS. Subsidiary vice jaws or pads made of wood, soft metal, etc., and fitted between the vice jaws to protect the surface of work held therein. *See* Chops.

VICTORIAN STYLE. *See* ENGLISH PERIOD STYLES, page 38.

VIENNA LIME. A polishing medium for steel. It is a mixture of the oxides of calcium (lime) and magnesium. It is prepared by calcining magnesian limestone, or " Dolomite," and must be used very soon after preparation, owing to the rapid loss of its polishing qualities. It is very cheaply produced and was at one time extensively used in American factories, mixed with alcohol or water and applied on boxwood laps. The whitish polish produced is inferior to that from redstuff or Diamantine (*q.v.*).

VIENNA REGULATOR. A weight-driven clock usually having a wooden pendulum rod, Dead Beat Escapement (*q.v.*), and made to hang upon a wall. Made in Austria and Germany. Many Vienna regulators are fitted with seconds dials, but the pendulums are not always seconds pendulums, and the train is such that the dials do not necessarily indicate seconds.

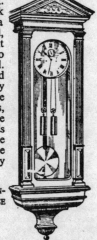

VIGNETTE. *See* ANTIQUE CLOCK CASE TERMS.

VIENNA REGULATOR.

VIMETAL. Trade name given to an unbreakable mainspring. Also the name of the alloy from which these springs are made. *See* Unbreakable Mainsprings.

VINE ORNAMENT. *See* ANTIQUE CLOCK CASE TERMS.

VIRGULE. An antique form of escapement introduced about 1750 after the Verge (*q.v.*) and the Horizontal (*q.v.*). It was intended as an improvement of the horizontal escapement. The action is as

follows:—Fitted to the balance staff is the long impulse pallet the body of which is shaped to form a roller with a recess cut into it. As the escape wheel rotates in the direction of the arrow, one of the upright teeth is held on the edge of the roller and as the balance rotates the tooth drops into the cut away portion and eventually to the impulse pallet when impulse is given to the balance. When the tooth drops off the impulse pallet the succeeding tooth drops on to the roller and so the cycle is repeated. The balance receives impulse in one direction only.

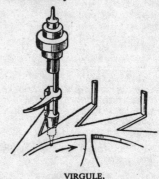

VIRGULE.

VIRGULE, DOUBLE. A similar escapement to the virgule, but arranged to give impulse to the balance in both directions. The action of this escapement is exactly similar to the Virgule (*q.v.*), but the cycle is repeated on the return vibration of the balance.

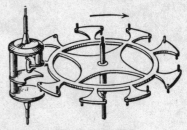

VIRGULE, DOUBLE.

VISCOSITY. Internal friction of fluids giving rise to a resistance to a change of form and resistance to flow. Coefficients of viscosity in c.g.s. units are:—Water 0·01; Glycerine 11; Air 0·00018; Symbol η. Fluid viscosity, in general, decreases with rise of temperature.

VOLET BALANCE. A form of balance used with an Elinvar (*q.v.*) balance spring. The bar or arm is made of brass and the rim of steel. Brass having a greater coefficient of expansion than steel, the balance changes in heat from the circular to an eliptical form. If groups of screws are arranged on the rim in a position at right angles to the arm, an adjustment can be made to compensate for the loss of elasticity of the balance spring for the same temperature change. This balance was invented by M. Volet and its principle may be understood by a consideration of the illustration. The dotted lines indicate the position, somewhat exaggerated, of the rim and temperature adjustment screws in heat. In recent years the same principle has been employed using Invar (*q.v.*) for the arm or bar and stainless steel for the rim. *See* Stainless Steel Balance, also Straumann Balance.

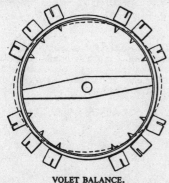

VOLET BALANCE.

VOLT. The unit of electrical pressure or potential.

VOLTAGE. Potential difference or electromotive force expressed in volts.

VOLTAGE AMPLIFIER. A thermionic valve circuit by means of which the output voltage obtained is an amplified version of the input voltage. Also known as a power stage.

VOLTAGE DROP. Specificially, a potential difference but applied generally to describe or define the " loss " in volts consequent upon a current flowing through a conductor, resistance, component, etc. *See* Kirchoff's Law, Ohms Law.

VOLTAGE MULTIPLIER. A resistance usually of a high accuracy and constancy applied in series with a voltmeter instrument, so as to enable the range of readings to be increased, *e.g.*, 0 to 100, 0 to 400, 0 to 750, etc.

VOLTAGE STABILISER. A device or circuit to maintain the voltage of a supply at a required figure over a range of current changes or varying loads.

VOLTMETER. An electrical instrument for direct measurement of the voltage or potential difference between two points.

VOLUME. The space occupied by a body.

VOLUTE. Spiral; in horology it is associated with the " flat " balance spring. When an overcoil is provided, the flat portion of the spring is referred to as the " volute." *See* Balance Spring.

VULLIAMY ESCAPEMENT. The Dead Beat Clock Escapement (*q.v.*) where the pallets are adjustable. Not used much in England but popular on the Continent. Invented by Benjamin Louis Vulliamy, about 1920.

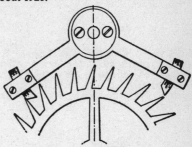

VULLIAMY ESCAPEMENT.

W

WAGON-SPRING CLOCK. *See* ANTIQUE CLOCK CASE TERMS.

WALL CLOCK. A clock made to hang on a wall, a mural clock. *See* Cartel; Vienna Regulator; English Dial; Act of Parliament Clock.

WARNING. The partial unlocking of the striking mechanism of a clock preparatory to its release at the precise moment required.

WARNING PIECE. The projecting block or piece that arrests the striking train of a striking clock between the interval of warning and release. A piece is used in chiming clocks for a similar purpose.

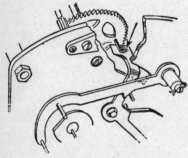

WARNING PIECE.

WARNING WHEEL. The wheel of the striking train fitted with a pin, which is arrested and released by the warning piece. A similar wheel is also to be found in a chiming clock and used for a similar purpose.

WARNING WHEEL.

WARWICK TIME STAMPING CLOCK. A device for stamping the time of arrival on correspondence, etc.

WATCH. Devised from the word "wæcc," used by the Saxons to designate "those who kept observation"—the sentry or guard, the watchmen of the night who called the hours. Even to-day time on board ship is measured by "watches." It was natural and convenient that the term watch should be applied to the first portable timekeepers introduced towards the end of the fifteenth century.

WATCH BOW. The ring fitted to the pendant of a watch and used as a form of attachment, by a chain, thong, etc., to secure it to a brooch or clip. *See* Bow.

WATCH BUTTONS. *See* WINDING BUTTONS and WATCH PART NOMENCLATURE.

WATCH CASE. The case into which the movement of a watch is fitted. There are many styles and types of watch cases. *See* WATCH CASE STYLES and PARTS OF THE POCKET WATCH CASE.

WATCH GLASSES. *See* STYLES OF WATCH GLASSES.

WATCH HANDS. *See* STYLES OF WATCH HANDS.

WATCH HOLDER. A form of stand made to hold a watch movement during assembly or adjustment. Several patterns are available. *See* Movement Holder.

WATCH MOVEMENT. The whole mechanism or works of a watch. *See* Full Plate; Half Plate; Three-quarter Plate.

WATCH PART NOMENCLATURE. Illustrations and accepted names in six different languages for various parts of wrist watches are given on the following pages.

WARWICK TIME STAMPING CLOCK.

WATCH PART NOMENCLATURE IN SIX LANGUAGES

(The numbers with the illustrations are the official Swiss spare parts numbers.)

Swiss Official Catalogue No.	English	American	French	German	Italian	Spanish
100	Bottom Plate	Pillar Plate	Platine	Unterplatte	Platina Anteriore	Platina de Debajo
105	Barrel Bar	Barrel Bridge	Pont de Barillet	Federhausbrücke	Pont del Barilletto	Puente de Cubo
110	Train Bar	Train Bridge	Pont de Rouage (Finissage)	Räderwerkbrücke	Pont Della Ruota	Puente de Rodaje
125	Pallet Cock	Pallet Bridge	Pont d'Ancre (Barette)	Ankerkloben	Pont dell'Ancora	Puente de Ancora

Swiss Official Catalogue No.	English	American	French	German	Italian	Spanish
121 or 122	Balance Cock	Balance Cock	Coq pour Spiral Plat or Coq pour Spiral Breguet	Unruhkloben	Pont del Bilanciere	Puente de Volante
180	Barrel (Complete)	Barrel (Complete)	Barillet Complet	Federhaus Komplette	Bariletto	Cubo Completo
770	Mainspring	Motor Spring	Ressort de Barillet	Zugfeder	Mola Mortrice	Muelle Real
190	Barrel Cover	Barrel Cover	Couvercle de Barillet	Federhausdeckel	Coperchio del Bariletto	Tapacubo

Swiss Official Catalogue No.	English	American	French	German	Italian	Spanish
195	Barrel Arbor	Barrel Arbor	Arbre de Barillet	Federwelle	Albero del Barilletto	Arbol de Cubo
200	Centre Wheel and Pinion and Cannon Pinion	Centre Wheel and Pinion and Cannon Pinion	Grande Moyenne Avec Chaussée (Roue des Minutes or Roue de centre)	Minutenrad Mit Minutenrohr Grossbodenrad	Ruota Centro Completo	Rueda de Centro Con Cañón de Minutos
210	Third Wheel and Pinion	Third Wheel and Pinion	Petite Moyenne	Kleinbodenrad mit Trieb	Ruota Intermedia Completo	Rueda Immediata con Piñion
220	Fourth Wheel and Pinion	Fourth Wheel and Pinion	Roue de Seconde	Sekundenrad mit Trieb	Ruota Secondi Completo	Rueda de Segundos con Piñion

Swiss Official Catalogue No.	English	American	French	German	Italian	Spanish
702–705	Escape Wheel and Pinion	Escape Wheel and Pinion	Roue d'Ancre	Ankerrad mit Trieb	Ruota Scappamento Completo	Rueda de Escape con Piñion
710	Pallets (Complete)	Pallet Fork and Arbor	Ancre Garnie	Anker mit Gabel und Ankerwelle	Ancora Completo	Ancora Completa con Tija
714	Pallet Staff	Pallet Arbor	Tige d'Ancre	Ankerwelle	Asse dell Ancora	Tija de Ancora
722	Compensation Balance (Complete with Breguet spring)	Balance Bi-Metallic (Complete with Breguet spring)	Balancier Bimétallique Complet avec Spiral Breguet	Komplette Zweimetallische Unruhe mit Breguetspirale	Bilanciere Compensato Completo con Spirale Bréguet	Volante Completa Espiral Bregurt

Swiss Official Catalogue No.	English	American	French	German	Italian	Spanish
	Compensation Balance	Balance Bi-Metallic	Balancier. Bimétallique	Zweimetallische Unruh	Bilanciere Compensato	Volante Solo
	Plain Balance	Mono-Metallic Balance	Balancier non Coupé	Die Unruh	Bilancie Pianore	Volante Simple
723	Balance Staff	Balance Staff	Axe de Balancier	Unruhwelle	Asse del Bilanciere	Eje de Volante
735	Balance Spring Breguet	Breguet Hair Spring	Spiral Breguet	Breguetspirale	Spirale Bréguet	Espiral Breguet

279

Swiss Official Catalogue No.	English	American	French	German	Italian	Spanish
734	Flat Balance Spring	Flat Hair Spring	Spiral Plat	Flachspirale	Spirale Plano	Espiral Plano
736–737	Balance Spring Collet	Hair Spring Collet	Virole pour Spiral Plat or Virole pour Spiral Breguet	Spiral-rolle	Spirale Virola	Chapa del Volante Espiral
738–739	Balance Spring Stud	Hair Spring Stud	Piton pour Spiral Plat or Piton pour Spiral Breguet	Spiralklötzchen	Spirale Pitone	Piton del Volante Espiral
302	Index (for Breguet Spring)	Regulator (for Breguet Spring)	Raquette pour Spiral Breguet	Rücker für Breguetspirale	Racchetta Spirale Bréguet	Raquete de Espiral Breguet
301	Index (for Flat Spring)	Regulator (for Flat Spring)	Raquette pour Spiral Plat	Rücker für Flachspirale	Racchetta Spirale Piatta	Raquete de Espiral Plano

Swiss Official Catalogue No.	English	American	French	German	Italian	Spanish
311	Top Balance End Piece	Cock Endstone	Coqueret	Rückerplättchen	Disco Contro Perno Posteriore del Bilanciere	Placa de Contrapivote
330	Bottom Balance End Piece	Foot Endstone	Plaque de Contre-Pivot pour Balancier	Decksteinplättchen für Unruh	Disco Contro Perno Anteriore del Bilanciere	Placa de Contrapivote
401	Winding Shaft	Winding Arbor	Tige	Aufzugwelle	Albero di Carica	Tije de Remontuar
410	Crown Wheel	Winding Pinion	Pignon de Remontoir	Transmissionsrad	Ruota a Corona Cricchetto	Rueda de Canto
407	Castle Wheel	Clutch Wheel	Pignon Coulant	Zeigerstelltrieb	Pignone a Corona	Rueda de Ranura
	Intermediate Wheels	Setting Wheels	Renvoi de Minuterie	Zeigerstellzwischenrad	Roata Intermedia di Messa All'Ora	Rueda de Transmisión

Swiss Official Catalogue No.	English	American	French	German	Italian	Spanish
260	Minute Wheel	Minute Wheel	Minuterie	Wechselrad	Ruota Cambio	Rueda de Minutería
250	Hour Wheel	Hour Wheel	Roue des Heures (Cannon)	Stundenrad	Ruota Ore	Rueda de Horas
240	Cannon Pinion	Cannon Pinion	Chaussée	Minutenrohr	Rochetto Calzante	Cañon de Minutos
435	Return Bar	Yoke	Bascule	Wippe	Leva	Báscula
440	Return Bar Spring	Yoke Spring	Ressort de Bascule	Wippefeder	Molla Della Leva	Muelle de Báscula

Swiss Official Catalogue No.	English	American	French	German	Italian	Spanish
45	Check Spring	Setting Lever Spring	Ressort de Tirette	Stellhebelfeder	Copri Leva Mella del Tiretto	Muelle de Terete
443	Pull-Out-Piece	Setting Lever	Tirette	Stellhebel	Tietto	Tirette de Puesta en Hora
415	Ratchet Wheel	Winding Wheel	Rochet Dessus	Aufzugspferrad	Rocchetto del Bariletto	Rochete de Cubo
420	Transmission Wheel	Crown Wheel	Roue de Couronne	Kronrad	Ruota Intermedia di Carica	Rueda de Corona

Swiss Official Catalogue No.	English	American	French	German	Italian	Spanish
423	Transmission Wheel Boss	Crown Wheel Washer	Noyau Rochet de Couronne	Ringkern für Kronrad	Tassello della Ruota Inter-media di Carica	Chapa de Rueda de Corona
425	Click	Click	Cliquet (Masse)	Sperrkegel	Cricchetto	Trinquete
430	Click Spring	Click Spring	Ressort de Cliquet	Sperrkegelfeder	Molla del Cricchetto	Muelle de Trinquete
630	Balance Jewel Hole	Cock or Foot Jewel	Pierre de Balancier	Lochstein für Unruh	Foro della Pietra del Balanciere	Piedra de Volante
	Centre upper 601 lower 602	Third upper 605 lower 606		Fourth upper 610 lower 611	Escape upper 615 lower 616	Pallet upper 620 lower 621
	Train Jewel Hole	Train Jewel	Pierre de Roue	Lochstein für Welle	Foro della Pietra del Ruoto	Piedra de Rodaje
648	Ruby Pin	Roller Pin	Cheville de Plateau (Ellipse)	Hebelstein	Bottone del Disco	Ellipses

Swiss Official Catalogue No.	English	American	French	German	Italian	Spanish
646	Entry Pallet Stone	Receiving Pallet Stone	Levée d'Entrée (Palette d'Entrée)	Ankerstein Eingang	Pietra di Leva d'Entrata	Boca del Ancora Entrada
647	Exit Pallet Stone	Discharging Pallet Stone	Levée de Sortie (Palette de Sortie)	Ankerstein Ausgang	Pietra di Leva d'Uscita	Boca de Ancora Salida
730	Double Roller	Double Roller	Plateau Double	Ankerplättchen Doppelte	Doppio Disco	Doble Platillo
	Single Roller	Single Roller	Plateau Simple	Ankerplättchen Einfach	Semplice Disco	Plato Simple
5170	Pillar Screw	Pillar Screw	Vis à Pilier	Pfeiler- schraube	Vite per Colonna	Tornillo del Poste

Swiss Official Catalogue No.	English	American	French	German	Italian	Spanish
5111	Bridge Screw	Bridge Screw	Vis de Pont	Brücken-schraube	Vite del Pont	Tornillo de Puente
5415	Ratchet Wheel Screw	Winding Wheel Screw	Vis de Rochet	Aufzugsperrad-schraube	Vite del Rocchetto del Bariletto	Tornillo de Rochete de Cubo
5420	Transmission Wheel Screw	Crown Wheel Screw	Vis de Couronne	Aufzugrad-schraube	Vite del Ruota Intermedia	Tornillo de Rueda de Corona
5101	Case Screw	Case Screw	Vis de Fixage	Werkbefestigend-schraube	Vite Ferma Cassa	Tornillo Para Fijar la Maquina en la Caja

Swiss Official Catalogue No.	English	American	French	German	Italian	Spanish
5102	Dog Screw	Case Screw, Half Head	Vis de Clef de Fixage (Demi-ronde)	Werkbefestigend-schraube Halbrund Gefräst	Vite per Cassa, Metá Testa	Tornillo Medio Redonda
5751	Dial Screw (Top)	Dial Screw (Top)	Clef de Cadran	Zifferblatt-schlüssel-schraube	Vite Per Mostra	Tornillo Sujeción de Esfera
5749	Dial Screw (Side)	Dial Screw (Side)	Vis de Chef Cadran (Côté)	Zifferblätter-schraube (Seite)	Vite Per Mostra, Lato	Tornillo Lateral de Esfera
	Jewel Screw	Jewel Screw	Vis de Pierre	Lochstein-schraube	Vite Per Disco Controperno	Tornillo del Rubi
5443	Pull-Out-Piece Screw	Setting Lever Screw	Vis de Tirette	Stellhebel-schraube	Vite del Tiretto	Tornillo de Tirete

Swiss Official Catalogue No.	English	American	French	German	Italian	Spanish
5435	Return Bar Screw (Shoulder Screw)	Yoke Screw	Vis de Bascule (Vis a Portée)	Zeigerstellhebel-schraube (Ansatz-schraube)	Vite del Leva	Tornillo de Bascula
5738	Stud Screw	Stud Screw	Vis de Piton	Spiralklötzchen-schraube	Vite del Pitone	Tornillo del Pitón
5425	Click Screw	Click Screw	Vis de Cliquet	Sperrkegel-schraube	Vite del Cricchetto	Tornillo de Trinquete
	Dial	Dial	Cadran	Zifferblatt	Guadrante	Esfera
	Hour Hand	Hour Hand	Aiguille des Heures	Stundenzeiger	Lancetta delle Ore	Minutero de Hora

SWISS OFFICIAL CATALOGUE No.	ENGLISH	AMERICAN	FRENCH	GERMAN	ITALIAN	SPANISH
	Minute Hand	Minute Hand	Aiguille des Minutes	Minutenzeiger	Lancetta dei Minuti	Minutero de Minuta
	Seconds Hand	Second Hand	Aiguille des Secondes	Sekundenzeiger	Lancetta dei Secondi	Secundario
	Centre Seconds Hand	Sweep Seconds Hand	Aiguille Seconde au Centre	Sekunde aus der Mitte	Lancetta dei Secondi al Centro	Secundario al Centro
	Winding Button	Winding Crown	Couronne de Remontoir	Aufzugkrone	Bottone di Carica	Corona de Remontar
	Bow	Bow	Bélière	Uhrbügel	Anello	Anello del Pendente

WATCH PENDANT. That part of a watch where the winding stem or button is located. Strictly, the pendant is the neck, tube, or chenier to which the " bow " is fitted, the winding button fitting over the pendant itself. Of recent years and for purposes of defining a certain position, especially in regard to timing, etc., the term " pendant " has referred only to the winding button: hence pendant right (P.R.); pendant left (P.L.); pendant up (P.U.) and pendant down (P.D.).

WATCH RACK. A rack to hold watches during positional timing.

WATCH RACK.

WATCH TIMER or WATCH RATE RECORDER. An instrument, almost invariably electronic, for indicating or recording the instantaneous rate of going of a watch or a clock with a balance escapement. There are two main types, the " visual ", on which the rate is shown by the movement of a trace on a cathode ray oscilloscope, and the " printer " by which the rate is indicated by permanent marks on a paper ribbon or disc, which may be removed. Both types usually have aural indications of the tick as well, and means of obtaining rates in different positions of a watch. Some timers are set to an outside standard, such as a good clock, but most have a quartz crystal oscillator standard built in. The principle of the instrument is to compare the rate of the watch by comparing a certain part of the amplified ticking sound with a signal generated by the quartz crystal oscillator. There is provision for watches with different trains. The main advantage of a watch rate recorder is that it gives going rates instantly without having to wait for 24 hours or so, and thereby speeds up the operation of timing and adjustment. It may also be used for fault finding.

WATER CLOCK. *See* Clepsydræ.

WATER-OF-AYR STONE. A stone similar in substance to slate and used with water for finishing brass. Found in Stair, Scotland. *See* Montgomerie Stone.

WATER POLO TIMER. *See* Timers.

WATERPROOF WATCH. A watch having a case specially designed to prevent the ingress of moisture. The principle generally employed is for the back, and bezel if there is one, to contact a plastic ring, forming an hermetic seal; the cover is either screwed or snapped into position. The pendant is sealed either by a system of screwing the winding button down on to a plastic ring, or, employing a plastic gland in the pendant for the pipe of the winding button to contact. There are several " systems " employed. *See* Atmospheric pressures on page 52.

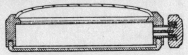

WATERPROOF WATCH CASE.

WATT. The practical unit of electrical power. It is equal to 1 joule per second. In a D.C. circuit the wattage is obtained by multiplying the current flowing by the voltage or pressure, *i.e.*:—

volts × amperes = watts.

In an A.C. circuit, this gives the " apparent power " due to the fact that the two quantities are not in phase. The sum thus obtained, is again multiplied by the " power factor " to give the true power.

1 horse power = 746 watts.

WATT-HOUR. The unit of electrical energy, *i.e.*, the work equivalent to 1 watt acting for 1 hour. It is equal to 3,600 joules. *See* Work.

WATTAGE. A term used to express the power dissipation of a circuit or component.

WAX. In horology the term is applied to any hard setting substance such as shellac, which softens or melts at a low temperature, and hardens quickly on cooling. *See* Wax Chuck.

WAX CHUCK. A chuck to which parts can be cemented with shellac or a similar substance: used for holding parts too delicate or too awkward for a normal chuck.

WAX CHUCK.

WAX POLISH. *See* ANTIQUE CLOCK CASE TERMS.

WEIGHT. A measure of the gravitational force acting on a body. If expressed in pounds-weight (gravitational units) this force is equal to the mass of the body in pounds. Thus the weight of a body is a measure of the mass content of that body.

WELDING. The joining or uniting of two metal surfaces by heating them to a melting or plastic temperature, so that they fuse together. A very commonly used form of construction in building up sheet metal objects such as boxes, covers, etc. A system of electrical arc welding, comprising a series of small unions, *i.e.*, fusion at a point, is termed spot welding, and has been applied to watch mainspring barrel hooking.

WESTERN ELECTRIC RECORDER. A recorder or timing machine which compares the vibrations of a watch with a known and controlled standard vibration of tuning fork. Agreement or variation of the watch vibration is automatically recorded on a travelling paper roll.

WESTERN EUROPEAN TIME (Universal Time (*q.v.*)). Greenwich Mean Time (*q.v.*).

WESTMINSTER CLOCK. Refers to the great clock at the Houses of Parliament, Westminster, and known as Big Ben, the name Big Ben originally referred to the great hour bell. The term " Westminster clock " also refers to any domestic chiming clock employing the Westminster chimes.

WET BATTERY. Another name for an Accumulator (*q.v.*) and sometimes applied to Primary Cells (*q.v.*) in comparison with the Dry primary cell (*q.v.*). A somewhat confusing term lacking precision.

WHEEL. A disc so mounted that it is able to rotate about a given centre. In the case of a toothed wheel, such as those used in horology, usually any gear having 20 or more teeth. An exception to this is an escape wheel which may have only 13 or 15 teeth.

WHEEL BAROMETER. *See* ANTIQUE CLOCK CASE TERMS.

WHEEL-CUTTING ENGINE. A

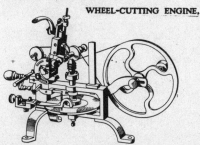

WHEEL-CUTTING ENGINE,

machine fitted with a count plate or suitably geared, for cutting the teeth of wheels.

WHEEL GAUGE. A plate with a series of progressively sized circular " sinks " used to size up the diameters of wheels. The sinks are graduated in $\frac{1}{8}$ mm. steps. Thus: $5\frac{0}{8}$, $5\frac{1}{8}$, $5\frac{2}{8}$, etc. Also known as an " Eighths Gauge."

WHEEL STRETCHING TOOL. A tool for increasing the diameter of a wheel or to "stretch" a portion of the periphery to a required diameter.

WHEEL STRETCHING TOOL.

WIG-WAG TOOL. A tool so devised that a reciprocating or backward and forward motion is obtained; used for polishing pivots. Also the term refers to the device as illustrated, a hand tool. The polisher, either a burnisher or soft metal charged with a polishing medium, is worked backwards and forwards on the pivot similarly to the Jacot tool operation, but the wig-wag causes the work to rotate at the same time.

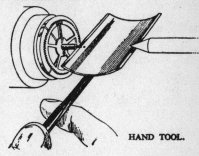

HAND TOOL.

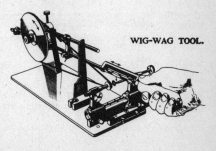

WIG-WAG TOOL.

WINDING BUTTONS

WINDING BUTTONS FOR CHRONOGRAPHS AND HUNTER OR HALF-HUNTER CASES

  Louis XV　 **Round**　 **Round**　 **Facette**

  Facette　 **Straight**　 **Breguet**　 **Straight**

  Breguet　 **Flat or Military**　 **Louis XV**　 **Louis XV Flat**

WINDER. *See* Key.

WINDER MAINSPRING. *See* Mainspring Winder.

WINDING BUTTON. *See* Button.

WINDING PINION. Another name for the Crown Wheel (*q.v.*).

WINDING SHAFT. *See* Stem.

WINDING SQUARE. The square or squared end of an arbor, shaft, etc., on to which the key is fitted to wind the driving spring or weights of the mechanism.

WINDING STEM. *See* Stem.

WIRE CHUCK. Another name for the split chuck or Collet (*q.v.*).

WIRE GAUGE. A plate pierced with a series of sized holes used in determining the diameter of wire. There are a number of standards, and some are applied to sheet metal also, but, in general the practice now is to size wire, metal, and twist drills directly in thousandths or similar fractions of an inch, or in tenths or hundredths of mm.

WOLF TOOTH GEARING. A form of gearing employing the Epicycloidal Curve (*q.v.*), and so designed that the curve comes into operation when the gears rotate in one direction only. Used in keyless work of some of the hand made types of Swiss watches.

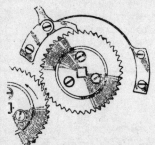

WOLF TOOTH GEARING.

WOODS FOR CLOCK CASES

Name	Where Grown	Other Names	Description
ACACIA ...	Gt. Britain and Continent of Europe.	—	Greenish yellow with reddish-brown veins. Used as veneer and inlay and bandings.
ALERCE ...	Chile, parts of N. Patagonia.	Alerzcolz Lahuan... ...	Red-brown in colour, often with alternate light and dark streaks. Usually straight grain. Fairly soft. Used solid. Weight 29 lbs. cu. ft.
ALERZHOLZ ...	*See Alerce.*		
ALDER ...	Europe, W. Asia, N. Africa, Japan.	Common Alder, Black Alder.	In its normal state this wood is not used for clocks but is used extensively for ply-wood. Occasionally found with a dark, twisted line figure, caused by insects or from burrs, and this can be used as veneer. Weight 33 lbs. cu. ft.
ANDAMAN ...	*See Padouk.*		
ANGICO ...	S. Brazil, W. Argentine.	Brauco, Armarello, Prio, Vermelho, Arapiraca, Jacare.	Reddish-brown, often regularly striped with darker colour. Mahogany like and lustrous. Hard. Weight 59 lbs. cu. ft.
ANGICO RAJADO.	Tropical and subtropical regions of world.	Over 180 Species. Serpent Wood, Zebra Wood, Cassie, Pashaco, Inga-Aana, Surinam, Snakewood.	Pale brown with irregular black or purplish stripes, conspicuous and characteristic, also with fine pencil-like striping of light coloured vessel line. Used as veneer and marquetry. Hard. Weight 70 lbs. cu. ft.
AMBOYNA ...	Amboyna and Aram, Islands of the Dutch E. Indies.	—	Rich yellowish-brown, very close " bird's eye " figure. Similar to Thuja. Used as veneer and as inlay and bandings. Hard.
ARAPIRACA ...	*See Angico.*		
ARMARELLO ...	*See Angico.*		
BIRCH ...	Gt. Britain	—	Used as a base for veneer; also to be found with a beautiful, rippled figure and when polished resembles East Indian satinwood. Hard. Weight 42 lbs. cu. ft.
BIRCH, CANADIAN YELLOW.	Canada and U.S.A.	Quebec Birch, Yellow Birch, Black Birch, Red Birch, Curly Birch, Gold Hard Birch, American Birch, Betula Wood.	Pale reddish-brown in colour. Fine and uniform with an attractive figure. This wood was stained and used as the first imitation mahogany. Used solid and as veneer. Hard. Weight 44 lbs. cu. ft.
BLACK EBONY	S. India, Ceylon, Burma and S. Africa	Cape Ebony	Usually jet black.
BLACK MAIRE	—	—	Wood of a similar character to Olive wood, beautifully figured.
BLACK PINE ...	New Zealand ...	Matai	Reddish-brown or bright cinnamon colour, silky texture, fine grain, rays and rings visible.
BLACK WALAUT.	U.S.A. and Canada	American Brown Walnut...	Dark brown to chocolate colour, almost black. Sometimes figured similar to mahogany. Used solid and as veneer. Hard. Weight 38 lbs. cu. ft.
BOMBAY EBONY.	Coromandel Coast	Coromandel Wood ...	Black with yellowish mottles or thin yellow stripes, of great beauty. Used as veneer.
BROWN EBONY	India, Burma, W. Indies.	—	Brown with darker blackish stripes and not so dense as the black ebony.

Name	Where Grown	Other Names	Description
Bubinga ...	Equatorial W. Africa Cameroons.	—	Pinkish to darker red. Roe and broken mottle figure, used as veneer.
Calamander Wood.	Ceylon	—	Dark brown, very hard with black stripes and figure.
Canary Wood	S. America ...	Tulip Tree, Yellow Poplar, Green Cypress.	Yellow with dark streaks. Somewhat resembles satinwood. Used solid and as veneer. An excellent wood as a base for paint. Hard. Weight 28 lbs. cu. ft.
Canela Parda	Forests of Parana. Argentine.	Brazilian Walnut	Olive to chocolate-brown, stained with oak stripes, somewhat curly, bright and lustrous. Hard.
Cherry ... Mahogany.	W. Africa	Makose	Popular substitute for mahogany. Close grain and fine varied figure. Used as veneer.
Chestnut, ... Sweet or Spanish.	S. Europe, Africa, N. America and England.	—	Similar to oak in appearance but redder and closer grain. When highly polished resembles sycamore. Sometimes used as a substitute for satinwood. Hard. Weight 38 lbs. cu. ft.
Curupay ...	See Angico.		
Ebony ...	India and Ceylon ...		The only black wood without markings. Although occasionally it is streaked with lighter markings. Rarely used solid but as veneer and as inlay. Sometimes small cases made from the solid wood. Hard. Weight 70 lbs. cu. ft.
Eleo Fermelho.	Tropical America ...	—	Dark red or purplish-red to reddish-brown. Closely resembles Cuban mahogany, but harder. Hard. Weight 56–63 lbs. cu. ft.
Elm	Gt. Britain	—	Light yellow in colour and takes a good polish. Logs are found richly figured cross cut as veneer and usually referred to as " pollared elm." Weight 39 lbs. cu. ft.
Gaboon ...	West Africa, French Congo, Spanish Guinea.	Gaboon Mahogany, Gaboon Wood, Okoume.	Light red-brown resembles African mahogany. Hard. Weight 25 lbs. cu. ft.
Green Ebony	India and W. Indies	Cocus Wood	Varies in colour, greenish black or brown. Solid.
Gum, American Red.	S.E. U.S.A., and in the mountains of Mexico.	Sweet Gum, Yellow Gum, Bilstead, Satin Walnut, Hazel Pine.	Reddish-brown with occasional dark streaks, handsome figure; used solid and veneer cut from certain logs with striking figure. Hard. Weight 34 lbs. cu. ft.
Harewood ...	—	Mousewood, Greywood ...	See Sycamore.
Holly ...	Gt. Britain	—	A beautiful white wood, used for marquetry work, stained or dyed various colours. Little used solid or as veneer.
Honeysuckle	New Zealand ...	Rewa	Two varieties, one reddish-brown and the other a light silver hue. Both similar figure to Lacwood or Plane Tree when cut radially.
Kingwood ...	Brazil	American Ebony, Blue Wood.	Rich dark brown colour a little lighter than rosewood but with stronger markings. When first polished it has a purple tinge and tones with age. Used solid and as veneer and for bandings. Hard.

Name	Where Grown	Other Names	Description
Kingwood ...	—	Violetwood...	—
Laburnum ...	Gt. Britain and the Continent of Europe.	—	Yellow streaked with brown to reddish-brown and sometimes a dark green colour. Used as veneer and cuttings from saplings used as "oyster pieces." Sometimes stained black and passed off as ebony. Hard.
Lignum Vitæ	W. Indian Isles, Guiana and Tropical America.	—	Dark brown streaked with black and dark green to greenish black. Used as veneer. Small cases sometimes made from the solid wood. One of the hardest and heaviest wood known. Weight 73 lbs. cu. ft.
Locust Wood	British Guiana ...	Surinam Teak	Dark brown to orange red and streaky in figure. Used as veneer.
Mahogany—Cuban.	West Indies, Cuba and San-Domingo.	Spanish Mahogany, San Domingo Mahogany, West Indies Mahogany, Jamaica Mahogany.	This is what may be termed the original mahogany. The Spaniards were the first Europeans to use this mahogany. Very close grain, with fine silky texture and may be beautifully figured with "fiddle-back," "mottle," "blister," "stripes," "roe," "crotch," etc. Heavier and harder than other mahoganies. Used solid and as veneer. Weight 48 lbs. cu. ft.
Mahogany—Central American.	Central America, Mexico, Peru, Brazil.	Honduras or British Honduras Mahogany, Costa Rica Mahogany, Mexican Mahogany, Nicaraguan Mahogany, Panama Mahogany, Tabasco Mahogany, Baywood.	Varies from light reddish-brown to yellowish brown to a rich dark red, similar to that of Cuban mahogany. A considerable variety of figure, such as "fiddle-back," "blister," "curl," "mottle," and "stripe." Lighter and softer than Cuban mahogany. Used solid and as veneer. Hard. Weight 34 lbs. cu. ft.
Maple ...	E. Canada, E.States of America.	Hard Maple, Sugar Maple, White Maple, Canadian Maple. Figured woods are known as Bird's Eye, Curly, Fiddle-back.	Creamy white to reddish tinge in colour. The Hard and Rock Maple of Canada is harder and is used in the solid and as veneer, especially the figured wood. Hard. Weight 47 lbs. cu. ft.
Marblewood	Andaman Islands ...	—	Alternate bands of black or brown and grey or yellow. Used as veneer.
Oak—American White.	N. America ...	White Oak	The colour varies from a pale yellow to a pale reddish-brown. Used solid. Hard. Weight 48 lbs. cu. ft.
Olive Wood	Europe	—	Greenish yellow with black cloudy spot and veins. Takes a high polish with oil and friction only. Used solid and as veneer. Hard.
Padouk ...	India, Burma ...	Andaman Redwood ...	Rich red or crimson colour streaked with black. Of great beauty. Close grain. Takes a fine polish. Used solid and as veneer. Hard. Weight 48 lbs. cu. ft.
Pear Tree ...	Gt. Britain	Fruit-wood...	Yellowish brown colour with no figure. Frequently used solid and stained black and polished, known as ebonised. Also used as thick veneers. Hard. Weight 40 to 44 lbs. cu. ft.
Peroba ...	Chiefly Brazil ...	Peroba Muida ... ... Peroba Poca ... ... Peroba Preta ... ... Peroba Rajada ... ... Peroba Reversa ... ... Peroba Tremida ... ... Peroba Revessa	Red with darker patches. White. Conspicuous black veins. Light red with large black patches. Dark with contorted grain. Yellow with lighter patches. Figure of bird's eye maple nature. Hard. Weight 44 to 53 lbs. cu. ft.

Name	Where Grown	Other Names	Description
Plane ...	E. Europe	Figured specimens known as Lace-wood, Silk-wood.	Young trees yellowish white; older trees medium brown. Close grain and takes a good polish.
Red Ebony ...	Mauritius	—	Reddish tint. Solid.
Rima	New Zealand	Red Pine	Deep red colour, figured dark or light streaks. Burrs produce fine veneers.
Rosewood ...	E. Indies, Brazil ...	—	Dark chestnut brown colour of fine figure and takes a good polish. Mahogany is often worked up as rosewood, being cheaper. Used solid and as veneer. Hard. Weight 60 lbs. cu. ft.
Satinwood ...	E. and W. India, and Ceylon.	Yellow Mahogany, Yellow Wood.	Both East and West Indian woods are cream to golden yellow in colour with the inner wood darker. Of the two the West Indian is the better. Smooth, fine grain and takes a fine polish. Peculiarly feathery figure of great beauty and sometimes a broad mottled figure resembling that of fine Cuban mahogany. Used solid and as veneer. Hard.
Silky Oak ...	Australia	Northern Silky Oak ...	Pinkish to reddish-brown in colour. Displays a well-marked irregular " silver grain." Oak wood type but not a true oak. Used solid and as veneer. Hard. Weight 38 lbs. cu. ft.
Snakewood ...	W. Indian Islands, chiefly Guiana.	Letterwood...	Nut brown colour spotted with black. Of great beauty. The sapwood is yellow, similar to box-wood. The former is used as veneer and the latter as veneer and for inlay and bandings. Hard. Weight 77 lbs. to 83 lbs. cu. ft.
Sycamore ...	Gt. Britain and temperate regions of Europe.	Plane Tree (in Scotland), Sycamore Plane. When treated with a thorough dying process which colours the wood grey, it is known as " Harewood."	An attractive creamy white to yellowish white darkening to a pale golden brown on exposure. Straight grain, fine texture, silky lustre. Curly and wavy grain sometimes found giving a rich "fiddle-back" figure. Used solid and the figured as veneer. Hard. Weight 39 lbs. cu. ft.
Tasmanian Oak.	Australia	Australian Oak, Victorian Oak.	Colour varies from ash to English oak and in many respects the latter, but lacks the characteristic " silver grain." Used solid. Hard. Weight 41 to 51 lbs. cu. ft.
Teak	Burma, India, Siam, Java, Indo-China.	—	Reddish brown in colour to deep brown when polished. Owing to its outstanding properties—extremely durable, strong, resistant to moisture, fire, acids and does not corrode metals—it is ideally suited for cases to be used in the tropics. Occasionally figured, when it is used as veneer, otherwise used solid. Hard. Weight 40 to 45 lbs. cu. ft.
Thuya ...	Africa	Thuja	When polished it is a rich brown colour, with small aureole figure centred with minute " bird's eye." Used as veneer. Hard.
Tulip Wood	Australia, Brazil ...	—	The Australian wood is close grained, beautifully marked with different shades from yellow to black, resembles olive wood. The Brazilian wood is yellowish-brown with stripes of a pinkish-red. The former used as veneer and the latter as inlay and banding. Hard. Weight 62 lbs. cu. ft.

Name	Where Grown	Other Names	Description
Walnut ...	Persia and the N.W. Himalayas.	Common Walnut	The Persian or Common Walnut is brown, veined and shaded with darker brown and black. The wood of the roots is often beautifully figured. Used solid and the fine figure as veneer. Hard. Weight 46 lbs. cu. ft.
Walnut—Black.	Eastern U.S.A. ...	American Walnut; Gum-Wood.	Rich brown to purplish brown in colour, usually straight grain, sometimes figured such as "roll," "mottle," etc., also burrs are found. Used solid and the figured as veneer. Hard. Weight 38 lbs. cu. ft.
Yew	Spain, Italy, Middle and Southern Europe.	—	Pale yellowish red colour to a darker colour. Fine grain, handsomely striped and often dotted like Amboyna wood. Used solid and as veneer. Hard. Weight 48 lbs. to 50 lbs. cu. ft.
Zebrono ...	W. Coast of Africa	Zebra wood	Light brown with regular darker stripes. Used as veneer.

Brown Oak, English ...   When the tree has lost its vitality, a form of decay known as "Foxiness" sets in. The strong acid in the wood turns it a warm brown colour but does not destroy its texture. Used as veneer.

Pollard Oak ...   ...   When the trees have been "polled" and stunted in growth. A wavy grain and variable figure is thus formed. Mostly used as veneer.

Bog, or Black Oak ...   Any oak will blacken if allowed to lie in a pond or bog. Used as veneer and for inlaying and some turnery.

WOOD CHUCK. A boxwood chuck used by watch-case makers. It comprises a solid or hollow cylinder of boxwood, which is turned out to fit the work tightly, thus holding it while being worked upon. Also a chuck for the lathe where a wood thread screw is fitted to screw wood on, e.g., a polishing mop.

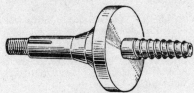

WOOD THREAD CHUCK.

WOOD ROD PENDULUM. A pendulum rod made of wood instead of metal. Its purpose is to minimise the effect of temperature changes on the rate of the clock. It answers very well, but it is very difficult fully to eliminate the effects of dampness or moisture.

WORK. The quantity of force expended. The unit of work is the foot-pound which represents the work done or energy expended in raising 1 pound mass vertically 1 foot against the force of gravity. Electrically, when the power in a circuit is 1 watt, work is done at the rate of 1 joule per second. Hence, 1 watt acting for 1 hour = 3,600 joules (see Watt-Hour).

WORKING DEPTH. The sum of the Addenda (q.v.) of a mating pair of gears.

WORM. A small gear, having a continuous spiral similar to a screw thread which meshes or engages at 90° to the plane of the driven gear or worm wheel. Usually employed where a high reduction and/or very smooth power transmission is required.

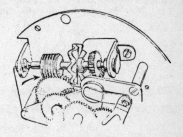

WORM.

WORM ESCAPEMENT. A form of lever escapement where the escape wheel is fitted on to a "worm" instead of a pinion. Invented by R. J. Clay in America.

WYLER BALANCE. A shock resisting system employing a balance specially designed to absorb the shock. The rim of the balance is attached to spring-like arms, so that when the watch receives a shock, the rim, the heaviest part of the balance, " gives," thus saving the balance staff pivots, etc. Used by the Wyler Watch Co.

WYLER BALANCE.

X

X. The usual symbol for electrical reactance.

X-PLATES. The two electrodes to which the horizontal deflecting voltages or signals are applied in a cathode-ray tube.

Y

YACHTING TIMER. *See* page 256.

YEAR CLOCK. A clock so designed that it will run for a year with one winding. Such clocks, usually weight driven, are distinct from the 400-day Clock (*q.v.*).

YOKE. An American term for Check Spring (*q.v.*).

YOUNG'S MODULUS. The coefficient of elasticity of stretching. It is the ratio of the stretching force per unit cross sectional area, to the elongation per unit length. The values of Young's modulus for metal are of the order 10^{12} dynes per sq. cm. *Vide* " Chambers's Technical Dictionary."

Y-PLATES. The two electrodes to which the vertical deflecting voltages or signals are applied in a cathode-ray tube.

YTIRE. Trade name given to an unbreakable mainspring. *See* Unbreakable Mainsprings.

Z

Z. The symbol for electrical impedance.

ZAANDAM CLOCK. *See* Dutch Clock.

ZENITH. The point in the heavens immediately above the observer's head. The maximum elevation of an object in the sky.

ZERO CUT CRYSTAL. A quartz crystal cut out with respect to its natural axes so that its temperature/frequency change, or coefficient, is zero. The type of crystal required for absolute frequency standards, as in the quartz clock. In practice, it may be a ring.

ZERO POTENTIAL. Another term for a point at Earth Potention (*q.v.*). It is also applied, however, to points in a circuit at zero potential relative to that circuit, but not necessarily at earth potential.

ZINC BALANCE. *See* Straumann Balance.

ZINC BLOCK. A piece of zinc plate about 3 in. × 2 in. and ½ in. thickness, used with Diamantine (*q.v.*) for polishing steel parts.

ZINC COMPENSATION PENDULUM. A pendulum, the bob being made of lead, and in which zinc is used as a means of compensation for changes of temperature. One form is a cylindrical lead bob resting on a collar attached to a steel tube which in turn hangs from the top of a zinc tube, the lower end of which rests upon the rating nut.

ZINC COMPENSATION
PENDULUM.

ZODIAC. In astronomy, a belt of the sky 16° wide, containing the apparent paths of the sun, moon and the chief planets. The Zodiac was divided into twelve signs of 30° each, as follows:—

SIGNS OF THE ZODIAC

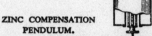 ARIES, the Ram. Mar. 21—Apr. 20.

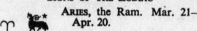 TAURUS, the Bull. Apr. 21—May 21.

GEMINI, the Twins. May 22—Jun. 21.

CANCER, the Crab. Jun. 22—Jul. 23.

LEO, the Lion. Jul. 24—Aug. 23.

VIRGO, the Virgin. Aug. 24—Sept. 23.

LIBRA, the Balance. Sept. 24—Oct. 23.

SCORPIO, the Scorpion. Oct. 24—Nov. 22.

SAGITTARIUS, the Archer. Nov. 23—Dec. 22.

CAPRICORNUS, the Goat. Dec. 23—Jan. 20.

AQUARIUS, the Water-Carrier. Jan. 21—Feb. 19.

PISCES, the Fishes. Feb. 20—Mar. 20.

ZONE, HOUR. *See* Hour Circle.

WORKSHOP HINTS AND HELPS

CEMENTS

To Make Paper Adhere to Iron and Steel

Rub the metal surface with an onion cut in half. Stick the paper on to the prepared surface with glue or paste.

To Cement Rubber to Metal

One part powdered shellac, 10 parts strong water of ammonia.

Place the powdered shellac in the ammonia water in a tightly stoppered bottle and leave for 3 to 4 weeks. The result will be a clear, transparent, liquid mass.

To use, spread the cement on to the rubber and apply to the metal. The cement softens the rubber but quickly evaporates leaving the rubber in its original condition.

To Cement Abrasive Cloth to a Lap

Mix 1 lb. of rosin, $\frac{3}{4}$ lb. paraffin, 2 ozs. Vaseline. Melt and mix thoroughly.

Clean the metal lap surface and make dry. Heat the lap and spread a covering of the cement. Rub the cloth down well to exclude all air.

To Cement Metal and Glass

Mix 2 ozs. thick glue, 1 oz. linseed oil, $\frac{1}{2}$ oz. turpentine. Boil the mixture for a short time until of a uniform consistency. Use boiling hot and clamp parts together immediately, leaving in position for about 2 days.

CLEANING SOLUTIONS

Acids and Alkalis—Warning

The storage, handling, and use of acids, alkalis, and strong reagents in general, requires care and comon sense. Such liquids can be very dangerous to the operator, particularly to the sight.

They should be stored in suitable containers distinctively labelled, coloured or shaped and away from other liquids, etc., with which they might be confused, or with which they might violently react if brought in accidental contact.

They should be kept in a position such that the container can always be firmly and securely handled. *It is dangerous to store them on a high shelf.*

A good supply of a suitable anti-acid and anti-alkali should be kept immediately available.

Ordinary corks should never be used as stoppers. Use only glass or rubber.

Never allow the contents to dribble down the outside of the bottle, and elsewhere; it will become unsafe to hold and menace everything touched.

Chemicals and Poisons

Use imagination and foresight in storing and handling all chemicals and particularly all substances of a poisonous nature. Care and cleanliness are essential if accidents are to be avoided; they are also necessary to the success of many operations.

To Clean Brass Castings

Mix $\frac{1}{4}$ part nitric acid, $\frac{3}{4}$ parts sulphuric acid, $\frac{1}{2}$ lb. domestic salt to each 10 gals. of the liquid.

Immerse the castings in the liquid for 30 seconds. Rinse thoroughly in boiling water and dry in sawdust.

To Clean Brass

Mix $1\frac{1}{2}$ ozs. nitric acid, 1 dr. saltpetre (potassium nitrate), 2 ozs. rain water. Let mixture stand a few hours before use.

Dip the article in the solution for a few seconds. Rinse in boiling water and dry in sawdust.

To Clean Nickel-Plated Pieces

Make up a solution of alcohol with 2% of sulphuric acid.

Immerse the piece for about 5 seconds, or a little longer if the pieces are very dull.

Rinse well in running water and dry with a soft linen rag.

COLOURING BRASS

To Give Brass a Yellow to Orange Colour

Well polish the article, then immerse it in a solution of 5 parts caustic soda to 50 parts water (by weight), and 10 parts of copper carbonate.

When the desired shade of colour is reached, remove the work from the solution, wash well in water and dry in sawdust.

Golden Yellow to Brown

Immerse in the following solution:—100 grains of lead acetate dissolved in 1 pint of water. Add a solution of sodium hydrate until the precipitate which first forms is redissolved. Add 300 grains of red potassium ferrocyanide.

At normal room temperature this solution will impart a golden brown colour but when heated to 125° F. a definite brown colour will result.

Gold Colour

Immerse the article in a boiling solution of 2 parts saltpetre, 1 part domestic salt, 1 part alum, 24 parts by weight of water and 1 part hydrochloric acid.

This will give the brass a rich gold colour.

Another Method

Immerse the article in a solution made of:—3 parts alum, 6 parts saltpetre, 3 parts sulphate of zinc, 3 parts domestic salt.

Take the article from the solution and heat it over a hot plate until it becomes black. Wash well in water, rub with vinegar and again wash with water and dry off. A good gold colour should result.

Antique Finish

A solution to produce a green antique colour is made as follows:—3 ozs. crystallised chloride of iron, 1 lb. ammonium chloride, 8 ozs. copper acetate, 10 ozs. domestic salt, 4 ozs. potassium bitartrate, 1 gal. water.

Small pieces may be immersed, the depth of colour depending upon the duration of immersion. Large pieces may be treated by application of the solution with a brush. Several applications may be necessary.

When the desired shade is obtained, the variegated appearance of naturally aged brass is obtained by stippling the article with a brush dipped in the solution.

To Silver Brass

Scrupulous cleanliness of the work and hands is essential for completely successful work.

Silvering paste. Grind together in a mortar 1 oz. of dry chloride of silver, 2 ozs. cream of tartar (potassium bitartrate) and 3 ozs. common salt. Add water to form a creamy, fairly thin paste.

To apply: Thoroughly and completely clean the work and do not handle the surface in any way thereafter. Dab a clean and fairly stiff brush into the paste and brush it on to the work using a circular motion. A frosted silver surface will result which should also be found to be quite uniform. Wash thoroughly in running water and dry; lacquer to prevent tarnishing and do not wrap or stand the work in or near any paper, cloth, etc., other than sulphur or acid-free quality.

Keep paste in a very dark glass or stoneware container, or quite away from light which has a deleterious effect upon it. On no account attempt to use " doubtful " paste. A smeary and patchy surface is bound to result.

To give the work a straight grain effect, dab a clean linen rag on to the paste and rub over the work backwards and forwards in straight lines.

To obtain a circular grain effect, make the work revolve and hold the charged rag on to the work.

A similar and equally satisfactory finish can be obtained by the use of a cork in substitution for the linen rag.

A good lacquer for silvered surfaces is Japan lacquer applied with a good clean-cut camel-hair brush.

On no account touch the treated surfaces at any stage.

Another method, particularly useful for silvering dials, to give a frosted effect.

(1) Silver nitrate 7 gms.; (2) Ammonia thiocyanate 7 gms., ammonia solution of sp. gravity, ·80, 5 gms., French chalk 40 gms., sodium thiosulphate 10 gms. (ordinary hypo photographic fixing salt), water 80 gms.

Dissolve (1) and (2) *separately*, mix and add solid hypo until precipitate re-dissolves. Add chalk and finally ammonia solutions until up to 100% quantity given above. Method of using, *e.g.*, re-silvering a watch dial. Note—the figures must be enamel, otherwise it will be necessary to repaint the figures. Place the dial flat on a sheet of cork. Clean the surface with powdered pumice and water using a brush, *i.e.*, a clean watch brush. Wash off in clean, running water. Apply the silvering solution with a clean brush, *i.e.*, a watch brush, using a circular motion. When the surface is fully silvered and white wash off in clean, running water. Do not touch the surface with the fingers at any time during the process.

Note:—It is advisable to mix the solution in sufficient quantity as required, or, store in a well-corked, dark bottle and keep away from the light. It is more economical to silver several dials at the same time.

Dry by dabbing the surface with tissue paper.

Lacquer with Japan to prevent tarnishing.

To Frost Brass

To give brass a frosted finish boil in caustic potash, rinse in clean water. Dip in nitric acid until all oxide is removed. Wash and dry off in heated boxwood dust. Lacquer while warm.

To Blacken Brass

Clean thoroughly and remove all grease. Immerse the work in chloride of antimony for a short time. Dry over a spirit-lamp or hot plate. Brush with a black-lead brush. Lacquer when finished.

Another Method

Clean the work bright and dip into nitric acid. Rinse well in running water and place in the following solution: hydrochloric acid 1 lb.; sulphate of iron 1½ ozs.; pure white arsenic 1½ ozs. When the work has turned quite black remove and rinse in running water. Dry in boxwood dust, polish with black-lead and lacquer when finished.

To Blue Brass

First warm the article then immerse in the following solution: 1 oz. chloride of antimony; 20 ozs. water; 3 ozs. hydrochloric acid.

Place solution in earthen vessel and suspend the work in the solution until it turns blue. When the desired colour is obtained, wash in water and dry in boxwood dust.

To Bronze Brass

Dip the articles in the following solution: mix equal parts of nitric acid, sulphuric acid and water. Take first the nitric acid and water adding the acid to the water, then add the sulphuric acid a little at a time.

To use, immerse the article first in boiling water and then into the acid solution and quickly back into the boiling water. Rinse well in clean water and dry in boxwood dust.

To Matt Brass

Make up a solution: 1 part sulphuric acid in 1 to 2 parts nitric acid and 1 part sulphate of zinc.

Allow solution to stand for 24 hours, then use hot. Immerse the article in the hot solution until the surface is as required.

The proportion of nitric acid will determine a fine or coarse grain.

Wash thoroughly in warm water, and dry off.

To Make Brass and Copper Bright

Make up a solution: by weight 100 parts nitric acid; 50 parts sulphuric acid; 1 part soot; 1 part salt.

Dip the work in the solution, wash well in clean water and dry off in sawdust.

To Recolour Bronze Articles

For renovation or recolouring of bronze, first clean thoroughly and remove all grease. Mix 1 part hydrochloric acid and 2 parts water. Apply solution to the article with a cloth. Allow to dry on the article and polish with sweet oil.

To Lacquer Brass

A good general purpose lacquer is made by dissolving 1 oz. of shellac in 1 pint of methylated spirits. Place the mixture in a well stoppered bottle in a warm place such as on or near a radiator, hot pipes, etc., for about a week shaking the bottle every day.

When the shellac has dissolved or appears to have dissolved as much as possible, filter the liquid through a clean cloth. It is then ready for use.

This lacquer is used cold but the article is slightly warmed and the work should be carried out in a dry atmosphere.

If the lacquer is not sufficiently heavy, *i.e.*, lacking in body, it should be boiled. Heat a piece of cast iron or a good brick and, when hot, remove all naked flames from vicinity. Place the pan containing the lacquer on the hot iron or brick and let it boil. The operation may be repeated as required. Lacquer should be applied with a well formed, soft camel-hair brush.

To Colour Brass White

Brass is made white by a coating of pure tin. Clean the brass thoroughly and boil or heat in a solution of water and sodium stannate and caustic soda with filings or small scraps of pure tin (not so-called sheet tin which is merely tinned iron).

The surface is very effective, durable, and untarnishable.

TO COLOUR STEEL

To Blue Steel Without Heat

The use of " blueing solution", obtained from a reputable gunsmith, is the simplest method.

Another Method

Arrange for a jet of steam to be directed into a wooden box. Place a dish or " bath " in the box containing the following:—
1 oz. iron chloride, 1 oz. ethyl alcohol, ¼ oz. strong nitric acid, ⅛ oz. copper sulphate, 1 quart water.

The vapour arising from this mixture forms a deposit on the steel articles placed inside the box. Some time may be required to obtain the desired colour but, when ready, remove the articles from the box and rub off with a cloth.

A Blueing Solution.

Dissolve 2 parts crystallised chloride of iron, 2 parts solid chloride of antimony, 1 part gallic acid, 5 parts of water.

Apply the solution with a small sponge and allow to dry in the air. Repeat several times then wash thoroughly in water and dry in sawdust. Rub with oil to deepen the shade.

A Steel Blue Enamel

Dissolve 1 part borax in 4 parts water. Soak 5 parts bleached shellac in 5 parts methylated spirit. Dissolve methylene blue in a small quantity of methylated spirit to the colour desired.

Heat the borax and water to boiling point and, constantly stirring, add the methylated shellac solution. Stir until all lumps are dissolved and then add the methylene blue solution.

To use, well clean the work to remove all traces of grease. Apply the enamel with a camel-hair brush.

The enamel may be stored in a well-corked bottle.

Brown Finish to Steel

Make up a solution: 1 oz. copper sulphate; 1 oz. sweet spirits of nitre; 1 pint distilled water. Apply four coats of the solution and allow to dry for several hours between successive coats. Brush over after each coating. After the last coating rub hard and allow to dry 24 hours.

This gives a reddish-brown colour without gloss. If desired the hue may be deepened by adding arsenic to the solution for the last coating.

To polish, use a wax polish of boiled oil, beeswax and turpentine. Rub well with a soft cloth as with furniture.

Black Finish to Steel

Make a saturated solution of caustic soda (sodium hydroxide) and add a small quantity of saltpetre (potassium nitrate) (a small handful to a 5-gallon solution). Boil for a short time and allow to cool. To use, bring solution to the boil, wire the articles to be treated and suspend them in the boiling solution. The steel will immediately turn grey and, eventually, black. Rinse in cold water, dry in sawdust, and oil with linseed oil. Wipe clean.

This process produces a fine, blue-black colour.

A Black Matt Surface to Steel

Mix 2 ozs. of powered tartar in 20 ozs. of water. Boil the articles in this solution until they turn yellow. Then place the yellow work in a further solution of copper sulphate. They will become coppered.

When this stage is completed, remove and place in a solution of sulphur-ammonia. They will now turn black. Remove from solution and rinse off in water.

After the rinse, mix a quantity of dry sawdust with sufficient sweet oil to render it slightly oily and rub in sufficient graphite to give the whole a blackish appearance. Place the work in the prepared sawdust in a metal container and shake well. Now place the container in an oven and roast the whole until the sawdust is reduced to charcoal. The articles are now removed and allowed to cool. They will have a good, black matt, non-reflecting surface.

A Black " Fill In " for Dials

Coat the whole surface of the dial with a shellac varnish making certain that all engraving is covered, and allow to dry.

Make up a paste of shellac, methylated spirit and lamp-black. Spread the paste well into the engraved lines, etc., leaving as little upon the other surfaces as possible. Allow to dry hard. Remove the superfluous paste and the varnish with fine emery paper. The dial may now be silvered. To brighten the filling, heat the dial slightly until the wax fillings just commence to move, then allow to cool and set hard.

HEAT TREATMENT OF STEEL

Glass-Cutting Drills.

Dissolve zinc in hydrochloric acid to saturation then reduce the solution by adding an equal volume of water. Heat the drill to cherry red and quench in the solution. Use without tempering and with turpentine as a lubricant.

Extreme Hardness

Mix 2 parts common salt, 1 part flour, 4 parts water into a paste. Heat the part to be hardened and dip into the paste so that the part is thoroughly coated. Heat now to cherry red and quench in rain water.

To Harden Metal-Cutting Tools

Mix 2 ozs. saltpetre (potassium nitrate); 2 ozs. salammoniac (ammonium chloride); 2 ozs. alum; ½ lb. common salt; 3 gals. rain water. Keep solution in a stone jar. Heat the tool to cherry red and quench in the solution. Relieve the hardening strains by warming the tool but do not temper.

To Protect Delicate Pieces While Hardening

Dissolve 2 ozs. pure castile soap in warm water to a thin paste. Add a little lamp-black until paste becomes fairly stiff.

Slightly warm the article and smear the paste over it. When dry, heat to a cherry red and quench in the usual manner.

The paste also protects the surface against scaling and parts so treated will require very little or no cleaning before tempering.

TO REMOVE HARDENING DISCOLORATION

After hardening, dip the article into muriatic acid and allow it to remain for a few seconds. Rinse off immediately in running water.

CASE HARDENING

To case harden steel or iron proceed as follows: Mix 7 parts by weight of potassium ferrocyanide; 1 part potassium bichromate; 8 parts common salt. Pulverise in a mortar and mix very thoroughly.

Heat the article to be hardened to a dull red and dip into the powder mixture. Repeat the process several times, reheating and allowing the powder to "soak" at each application.

The depth of hardening will depend upon the number of times the process is followed.

Finally heat to a cherry red and quench in the normal manner.

Another Compound

This compound is used in the same way as above. 1 part ammonium chloride; 3 parts potassium ferrocyanide; *or* 1 part potassium ferrocyanide; 2 parts bone dust and 2 parts ammonium chloride.

Proprietary Compounds

There are a number of compounds marketed which will be found quite satisfactory. The makers' instructions should be followed carefully.

TO ANNEAL STEEL

Cover the article with fire clay and heat to a cherry red. Allow several hours to cool and as uniformly as possible.

METAL POLISHING COMPOUNDS

A good brass polishing and cleaning compound is made by mixing 1 oz. oxalic acid, 6 ozs. rotten-stone and kerosene oil to work into a paste.

Apply with a cloth or brush and polish with a soft brush or cloth. For a good surface in all metal work any cloth used should be dust free and preferably washed. Minute particles of dust and grit collected by polishing cloths can cause an almost imperceptible scratching of the surface which nevertheless mars the mirror-like finish otherwise obtainable.

A LIQUID POLISH FOR BRASS

1 quart rain water; $1\frac{1}{2}$ ozs. powdered rotten-stone; 2 ozs. pumice-stone powder; 4 ozs. oxalic acid.

Mix well together and allow to stand 2 or 3 days before using. Shake up well before use and apply with brush or cloth as above.

TO REMOVE RUST FROM STEEL

Brush the parts well with a paste made up as follows: $\frac{1}{2}$ oz. cyanide of potassium; $\frac{1}{4}$ oz. castile soap; 1 oz. whiting and sufficient water to make a paste.

Wash after brushing in a solution of $\frac{1}{4}$ oz. cyanide of potassium to 2 ozs. water.

Finally wash clean in water and dry in sawdust. Potassium cyanide is very poisonous.

Another Method

Make a solution of sulphuric acid in water. *It is very important that the acid is added to the water and not vice versa.*

To prepare such a bath, add the sulphuric acid drop by drop to the water, stirring all the time. Dip the rusted article in the bath to try the effect and continue the slow addition of the acid until the solution removes the rust cleanly. Allow the parts to soak in the bath until all rust is removed.

Remove the articles and wash in a solution of common household soda in water. Dry and immerse in benzine. Finally dry as much as possible with a linen rag and then in sawdust.

SOLDER AND SOLDERING

SOFT SOLDER

Consists of lead and tin. The melting point varies according to the tin content and rises gradually, up to 67% tin, to the melting point of tin. Common solder contains 2 parts lead, 1 part tin.

A flux is made by dissolving strips of zinc in hydrochloric acid which gives a saturated solution of zinc chloride.

This flux is good but the parts soldered require careful and complete washing afterwards as the acid liberated by the operation will rust ferrous metals and can thus cause considerable trouble. For this reason it is not considered a "safe" flux, particularly in electrical work.

A non-rusting flux in the form of a paste is made as follows: 1 lb. Vaseline or petroleum jelly; 1 oz. chloride of zinc.

A liquid flux is made from a saturated solution of zinc chloride to which is added ¼ part ammonia. Dilute the whole with an equal quantity of water: wash well with water to prevent corrosion.

ELECTRICAL FLUXES

For very exacting work in electrical connections rosin alone is used, the copper surfaces being carefully cleaned beforehand.

Proprietary fluxes are obtainable and, in general, it is important for their full action to be realised that the soldering is carried out at the full temperature with sufficient duration to ensure the solder runs well.

Zinc and acid types of flux should never be used in electrical work of any permanency. It is almost impossible to prevent ultimate corrosion of the parts adjacent although the " join " may remain sound in itself.

HARD SOLDER

Silver is used in the manufacture of hard solder also known as "silver solder." There are three grades, Hard, Medium, and Easy.

The hard solder is composed of 70 parts silver, 30 parts copper.

Easy solder consists of 49·24% silver, 34·36% copper, 16·40% zinc.

Borax and water is used as a flux, and powdered boracic acid may also be used.

GOLD SOLDER

Three grades are usually used, similar to silver solder, namely, Hard, Medium, and Easy. Hard is composed of 1 oz. fine gold; 6 dwts. fine silver; 4 dwts. copper wire. Medium—1 oz. fine gold; 10 dwts. fine silver; 10 dwts. copper wire. Easy—1oz. fine gold; 1 oz. ½ dwt. fine silver; 1 oz. ½ dwt. copper wire.

Borax and water is used as the flux.

STAINLESS STEEL FLUX

For soldering stainless steel, the ordinary fluxes are unsatisfactory and a strong solution of phosphoric acid is used.

This has persistent corrosive powers and the work must be boiled in strong soap solution for several minutes after soldering.

BRAZING

A form of hard soldering employing a brass spelter instead of silver.

A good all-purpose spelter is: 44% copper; 50% zinc; 4% tin; 2% lead. A good flux is borax, boric acid, and water.

TO BRAZE STEEL WITHOUT HEAT

Make up a solution: ¼ oz. hydrofluoric acid; 2 ozs. brass filings; 1 oz. steel filings: allow to stand until filings are dissolved. Store the solution in an earthenware or rubber vessel. To use, touch each part to be united with the solution and clamp them together. The acid is used for etching glass and is dangerous and poisonous.

PLATING

BRASS COATING

To coat iron or steel articles with brass, immerse them in a solution of: ½ oz. sulphate of copper; ½ oz. stannous chloride; 2 pints water. Stir the articles in the solution until the required colour is obtained.

TIN PLATING

The following solution gives a white finish similar to that of chromium. The articles must be polished and cleaned before treatment.

Immerse the work in a solution of sodium stannate and caustic soda (heated to dissolve). Add filings or scraps of pure tin. Boil the work in the solution until the desired colour is obtained.

MISCELLANEOUS HINTS

To remove loose pieces from a hole, *e.g.*, broken blade of a drill, work up a piece of beeswax to a point, press into the hole and withdraw sharply. If the part is loose it will become embedded in the wax and be removed.

A threaded piece broken into a blind hole may sometimes be removed by patient working with one, or two, needle points. Examine the work under a glass to see if there is any sign of looseness. The method is seldom successful if the piece is in tight, but can be tried before other methods are attempted.

To remove a broken-in steel screw or drill from brass, prepare a saturated solution of alum. Immerse the whole work in the solution for several hours when the steel piece will be eaten away. The action is considerably accelerated by boiling the solution. The brass may be discoloured but will not otherwise be affected. All other steel work must be taken off or prevented from coming into contact with the solution.

If the steel part is below the level of the brass, make sure that no bubble of air is preventing the solution reaching the steel.

This sometimes happens in a cold solution and will of course prevent any action on the steel taking place.

———

Certain grease marks may sometimes be removed from leather in the following manner. Place sheets of blotting paper over and under the article. Dust powdered magnesia freely on and under the stain, and press over all with a hot iron.

———

LUBRICANT FOR SMALL OILSTONES

Kerosene oil is probably the best lubricant as it not only allows the stone to " bite " but keeps it clean and sharp. Failing kerosene, paraffin is good.

———

TO DRILL HOLES IN GLASS

Holes of reasonable size can be drilled with copper or brass tubing, the outside diameter being equal to the size of the hole required.

The tube should be made to revolve at high speed with carborundum and light oil as the cutting medium.

The carborundum embeds itself in the softer metal and acts as a lap. Support the glass on several sheets of blotting paper or a piece of thick felt to provide an even, wide support.

Small holes are drilled with a solid drill shaped as for drilling brass, i.e., pointed, and hardened in sulphurous acid, untempered. Use turpentine as a lubricant when drilling.

———

TO CUT PLATE GLASS

To obtain a good, clean, straight edge, cut with diamond in the usual manner employing a straightedge as a guide, and a good, steady, single stroke. Heat an iron or steel rod of $\frac{1}{4}$ in. diameter to a dull red and lay along the length of the cut. Keep in position for 3 or 4 minutes when the glass will crack along the cut leaving a clean and uniform surface to the edge.

———

MIXING PLASTER OF PARIS

Sprinkle the plaster of Paris *on to* the water stirring the while; do not add water to the plaster when mixing.

———

TO IDENTIFY IRON AND STEEL

A simple acid test to determine whether a piece of metal is iron or steel—touch with nitric acid using a wooden dipper. Wash off in water and examine the stain. If steel, a black stain will be found. If iron, a blue stain.

———

TO CLEAN MERCURY

Place a 10% solution of nitric acid in an iron ladle and pour in the mercury. Bring the ACID to the boil and allow to cool. Dirt and grease will rise to the top leaving the clean mercury in the ladle bowl.

Care must be taken not to boil the mercury as the fumes then given off are dangerous.

To refresh mercury not seriously contaminated a permanent apparatus may be easily set up as follows: a glass cylinder of about 3 ft. length is clipped securely to a backboard standing on a heavy base. The upper end of the cylinder is closed with a rubber cork which takes a small filtering funnel and short glass tube. The lower end is closed with a rubber plug firmly fixed and taking a glass cock or stopper.

The glass tube is nearly filled with a solution of nitric acid.

To use, the affected mercury is slowly dribbled into the funnel which will cause it to " pellet " as it falls into the column of the acid through which it passes to the bottom. The clean mercury may be drawn off at the cock.

———

TO RE-SHARPEN FILES

First clean the files to remove all grease by soaking in petrol or, a better method, boiling in a 10% caustic soda and water solution. Dry well before proceeding with next stage. Place the clean files in an enamel dish in such a manner as to leave all surfaces as free as possible. If several are to be treated they may be placed on short lengths of wire separating them one from another.

Cover the files with water and slowly add sulphuric acid until a solution about 25% acid is obtained. It is essential that the acid be added slowly as considerable heat is generated which expedites the action, but may also cause a violent eruption if the acid is poured in quickly in bulk.

Fine files are sufficiently sharpened in about five minutes and coarse files in up to twenty minutes.

Remove from the bath when ready, well wash in water or a solution of ordinary household soda to neutralise the acid, and dry.

ATTENTION TO DRY CELLS

The modern " dry " cell or battery such as is used in instruments, clock and bell systems gives very good service and is thoroughly reliable. Occasionally, however, a battery may develop a sudden fault or loss of voltage and it is good practice at once to test the voltage of each individual cell—preferably " on load." A single faulty cell can otherwise escape detection for some time.

A swelling or bulging of the cell case, sweating or leakage of the contents, and soft places in the jacket, indicate that the cell is due for replacement although it may still be working satisfactorily.

Beads of moisture or a layer of damp extending across the bitumous top should be wiped off clean and dry. Such a film may indicate a deterioration of the cell but it also occurs in normal working and protection against the formation of a leaking electrical path formed by dust settling thereon is one reason for enclosure of a dry cell battery in a box.

Although sturdy in construction dry cells must not be dropped or very roughly handled, as the carbon central pole is liable to fracture, or the centre terminal cap displaced. The cap can be resoldered, using a large hot iron. But cells suspected of having been dropped should never be used.

Excepting for purely temporary purposes, attempts to " resore " these cells by heating, forcing in sal-ammoniac solution, etc., are not practicable and are not recommended.

Cells used in electrical instruments, e.g., multi-range meters, etc., are usually very reliable. They require replacement at intervals and variable readings, a continually varying " zero " position of the needle, are signs that the battery should be examined.

CARE OF ACCUMULATORS, STORAGE BATTERIES

The two main types in general use, i.e., the lead-acid and alkaline-nickel-iron cells, both require periodical inspection and correct usage to maintain their life and efficiency. Instructions are normally affixed to the cases or issued with the accumulators and these should be followed as exactly as possible.

In the case of lead-acid types, the correct specific gravity acid solution should be used.

It is equally important to obtain the correct alkaline electrolyte for the particular make of accumulator.

Probably neglect ruins more accumulators than are ever worn out by legitimate use.

They may require less frequent attention than other tools or apparatus. This does not mean " no attention at all until too late."

Lead-acid types may be permanently damaged by allowing the voltage to fall below the stated minimum, continuing to use the battery until exhausted, and neglecting to recharge. The voltage must be checked when " on load," otherwise the true state of the battery cannot be ascertained.

There is no method of restoring a lead-acid cell seriously damaged excepting by reconditioning equivalent to remaking.

Corrosion and sulphation of the cell terminals and connections can be prevented by coating with water-free grease. Vaseline is not always ideal for this purpose.

For " topping up " the electrolyte, tap water is sometimes used but in such cases the water happens to be suitable. It is not so in all parts of the country or in all parts of one area. Iron, lime, and acidic contents will cause trouble. Distilled water is preferable.

Overcharging, i.e., charging at an excessive rate causes internal damage and loss of electrolyte. Merely " topping-up " in this case with water alone worsens the position. The electrolyte must be replaced and it must be of the correct specific gravity.

Incipient or minor internal sulphation can be arrested or sometimes eliminated by a continuous process of alternate charging and discharging in gradually lengthening periods until the cell or battery is, in fact, worked up to its fully operating condition. The charge and discharge rates may be slightly in excess of the standard rate in commencing the treatment, but must not be excessive.

A charging room must be well ventilated and no naked lights or flames allowed therein.

In general, the alkaline type of cell can withstand neglect and harsh treatment more successfully than the lead-acid. These batteries are fitted with a special type of vent which acts as a non-return valve. It should be kept clean and free from dirt.

It is repeated that the makers' instructions should be followed if the full life and service is to be realised.

These brief notes do not fully cover the subject and further information should be sought in technical literature.

SUPPLEMENT

A LEXICOGRAPHER attempting to set bounds to the English language must summon all his courage and skill when he proposes to limit and define the language of the technician, and particularly so when he approaches the language, both ancient and modern, of the horologist.

Beside the invention of so many of the mechanisms now taken for granted, the makers of clocks (originally) and of watches (subsequently) invented the terms and phraseology to identify and describe them, originating, in the process, special tools with special names. Thus it comes about that few crafts have such a wealth of words of special and, often, of unique significance. The horologist has his own names for his specialities and tools, sometimes more than one for the same thing. And where two or more are apt, or equally descriptive and equally well known, it is difficult to say which is right; which should be used and which ignored. So the writer of books on horology finds the choice of words before him more lavish than precise, a difficulty which was before me in writing *Practical Watch Repairing*. The inclusion of a glossary appeared a way to overcome it. But the glossary in itself became nearly as large as the book ! So the only other way was to complete the glossary, deal with the definitions on encyclopedic lines and to do the job thoroughly with hundreds of illustrations and hang the expense ! Fortunately this was also the publisher's opinion.

Although researches have been made to include every technical horological word it is vain to hope that nothing has been overlooked or that mistakes have not been made. Alternatives, where known, have been given with a cross reference to the term considered to be correct or the most used. Names of makers are not included (Baillie's *Watchmakers and Clockmakers of the World* presents a book full of them), unless the name has become synonymous with a particular article or invention, such as Breguet balance spring, Graham deadbeat escapement, Guillaume balance, etc. Another encyclopedic feature of this book is the arrangement, in separate sections, of certain groups of words having related usage, such as antiquities, woods, marbles, chimes, and so on; an arrangement which assists the seeker for a word as well as for a definition.

While every care has been taken to ensure accuracy and, also, to include every descriptive word used in all the departments of horology, it is realised that errors and omissions are inevitable. These will be repaired in later editions. Information and advice on these points will be received with gratitude. As the publisher's favourite literature appears to be guide books, he suggested I should here include an extract from the introduction to one of them because it seems to imply more than it actually says, and will I hope, convey to the reader what might make little impression if put in more conventional language; to quote the guide book:

" Should any defect be discovered, let everybody denounce it freely for the sake of public utility and should we be deserveful of praise be it only complimented our wilfulness and our utmost cares in tracing up the best possible way the truth to represent it clearly to all our readers."

Obviously, assistance in the compilation of this book has been sought from all and sundry, and in every case freely given. But I would like to place on record my special thanks to Mr. Maurice C. Aimer who supplied most of the matter relating to subjects met with in dealing with the quartz crystal clock and timing machines, and who also assisted in arranging the entire book in alphabetical order and added much to the copy.

To Mr. E. A. Ayres, the artist, who has patiently given much thought and time and helped in no small measure to create what must be a unique collection of drawings.

To Mr. H. B. Boulton, the author of books relating to woods and timber, who has helped with the section on woods suitable for clock cases.

To the Dennison Watch Case Co., Ltd. for their help when compiling the section on watch cases.

To Mr. Percy Dawson, the authority on antique clock cases, who has kindly read through the copy relating to antique clock case terms and to M. Leon Leroy of Paris, for his help with the French period clocks.

To the late Phillip Clowes, who loaned specimens of horological work for purposes of illustration.

To Mr. Malcolm Gardner, the authority on horological literature, who has helped in finding references to many subjects.

To the late Mr. Courtenay Ilbert, who placed at my disposal his collection of horological subjects and gave access to his library.

To Mr. Hillyard T. Stott, who has placed to my disposal his glossary of electrical terms.

To Mr. W. O. Davis, for permission to use his definitions on gearing, taken from his book " Gears for small mechanisms ".

To Mr. Robert Webster, for his knowledge and industry in revising the section on Marbles and Ornamental Stones.

My grateful thanks to Professor D. S. Torrens, for considerable help in reading through, correcting, and adding to the copy.

It is not possible to enumerate all who have helped, but I would like them to know that their assistance is much appreciated.

D. DE CARLE.

Pinner

A

ABBESS WATCH. A Swiss watch of about the middle of the 16th century in the form of a cross, worn round the neck. Usually made of rock crystal.

ABRASIVE. (*See* page 9). The abrasives used in the clock and watch industry are oil-stone dust, which is, as its name implies, powdered oil-stone mixed with *clock* oil to a consistency of a fairly stiff paste, and used as a preliminary to polishing with diamantine. Diamantine or its substitute is a white powder mixed with watch oil and great care must be taken in the preparation. As much diamantine as can be picked upon a quarter of an inch of a pocket knife blade is placed on a zinc block (made specially for this purpose. *See* Polishing Block) and one drop of *watch* oil is applied. This is then beaten with a freshly filed iron polisher, wiped scrupulously clean, adding another drop of oil if it is not possible to form a thick hard paste. When the hard paste is formed it is applied to the polisher with the knuckle of the thumb, knocking the knuckle onto the paste and then on to the polisher, to transfer a minimum amount of paste. Refer to "Practical Watch Repairing", by D. de Carle.

ACANTHUS. (*See* page 15). Stylised from the Mediterranean Acanthus plant. Represented conventionally in decoration.

ACCUTRON. Trade name of the first transistorised tuning fork watch (used instead of a balance wheel and spring). Also called a "sonic watch".

ACORN CLOCK. An American Shelf Clock (*q.v.*) roughly in the shape of an acorn.

ACTION. (*See* page 9). With watches, in particular, it is essential to obtain a good action—three-quarters of a turn of the balance in each direction—to ensure good timekeeping especially when timing in positions. To determine the extent of the arc of vibration of a balance, note the position of the arm of the balance from the centre to the outer edge, *i.e.* when the balance is quiescent, and as the balance vibrates it will be observed that the part of the arm will appear to cross over, which is equal to one complete turn of the balance —a half turn on each side. Keep the vision steady and observe the arm creep up to another quarter of a turn which equals one and three-quarter turns. With an arc in excess of this, there is the risk of the ruby pin knocking the back of the lever notch, known as "knocking the banking". Refer to "Practical Watch Springing and Adjusting", by D. de Carle. *See* Arc.

ADJUSTED. (*See* page 10). The Swiss have decreed that the word Chronometer (*q.v.*) shall be the indication of an adjusted watch. Hitherto the word "chronometer" refered to a timepiece with a detent escapement. Nevertheless, the name "chronometer" applied by the Swiss does not necessarily imply quality, only that the watch has satisfied certain tests at an Official Bureau. *See* Testing Standards, page 242. It is possible for low grade watches to be marked "chronometer".

ADOS CLOCK. The name given to an eight-day folding travelling made by Le Coultre, Switzerland. Sometimes referred to as a Camera Clock.

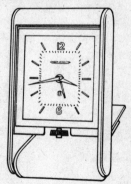

ADOS CLOCK.

AIRY'S BAR. (*See* page 10). Sir George Airy, who was Astronomer Royal, took great interest in the timing of marine chronometers and found that to adjust for changes of temperature was difficult, because moving the two weights equally, so as to keep the balance in poise, was well-nigh impossible. The bar he introduced in 1871 overcame the difficulty. Refer to "The Marine Chronometer", by R. T. Gould.

ALARM or ALARUM. A clock or watch which rings or alarms at a predetermined time. An alarm was probably the first form of mechanical timekeeper, dating from the 14th century, used to alert the sexton or watchman to toll a bell to call a religious community to prayer or to sound a curfew. It was not a timepiece or clock in the true sense, but a warning for a bell to be tolled manually, calling monks to prayers, and so on. *See* Cricket Watch, Recital Alarm Clock, and Tea Time Clock.

ALNICO. Aluminium, nickel and cobalt alloy used as strong magnets in horology.

ALTAR CLOCK. During the latter half of the 17th and first half of the 18th centuries, wooden clock case designs were influenced by the shapes of the alter reredos. Such clocks were more popular on the Continent than in England.

ALTAR CLOCK.

ALTITUDE DIAL. A portable form of sun-dial dating from about the seventh century. The timekeeping depends upon the height of the sun and therefore the length of its shadow.

ANTIQUE CLOCKS
PERIODS OF FRENCH CLOCK STYLES
see also pages 45-47

LOUIS XIV
DESIGN OF MAROT.

LOUIS XV
ORMOLU.

LOUIS XV
ORMOLUON
VERNIS MARTIN DECORATION.

LOUIS XIV
REGULATOR CLOCK.

LOUIS XVI
ARCHITECTURE STYLE
WHITE MARBLE AND ORMOLU

LOUIS XVI
CARTEL BRONZE GILT.

LOUIS XVI
DIRECTOIRE
WHITE MARBLE AND ORMOLD

EMPIRE
BRONZE GILT BLACK FIGURES.

LOUIS XVI
FOUR GLASS REGULATOR.

ANNIVERSARY CLOCK. In America, the Four Hundred Day Clock (*q.v.*) is referred to as an anniversary clock. The term also refers to a clock which runs for one year after winding.

ANNULAR BALANCE. (*See* page 15). The name distinguishes it from the Foliot (*q.v.*), which is a form of balance.

APPOINTMENT CLOCK. A clock operated slot machine. The time of the appointment required is written on an ivorine tablet and at the appointed hour the tablet is ejected and an alarm rings. Made at the end of the 19th century.

ARMOURED CRYSTAL. Watch glass with inner reinforcing ring.

ARROW CLOCK. An arrow, fixed to a chain, travels round the frame of a mirror. Twelve beads or other decoration act as the hours. The chain is motivated by a clock. Said to have been devised by Grollier de Serviere, 17th century.

ARROW
CLOCK

ART NOUVEAU. New Art. About 1925, clock cases and jewellery appeared made of pewter—and jewellery also of silver—with some enamel decoration of blue hues to peacock colours, following the artistic revival of the time, led by William Morris. Some watch cases were made about 1905, but Art Nouveau did not become popular until the revival in 1925. The clock cases were usually fitted with French drum time-piece movements.

ARTIFICIAL CLOCK. Upon the intro-duction of mechanical clocks, in the second half of the 14th century, they were referred to as "artificial clocks" to distinguish them from sundials and water clocks. A book was published entitled "The Artificial Clock Maker" by Wm. Derham, 1696. This is not about the craftsman, but the mechanical clock.

ASTROLOGICAL CLOCK. A rare Table Clock (*q.v.*) of the 17th century which, in addition to showing the time of day, also shows some astrological information. Usually of German make.

ATMOS CLOCK. (*See* page 15). As the motive power to wind the mainspring, Le Coultre Co., of Switzerland, now use an aneroid (*q.v.*). Otherwise the clock is the same as the original.

AUGSBURG CLOCKS. About the middle of the 16th century, the main centre of domestic clock production was Augsburg,

Germany. The original Augsburg clocks were Table Clocks (*q.v.*).

AUXILIARY DIAL. The dial or dials of a clock or watch giving subsidiary information in addition to the time of day.

B

BACKWIND WATCH. Winding button on the rear of the watch. Used in smallest watches. Setting buttons on some electric watches are on the back.

BACK PLATE. The plate of a clock to which the back cock (*q.v.*) is attached. The plate under the dial is the front plate, so the other plate is the back plate.

BALANCE. The oscillator, usually in the form of a wheel, which with a balance spring is the time controller of many clocks and watches. It operates with the escapement. Some early balances were in bar form. *See* Bar Balance and Foliot. All are now wheel balances. *See* Compensation Balance, Volet Balance and Guillaume Balance.

BALANCE, PLAIN. Used in Volet Balance (*q.v.*) compensating systems. *See* WATCH PART NOMENCLATURE, page 275.

BALL and TAPE CLOCK. An early form of ball-shaped clock hanging on a tape. The clock descends at a controlled rate to expose the tape in which the hours are marked. Lifting the ball "rewinds" the tape into the movement. A form of Falling Ball Clock (*q.v.*)

BALL AND TAPE CLOCK

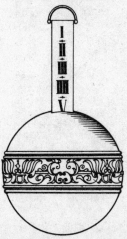

BALL WATCH. A spherical watch worn suspended by a chain or cord from the neck. Vast numbers of these watches were made in Switzerland about the middle to the end of the 19th century. They are of fine quality, with gold, enamelled and engraved cases. Winding is effected by rotating the upper half of the case. The mechanism is built on three tiers, the mainspring, train of wheels and then the escapement, either Lever (*q.v.*) or Cylinder (*q.v.*). Eventually a lower grade of watch was produced by the Swiss from about the early part of this century. Such watches are usually in gilt metal cases, enamelled and engraved. They are distinguishable by a winding button as the bezel or upper half of the case was no longer used for winding.

BALL-DRIVEN CLOCK. A rare form of clock, invented in about the middle of the 17th century, where a heavy ball slowly runs down a series of inclines and its weight bearing on the supports provides motive power to the clock movement. When a ball reaches the end of its journey, it drops into a drawer and releases another ball at the top of the clock. As a rule there are six balls which provide power for 24 hours, when the balls are replaced at the top of the clock.

BANKING, MAGNETIC. Used in electrical watches. The indexing pallet, which drives the hands, is made to bank by small magnets, since there is no mechanical draw (*q.v.*).

BAR BALANCE. An early form of oscillator to control clocks and watches. *See* Foliot and Balance.

BAROMETRIC COMPENSATION. There are two main methods of correction of the Barometric Error (*q.v.*): (1) To fix to the pendulum itself, either a small mercurial barometer to rise or fall or a permanent magnet fixed to a barometer to attract a magnet fixed to the pendulum. (2) To place the pendulum in a hermetically-sealed container where the pressure of air can be kept constant.

BAROMETRIC ERROR. Barometric pressure slightly affects the rate of pendulum clocks, and of chronometers, especially where the temperature weight or screws of the balance protrude and cause air resistance.

BAROMETRIC PRESSURE. The pressure of the air causing density of the air. *See* Barometric Error.

BASLE TIME. In the 14th century, Basle, Switzerland, counted its time from mid-day but referred to it as one o'clock. Later this was changed to universal practice.

BASSE-TAILLE ENAMEL. Fr. Base Cut. A form of enamel watch dial where the base is engraved and then covered with a thin layer of coloured transparent enamel. Date about 1600.

BATTERSEA ENAMEL. A loose term for English enamelled watch cases, etc. The Battersea Enamel Factory, in Battersea, London, started about 1750 and closed in 1756. The new process was to take the colour of engraved plates on to paper and transfer them to the surface to be enamelled. The work was carried on in Bilston, Staffordshire, and elsewhere.

BATTERY CLOCK. An electrically-powered clock employing an electric battery, first introduced by Alexander Bain, 1840. Modern battery clocks are in two main categories, those in which a battery winds a normal spring-driven clock at short intervals and those in which the balance is driven electro-magnetically by the battery and in which the balance also drives the hands.

BATTERY WATCH. The battery used in an electric watch is a dry energy cell— usually a mercury cell—measuring about five-sixteenths of an inch in diameter and less than one-eighth of an inch in thickness and lasts for about one year or even longer. *See* Electric Watch, Tuning Fork Watch and Quartz Crystal Watch.

BILSTON ENAMEL. Late 18th and early 19th century enamelled boxes and watch cases etc., were produced in Bilston, Staffordshire. They followed Battersea enamels, and were made by a similar system of production. A Bilston factory has again started to operate.

BIM-BAM CLOCK. Another name for Ting-Tang Clock (*q.v.*).

BINNACLE CLOCK. A form of Ship's Bell Clock (*q.v.*).

BISSEXTILE. The continental term for Leap Year.

BLACK FOREST CLOCK. A vast number of what may be termed novelty clocks have been and are produced in the Black Forest, Germany, which also makes huge numbers of lower grade alarm and travelling clocks. *See* Four Hundred Day Clock, Flying Ball Clock, Cuckoo Clock and Tellurion Clock.

BOB PENDULUM. The type of pendulum where the rod—usually thick brass wire—is fixed to the pallet arbor and the bob screws direct on to the rod. There is no suspension spring or rating nut. Usually found in antique verge clocks and the V.A.P. (*q.v.*) French clocks. *See* Antique Clocks, page 19.

BOLT SPRING. Used in some keywind watches to keep the bolt in the desired position.

BOOK CLOCK. A small desk clock in the form of a book which became popular in the latter part of the 16th and early 17th centuries. The fashion was revived by the Swiss between the two Great Wars.

BOUDOIR CLOCK. While boudoir suggests a lady's room, the term Boudoir Clock has become associated with a particular style of English clock and more especially with the make and finish of the case. Many such clocks were made by Cole from about 1860 to the end of the century; the dials were signed by such London retail jewellers as Hunt & Roskell, and Payne, both of Bond Street. The cases are made of brass, profusely engraved and gilt. Dials are silver with blued steel hands. Some of these clocks are to be found in the form of a swing dressing table mirror.

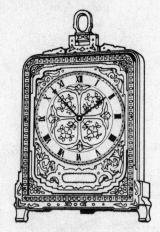

BOUDOIR CLOCK.

BOULLE. *See* Buhl.

BRAKE PLATE. The mechanism that avoids backlash of the seconds hand in chronographs.

BRAS EN L'AIR. A timepiece where the time is indicated by a figure of a man or woman, its right arm pointing to the hours on a sector and its left arm to the minutes on a similar type of dial. Some showed the time only when the pendant was depressed which raised the arms. Sometimes the hands held weapons that pointed to the time. Normally the hours, 12, 1, 2, etc. to 12, were shown on the right, and the minutes, 0 to 60, on the left. When the arms always point to the time, they jump back when they reach the ends of their respective scales.

BROCOT ESCAPEMENT. (*See* page 71). This escapement was popular with French clockmakers, who designed clocks with the escapement visible on the front of the dial.

BUTTERFLY NUT. A winged nut sometimes found above the suspension spring of antique clocks, for the purpose of final regulation. A feature of some long case clocks made by Joseph Knibb is a butterfly piece—not a nut— to hold while making adjustment to the nut upon which the pendulum bob rests. This system holds the pendulum rod firmly, thus protecting the suspension spring.

C

CAMERA CLOCK. *See* Ados Clock.

CANDLE CLOCK. A marked candle to denote the passing of the hours. As the candle burns away so the passing of time is observed. King Alfred's biographer, Asser, records that Alfred made use of candles as timekeepers so as to regulate his work. Each candle burned away in four hours.

CANONICAL HOURS. A system employed in European monasteries in days before the mechanical clock to divide daylight hours into prayer times. Originally there were three, which were increased over many years to seven.

CAPUCIN. Another name for Chamber Clock (*q.v.*). *See* Antique Clocks, page 22.

CENTRE OF GYRATION. That point in which the whole mass of a rotating body might be concentrated without altering its moment of inertia.

CHAISE WATCH. A large pocket style watch—about three to four inches in diameter—too large to be worn in the waistcoat pocket. Made to fit into a pocket fixed inside a horse-drawn carriage. Popular during the 18th century.

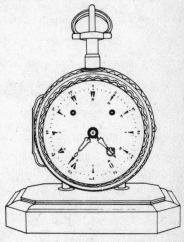

CHAISE WATCH.

CHAMPLEVÉ ENAMEL. An early form of watch case enamelling, where the metal is carved and the hollows filled with various coloured glass powder. The case is then fired until the glass is formed. Then the surface is polished, giving the effect of metal inlaid with glass. Cloisonné enamel has a similar effect with the difference that the hollows are formed by soldering strips of metal to the surface.

CHESS CLOCK. A clock made to register the length of time between each move on the chess board. A combination of two identical clocks is used, one for each player. When a move is made a knob is depressed which stops the players clock and automatically raises the knob of the other clock to start it. A small red flag on the dial is raised when the time for a move has expired.

CHINESE DUPLEX. (Double Duplex). Duplex escapement with crab-claw teeth. The escapement receives impulse in only one direction, and the seconds hand jumps in seconds. Popular with watches for the Near and Far East. Bovet Fleurier produced many such watches.

CHRONOMETER CLOCK. A clock fitted with a Chronometer Escapement (*q.v.*) *i.e.*, Spring Detent escapement.

CHRONOSCOPE. An instrument where a Chronograph (*q.v.*) mechanism is set into motion by the action of a pair of electromagnets, thus eliminating the personal error of the operator pressing the button of the conventional chronograph or stop watch. Chronoscope also refers to a watch where apertures are cut in the dial revealing discs upon which the hours and minutes are marked. Some watches are provided with sun and moon discs, minute hand, and hours marked upon a disc observable through an aperture. Such dials were made of metal in the 17th century and, in the early part of the 18th century, enamel dials were used.

CIVIL TIME. Two 12 hour periods starting at midnight.

COACH CLOCK. During the 18th century, clocks—really large watches—were made either to hang or fit into pockets inside coaches. *See* Chaise Watch and Sedan Clock.

COLUMN CLOCK. Fashionable in France about the early part of the 18th century. This style of clock developed from a pedestal upon which a clock with a short pendulum was placed. Eventually the clock case and pedestal became an integral case. Later the long pendulum was introduced into the case and the French "grandfather" clock resulted.

COLUMN CLOCK

COMBINATION CLOCK. Usually a travelling clock with a combination of other instruments in addition to the time-of-day clock. The popular combination is a clock and a separate dial for a barometer or calendar and perhaps, between the two dials, a thermometer. Some combination clocks have four and even six dials, *e.g.* time, thermometer, calendar, barometer, hygrometer and compass.

COMPASS DIAL. A sundial incorporating a compass enabling the time to be ascertained from the sun's direction. First made its appearance early 15th century.

COMPENSATION CURB. A device used in some watches of the late 18th and early 19th centuries, where one index pin is fitted to the Index (*q.v.*) and the other is fitted to a bi-metallic strip, or the end of the strip acts as a pin. When ambient temperature increases, the space between the pins is enclosed, thus making the watch tend to gain and thus compensate for its tendency to loose in heat. Breguet used this system extensively on his cylinder escapement watches and may have invented it. A similar system was used by the English watch and chronometer makers Arnold and Earnshaw. While satisfactory up to a point, the system has the disadvantage of disturbing the Isochronism (*q.v.*) of the watch, but this would not be a serious handicap when considering the rating of a watch fitted with a cylinder escapement.

COMPOUND PENDULUM. A pendulum pivoted or suspended at or near the centre of the pendulum rod with one bob or weight attached to the bottom and another to the top of the pendulum rod. The top weight can be adjusted. Long periods of vibration can be obtained with a comparatively short pendulum, as in some Gravity Clocks (*q.v.*).

CONSTANT FORCE ESCAPEMENT. Where the force to drive the pendulum is independent of the clock mechanism. This is achieved by an arm on each side of the pendulum rod being lifted by the clock mechanism and then allowed to rest on the pendulum rod. The weight of the arm resting on the pendulum rod keeps the pendulum vibrating. Lord Grimthorpe has been given credit for the invention of the Double Three Legged Escapement (*q.v.*) when he designed Big Ben in 1852 but the principle was used by Bloxham in 1850. Also Mudge; Katir; Massy and Peers, devised similar escapements. There are also constant force devices that are spring instead of weight operated and used in portable clocks with balances. *See* Remontoire.

CORDLESS CLOCK. An American term for a Battery Clock (*q.v.*) to distinguish it from a Mains Clock (*q.v.*) with a wire lead.

COTTAGE CLOCK. A miniature bracket style clock of about seven to eight inches high and about two inches deep. Originally these clocks were fitted with 30-hour verge watch movement, and were made about the end of the 18th century.

COTTAGE CLOCK.

COUNT WHEEL. *See* Locking Plate.

COUP PERDU ESCAPEMENT. *See* Galileo's escapement.

CROSS BEAT CLOCK. In the 16th century, Jobst Burgi, the Swiss clockmaker, modified the Verge Escapement (*q.v.*). Two bar balances were employed with the object of increasing the accuracy of the verge escapement. Also known as the Two Bar Balance Escapement.

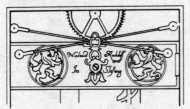

CROSS BEAT CLOCK.

CRYSTAL LIFTER. Tool that constricts the circumference of a plastics crystal, allowing it to be lifted from its bezel.

C.M.O.S. Complementary metallic oxide semiconductor used in transistorised timepieces.

CUVETTE. Dust cap for watches.

D

DECIMAL CLOCK. *See* Decimal Clock Dial, and French Period Styles, page 45.

DIALING. Refers to the art of designing, making and positioning sundials.

DIGITAL CLOCK. A clock where in place of the conventional dial and hands, figures (digits) appear to indicate the time of day, *e.g.* 15.45 (on those showing time on a 24-hour system). On some clocks, seconds are indicated, also the date. *See* Flick Leaf Clock.

DIGITAL CLOCK.

DIURNAL. In astronomy it refers to a period covering a mean Solar Day. *See* Greenwich Mean Time.

DOUBLE STRIKING CLOCKS. A clock which repeats the hours at approximately two minutes after the correct time has been struck. The system dates from the 17th century. It was used in some public as well as domestic clocks. *See* Dutch Striking.

DOUBLE TOOTH DUPLEX ESCAPEMENT. Similar in action to the Duplex Escapement (*q.v.*) but has two locking teeth, one of which gives slight impulse. Also known as "Chinese Duplex".

DRUM HEAD CLOCK. A circular clock with a base, usually of English make, used in such places as offices, banks, etc., popular during the latter part of the 19th century.

DUMB-BELL BALANCE. The dumb-bell appearance of the balance of an antique watch fitted with the Foliot (*q.v.*) balance. It consists of a bar with a ball at each end and is the predecessor of the annular or circular balance. *See* Balance.

DUOFIX. Device using combination cap

and hole jewels in combined setting. Not a shock device.

DRUMHEAD CLOCK.

E

ELECTRIC WATCH. (*See* page 122). A battery-driven watch where electric power is used in place of a mainspring, but with the difference that the mainspring drives the train of wheels to the escapement. The battery-driven watch is motivated from the escapement through a train of wheels to the hands indicating the time of day. Batteries are also used in Tuning Fork and Quartz Crystal Watches (*q.v.*).

ELEPHANT CLOCK. A model of an elephant with a clock on its back. Sometimes the elephant is of bronze and the rest of the clock gilt. Popular during the Regency and Louis XVI periods. *See* French Period Styles, page 45.

EN GRISAILLE. Enamel painting with grey background.

EN PLEIN. Describes antique watches fully crowded with jewels, pearls, etc.

EN QUEUE. Straight line train of gears in timepiece.

ENAMEL. Enamel is glass composed of silica, red lead, and potash. It is normally colourless and called flux, but coloured when fused with oxides of metals. it was and still is the practice of manufacturers to send items such as watch cases, clock cases and parts of cases, boxes, ornaments etc., to the enamel factories for them to embellish. *See* Basse-Taille, Battersea, Bilston, Champlevé, Cloisonné, Flinqué, Guilloché, Niello and Paillonné.

ENGLISH FOUR GLASS CLOCK. Rectangular clock with glass panels to the sides, back and top of case. Usually with a fuse movement, either timepiece or strike, about seven to twelve inches high, in a case of mahogany, satin wood, and ebony veneered.

ENGLISH FOUR GLASS CLOCK

ENGLISH PERIOD STYLES. (*See* page 44). Quarter hour divisions only on dials of clocks with hour hand only up to 1600.

EPACT. (*See* page 125). Excess of the Solar year over 12 lunar months, about 11 days.

EPOXY RESIN. Resinous, two-part adhesive forming a permanent, strong bond.

EQUATION CLOCK. A clock which automatically registers the Equation of Time (*q.v.*). Such clocks are rare and date generally from the latter part of the 17th to the middle 18th century. Some clocks of this period are provided with a dial and hand which is manually adjusted after consulting an equation table.

ESCAPEMENT. (*See* page 126). *See* escapements as follows: Brocot; Chronometer; Detent; Cross Beat; Club Tooth;

Crank; Crown Wheel; Dead Beat; Double
Three Legged; Duplex; English Lever;
Grasshopper; Grimthorpe, Lord; Half
Dead Beat; Karrussel; Le Paute's; Lever;
Litherland; Lobster claw; Magnetic; Mani-
velle; Mudge's; Pin Pallet; Pin Wheel;
Pivoted Detent; Platform; Rack Lever;
Reid's; Riefler; Resilient; Right Angle;
Savage's; Semitangential Lever; Straight
Line; Tic Tac; Tourbillon; Three Legged;
Verge, Virgule; Virgule, Double;
Vulliamy's.

ÉTABLISSEUR (Swiss term). The owner
or controller of a watch factory where
Ebauches (*q.v.*) are finished and made into
complete watches. The établisseur may
finish the ébauches in his own factory or
send to a small workshop where the owner,
known as a Termineur, carries out certain
work but does not complete the watch.

F

FAHRENHEIT SCALE. (*See* page 127).
The fixed points are freezing 32° and boiling
212°. Most countries have changed or are
changing from this or another scale to
Centigrade or Celsius in which the fixed
points are freezing 0° and boiling 100°. *See*
Temperature Conversion Table.

FALLING BALL CLOCK. A spherical
clock, the weight of which provides the
motive power. The ball is suspended by a
cord. The time is indicated by a figure such
as a cherub, pointing to the hour, which is
marked on a rotating band around the
centre of the ball. These clocks first made
their appearance during the 15th century.
A falling ball clock of more recent date is
furnished with a tape upon which are
marked the hours and as the ball descends
so the time of day is exposed. Both types of
clocks are wound by manually raising the
ball until the cord or tape disappears into
the ball.

FAN CLOCK. A fan with numerals on the
folds. As the fan unfolds, so the time is
revealed. The illustration shows 12 mid-day
and when fully unfolded the fan snaps back
to the closed position. Reputed to have
been invented by Grollier de Servière, about
1650.

FAUSSE MONTRE. (Fr. Dummy watch).
Fashionable about the last quarter of the
18th century. Used to counterbalance the
live watch at the other end of the waistcoat
chain.

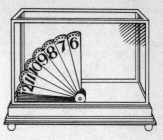

FAN CLOCK.

FIRE CLOCK. A system where weights
are made to drop into a pan to make a
sound like a gong by a slow burning fuse
severing the thread to which the weights are
attached. The time at which the weights are
to fall can be adjusted by the fuse. Of
Chinese origin, 18th century.

FLINQUÉ ENAMEL. A form of enamelling of the latter part of the 17th century
where hand engraving was covered with a
layer of coloured transparent enamel.

FLIP-FLOP. Circuit with valves or
transistors in which one section is conducting while the other is cut off (delayed with
resistors) but soon takes over while the
opposite section becomes dormant. Used
in electronic timepieces as a timing element.

FLOATING BALANCE. A balance for
clocks suspended by a Duo-in-uno hairspring (*See* page 58), and supported by a
wire through the hollow balance arbor.

FLOATING HOUR DIAL. *See* Wander-
ing Hour Dial.

FLORAL CLOCK. Edinburgh Castle,
and the gardens in Geneva, Switzerland,
among many other places, have clocks in
the ground, the dial laid out in bedding
plants. Some have striking and even
cuckoo mechanisms.

FLUX. *See* Enamel.

FLYING BALL CLOCK. Sometimes
referred to as the flying pendulum clock and
also Villard's rope escapement clock
(invented c. 1240). There is no escapement
as such to this clock. The pendulum acts as
the escapement as well as the controller. A
centre post rotates freely, turned by the
clock, and has a thread and ball attached
to it. As it swings, its course it is obstructed
by a post on the outer edge of the base

around which the thread with the ball attached becomes entwined. When it unwinds, it swings round and the action is repeated. Such clocks are produced in Germany at the present time as a novelty.

FLYING BALL CLOCK.

FOLDING CLOCK. *See* Three Fold Clock, Combination Clock, Calotte Clock and Camera Clock.

FORM WATCH. A watch in the form of an article other than the conventional shape, such as a musical instrument, fruit, ladybird, beetle, butterfly, etc. Some such watches are beautifully made, enamelled and set with stones. Usually for use on a table, etc. They are not convenient to wear.

FOUNTAIN CLOCK. A French clock with a spiral of glass rotating to give the impression of water issuing and running into a basin. Some such clocks have a number of fountains. Another theme was a jet of wine—red glass spiral—running from a barrel into a basin, with a figure of Bacchus sitting astride the barrel. Fountain clocks are usually fitted with eight-day movements and the fountain part operates independently of the clock movement and runs for about four hours after each winding. Date about the middle of the 19th century.

FOUR HUNDRED DAY CLOCK. (*See* page 131). In America, the Four Hundred Day Clock is sometimes referred to as an Anniversary Clock.

FREE SPRUNG. A watch with balance and spring but no index. For purposes of regulation, screws on the balance where used.

FREED BRIDLE. Connection from battery to earth in electrical timepieces.

FOUNTAIN CLOCK.

FRENCH FOUR GLASS REGULATOR. A gilt metal clock with glass panels at the sides and back of the case and a glass door in front. The movement is fitted with a Gridiron (*q.v.*) or a mercurial (*q.v.*) pendulum and also with a lenticular (*q.v.*) bob.

G

GALILEO'S ESCAPEMENT. A unique escapement contrived by Galileo during the first half of the 15th century. Also known as the Coup Perdu (lost beat) escapement because impulse is imparted to the pendulum at alternate beats.

GARNIER, PAUL, ESCAPEMENT. A vertical form of escapement employing two escape wheels acting on a pallet fitted to the balance staff. This escapement is a modification of Debaufre's escapement. The Garnier escapement is to be found in carriage clocks made by him. Invented about 1830 in Paris.

GOVERNOR OF REPEATING WATCH. A form of escapement for the repeating train of a watch. There are three systems in use:—

(1) Pallets and an escape wheel. The speed of repeating mechanism is controlled by a projection of the pallets banking on a pin which is drilled eccentrically in the end of a screw. As the pin is made to turn closer to the pallets, so the speed of the train is increased.

(2) A pinion gearing into the last wheel of the repeating train. The upper pivot hole of the pinion is drilled eccentrically into a screw bush. As the bush is turned to deepen the depth of the pinion into the wheel, so the speed is lessened.

(3) A disc with two weighted, pivoted arms, with springs bearing upon them. The disc is fitted on the extended pivot of the terminated pinion. As the disc revolves so the arms are thrown outward. To increase speed the springs are made to bear harder on the arms and to lessen speed, the springs are made to bear lig'ter.

GUILLOCHET ENAMEL. A form of transparent, coloured enamel, on an engine-turned base. Popular in the latter part of the 19th and early 20th centuries.

FRENCH FOUR GLASS REGULATOR

LANTERN CLOCK HANDS

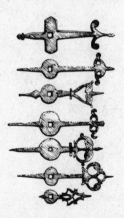

SIMPLE HOUR HANDS DATING FROM CIRCA 1630 (TOP) AND DEVELOPING TO THE STYLE ILLUSTRATED AT THE BOTTOM ABOUT 1680 AND EVEN LATER

ENGLISH CLOCK HANDS

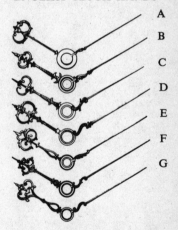

A
B
C
D
E
F
G

A ⎫
B ⎬ EARLY STYLE OF HANDS
C ⎬ FAVOURED BY JOSEPH KNIBB
D ⎭ AND WM. CLEMENT UP TO
       CIRCA 1700.

E ⎫ STYLE OF HANDS FAVOURED BY
F ⎬ THOMAS TOMPION; JOHANNES
G ⎭ FROMANTEEL UP TO CIRCA 1700.

ENGLISH CLOCK HANDS
FOR LONGCASE AND BRACKET CLOCKS FROM CIRCA 1665 TO CIRCA 1700.

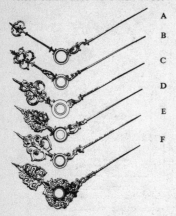

A
B
C
D
E
F

A ⎫ STYLES FAVOURED BY JOSEPH KNIBB
   ⎬ AND HIS CONTEMPORIES, UP TO
B ⎭ CIRCA 1700.
C ⎫ STYLES FAVOURED BY THOMAS
D ⎬ TOMPION AND HIS CONTEMPORIES
E ⎭ UP TO CIRCA 1700.
F ⎱ STYLE FAVOURED BY CHRISTOPHER
     GOULD CIRCA 1700.

ENGLISH CLOCK HANDS
FOR LONGCASE AND BRACKET CLOCKS FROM CIRCA 1700 TO CIRCA 1750.

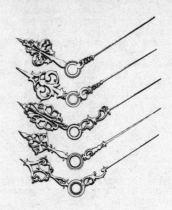

THESE HANDS ARE WHAT MAY BE
TERMED ORDINARY STYLES FOUND ON
CLOCKS OF THE FIRST HALF OF THE
18TH CENTURY.

ENGLISH CLOCK HANDS
FOR LONGCASE AND BRACKET CLOCKS FROM CIRCA 1750 TO CIRCA 1850 AND EVEN LATER.

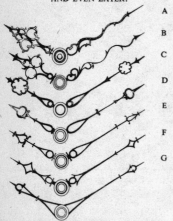

A
B
C
D
E
F
G

A ⎫ STYLE FAVOURED
B ⎬ FROM CIRCA 1750
C ⎭ TO CIRCA 1800.
D ⎫
E ⎬ STYLE FAVOURED FROM CIRCA 1800
F ⎬ UP TO CIRCA 1875.
G ⎭

EARLY WATCH HANDS
FOR ONE HAND WATCHES

1
2
3
4

1. GERMAN STYLE, CIRCA 1575.
2. ENGLISH STYLE, CIRCA 1620.
3. ENGLISH STYLE, CIRCA 1635.
4. ENGLISH STYLE, CIRCA 1675.

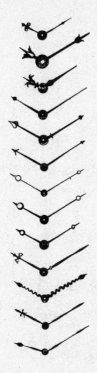

1. THOMAS TOMPION STYLE CIRCA 1675.

2. TULIP STYLE CIRCA 1690.

3. TOMPION STYLE CIRCA 1705.

4. JOHN ARNOLD STYLE CIRCA 1780.

5. JOHN ARNOLD STYLE CIRCA 1780.

5. FRANCIS PERIGAL STYLE CIRCA 1780.

6. RECORDON STYLE CIRCA 1785.

7. BREGUET STYLE CIRCA 1780.

8. BREQUET STYLE CIRCA 1790.

9. BREGUET STYLE CIRCA 1810.

10. MUDGE STYLE CIRCA 1800.

11. ROBERT ROSKELL STYLE CIRCA 1830.

12. JAMES MCABLE STYLE CIRCA 1880.
    ALSO WITH FLEUR DE LYS ON THE MINUTE HAND.

13. SPADE HAND, POPULAR FROM ABOUT 1800.

HEBDOMAS WATCH. (Greek, seven). An eight-day Swiss watch with the lower part of the dial cut away—usually about one-third—exposing the balance of the watch movement. The watch is wound every seven days.

HERTZ. The unit of frequency of electricity; one cycle per second., abbreviated to Hz, named after the German physcist, Henrich Rudolf Hertz.

HOROLOGE, HOROLOGIUM. Terms used in old writings to define a mechanism for measuring time.

HYGROMETER. An instrument for measuring the humidity of the air.

I

INCENSE CLOCKS. A form of time recorder used in China and Japan. A flat tray divided into sections, somewhat like a maze and marked off into hours or the local time. These sections are packed with joss—stick or incense. Lighted from the centre, they burnt outward, indicating the passing of time as the incense burns away.

ITALIAN TIME. The day divided into 24 hours starting from sunset. Public striking clocks struck up to 24 strokes. This system persisted for several centuries and eventually clocks were made to strike up to 12 hours and to indicate time in the conventional manner.

J

JAPANESE CLOCK. *See* Pillar Clock.

K

KINGS AND QUEENS OF ENGLAND.

1046–66	Edward the Confessor
1066	Harold
1066–87	William I
1087–1100	William II
1100–35	Henry I
1135–54	Stephen
1154–89	Henry II
1189–99	Richard I
1199–1216	John
1216–72	Henry III
1272–1307	Edward I
1307–27	Edward II
1327–77	Edward III
1377–99	Richard II
1399–1413	Henry IV
1413–22	Henry V
1422–61	Henry VI
1461–83	Edward IV
1483	Edward V
1483–85	Richard III
1485–1509	Henry VII
1509–47	Henry VIII
1547–53	Edward VI
1553	Lady Jane Grey
1553–58	Mary I
1558–1603	Elizabeth I
1603–25	James I
1625–49	Charles I
1649–60	Interregnum (Cromwell)
1660–85	Charles II
1685–88	James II
1688–94	Mary II
1694–1702	William III
1702–14	Anne
1714–27	George I
1727–60	George II
1760–1820	George III
1820–30	George IV
1830–37	William IV
1837–1901	Victoria
1901–10	Edward VII
1910–36	George V
1936	Edward VIII
1936–52	George VI
1952	Elizabeth II

L

LAMP CLOCK. There is evidence that a form of lamp was used to indicate the passing hours at about the time King Alfred used the Candle Clock (*q.v.*). Oil would be placed in a glass vessel with markings and as the oil burnt away so the hours would be noted. Also a Night Clock (*q.v.*) where a lamp shade is marked with the hours and revolves. The time of day is indicated by a pointer fixed to the body of the lamp.

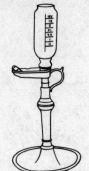

LAMP CLOCK I

LAMP CLOCK II.

LION CLOCK. A clock, usually of French make, which is a bronze lion on a marble base with an ormolu clock on its back. The clocks were made about the middle of the 18th century.

LIQUID CRYSTAL. A term used in connection with some digital quartz crystal timepieces. A sandwich of very thin sheets of glass with a clear liquid crystalline material between them. A small charge of electricity across the plates causes the liquid to turn milky.

M

MAGIC LANTERN CLOCK. *See* Projection Clock.

MARINE CLOCK. *See* Ship's Clock and Ship's Bell Clock.

MEAN SOLAR TIME. Time as indicated by the sun after allowance has been made for the Equation of Time (*q.v.*). Mean Solar Time is our standard of time. *See* Greenwich Mean Time.

MERCURIAL GILDING. A form of gilding where powdered gold of high quality is made into paste with mercury (amalgam) and rubbed on to the metal which is then heated. The mercury vaporizes, causing the gold to amalgamate with the metal. This method is also known as fire gilding. Modern gilding is by an electro-chemical system. Mercurial gilding is extravagant, costly, and dangerous to health. Many French clock cases were mercurially gilt and at a later period many were heated (sweated) to extract the gold, thus depreciating the value of the clock.

MERIDIAN WATCH. A watch indicating the time of day in different parts of the world. Usually a number of subsidiary dials showing the times in the principal cities of the world.

MONSTRANCE CLOCK

MONSTRANCE CLOCK. A clock, usually of German make, in the form of a monstrance used in Roman Catholic Churches. Made in the 15th century.

MORBIER CLOCK. *See* Comté Clock.

MUSK APPLE CLOCK. A globe-shaped small clock, worn from the neck by a cord. The dial is on the under side. The name is taken from the perforated ball filled with musk or fragrant herbs to counteract disagreeable odours.

N

NAPOLEON. The Demi-hunter Watch (*q.v.*) said to have been invented by Napoleon I. Also a mantel clock in the shape of the hats worn by Napoleon I.

NAPOLEON CLOCK. A name referring to the shape of the case of a clock; based on the style of hat worn by Napoleon I.

NAPOLEON CLOCK.

NAUTICAL DAY. The nautical day starts when the sun is on the meridian. The day is divided into an afternoon watch of four hours; two day watches of two hours each; middle watch; night watch; morning watch, and forenoon watch, each of four hours, completing the day. *See* Ship's Bell Clock.

NEF CLOCK. A clock incorporated in a model of a ship or galleon. Such clocks are antique works of art, c. 1575, and are not Ship's Clocks (*q.v.*).

NEUCHATELOISE CLOCK. Swiss clocks made in the style of French, Louis XIV and XV periods. *See* French Period Styles, page 000. Neuchateloise clocks are made of wood and decorated with coloured lacquer and ormolu mounts.

NIELLO. A form of semi-hard black enamel decoration used as a rule on silver watch cases. The design is deeply engraved and filled with an alloy of silver, lead and copper with sulphides, the case is then heated. The sulphides remain black. Niello work was in use, as early as the first part of the 17th century, but was more commonly found in the latter part of the 18th and early 19th centuries. The pattern is somewhat similar to marquetry inlay, the silver, picking out the design. Also known as Tulla Work, from Tulla, a Russian town where the work originated.

NIGHT CLOCKS. Clocks of the 17th century, both Bracket (*q.v.*) and Long Case candle will shine through. A segment of the dial is cut away and pierced discs appear indicating the time of day. *See* Lamp Clock.

O

OIGNON WATCH. (Fr. Onion). Refers to a large thick or fat watch of imagined onion shape. Not as large in diameter as a Chinese Watch (*q.v.*). Usually about 1 inch thick.

ORGAN CLOCK. A pipe organ operated by a pin barrel similar to a musical clock (*q.v.*). Instead of a comb providing a tune, the pipes of the organ are blown. The time of day is indicated by either a conventional clock dial and hands, or a revolving sphere with the hours marked round its circumference and the hand of a figure pointing to the time of day. The clock is usually positioned on top of the organ. Such clocks were made about the middle of the 18th century.

ORRERY CLOCK. An Orrery (*q.v.*) which is attached to and operated by a clock. Raingo of Paris, a famous French clockmaker, specialised in orrery clocks and his clocks are referred to as Raingo Clocks. (*q.v.*). They were made in the first quarter of the 19th century.

OSCILLOSCOPE. TV type of instrument to observe sound or electronic wave patterns when studying timepieces.

P

PAVÉ. "Paved with diamonds".

PARACHUTE INDEX. Chute. *See* Shock Resisting Watch.

PAILLONNÉ ENAMEL. (Fr. Spangle). A method of enamelling where pieces of gold foil, *e.g.* stars, fleurs de lis, etc., are

applied and then covered with transparent enamel or flux. Vast numbers of watch cases in this style were produced in Switzerland during the last part of the 19th and early 20th centuries.

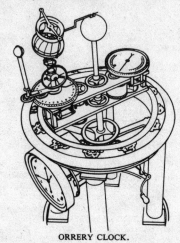

ORRERY CLOCK.

PECTORAL WATCH. An antique watch in the form of a cross, skull, etc., made to rest on the chest.

PEDESTAL CLOCK. *See* Column Clock and Term Clock.

PEDOMETER. An instrument, usually in the form of a watch, for measuring distances. The instrument is supported in an upright position on the person; the movement caused by walking keeps a weighted lever moving up and down and motivates gearing to register the distance covered. *See* Automatic Winding Watch.

PETITE SONNERIE CLOCK. Generally refers to a carriage clock striking ting-tang at the quarter and half hours but not striking the hours at each quarter, as does a Grande Sonnerie Clock (*q.v.*).

PICTURE CLOCK.

PICTURE CLOCK. A picture including a church or tower with an actual clock set in it, made about the middle of the 18th century. Such clocks were, as a rule, fitted with 30 hour verge watch movements. In recent years the Swiss have made picture clocks fitted with eight-day movements.

PILLAR CLOCK. A Japanese clock used in Japan before 1873. It is in the form of a flat pillar about thirty inches high and about six inches wide. The weight-driven mechanism was enclosed in a form of hood, somewhat similar to a hanging Dutch clock. The time is indicated by a pointer attached to the weight moving over a scale fixed on the trunk of the case. There is no dial and no hands. As the Japanese day was divided into different hours for different months of the year, a suitable scale would be used. Some such clocks were provided with the scale for all the months, in which case the pointer was adjusted to move over the appropriate scale.

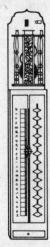

PILLAR CLOCK.

PIQUÉ WORK. A form of decoration on watchcases. Usually refers to inlay of gold or silver in an outer, or pair case. It also can refer to a leather covered pair case decorated with gold or silver pinheads.

PLANISPHERE CLOCK. A clock made to operate a planetarium. *See* Planetarium. Also a clock in which a star map is incorporated.

POLOS. A form of sun-dial where a staff or stick is fixed perpendicular in the centre of a basin-like plate; lines are marked for the twelve daylight hours.

PORTFOLIO. *See* Calotte, also Three Fold Clock.

POST CHAISE CLOCK. *See* Sedan Clock.

PROJECTION CLOCK. A form of magic lantern clock projecting the time of day on to a wall or ceiling at will. Originally made in France about the middle of the 19th century, and more recently in Germany, where the image of the dial and hands is projected onto the ceiling.

PULL QUARTER CLOCK. *See* ANTIQUE CLOCK CASE TERMS.

PURITAN WATCHES. Watches made in England in the early 17th century. Perfectly plain, oval shaped, in silver, with no decoration at all. They were worn in conformity with the Puritan period of Cromwell, 1649-60. Sometimes referred to as Cromwellian-style watches.

Q

QUARTZ CRYSTAL BATTERY DRIVEN WATCH. A watch with a miniaturised quartz crystal oscillator as its timekeeping standard. The first movements in 1967 measured about one and one-third inches square and about one-eighth of an inch thick, compared with the first quartz clock, which measured some nine feet high, seven feet wide and three feet deep. The development was financed by a consortium of Swiss manufacturers forming The Centre Electronique Horloger S.A. in Neuchâtel. C.E.H. state that the watch is built to withstand the shocks, temperature variations and humidity that occur in normal wear. The timekeeping properties are remarkable, six times more accurate than the Tuning Fork Watch (*q.v.*) and twelve times more accurate than the finest precision mechanical watch. The error of the quartz watch is approximately thirty-six seconds a year. The quartz crystal is a thin bar connected to an oscillating circuit. It flexes at a fixed frequency owing to its piezo-electric properties and keeps the oscillations constant. The frequency is broken down electronically by binary circuits until it is low enough to drive a small motor that turns the hands through motion work. The circuits and motor are powered by a replaceable mercury cell. Several variations of the basic circuit were subsequently developed. Most have an oscillator frequency of 8192 Hz. In 1970, the Hamilton Company announced a solid state quartz crystal watch with no moving parts, the time being shown digitally at a touch of a button.

R

RACK CLOCK. *See* Gravity Clock.

RAILWAY CLOCKS. Up to the middle of the 19th century and for some time after, clocks in railway stations were set to show local time. As railways were extended, it was found necessary to introduce "railway time", and later G.M.T. (*q.v.*). Leaflets were issued by the railway companies giving conversion from local time to G.M.T.

RAINGO CLOCK. Among other fine domestic clocks, Raingo of Paris in the early 19th century, made clocks incorporating an Orrery (*q.v.*). The orrery is operated by the clock mechanism. The name Raingo has become synonymous with an orrery clock.

RECITAL ALARM CLOCK. An eight-day alarm clock which repeats the alarm every 24 hours without resetting.

RELIGIEUSE CLOCK. A French clock of the later part of the 17th century and early 18th centuries in a black wooden case. Simple in outline and beautifully inlaid, ormolu mounted. *See* French Period Clock Styles, page 45.

REMONTOIRE CLOCK. A clock with device to provide constant power to the escapement to improve timekeeping. *See* Constant Force Escapement.

RING DIAL. A form of portable sundial in the shape of a serviette ring. The sun would shine through a small hole, indicating the time on a scale of hours marked on the inside of the ring.

RODICO. Plastic substance used to clean or pick up dirt and oil from watch parts.

ROLLER. In horology it refers to the circular plate fitted to the balance staff of a timepiece, into which the ruby or impulse pin is fitted.

ROMAN NUMERALS.

I	II	III	IIII or IV		V	VI	VII	VIII
1	2	3	4		5	6	7	8
IX	X	XI	XII	XX	XXX	XL	L
9	10	11	12	20	30	40	50
C	D	M					
100	500	1,000					

For example, MLMLXXV —

M	L M		LXX	V	
1000	(100-1000—900)		70	5 —	1975

ROPE ESCAPEMENT. *See* Flying Ball Clock.

S

SCARAB WATCH. A Form Watch in the shape of a beetle. The scarab is the sacred beetle of ancient Egypt.

SCRATCH MOULDING. The shallow moulding found on some antique clocks. The cut is marked with a scraper formed to the required design. For a bold moulding a plane would be used.

SVERES CLOCK. French clock case made wholly of Sévres china or an ormolu clock with Sévres china plaques.

SHADOW CLOCK. One of the earliest forms of sun clocks—not a sundial—because there is no dial as such. Used in Egypt about 2,000 B.C., it consists of a rectangular bar with notches or lines marked upon it to denote the time of day. Attached to the end of this bar is a short post and to this post another bar is attached at right angles to the base bar. The T part is pointed to the sun and the shadow cast by it falls on to the notched base bar.

SHELF CLOCK. The American name for a Bracket Clock (*q.v.*).

SIDERIAL TIME. (*See* page 226). Should read "A Siderial day is approximately 3 minutes 56 seconds shorter than the mean solar day".

SILENT ESCAPEMENT. *See* Gut Pallets.

SKELETON DIAL. A Chapter Ring (*q.v.*) in which the metal around the numerals is cut away—fretwork—leaving the numerlas attached to the ring by tabs. In some instances the minute circle is also cut away. This system was fashionable during the latter part of the 17th and early 18th centuries, and is usually to be found on fine clocks.

SPEAKING CLOCK. *See* TIM.

SPLIT PLATE. In some 17th century bracket clocks, the Back plate (*q.v.*) is cut down the centre, making two plates, thus faciliating repair work; the timepiece part of the movement for instance can be attended to without dismantling the whole of the movement. Split plates are to be found only in striking clocks.

STAGE COACH CLOCK. The style of clocks used in hosteleries, the stopping places of stage coaches, during the eighteenth century. The predecessor of the Act of Parliament Clock (*q.v.*), it was usually a wall clock with a long pendulum and large open dial, two or more feet across, and made of wood like the case.

STAGE COACH CLOCK.

from the outside were seen to strike the hours on bells. Date, latter part of the 14th century. During the 15th and 16th century dials and hands were introduced.

STRUT CLOCK. A clock with a hinged strut at the back similar to an easel to enable it to be stood up.

SWING CLOCK. Refers to French clocks where a cupid seated upon a swing is the pendulum. The cupid swings backwards and forwards and not from side to side like a conventional pendulum. Made during the latter part of the 18th century.

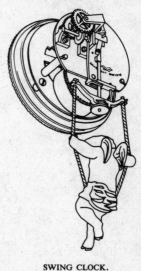

SWING CLOCK.

T

STEM WINDING. Where the mainspring is wound by a button fitted to the winding stem or shaft. A method which succeeded the key wind system.

STRIKE SILENT DIAL. A subsidiary dial of a clock—usually a Bracket Clock (*q.v.*)—with a hand which can be moved to strike or to make silent. To be found in clocks from the last quarter of the 17th century becoming popular during the 18th and 19th centuries.

STRIKING JACK. Very early Turret Clocks (*q.v.*) or tower clocks were not fitted with dials and hands. They just struck the hours and at a later date figures of men, known as jacks, jacomarts or striking jacks,

TACT WATCH. (Fr. feel). (*See* page 238). The "Montre à tact" was invented by A. L. Breguet about 1800. Breguet made it as an alternative to a repeating watch. Some versions had the indicator or index on one side and the normal time of day hands on the other side.

TAPE RECORDER. An instrument used in watch testing laboratories for checking the rate of timekeeping of watches, etc. Two tapes are used. One is connected to a standard timekeeper, which marks the tape each second. The other is connected to the watch under test. The two tapes are then compared thus eliminating any personal error.

TEA TIME CLOCK. A form of alarm clock incorporated into a fixture with a specially designed electric kettle and a tea pot. At a pre-determined time, the kettle is made to boil and pour the water into the tea pot. Finally an alarm sounds. Also referred to as "Teasmade".

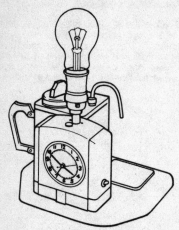

TEA TIME CLOCK.

TELLURION CLOCK. A clock of either French or Swiss origin in which a mechanism somewhat similar to an Orrery (*q.v.*), surmounts the dial. In addition to time of day, the clock indicates the age of the moon on a scale, and has a four year calendar, indicating day and night, spring, summer, autumn and winter. Dated about the early part of the 18th century.

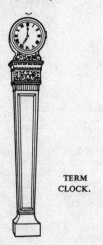

TERM
CLOCK.

TERM CLOCK. A form of pedestal or Column Clock (*q.v.*) standing five to six feet high, where the case tapers down from a round clock at the top to a supporting base. Usually of French make but sometimes English. Date early 18th century.

TERMINEUR. (Swiss term). *See* Établisseur.

THERMOGRAPHIC CLOCK. A clock similar to the Barograph (*q.v.*), but in place of an aneroid a bi-metallic strip is used to operate the pen, in order to register changes of temperature.

THREE FOLD CLOCK. A travelling clock made of leather, plastic or metal. The clock is fitted on to a centre panel which is hinged. There are two outer parts to the case and as they close together, the centre panel with the clock is enclosed.

THREE FOLD CLOCK.

TIC-TAC ESCAPEMENT. A recoil escapement embracing one and sometimes two teeth. This form of escapement is to be found in V.A.P. Clocks (*q.v.*). It was also employed in some early English bracket clocks. Sometimes referred to as "drum escapement".

TIM. If the letters TIM or the numbers 123 are dialed on the telephone, the exact time will be announced by the "speaking clock", housed at the Post Office Research Station, Dollis Hill, London, N.W. At, say, 20 minutes past 11 o'clock, the voice will announce "At the third stroke it will be 11.20 precisely", followed by three pips, and so on every ten seconds; the word "precisely" is included after the minutes, not the seconds. While in Paris in 1933, G.P.O. officials became interested in the speaking clock just inaugurated in that city. It was decided to develop a similar system in this country. The project was entrusted to Dr. E. A. Speight, of the Dollis Hill Research Station, who devised an entirely new system, employing a free pendulum clock designed expecially for the purpose. The error of TIM is said to be never greater than one-tenth of a second. TIM was brought into service in the afternoon of 24th July 1936. A quartz crystal clock is now used as the time standard.

TIME RECORDING STAMP. *See* Warwick Time Stamp Clock.

TIME SIGNALS. It is on record that in 1835 G.M.T. was available at certain Post Offices. Direct lines had been established from Greenwich Observatory. In 1877, The Standard Time Co. was established and signals were available by telegraph wire, when a bell was made to strike one blow every hour. In 1924, the first "six pips" signal was heard on wireless sets. Up to 1835, City of London chronometer, clock and watch makers, checked their standards by sundial observations, using Equation of Time (*q.v.*) tables. When no sun was overcast, a watch was taken—by horseback (there was no rail) to Greenwich—the time checked at the Observatory and distributed to certain London houses.

TING-TANG CLOCK. (*See* page 258). Also known as Bim-Bam Clock. *See* Chimes.

TORTOISE CLOCK. One of the many novelties contrived by Grollier de Serviére of France, about the end of the 17th century. A metal dish or plate—usually pewter or brass—with the hours engraved on the flange is filled with water and a model of a tortoise floats upon it. A piece of iron is fixed to the tortoise. The plate is placed upon a stand where a clock movement is fitted and a magnet is fixed to what would be the hour wheel socket. As the clock goes, so the magnet rotates and attracts the tortoise with it. Sometimes referred to as Turtle Clock. Many modern versions of the Tortoise Clock are to be seen; usually fitted with an eight-day movement.

TRANSISTORISED CLOCK. A battery-driven clock employing transistors, to eliminate mechanical switches and therefore contact troubles. First used about 1960.

TULLA-WORK. *See* Niello.

TUNING FORK BATTERY DRIVEN WATCH. In 1950, Max Hetzel, a Swiss electronics engineer, introduced the tuning fork as the controlling element in a watch in place of the conventional escapement. It had been appreciated for many years that a tuning fork was a stable source of frequency if made of a metal not affected by changes of temperatures and that it could be kept in operation by and also control an oscilating circuit by using an electro-magnetic transducer. In 1959, the Bulova Watch Company of New York, with Hetzel as their physicist, introduced a commercial version of the watch called the Accutron. The watches were later produced also at the Bulova factory in Bienne, Switzerland. The tuning fork watch is now made, under licence, by other manufacturers and offered for sale under the name of the manufacturer. The rate of timekeeping is in the region of one minute per month in wear.

TURTLE CLOCK. *See* Tortoise Clock.

TWO BAR BALANCE ESCAPEMENT. *See* Cross Beat Clock.

U

URN CLOCK. A French clock in the form of an urn or vase. The time of day is indicated by rotating bands, one marked with the hours and another with minutes. A figure or pointer of some kind, fixed to the body of the clock, points to the time. First appeared about the middle of the 18th century.

URN CLOCK.

V

V.A.P. CLOCK. A French Drum (*q.v.*) timepiece clock, made by Valonge, of Paris.

The initials form the trade mark. Fitted with a Tic-Tac Escapement (*q.v.*) either with Short Bob Pendulum (*q.v.*) or balance and balance spring. Where the balance is employed, a unique feature is that the escape wheel and pallets are pivoted between the two main plates of the clock and the lever is shaped so that it operates on the face of the back plate where the balance is situated. First appeared about the middle of the 18th century.

VERNIS MARTIN. Four brothers, Guillaume, Simon, Etienne and Robert Martin were carriage builders and cabinet makers in France. Two of the brothers, Robert and Etienne, invented a lacquer in 1730 which was used extensively on clocks. At the height of their fame they had three workshops in Paris, one of which was still in existence in 1785.

VISIBLE ESCAPEMENT CLOCK. A clock in which the escapement is visible from the front. Much favoured by the French. *See* Brocot, and French Four Glass Clock.

W

WAG-ON-THE-WALL CLOCK. An American term for a wall clock in which the pendulum and weights are exposed to view.

WARWICK TIME STAMPING CLOCK. A clock with a rubber stamp of a clock dial and hands, fixed to the back of the clock, which functions with the going of the clock. The stamp is inked on an ink pad and then printed on the document so that it indicates the time. This device first appeared about 1880. Made by the Warwick Time Stamping Company.

WATCH PAPERS. It was the custom during the 18th and 19th centuries, and to a lesser degree during the early part of the 20th century, for watch repairers to place inside the back cover of a pocket a disc shaped label. Some of these papers are handsomely decorated and printed, giving the name and address of the craftsman. Some of the later papers give the date of the repair and suggest when the watch should be cleaned, etc. The papers are interesting and are the subject of some collectors.

WATCHMAN'S CLOCK. *See* Tell-Tale Clock.

WORLD TIME CLOCK. A clock showing the time in various capitals of the world. There are many systems and the one illustrated is by Luxor of Switzerland. As an example, if the time in London is 9 a.m., the outer ring is turned so that the London, Madrid and Algeria section is brought into line with the figure 9 on the 24 hour ring. New York Time will be noted as 4 a.m., and Bombay as 2 p.m., indicated by the dark part of the 24 hour ring.

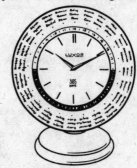

WORLD TIME CLOCK.

Z

ZAPPLER CLOCK. A small pendulum clock made in Austria, in the early 19th century. The short light pendulum swings in front of the dial. Sometimes there are two pendulums, swinging in opposite directions.